ROUND SALAD BOWLS

DIAMETER (in.)	CAPACITY
5	10 oz.
6	12–14 oz.
8	40 oz.
10	2 qt.
12	4 qt.
15	8 qt.
18	15 qt.
23	36 qt.

CAN SIZES

DESCRIPTION	VOLUME	WEIGHT	NUMBER = #10
6 oz.	$\frac{3}{4}$ cup	6 oz.	—
8 oz.	1 cup	8 oz.	12
No. 1 (picnic)	$1\frac{1}{4}$ cup	$10\frac{1}{2}$ oz.	—
No. 300	$1\frac{3}{4}$ cup	$15\frac{1}{2}$ oz.	—
No. 303	2 cup	1 lb.	7
No. 2	$2\frac{1}{2}$ cup	$1\frac{1}{4}$ lb.	5
No. $2\frac{1}{2}$	$3\frac{1}{2}$ cup	1 lb. 13 oz.	4
No. 3 cyl.	$5\frac{3}{4}$ cup	2 lb. 14 oz.	2
No. 10	12 cup	6 lb. 9 oz.	—

F-V

St. Louis Community College

Library

5801 Wilson Avenue
St. Louis, Missouri 63110

Buffets

A GUIDE FOR PROFESSIONALS

Buffets

A GUIDE FOR PROFESSIONALS

Georges C. St. Laurent, Jr.

Chet Holden

JOHN WILEY & SONS

New York Chichester Brisbane Toronto Singapore

Cover photo: Riccardo Marcialis
Production supervisor: Fred Schulte
Interior design: Laura Ierardi
Cover design: Dawn L. Stanley

Library of Congress Cataloging in Publication Data

St. Laurent, Jr., Georges C.
    Buffets: a guide for professionals.

    Bibliography: p.
    Includes index.
    1. Buffets (Cookery)   2. Quantity cookery.
I. Holden, Chet. II. Title.
TX738.5.S73 1986   642′.4   85-22677
ISBN 0-471-81874-7 (College ed.)

Printed in the United States of America

10 9 8 7 6 5 4 3 2 1

Dedication

The authors respectfully dedicate *BUFFETS*
to Mrs. Eleanor "Toodie" St. Laurent,
and her sons Georges III and William.

Preface

In his delightful book Ma Gastronomie, *the late French master chef Fernand Point reflected: "If the divine creator has taken pains to give us delicious and exquisite things to eat, the least we can do is prepare them well and serve them with ceremony." Nowhere is this more true than in the vast and wonderful realm of buffets.*

Every time we set up banquet tables, drape them with crisp linen, and polish the chafers, we present a food-service format that enables us to transcend the cuisine of this nation and all others. All countries or cooking styles are represented in this culinary bandwagon, as are all segments of the American food-service industry. From morning to midnight, juice bar to happy hour, Sunday brunch to Monday night football . . . the sun never sets on the world of buffets.

The treatment of so vast a subject is a challenge. The question is not so much where to begin but, rather, where to end. What we have done with Buffets *is to offer bits and pieces, a taste of this and a sample of that, in much the same way our subject itself comes to life on food-service tables. Each subject will be "garnished" in a different way, as if the very world of cooking might join our food parade. It is our intention that each chapter should stand as a building block of information, firm in its own content yet stronger when combined with the material from others.*

A GLOBAL PERSPECTIVE. Yes, there is indeed a world *of buffets. We offer a guide to a score of countries, their foods, and their customs. From within the quiet valleys of a far-off land come ideas that can take their place on your buffet tables. Come one, come all to this wonderful world of foods!*

HERBS AND SPICES. If there is a key to unlocking the treasures of ethnic cookery, surely it will be found within the array of herbs and spices that have traveled from around the globe to lend airs to our own kitchens. We will review dozens of these seeds, nuts, and leaves and offer you some suggestions for how best to use each of them.

APPETIZERS. Buffet favorites throughout the culinary universe, in some cultures appetizers actually represent the entire buffet array. We will look at some of these appetizer settings and suggest ways of incorporating them in your buffet presentations.

SALADS.   Salad ingredients are listed on market sheets throughout the year, but at some times the quality and economy of fruits and vegetables definitely encourage their use in meal planning. We will look at the seasons for our nation's vitamin-rich harvest.

SOUPS.   Soups appear on more international menus than perhaps any other course, and every country has a few that stand as national favorites. We will highlight a soup from each of almost 50 countries and domestic recipes as well—every one a proven success.

MEATS.   Viewed in terms of their place in global cookery, meats are discussed in a way that includes a taste of Greek lamb, Chinese pork, British beef, German sausage . . . and more.

SEAFOOD.   Considering the multitude of species available, seafood can be a real mystery in food planning. But in Chapter 7 you will learn to separate varieties into interchangeable and, therefore, highly usable lean/fat categories.

POULTRY.   Every nation of this world cooks and serves poultry, be it duck or quail, chicken or goose, turkey or Cornish hen. We will take a country-by-country look at some long-standing multinational favorites.

SIDE DISHES.   Vegetables will be presented by their country of origin, so you can learn in just which cooking styles they naturally appear. Are potatoes appropriate in the Orient, or might they best be served on a Brazilian buffet?

DESSERTS.   Creativity in desserts is of paramount concern for buffet planners who must continually find new dishes to tempt and tantalize. Buffets offers a profile of dessert classics to help keep the meal's end at the top of any menu's excitement.

BRUNCH.   This is a profitable meal for food-service buffets, and one that often focuses on eggs. We will borrow from some French classics to suggest a hundred ways in which to cook these brunchtime specialties.

Our "buffet" will offer an array of tastes and textures, a panorama of color and cooking. We hope that your moments of reading and the menus you plan will be influenced by the subjects we have chosen. But more than that, if we encourage you to continue the search for another buffet theme, another dish to add to your menu repertoire, then our efforts will have been successful.

CARE, the worldwide food relief agency, once circulated a simple wall poster that stated: "If you give a man a fish, you feed him for a day. If you teach a man to fish, you feed him for his lifetime." We sincerely hope that Buffets *will teach you something lasting about a truly universal style of service.*

GEORGES C. ST. LAURENT, JR.
CHET HOLDEN

About the Recipes

You will find more than 300 recipes in the pages that follow.
We have attempted to provide a broad cross section of ethnic
as well as regional American foods so that you can add to your existing
buffet menus or perhaps gain insight into new themes for service.
It was not our goal to dictate complete buffet menus but to
spark interest in the subject and to prompt additional research.

Every recipe includes quantities for testing as well as for service.
In a buffet environment, it is difficult to establish exact
portion quantities because guests are invited to help themselves.
However, we have suggested 8 portions for the test quantity
and 50 for service. Your experience will allow you to fine-tune these
quantities through repeated use.

We have also included suggestions for proper service of each dish
and some hints on variations. Garnishing ideas will be discussed in
the chapter on buffet layout. We hope that the remaining text
material will help you to supplement each recipe with seasonings and
ingredients that are appropriate for each dish. Through experimentation
in cooking and service, the world of buffets can become a profitable
part of your menu repertoire.

Table of Contents

Acknowledgments

We are grateful for the assistance of several good friends and colleagues, whose kind words and deeds had great impact on the content of the following pages. We thank them with sincerity and respect.

Brother Herman E. Zaccarelli—Director of Purdue University's Restaurant, Hotel and Institutional Management Institute.

Ferdinand E. Metz—President, The Culinary Institute of America, Hyde Park, New York.

The International Foodservice Editorial Council—Several of whose members donated time, recipes and the beautiful photographic plates that grace several pages within the book.

The Professional Review Committee—Several professionals from the field of foodservice who spend many hours reading, reviewing and—thankfully—correcting manuscript.

Judith Joseph—Editor, John Wiley and Sons, Inc. who supported the project with enthusiasm and constructive support, literally from its very genesis.

We also acknowledge the following individuals for their contributions: John R. McDonald, The Southeast Institute of Culinary Arts/St. Augustine Technical Center; Patrick Sweeney, Johnson County Community College; Mike Jung, Hennepin Technical Centers; Valeria S. Mason, State Department of Education, Gainesville, Florida; Philip Panzarino, New York City Community College; Herb Traub, Pirates' House, Savannah, Georgia; Gayle M. Müller, Keystone Junior College; and George Dragisity, University of Houston.

G. C. ST. L., Jr.
C. H.

One

Buffets: A Global Perspective

The development of any national cuisine is a function of various factors. Just as climate and geography are surely influential, so too are social and religious customs. Around the world, when people gather to observe and celebrate traditional occasions, very often the focal point is food. Great buffet tables are laden with fare of all descriptions. So let's look at some international themes that you might consider adding to your list of buffet possibilities.

Austria. Austrian cooking (often called Viennese) is one of the world's more heterogeneous culinary styles, reflecting influences of Italy, Hungary, Poland, Rumania, France, and Germany. This mixed-bag cuisine presents Viennese fried chicken beside boiled beef with chives, apple sauce with horseradish, and slices of Sacher torte. Pastries are legion, and when it comes to buffets, Austrians gather in hordes. Whether it's the chic Viennese Opera Ball, a candlelit New Year's Eve, or a pre–Lenten herring feast, Austrians revel in buffets. All of Austria's culinary festivities offer suggestions for American menu writing; check your calendar, as the Austrians do, for "pudding week," "dumpling week," or "game week."

Czechoslovakia. A blend of Eastern European foods join German and Austrian influences in the Bohemian style of Czechoslovakia. Smoked Prague ham is famous, as are buffets that celebrate the use of pork. Lard is the choice over butter, and sausages are national favorites. Sour cream and sauerkraut, pickles and dumplings are Czech favorites. Fish (be it trout or prized carp) are often the centerpiece for Christmas buffets, while broiled lamb, gnocchi, pickled vegetables, and a variety of bread are highlights of the nationally popular picnics. If you want to duplicate a Czech fishing festival, set the table in green linen and drape it with netting; be sure to have beer and Riesling wine to accompany the meal. Traditional with Czech men is a stag party in honor of someone's fiftieth birthday; hunt festivals in the fall honor the tradition of setting all glasses to the left (leaving room on the right for weapons) and the use of round tables to assure equal status for all.

Denmark. The most famous Danish buffet is a culinary art form in its own right: The *smørrebrød* (translating simply to "bread and butter") is a buffet of open-faced sandwiches with literally hundreds of variations. Resting atop thin slices of diverse breads are profuse combinations of eggs, radishes, pickles, sardines, anchovies, lettuces, shrimp, onions, cheese, sour cream, capers, potatoes, and caviar . . . and that is just the tip of a very tasty Danish culinary iceberg. But buffets are not limited to the *smørrebrød* in this country known for hams and bacon. On Christmas Eve there is a grand feast with pork, goose, traditional rice dishes, and apple cake with cream; Christmas Day is characterized by much simpler fare, with liver pâtés and bread. Breakfast pastries known throughout the world as "Danish" are here called "Vienna breads" and are popular on the breakfast bar with juices, butter, and jams. Danes serve boiled cod at the New Year's Eve fête and always offer aquavit to drink. Traditional buffets also include the Round Year party, a celebration held every decade from an individual's tenth birthday to the one-hundredth and beyond; fruited cakes are bedecked with whipped cream for these occasions.

Finland. Rains fall frequently in this Scandinavian land, all the better for her wondrous wild mushrooms and ever-popular potatoes; it is said that the latter rival any spud on earth. The sea offers Finns a bounty of species, including the favored herring. Buffet season is an all-year affair, with high points that include the Christian holidays of Easter, Advent, and Christmas. A customary dish on the yuletide buffet is almond rice, a seasonal specialty in which nestles a hidden nut, awaiting the first single person to find it and "assuring" marriage within the year. May Day is a secular observance, as the coming spring is a welcomed break from the long and trying winter months. The May Day buffet is actually a breakfast that follows a full night of revelry; herring, in many styles, steals the show and is complemented with breads, golden butter, and the omnipresent schnapps and beer. Once the summer has fully unfolded, Finns celebrate Midsummer's Eve, a bonfire-torched affair that features, among other favorites, Russian-influenced blinis and vodka.

France. What has yet to be said about the cuisine of France! Perhaps only China can compete with this European nation when it comes to an influence on global cooking. To look at France is to look at a country of regions, each brimming with opportunity for buffet themes. Take Normandy, for example. Offer guests poached fish with sorrel or sauteed veal with mushrooms and apples. From the Alsace region, offer pork in almost any form (it's the region's favorite meat) or spark up some pheasant with sausages and sauerkraut for a variation on the *choucroute* theme. The Burgundy region brings great wines put to wonderful use in the classic chicken dish known as *coq au vin.* Another Burgundian delight is *gougère,* a feather-light pastry made to nibble with wine; with or without a sauce to accompany, this cheesey, choux-based pastry will enliven your buffet. The Lyonnaise region, known for its great restaurants, is also famous for its cheeses. Offer a selection of cheeses and a brioche dough with sausage *(saucisson en brioche)* and glasses of wine for a buffet delight. For a taste of Provence, intermingle slices of tomato and zucchini in a steam table pan; top with sautéed garlic, onions, eggplant, and peppers; drizzle with olive oil and bake.

Great Britain. Long the subject of snide culinary references, British cuisine in fact offers wonderful meats and game to accompany her abundant fruits and rich Cheddar and Stilton cheeses. Buffets range from a high tea and formal wedding luncheon to perhaps the grandest British meal, breakfast. Porridge and other cereals, fruits, bacon, ham, sausage, eggs, breads, and traditional finnan haddie are offered daily; on special occasions, like a hunt breakfast, there are hors d'oeuvres, cold meats, and more hot fish to bolster the buffet. Sporting people to the end, Britons take special pains at buffets that celebrate the Henley Regatta in June (strawberries and thick Devonshire cream) or Derby Day at Epsom Downs; cold meats (pâtés, gallantines, terrines) or fish (poached lobster or salmon) will receive special buffet treatment. And no summer is complete without the Ascot races and their parades of food and drink, pomp and circumstance. At yuletide, the turkey displaces the regal goose on many buffet tables, but flaming plum pudding remains a tradition. In fact, puddings of many kinds are often featured in British cuisine.

India. The foods of this country reflect very clearly the influences of religion and geography, as both Hindus (who are vegetarian) and Moslems (who are not) populate this vast nation. Whether the buffet is free of meat according to Hindu tenet or replete with lamb and chicken (especially flavorful is kiln-roasted henna-red "tandoori-style"), Indian food is spirited and colorful. The most famous spread is curry. Custom calls for guests to be offered trays with five small bowls (a buffet already!); patna (medium-grain) rice fills one, while chutney, pickled vege-

tables, coconut, and *pappadums* (spicy pepper wafers) are offered in the others. Indian curry is not the prepared powder commonly available here but, rather, a mixture of herbs and spices ground daily to a paste for specific foods. Other items on an Indian buffet may include *sambals* (Indian appetizers), *chapattis* (flat breads), and *samosas* (fried puffs filled with many wonders.) Translated loosely as "pepper water," *mulligatawny* is a fiesty Southern Indian soup that has enjoyed Western popularity. In any Indian buffet, sweets (called *meetais*) are absolutely necessary; essential to every meal, meetais are often brought to a party by guests, who have made them at home. Also critical to most Indian food is *garam masala*, a spice blend that varies from one cook (or food) to another. Variations abound, but garam masala is always ground fresh.

Italy. The first European cookbook ever published emanated from Italy 18 years before Columbus set sail for the New World; to this day Italian cuisine enjoys enormous popularity. Just about any occasion is celebrated with buffet assortments, be it a New Year's Day lentil dish ("lots of lentils bring lots of money") or a predinner antipasto selection of meats, cheeses, artichokes, and olives. The predominantly Roman Catholic population has established a number of church-related holidays that lend themselves naturally to food. Epiphany (in English, the Twelfth Night) is January 6; Carnival (Shrovetide) is a time for fritters and lasagna, especially in Naples. Easter is a day for lamb, and the following day, Easter Monday, is traditional as the *pic-nic de Pasquetta* or the first picnic of the new spring; roast chicken and frittata slices are served with cheeses and jugs of wine. All Hallows is a family time where pastries and marzipan figures that represent famous characters are served. On Martinmas (November 11), chestnuts are served (traditionally alongside a bonfire) with wine. For Christmas Eve, there is a vast seafood buffet; the chafers of this peninsular nation are filled with squid, octopus, clams, mussels, and fish of all descriptions.

Japan. The culinary displays of this nation bring buffets to magnificent heights. Japanese chefs are masters of the knife, and when these talents are applied to ice carvings, the effects are dramatic. Sushi and sashimi arrangements take on mosaic charms; and then there are the *bento*, literally "picnic box," foods. *Yakitori* are grilled chicken strips served on a skewer with soy sauce, tempura are batter-fried meats and vegetables served with dipping condiments, and *onigariyaki* is a seafood kebab with shrimp or mussels; each can be prepared by cooks behind the buffet line for guests as they pass by. Soup is served at every Japanese buffet, be it *akadashi* at breakfast (a red miso soup often served with tofu), *sumashijiru* at lunch (a clear chicken soup), or *hamaguri no ushio jiru* at dinner (a clam consommé). Pickled vegetables are also popular, as are many kinds of fish; remember, Japan is comprised of a chain of islands. Steamed rice (*gohan*) is a Japanese standard. Most Japanese buffets end rather simply, with freshly cut fruits arranged artistically. Garnishes of serrated palm leaves and small bowls of piquant green horseradish (*wasabo*) help to decorate the Japanese buffet table.

Mexico. One of the food industry's most popular ethnic trends, Mexican cookery has withstood the test of time. With a blend of Indian and Spanish touches, Mexican food can form a central theme for your buffet schedules—and it's not all tacos and beans. Take the piñata party. The celebration of a birthday can prompt the breaking of a piñata stuffed with candies, balloons, and other treats. Or feature an afternoon *merienda*, a Mexican variation of the British tea party. Coffee is the choice now, though, accompanied with pastries and Mexican coffee—equal parts of steaming brew and hot milk. Two festive occasions to celebrate with a Mexican flare are January 6, the traditional Twelfth Night, and May 5, *El Cinco de Mayo*, the Mexican day of Independence. Don't stick to the Tex-Mex favorites, but venture instead into the Yucatán for lime soup or garlic-laced pompano fillets. Look to the hill country for the Mexican standard, *mole poblano*; use chicken or turkey as you wish. One can also savor the southern coast of Mexico by offering *camarones en frio*, which are cold marinated prawns lusty with cilantro, garlic, and lime.

The Netherlands. Dutch cuisine reflects not only the bounty of that country's fields and canals, but also the heritage of courageous sailors who unlocked the treasures of exotic Spice Islands. Indonesia, first settled by the Dutch, has contributed the now-famed *rijsttafel* (rice table) to our journey through buffets. Rice holds center stage (literally) but the supporting cast includes a panoply of zesty dishes: fruits, meats, vegetables and fish are served in tidbit portions, made fiery hot with pungent sauces. Be sure to offer cooling tumblers of chilled beer or tea; remember, too, that the rijsttafel tradition excludes the use of knives in favor of forks and spoons. On the holiday side, the Dutch celebrate New Year's Eve in the home of friends, starting with coffee before proceeding through wines and stout Genever gin; herring is exceedingly popular, as are veal, pork, and chicken. Appetizers on a Dutch buffet will employ shrimp, eel, and oysters that are smoked, salted, marinated, in dill sauce, with tomatoes, and even raw. If early December is in need of an event, follow the Dutch lead with a St. Nicholas Day affair; every December 5, the Dutch celebrate with a grand buffet and then conclude with the tradition of offering all guests their own initials, struck from pure chocolate.

Norway. A land of crystal waters and scarlet cranberries, Norway offers countless variations on the buffet theme. Its fjords yield crayfish; its seashore offers lobster and cod; and its fields offer a great variety of fruits and vegetables. Lamb is prevalent for entrees, beef is stewed with beer and cabbage, and rice desserts are favorites. After the long winter, Norwegians gather to celebrate their national day on May 17; this is the time to flaunt great salmon with hollandaise sauce and cucumbers and strawberries and cream to end. Later in the summer come Midsummer Eve (June 24) and Olsok Day (July 29)—both occasions for grilled or thinly sliced dried lamb. August 8 brings the opening of crayfish season, and in September lobsters make their debut, accompanied by mounds of toast and rich mayonnaise; game begins to appear at this time too. The yuletime *Julebord* is a festive occasion that runs for weeks (December 5 through 20) and is characterized by vast buffets of hot and cold foods. New Year's Eve in Norway is another dining occasion, featuring traditional Norwegian breads (flat, square, thin, thick, black, white) with butters and some favorite cheeses.

Spain. The cookery of Spain reflects its turbulent past. The Romans invaded and brought olive oil. The Moors invaded and brought saffron and rice, without either of which *paella* could not exist. Then when the Spanish set out to do some conquering on their own, they counted among their booty the potato, the tomato, the pepper, and chocolate. The most prolific display of these and other foods is the *tapas* buffet (see Appetizers), a wondrous assortment of tidbits enjoyed with sangria or sherry before a later-evening meal. Andalusia, home of flamenco dancing, is a southern region whose shores produce legions of seafood varieties. This is also the home of another American favorite, gazpacho. The Basque region of Spain celebrates its shepherds with a number of lamb dishes, many of which are served with potatoes. Where the sea meets the herds, a result is salt cod and tomatoes, bean dishes, and famous *chorizos* (sausages). If you wish to put a touch of Catalonia on your buffet table, get out the red pepper and wine; this Spanish district is famous for its feisty sauces. Valencia is the home of a buffet-in-a-pan, the famous paella. Combining the best of sea, shore, and field, paella offers anyone the chance to prepare a buffet with true Old World charm.

Sweden. From the land of the *smörgåsbord* come a number of reasons to gather around the buffet table. Whether it

is Easter (complete with blue and yellow eggs and multicolored feathers) or Midsummer's Eve (with seemingly omnipresent salmon and remoulade sauce), the Swedish are big on buffets. A "morning after the night before" tradition in Sweden is the Vikings table, with herring dishes at its center; salmon, hash, sausages, and cheese are washed down with coffee and glasses of aquavit. But it is the smörgåsbord that puts Sweden on the global buffet map. Not one table, but many, are needed. The first, smallest, table offers breads and cheeses, assorted herring again, and boiled potatoes. Then a larger table offers forms of salmon, prawns, sausages, pâtés, roasts, ribs, chicken, lamb, and ham and salad. Still another table might feature wild mushrooms, omelets, ragouts, and vegetables. Also important to a smörgåsbord is the small cocktail table at the front of the room with beers and aquavit. Just as important is the dessert collection of fruits and cheeses and Swedish black bread.

Switzerland. This country of 22 provinces (or cantons) offers at least that many specialties for buffets. Whether it's regional wines and fruits toward the Italian border, nuts and desserts of the high valleys, or the most common Swiss treat of all, cheese, Switzerland is a harvest basket of foods. A variation on the time-honored Swiss fondue is the raclette of the Valais district. Guests at a buffet queue up for oozy slices of warmed cheese that are scraped off a large chunk and served with bread, salad, and wine. Other folks might be drawn to crudités, a favorite offering of raw vegetables and dips. The Harvest Festival of the Bernese Emmenthal (same name as the famed large-holed cheese) features great sheets of plaited breads, a

traditional pork and veal stew, and the celebrated *Berner platte:* grand sausages and beans or sauerkraut. Desserts might be meringues with whipped cream and coffee laced with cherry kirsch. The canton Fribourg celebrates the *Benichon,* a tribute to fruits and the earth. Breads again are featured, as are soups with vegetables and marrow bones. A special mustard (with the same name as that of the region) is offered with spiced pears and cooked wine; the roasted leg of lamb is served with carmelized apples and pears and the region's grapes. As always, cheeses and eau-de-vie, a clear brandy, end the buffet affair.

Tunisia. Like paella and bouillabaisse, Tunisia's *couscous* is a spicy, one-bowl, full-meal buffet combination of grain (usually semolina) steamed over pots of lamb, chicken, and vegetables; pork is never served. Slices of melon offer a refreshing counterpoint for the feisty tomato-laced sauce. A holiday celebrated by this Islamic nation is Prophet's Day (or *Mouled*), which offers the opportunity to present a great Tunisian favorite, *assida.* This is a sweet served with pastry cream and fruits and is shared throughout the land. Date and walnut cakes are also popular. Fruits are a big part of Tunisian cookery, as are hors d'oeuvres. Not served to begin a meal but throughout, appetizers can take many forms. Fish is popular along the coastline, where it is served as part of the traditional wedding feast. In fact, a fish is placed at the doorstep of the new couple so, as they step over it the day after their betrothal, they will be blessed with good health and a protected home. Although wine is not generally imbibed in Tunisia, a good rosé would complement a regional buffet.

Review Questions

1. What are four factors that influence an ethnic cuisine?

2. What country is known for Prague ham?

3. What is a Danish *smørrebrød?*

4. What is a tradition of the Dutch St. Nicholas Day?

5. What country claims the first-ever European cookbook?

6. Briefly explain the influences that produced Spanish paella.

Two

Herbs and Spices: The Bark is the Bite

Herbs and spices, which have been sought throughout history for their preserving and flavor-enhancing qualities, can help you to duplicate dishes that their use over time has created. Stored air-tight, cool and dry, and ground a bit before each use, herbs and spices stand ready to guide you through the wonders of multiethnic cuisines.

HERBS

Basil. The French often call basil the "royal herb" in recognition of its culinary diversity; in Greek, the word means "king." The clove/pepper aroma and taste of basil is a natural with lemon and garlic and balances well with mint; a native of India, it has traveled throughout all of Europe and into such New World cooking styles as that of Chile. A classic with tomatoes, try basil with corn, zucchini, peas, and eggplant; seafood, sausages, lamb chops, and eggs will also benefit. Fresh cucumber salad with basil, mint, and yogurt will showcase its Mediterranean heritage.

Bay Leaf. A primary bouquet garni herb, one well at home in hearty stews, this Middle Eastern herb was used in an-tiquity to honor kings and victors; classic in the French cuisine, a variety of this aromatic plant is now cultivated in California. Best used while green, not dry and brittle, bay leaves should always be added in moderation and removed before service. Pickling brines and marinades often call for bay leaves, as do poaching liquids for poultry and seafood. Cabbage soup, chowders, curries, rice dishes, and stuffings, along with roasted poultry and lamb, are just a few of its many uses.

Caraway. Available in leaf and seed form, this versatile herb has been in use since 5000 B.C.; once thought to settle stomachs, it has become a major culinary ingredient in several cuisines. Offering a taste profile of dill and anise, caraway shows up in Scandinavian, Polish, and Hungarian dishes as well as in the cordial Kummel; it is a major flavoring in rye bread. Try adding caraway seeds to sauerkraut and cabbage, baked apples, potato salad, cakes, carrots, beets, noodles, and goulash; the leaves are ideal for stews, meat loaf, green salad, and eggplant.

Chervil. Native to southwest Asia, chervil contributes a light anise flavor to fish and chicken dishes, omelets, soups, and sauces. A relative of the carrot family, chervil is combined with tarragon, chives, and parsley to form the French blend *fines herbes*. This delicate herb, best added after cooking, enhances potato salad, cream cheese, cottage cheese, and freshly sliced tomatoes; spinach, peas, and beans celebrate its touch as well.

Chive. Another member of the fines herbes group, this native of Greece and Italy grows wild in many places, as do other relatives of the onion (actually, lily) family; its name is derived from the Latin "rush leek." In addition to the mild onion flavor of the snipped green stalks, chive offers delicate purple flowers that have been revered for their culinary beauty since they were first mentioned as being present in the gardens of Charlemagne. Try chives in mashed potatoes, green beans, asparagus soup, scrambled eggs and omelets, cream cheese, mayonnaise dressings, soups, salads, and, of course, vichyssoise.

Coriander. A multifaceted flavoring plant, the seeds of this native of North Africa have worked their way into cuisines of South America, Mexico, and China and into *garam masala* of India; the leaves of the herb are called cilantro, fresh coriander, or Chinese parsley. Coriander possesses a strong flavor, reminiscent of lemon and lavender, with a subtle metallic suggestion. Try the ground seeds on roast pork and in pastries, sausages, stuffings, curries, and stews; the leaves impart a true Mexican flavor to sauces, seafood, guacamole, and light cheese dishes.

Dill. Named for the Norse word meaning "to lull," and once used to induce sleep, dill is applied to cuisines as far reaching as Greek, Scandinavian, European, and Slavic. Dill resembles fennel in foliage and offers both seed and leaf for culinary use. Dill is as critical to the Swedish marinated salmon known as gravlax as it is in Russian cookery; in the latter, dill is often married to yogurt or beets. Dill leaf can be used in your kitchen to flavor potato salad, vinegar, shellfish poaching liquids, stuffed eggs, green beans, and sauerkraut; use the seeds for breads, bean soup, steamed artichokes, stews, cucumber dishes, pickles, and sausage.

Fennel. One of the more versatile herbs, fennel produces leafy stalks, seeds, and edible bulbs that are cooked like turnips; of Mediterranean origin, fennel has found its way into the cooking of France, Italy, and the countries of Scandinavia. Fennel seeds are exceedingly strong, yielding one signature flavor of Italian sausages; they also do well in sauerkraut, apple pie, bean soups, shellfish dishes, candies, and beets. Stalks are much milder, finding their ways into preparations of grilled fish, potato salad, spinach, sweet pickles, and soups.

Marjoram. Related to, but milder than, oregano, marjoram is another member of the mint family; its Greek name means "joy of the mountain," a tribute to both its quality and origin. Marjoram is termed the "sausage herb" by German cooks and is touted for the same qualities by the sausage-loving British. Of the available varieties, that labeled "sweet" has the most far-ranging culinary uses. Herb breads, stuffings, and egg dishes benefit from marjoram, as do chowders, beans, meat pies, and roast lamb, duck, and beef. Marjoram can often be used in place of oregano.

Mint. Early Egyptians prized mint for paying tithes and a variety of pharmaceutical and hygienic uses, and probably introduced it to the Romans; it then made its way throughout Europe, where the two culinary varieties, spearmint and peppermint, thrived. Mint is popular in such Middle Eastern dishes as Lebanese *tabbouleh* and has long been regarded for its marriage to roasted lamb. Additional mint magic can be created in apple sauce, stewed pears, and fruit salads; other uses include carrots and peas, cucumbers and yogurt, cream cheese, and pea and bean soups.

Oregano. A member of the mint family, and essential to Greek and Italian cooking, this major herb is also termed "wild marjoram" and "Mexican sage"; of Syrian origin, oregano traveled far and wide, eventually being carted to Mexico by Spanish settlers. Its pungent taste and aroma find their ways into chili dishes, salad dressings, sautéed onions, omelets, zucchini and bean dishes, eggplant, and shrimp salad. A natural with tomatoes, oregano can simply be sprinkled over fresh slices with vinaigrette dressing.

Parsley. Although the ancient Greeks disdained its culinary uses for decorative wreaths, parsley has gained quite a following in contemporary European cookery. A major ingredient in Lebanese tabbouleh, parsley is a constituent of both fines herbes and bouquets garni; it combines with olive oil and garlic to form French *provençale*. Many forms of parsley exist, one of which has become ensconced in Chilean and other South American cookery styles. Soups and salads, stews and casseroles all benefit from a touch of fresh parsley, as will potatoes, rice, mushrooms, meatballs, and dumplings.

Rosemary. A Mediterranean evergreen, rosemary grows along the shore, well within range of the sea's salt spray; "the plant of memory," rosemary is often called the most beautiful and fragrant of all herbs. Taken to England by the Romans, rosemary quickly became an all-European favorite, both in cooking and as a widely used ingredient in medicinal concoctions. In addition to its regal status with roast lamb, rosemary fares well with chicken, pork, stuffings, and dumplings; stews and soups like minestrone really benefit from its presence. Try rosemary with green beans, with orange slices, and in herbal jelly.

Sage. Native to Mediterranean shores, sage was carried by the Romans to England, and from there it traveled to China. In addition to culinary uses, sage was peculiarly steeped and consumed as an age-reducing tea! The strong presence of sage can be toned down with chopped parsley, but its characteristic flavor is welcomed in bread stuffings, sausage, and seafood chowders; cheese sauces and omelets also benefit from careful addition. A natural with pork, sage does wonderful things for veal, game, cream soups, and lima beans.

Savory. A member of the mint family, savory has traveled from native France and Spain to touch the foods of many countries. With a flavor reminiscent of thyme, savory has often been called the "green bean herb," a clear reference to its favorable influence on that vegetable. Savory is available in winter and summer varieties, the latter of which is more highly prized. Try savory in stuffings, meat loaf, chicken dishes, baked onions, asparagus, artichokes, scrambled eggs, cabbage dishes, fish, and peas.

Sorrel. Found predominately in the cooking of England and France, the use of this herb has been recorded since 3000 B.C.; ancient Egyptians and Romans mention its presence in salads. Acidic in flavor, the green leaves must be used sparingly in salads, but can be cooked to great benefit with spinach, cabbage, and beet greens. Sorrel soup is a French classic, and in a sauce, sorrel is served with lamb, beef, and fish; it can also be used in scrambled eggs and omelets.

Tarragon. Another constituent of fines herbes, tarragon lends its aniselike flavor to the classic sauce bearnaise. Native to France and Spain, the dominating flavor of tarragon evidently prompted early users to favor its application to dragon bites! When used with discretion, tarragon complements cream sauces for chicken, veal, and fish and mayonnaise dressings for shrimp; quiches, carrots, omelets, salmon, vinegars, and compound butter are also tarragon candidates.

Thyme. Once used to symbolize strength and bravery, thyme has a strong flavor and must be used with care; many varieties of culinary thyme are found in its native Greece, in French bouquets garni, and throughout European cookery. Combining well with dill and oregano, thyme also marries nicely with brandy, leeks, cream, or wine. Most roasts, meat loaf, and fish dishes can benefit from thyme, as can seafood chowders, other soups, omelets, and various rice dishes; a natural with tomatoes, it also enhances onions, potatoes, and zucchini.

SPICES

Allspice. A berry from a West Indies tree, allspice offers a unique aromatic suggestion of cinnamon, nutmeg, and clove; picked while still green and then dried, it is available whole or ground. The Spanish call this subtly sweet spice *pimento*. Present in Lebanese and Scandinavian cookery, allspice is ideal for marinades and curries, ketchup, and pickles. A touch does wonders for cabbage, potato, and cauliflower soups; puddings, spice cakes, and mincemeat are some dessert uses. Try it in tabbouleh salad, tomato sauce, spinach, and stuffed eggs.

Anise. Thought to be a native of Egypt, this sweetly aromatic seed provides a flavor reminiscent of licorice; it can be found in the cuisines of France, Italy, Mexico, North Africa, South America, and the Middle East. Anise runs the gamut from aperitif to dessert, providing the distinctive flavor of French pernod and Italian sambucca, and it appears in various cookies and breads. A member of the carrot family, anise graces soups, stocks, tomato sauce, baby carrots, halibut steaks, poached pears, and citrus

fruits. A variety known as "star anise" is a versatile performer in Chinese cuisine.

Cardamom. An Asian relative of the ginger family, cardamom has found its way into such dishes as Scandinavian pastries and Indian curries. The sweet/sharp flavor of these small seeds blends well with cinnamon and cloves, is reminiscent of ginger, and must be used with discretion. Ground cardamom does well with rice, carrots, melon, and yogurt; try a touch in pancake and waffle batters, as well as in grape jelly. The whole seeds are used to make cordials and also add zest to cups of espresso.

Chili Powder. Not a true spice, this is a blend of flavoring agents whose combination produces the familiar product. Chili pepper, cumin, oregano, garlic powder, and salt are in most blends as might be cloves, allspice, anise, and coriander. A common ingredient in Mexican and Tex-Mex cookery, chili powder can also be used in dips, cocktail spreads, guacamole, barbecued chicken and meat, French dressings, and sausages; combining it with tomato sauce results in an omelet filling.

Cinnamon. Discovered by the Dutch on the island of Ceylon (now Sri Lanka), cinnamon is derived from the bark of a tropical tree; quite mild in its pure form, cinnamon is less piquant than its cousin cassia, which comprises most commercial ground blends. Cinnamon has become a major flavoring in such cuisines as those of Mexico, Greece, Scandinavia, and Africa, to name but a few. Add a touch to chili, moussaka, baklava syrup, mincemeat, and French toast batter. Cinnamon will also sparkle in puddings, breads, sweet potatoes, curries, chocolate items, and fruit desserts; it is a standard in pumpkin pie.

Clove. One of the more aromatic spices, whole cloves are produced by drying the plucked unopened blossom of a bushy tropical tree; native to Madagascar, the Philippines, and Indonesia, the clove is bright red when picked and dark brown when shipped whole or ground. Always removed before service, whole cloves are excellent in marinades, roasted hams, meat stews, pickles, poached fish stock, and sauerbraten. Ground cloves should be carefully tested with fruit compotes and soups, hot drinks, chocolate pudding, beets, and various stuffings for meat and game.

Cumin. Native to Iran and the Mediterranean area, cumin is distributed around the world; it flavors cooking in Europe, Africa, India, South America, the Middle East, and Mexico, where it bears the name *comino*. A relative of the carrot family, cumin provides the aroma and flavor known by anyone who cooks with chili powder; it is also a constituent of curry powder and *garam masala*. If you desire stronger flavor, carefully roast the seeds before grinding them or adding whole to corn soup, guacamole, carrot salad, bean dishes, pepper salad, rice, chicken, potatoes, or any number of fish and shellfish dishes.

Curry Powder. Rather than a single spice, curry powder is a mixture whose distinctive flavor emanates from a blend of such spices as ground clove, chilis, ginger, turmeric, fenugreek, cardamom, and coriander—to name just a few. Associated with Indian cookery, curry powder is an Anglicized version of garam masala, spice blends that are prepared specifically for a particular dish. Strong in character, a touch of curry powder goes a long way with stuffed eggs, crêpe fillings, shellfish dishes, French dressing, rice, stewed pears, lamb entrees, and soups such as chilled Crème Senaglaise.

Fenugreek. This slightly bitter member of the pea family provides the classic aroma one associates with curry powder; a typical ingredient in garam masala mixtures, this seed (either whole or ground) is often used in conjunction with such other blended spices as cumin, fennel, and mustard. While some suggest that a taste of fenugreek reminds them of maple syrup, its more currylike aroma complements potato dishes, soups and stews, okra, lentils and other dried bean dishes, eggplant, and pickled vegetables.

Ginger. The presence of the gnarled root of the ginger plant is strong in Indian and Chinese cuisines, although it has long been one of the most valued spices throughout the culinary world; the perennial favorite gingerbread is thought to have been first baked in Greece in 2800 B.C.! The hot, spicy roots are grated and added to a variety of dishes and are constituents of garam masala. Ginger laces sauerbraten and other pot roasts, is familiar in pumpkin pie and chutney, and can also lend its charms to sweet potatoes, papayas, avocados, and canned fruit; try it in chicken dishes, with fish, and in spice cakes and cookies. When purchasing ginger, look for a smooth, greenish surface; when brown and wrinkled, the roots are woody.

Juniper. This berry from the juniper pine (actually a cypress tree) provides the principal flavor of distilled gin; bittersweet and strong to the taste, dark juniper berries should be counted and crushed before adding to most dishes. When combined with garlic and brandy, juniper is a popular spice in Polish kitchens; also, cooks in the British Isles have long sung its culinary praises. Try juniper in marinades and pâtés, in game dishes, and with lamb, Cornish hens, and braised pork; chicken salad, cabbage, baked beans, and stuffings are more possibilities.

Mace. Harvested as a brilliant red lacy covering from the nutmeg fruit, mace reaches the kitchen from its native Indonesia as a deep, reddish-brown powder; if available whole, the correct name for a piece of mace is blade. Although it is little used in its country of origin, mace interchanges with nutmeg in the cuisines of such countries as Italy, South Africa, Hungary, and England; it is sometimes called the pound cake spice. Mace is used in a variety of desserts that include cherry and chocolate items, preserves, and gingerbread; it also lends interest to carrots, oyster stew, fish sauces, pickles, red cabbage, and beans.

Mustard. One taste of the bright-yellow concoction served in many Chinese restaurants will be sufficient to corroborate the reputation for piquancy of ground mustard; mixed with warm water and allowed to stand for 10 minutes, mustard produces quite a whallop, greatly enhancing slices of British roast beef as well as egg rolls and wontons. Two kinds of unground seeds are available: yellow are mildly flavored and hot; black are more pungent, but also more tame. Try a judicious amount of ground mustard powder in mashed potatoes, cheese and cream sauces, pork chops, and eggs; whole seeds are used in pickling brines and marinades and are tossed in with salad greens.

Nutmeg. Plucked from trees up to 40 feet tall, nutmeg is cloaked with an aril of mace; when removed from its yellow-green shell, the pecan-sized spice is shipped from its native Indonesia. Nutmeg first made its way through India as one of the key spices to reach Europe and one that Columbus sought to discover in his travels. Though he never found this treasured spice, nutmeg ultimately reached the kitchens of the world and is now used in custards, puddings, doughnuts, and eggnog; nondessert dishes include spinach and cauliflower, cream sauces, cheese dishes, mushrooms, vegetable purées, and cornmeal gnocchi.

Paprika. One of many Capsicum peppers discovered in the New World, paprika has become indelibly associated with Hungarian cookery, although it was initially developed in Turkey; varieties are now raised in Spain and California as well as throughout Eastern Europe. The best paprika is deep to bright red in color; Hungarian is typically piquant, while Spanish is most often sweet. Exceedingly high in vitamin C, paprika finds its way into sausages and marinades and adds flavor to soups and chowders, chicken and shellfish, mayonnaise and sour cream dressings, and dishes that feature pork and veal. Its flavor blends well with caraway and garlic.

Pepper, Black. This is the one that started it all! Once more valued than human life, the small kernel of the *Piper nigrum* family prompted Christopher Columbus and others like him to seek its source and thus control its supply and price. Native to India and to the Indone-sian Spice Islands called the Moluccas, true black pepper is picked while green and spread in the sun to dry. White pepper is the very same berry that is allowed to ripen on the tree; its hull is removed and its core is bleached. Green peppercorns are merely unripened berries that are immersed in brine (among other preservatives) and sealed. This king of spices has been used to ransom cities and, less aggressively, to stimulate the appetite; its culinary uses run the gamut from lacing an iced aperitif vodka to a dessert of pepper-strewn pears. No vegetable, sauce, soup, or entree — or any other food type — would be inappropriately caressed by a kiss of *Piper nigrum* pepper.

Pepper, Hot and Sweet. When Columbus sailed forth to discover a western route to India, it was for spices — especially pepper — that he searched. When he encountered various plants with pods of green, yellow, and red fruit, and he tasted their piquancy, he mistakenly assumed them to be peppers and named them so. Thus a confusion resulted that has lasted to this day. Dozens of varieties of these Capsicum varieties exist, including such common ones as paprika, cayenne, chilis, and sweet bell. A part of the same organic family that provides tomatoes and tobacco, red pepper returned with Columbus to Europe and from there it circled the globe; the cuisines of China, Africa, Europe, Japan, Korea, India — almost everywhere — share with Mexico and Central and South America the use and appreciation of the red pepper family. From bell pepper sweet to the hell fire of Yucatán *habañeros*, the Capsicum family is a large one indeed. With the expanding popularity and availability of typically Mexican peppers, it is a good idea to become familiar with the piquant properties of some of the more common types. Hot: *jalapeño, serrano, habañeros, chilacas, guero, pasilla, guajillo, chipotle, seco.* Mild: *poblano, ancho, mulato, cascabel.* Care should be taken when handling these often fiery little pods, especially when removing their seeds and veins; always wear gloves and never rub your eyes during or directly after handling.

Saffron. One of the world's most expensive spices, saffron is derived from a tiny Spanish crocus plant; the orange stigmata that each 3-inch plant produces are plucked and then dried to yield their treasure. Saffron contributes a brilliant yellow color and distinctive metallic flavor that are renowned in the cookery of Mediterranean Spain, Italy, and the south of France; Mexican cooks use *achiote* to duplicate the color, though not the flavor, in some of their foods. Saffron is critical to such classics as paella, bouillabaisse, and arroz con pollo. To use, dissolve stigmata "threads" in warm water until the color is obtained.

Sesame Seed. Called Benne seeds along our Atlantic coast, sesame seeds found their way here from western Africa; they are used in the cuisines of China, Korea, Mexico, and the Middle East, in their natural pale color, toasted to a golden brown, or pressed into richly flavored oil. High in fat content, sesame seeds should be watched carefully to prevent burning while toasting. Other than baking applications, sesame seeds are used in salads, candy (halvah), meat loaf, spinach, poultry stuffing, *tahini,* and many cream pies; in Mexican cookery, they are a key ingredient of the classic *mole poblano.*

Turmeric. The source of the yellow hue in curry powders and prepared mustards, turmeric is sometimes called a "poor man's saffron." Native to India and Jamaica, turmeric is obtained by grinding the root of a plant related to ginger; slightly bitter in taste, it is a key constituent of the Indian spice mixture garam masala. Try conservative amounts of turmeric in curry and rice dishes, chutneys, seafood, chicken, and vegetables.

Review Questions

1. What herbs constitute a bouquet garni?

2. What makes up the fines herbes mixture?

3. What is another name for cilantro?

4. What herb is required for gravlax?

5. What do German cooks call the sausage herb?

6. What two herbs are prevalent in tabbouleh?

Three

Appetizers: A Time and A Place

Just as there are no limits to the time of day or meal occasion for the service of buffet appetizers, neither are there limits to their ethnic flavors. In fact, within the fabric of many cuisines there is a special place for appetizers alone, a time when people gather to hone their wits and whet their appetites . . . with savories and socializing around an appetizer buffet. Whether you offer appetizers on a buffet table or in the cocktail lounge, ideas from many countries provide several ways for creative world's fare to grace your menu.

CHINESE *DIM SUM*

Literally meaning "touch the heart," these Chinese stuffed pastries have been a part of Oriental cuisine since the ages of the Sung Dynasty, more than 300 years before the travels of Marco Polo. Wontons, egg rolls, and "pot stickers" are some of the general categories, and within each is a wealth of Chinese appetizers that can be prepared from fresh or premade wrappings. Wontons can be filled with meat or fish and then steamed or fried. *Siu mai* (small dumplings made in wonton wrappers) contain seasoned ground shrimp and pork; gentle steaming prepares them for the buffet table. Egg rolls, a direct descendant of spring rolls, are filled with shredded meats and vegetables before they are deep fried for ser-

vice. Pot stickers, or *jao tze*, are pork- and shrimp-filled hot water pastry circles that are folded into three-sided pockets and steamed, either with or without a preliminary frying step. Shrimp toasts are a deep-fried item made by spreading bread triangles with a puréed mixture of shellfish and egg whites; *ga li gai goh* are a similar preparation of curried chicken on strips of pie dough. In addition to these dim sum appetizers, Chinese cooks also prepare such "picnic" foods as smoked tea duck, fried chicken wings, barbecued spareribs, tangy stir-fried shrimp, piquant noodle salad, and marinated vegetables; like their Japanese counterparts (see section on Japanese *zensai*), these delights can be served warm or chilled. Most Chinese appetizers are delicious with soy sauce, rice wine vinegar, sweet/sour sauce, or *hoisin* sauce; beer and sake are appropriate beverages.

GREEK *MEZES*

When the time draws nigh for some *mezethakia*—an assortment of Greek appetizers that combine to form a buffet of vast delights—beverages such as ouzo or roditis help to set a gala food theme. Greek canapés are popular items, spread thickly with caviar, sardines, or anchovy slices; crackers can be used to dip into yogurt spreads or a mixture of eggplant,

olives, and capers. Greek sausage, called *loukania*, is rich with meat, garlic, cinnamon, pepper, and orange peel; herring is smoked and served with olive oil. Little pastries are filled with cheese, spinach, or lamb; mussels are stuffed with rice and herbs; grape leaves burst with lamb, scallions, mint, and dill; cucumbers form "boats" for chopped shrimp, crab, and creamed cheese. Vegetables such as eggplant and zucchini are often frittered and fried; cheese wedges, called *kasseri tighanito*, are flamed with brandy and doused with lemon. Samples of souvlakia are appetizer portions of skewered lamb or chicken, served with slices of pepper and onion. If you want to complete the picture with another appropriate wine, complement ouzo and roditis with piney, yellow retsina.

INDONESIAN *RIJSTTAFEL*

The translation is "rice table," but the practical meaning is lots of good food! This Dutch-Indonesian classic has been toned down dramatically from a pompous history, but still features meats and vegetables in panoramic presentation; accompanied by small bowls of condiment *sambal* and steamed rice, items on a rijsttafel welcome guests to test and sample. Perfect for the stand-up buffet, Indonesian *satés* are skewers of grilled poultry, shrimp, or meat; peanut sauce is a favorite accompaniment. Curried chicken, spiced eggplant wedges, shredded beef and spiced pork, shrimp wafers, fried tofu cubes, spiced hard-boiled eggs, and coconut-flavored fried chicken are just some of the items that could be served in appetizer-sized pieces. Fried banana slices, barbecued ribs, and vegetable curries and dipping sauces can tempt participants in a rijsttafel to cool their palates with a tropical cocktail or iced tea; palm leaves and coconuts provide a touch of atmospheric garnish.

ITALIAN ANTIPASTO

Meaning "before the pasta," these traditional favorites are welcomed at any time and can stand on their own as a buffet drawing card. When raw vegetables or grilled pepper strips need a dipping sauce, *bagna cauda* is the choice; rich with garlic and tangy with anchovies, this is a specialty of the Piedmont area. Chicken livers are ground with prosciutto and spread on toast slices, shrimp are mixed with rice and peppers, mussels are steamed with lemon and parsley or baked with vinegar and garlic, and olives are stuffed with ground meats and cheese for some other regional specialties. All antipasto platters must include slices of flavorful sausages and creamy Italian cheeses, and mushrooms, carrots, and artichoke hearts are marinated in oil and vinegar; melon slices or figs with ham are also common antipasto constituents. The *frittata* is an Italian omelet and often finds its open-faced way onto antipasto presentations; artichokes, spinach, zucchini, and onions are just a few of the

possible toppers for wedge-shaped servings. Octopus and squid, fried or marinated in ubiquitous garlic and olive oil, will also be popular. Loaves of crisp bread and carafes of dry white or red wine will complete the scene for an Italian appetizer antipasto buffet.

JAPANESE *ZENSAI*

Closely related to the Japanese *bento* (picnic box foods), which are items planned to be eaten at room temperature, zensai are tidbits served before a main meal that can be warmed or cool, but always presented with an eye toward garnish and delicate slicing. The variety of shellfish available to Japanese cooks contributes to zensai assortments, as do carrots, cucumber, and daikon, the Japanese white radish. Sushi is a classic Japanese presentation of short-grain rice rolled with raw fish, mushrooms, ginger, or smoked salmon; the mixtures are wrapped in sheets of kelp before being sliced into bite-sized pieces. Sashimi, on the other hand, is a presentation of deftly sliced or cubed raw fish, served with carved vegetables and that piquant Japanese horseradish, *wasabe*. Shrimp also take their place on a zensai table, either breaded and fried or grilled with a sauce. Stuffed mushrooms, broiled oysters, steamed clams in a sweet sauce, chopped duck steamed in sake, marinated asparagus and rounds of cucumbers stuffed with crab meat and vegetables are additional zensai offerings. Sake and beer are traditional beverages, while such dipping sauces as mustard, soy sauce, and horseradish find their places among these delicate foods.

RUSSIAN *ZAKUSKI*

Although wind and snow may blow across the frigid plains, all's warm when zakuski time draws nigh. This Russian appetizer assortment spreads across both tabletop and culture, and although such an "official" excuse like the Easter celebration poses a definite call for zakuski, virtually any occasion for gathering a group will do. Flavored vodkas and varied loaves of sliced rye breads are almost as profuse as the foods traditionally served, each in its own bowl: marinated vegetables such as radishes, cucumbers, carrots, celery, and beans; caviar of as many sorts as feasible, served with garnishes of onions and sour cream; pickled mushrooms with julienne strips of carrots and celery; smoked salmon; creamed and marinated herring; cheeses and sausages of great diversity; pâtés; oysters, anchovies, sardines, and other seafood; pastries filled with mousses of fish or meat; and vodka, vodka, vodka—icy cold from the freezer or flavored with lemon, pepper, or buffalo grass.

SPANISH *TAPAS*

The scene shifts to a setting sun over the broad Atlantic, fiery red light flooding the assembled foods. It is time for tapas, the Spanish assortment of individual foods designed to be taken in small doses of large variety, ideally well before a formal meal. Some of the literally dozens of comestibles on a tapas array might include cheeses and fruits; ceviche of fish or scallops—tart with lemon or lime; calamari, fried or in marinade; chorizo and other sausages, grilled with a piquant sauce or simply sliced and offered chilled; pâtés of seafood; pasta salads; fried squid stuffed with seasoned pork; sautéed frog legs, shining with a deep red tomato sauce; skewers of lamb or shrimp, with a drape of olive oil, garlic, and paprika. An occasion in its own right, a tapas theme might be enhanced by guitar and flamenco, pitchers of fruity sangria, or slightly chilled glasses of hearty dry sherry. Regardless of the beverage, the list of foods, as well as the reasons to serve them, go on and on.

TURKISH *RAKI* TABLE

Often refered to as "lion's milk," Turkish raki is a brandy-type beverage flavored with anise; similar to both Greek ouzo and French pastis, raki turns cloudy when diluted with water. Diluted to the taste, or taken straight from the bottle, raki has spawned the raki table, a Turkish social institution focused on the beverage and an array of cocktail appetizers. Often extending into the wee hours, a raki table offers Americans a taste of another cultural buffet event. Cold dishes include feta cheese and olives of many descriptions, sliced tomatoes and cucumbers with a dipping sauce of cheese and herbs, sardines, and marinated native bonito. Snow almonds, in a unique method for serving these nuts, are first soaked in water, then rubbed and drained, and presented in a bowl filled with ice. Warm selections on the raki table might include cheese or meat-filled *boereks*, little packages of phyllo dough that are baked to a golden brown; *hanim parmagi* are little fingers of deep-fried spiced ground beef; *yalanci dolma* are the Turkish version of miniature stuffed grape leaves; fried mussels are served in a variety of ways, including with a *tarator* dipping sauce of pine nuts and garlic. Rosé wine or chilled beer make suitable alternatives to the "lion's milk" if a more subdued "roar" is desired.

Baked Clams

INGREDIENTS	TEST QUANTITY: 8	SERVICE QUANTITY: 50	METHOD
Littleneck clams, shucked and chopped	2 doz.	12 doz.	Distribute chopped clams in open shell halves.
Butter, melted, unsalted	1 cup	3 lb.	Combine and divide among shells.
Almonds, chopped	$\frac{1}{4}$ cup	$1\frac{1}{2}$ cups	
Tomato, medium, peeled, seeded, chopped	2	4 lb.	
Green pepper, minced	$\frac{1}{4}$ cup	$1\frac{1}{2}$ cups	
Garlic, minced	5 cloves	3 tbsp.	
Shallots, minced	$\frac{1}{4}$ cup	$1\frac{1}{2}$ cups	
Parsley, chopped	$\frac{1}{2}$ cup	3 cups	
White wine, dry	$\frac{1}{4}$ cup	$1\frac{1}{2}$ cups	
Bread crumbs, very dry, sifted	$\frac{3}{4}$ cup	1 lb.	
Salt	to taste	to taste	
Pepper, black, freshly ground	to taste	to taste	
Paprika	to taste	to taste	
Bread crumbs	$\frac{3}{4}$ cup	1 lb.	Sprinkle over.
Parmesan cheese, grated	$\frac{1}{4}$ cup	$1\frac{1}{2}$ cups	
Butter, melted	$\frac{1}{2}$ cup	$1\frac{1}{2}$ lbs.	Sprinkle over. Bake at 350°F until golden, about 10 minutes.

SPECIAL HANDLING FOR BUFFET SERVICE: *Serve these northeast American favorites from a heated tray or shallow insert pan set over dual heating units. Keep covered to maintain optimum heat level. If desired, substitute chopped fresh spinach for the parsley, and add grated Parmesan cheese to the bread crumbs.*

Baked Oysters

INGREDIENTS	TEST QUANTITY: 8	SERVICE QUANTITY: 50	METHOD
Oysters, opened, on half-shell	8	50	Place half-shells on sheet pan(s) lined with rock salt.
Butter, melted, unsalted	3 tbsp.	1 cup + 2 tbsp	Combine and brush over oysters.
Lemon juice, strained	2 tbsp.	$\frac{3}{4}$ cup	
Worcestershire sauce	1 tsp.	2 tbsp.	
Salt	to taste	to taste	
Pepper	to taste	to taste	
Hot pepper sauce	to taste	to taste	
Bread crumbs, fine, fresh	$\frac{1}{2}$ cup	3 cups	Combine and divide among oysters. Bake in pans lined with rock salt at 425°F until well warmed, about 5 minutes. *Offer with lemon wedges.*
Shallots, minced	1 tbsp.	$\frac{1}{3}$ cup	
Bacon, fried, crumbled	$\frac{1}{2}$ cup	3 cups	
Bacon grease	2 tbsp.	$\frac{3}{4}$ cup	
Green peppers, minced	1 tbsp.	$\frac{1}{3}$ cup	
Parsley, chopped	1 tbsp.	$\frac{1}{3}$ cup	

SPECIAL HANDLING FOR BUFFET SERVICE: *Serve very warm from heated tray or from shallow insert pans set over dual heating units. Keep covered to maintain optimum heat level. Offer as an appetizer or as a unique shellfish entree, accompanied by various side dishes. Add finely diced Chinese cabbage or red peppers for variation.*

Broiled Clams with Mustard Butter

INGREDIENTS	TEST QUANTITY: 8	SERVICE QUANTITY: 50	METHOD
Butter, soft, unsalted	$\frac{1}{2}$ lb.	3 lb.	Combine until well mixed.
Scallions (greens only), minced	$\frac{1}{3}$ cup	2 cups	
Celery, minced	$\frac{1}{3}$ cup	2 cups	
Mustard, Dijon type	$\frac{1}{4}$ cup	$1\frac{1}{2}$ cups	
Worcestershire sauce	2 tsp.	$\frac{1}{4}$ cup	
Parsley, chopped	2 tbsp.	$\frac{3}{4}$ cup	
Lemon juice	to taste	to taste	
Salt	to taste	to taste	
Pepper	to taste	to taste	
Tabasco	to taste	to taste	
Steamer clams, scrubbed	16	100	Open. Release clam, but leave in half shell. Divide butter mixture smoothly over clam. Place clam shells on sheet pan(s) lined with rock salt. Chill to set butter mixture.
Bread crumbs, fresh, fine	$\frac{2}{3}$ cup	$\frac{1}{2}$ lb.	Combine and sprinkle over clams. Broil until golden and bubbly, about 3 minutes. Offer with lemon wedges.
Parsley	2 tbsp.	$\frac{3}{4}$ cup	
Garlic, minced	1 tsp.	2 tbsp.	

SPECIAL HANDLING FOR BUFFET SERVICE: *Serve very warm from heated platter or from shallow insert pans over dual heating units. A perfect dish for your clambake assortment; with a touch of soy sauce, these clams could accompany Japanese sushi or sashimi buffets as well. Long-neck bottles of iced beer would be a refreshing accompaniment.*

California Olive Cheese Balls

INGREDIENTS	TEST QUANTITY: 8	SERVICE QUANTITY: 50	METHOD
Cheddar cheese, sharp, grated	$\frac{1}{4}$ lb.	$1\frac{1}{2}$ lb.	Cream together.
Butter, soft, unsalted	2 tbsp.	$\frac{3}{4}$ cup	
Flour, all purpose	$\frac{1}{2}$ cup	3 cups	Blend into cheese and butter, using water only if necessary to form a dough. Roll out thinly. Cut into pieces large enough to cover olives. Adjust salt as necessary.
Salt	$\frac{1}{4}$ tsp.	$1\frac{1}{2}$ tsp.	
Red pepper, ground	dash	$\frac{1}{4}$ tsp.	
California black ripe olives, pitted, jumbo	16	100	Wrap each with dough to cover completely. Place on sheet pans and bake at 400°F for 12 to 15 minutes.

SPECIAL HANDLING FOR BUFFETS: *Serve very warm from shallow insert pan(s) set over dual heating units. Do not cover or balls will become soggy. Insert a pecan or walnut half in each olive before wrapping.*

Cantonese Fried Chicken Wings

INGREDIENTS	TEST QUANTITY: 8	SERVICE QUANTITY: 50	METHOD
Soy sauce	3 tbsp.	1 cup + 2 tbsp.	Combine in stainless steel bowl.
Hoisin sauce	1 tsp.	2 tbsp.	
Rice wine	2 tbsp.	$\frac{3}{4}$ cup	
Scallions (greens and whites), crushed, chopped	$\frac{1}{2}$ cup	3 cups	
Ginger root, grated	1 tbsp.	$\frac{1}{3}$ cup	
Horseradish, grated	$\frac{1}{2}$ tsp.	1 tbsp.	
Garlic, crushed	1 tsp.	2 tbsp.	
Red pepper, crushed	1 tsp.	2 tbsp.	
Sherry, dry	$\frac{1}{4}$ cup	$1\frac{1}{2}$ cups	
Sesame oil, Oriental	2 tbsp.	$\frac{3}{4}$ cup	
Salt	1 tsp.	2 tbsp.	
Pepper	$\frac{1}{2}$ tsp.	1 tbsp.	
Chicken wings, halved	3 lb.	18 lb.	Add. Marinate for 2 hours. Remove and reserve. Strain marinade and reserve.
Lemon juice, strained	$\frac{1}{4}$ cup	$1\frac{1}{2}$ cups	Combine. Add to reserved, strained marinade. Heat just to a simmer, or until thickened. Pour over chicken wings.
Chicken stock	$\frac{3}{4}$ cup	1 qt. + $\frac{1}{2}$ cup	
Sugar	2 tbsp.	$\frac{3}{4}$ cup	
Cornstarch	2 tsp.	$\frac{1}{4}$ cup	
Salt	$\frac{1}{2}$ tsp.	1 tbsp.	
Eggs beaten well	2	1 dozen	
Cornstarch	as needed	as needed	Shake excess liquid from wings. Dredge in cornstarch. Shake off excess. Fry in 350°F oil until golden. Place on paper to drain. Turn oil to 425°F and fry wings again until crisp and golden.

SPECIAL HANDLING FOR BUFFET SERVICE: *Serve warm from heated platter or from shallow insert over single heating unit. Offer in any Oriental or Polynesian setting or simply as a finger-food pickup on any occasion. Serve with dipping sauces of mustard, sweet-sour sauce, or even your favorite barbecue sauce.*

Cantonese Shrimp Toast

INGREDIENTS	TEST QUANTITY: 8	SERVICE QUANTITY: 50	METHOD
Shrimp, raw, peeled, minced	$\frac{1}{2}$ lb.	3 lb.	Combine in bowl.
Peanut oil	1 tsp.	2 tbsp.	
Flour, all purpose	$\frac{1}{4}$ cup	$1\frac{1}{2}$ cups	
Baking powder	$\frac{1}{4}$ tsp.	$1\frac{1}{2}$ tsp.	
Egg, beaten	1	6	
Salt	1 tsp.	2 tbsp.	
Ginger root, grated	1 tsp.	2 tbsp.	
Cilantro, chopped	$\frac{1}{2}$ tsp.	1 tbsp.	
Bread slices, quartered, toasted	6	36	Spread with shrimp mixture. Fry in 350°F oil, shrimp side down, for 2 minutes. Turn over. Fry 1 minute more.
Vegetable oil	as needed	as needed	

SPECIAL HANDLING FOR BUFFET SERVICE: *Serve warm from heated platter or from shallow insert pan set over dual heating units. Perfect for cocktails or as part of an Oriental or South Pacific buffet, shrimp toasts can be prepared well ahead of time and frozen for later (oven) reheating. These are ideal for using up small or broken shrimp and can be bolstered with chopped scallops.*

Caribbean "Hot and Cold" Fish

INGREDIENTS	TEST QUANTITY: 8	SERVICE QUANTITY: 50	METHOD
Red snapper filets (small), sliced	1 lb.	6 lb.	Dredge. Shake off excess flour mixture.
Scallops, sliced	1 lb.	6 lb.	
Flour, all purpose	1 cup	1½ lb.	
Salt	1 tsp.	2 tbsp.	
White pepper	¼ tsp.	1½ tsp.	
Cayenne	1 tsp.	2 tbsp.	
Cinnamon	½ tsp.	1 tbsp.	
Olive oil, hot	½ cup	3 cups	Sauté until golden. Place in shallow pan(s).
Onions, julienned	1 lb.	6 lb.	Combine in sauce pan(s). Bring to a boil.
Green bell peppers, julienned	¼ lb.	1½ lb.	Reduce heat, cover, and simmer for 5 min-
Carrots, thinly sliced	⅓ lb.	2 lb.	utes. Let cool. Pour over fish. Refrigerate for
Celery, julienned	⅓ lb.	2 lb.	24 hours. Allow to rest at room temperature
Thyme	½ tsp.	1 tbsp.	shortly before service. Drain and arrange fish
Ginger, grated	½ tsp.	1 tbsp.	on service piece(s). Garnish appropriately (see
Salt	1 tsp.	2 tbsp.	Chapter 13, page 367).
Peppercorns, black, crushed	½ tsp.	1 tbsp.	
Red pepper, crushed	1 tbsp.	⅓ cup	
Lime juice, strained	½ cup	3 cups	
Orange juice	½ cup	3 cups	
White wine, dry	1 cup	1½ qt.	

SPECIAL HANDLING FOR BUFFET SERVICE: *Serve chilled from platter or shallow insert pans. Garnish with decorative green parsley or cilantro, along with slices of lemon and lime.*

Serve during any Caribbean or South Seas buffet or as a smorgasbord offering. Check the text of the seafood chapter (Chapter 7) for possible substitutes for red snapper.

Chimichurri Sauce (for Argentine empanadas)

INGREDIENTS	TEST QUANTITY: 8	SERVICE QUANTITY: 50	METHOD
Vinegar, red wine	$\frac{1}{2}$ cup	3 cups	Beat well.
Olive oil	$\frac{2}{3}$ cup	1 qt.	
Dry mustard	1 tsp.	2 tbsp.	
Onion, minced	1 cup	2 lb.	Combine and whip into vinegar-oil mixture.
Green olives, chopped	1 tbsp.	$\frac{1}{3}$ cup	Cover and allow flavors to blend for several
Parsley or cilantro, chopped	$\frac{1}{2}$ cup	3 cups	hours. Mix well.
Scallions (greens only), chopped	1 tbsp.	$\frac{1}{3}$ cup	
Garlic, chopped	2 cloves	12 cloves	
Brandy	1 tbsp.	$\frac{1}{3}$ cup	
Oregano	2 tsp.	$\frac{1}{4}$ cup	
Pepper	1 tbsp.	$\frac{1}{3}$ cup	
Cayenne	2 tsp.	$\frac{1}{4}$ cup	
Salt	to taste	to taste	

SPECIAL HANDLING FOR BUFFET SERVICE: *Serve chilled or at room temperature. Offer "on the side" as accompaniment for Argentine empanadas or grilled red meats.*

Cocktail Hour Dipping Sauce

INGREDIENTS	TEST QUANTITY: 8	SERVICE QUANTITY: 50	METHOD
Chili sauce	1 cup	$1\frac{1}{2}$ qt.	Combine in blender or food processor. Blend until well mixed. Chill completely.
Lemon juice	1 tbsp.	$\frac{1}{3}$ cup	
Horseradish	1 tbsp.	$\frac{1}{3}$ cup	
Worcestershire	1 tbsp.	$\frac{1}{3}$ cup	
Scallions (greens only), chopped	$\frac{1}{4}$ cup	$1\frac{1}{2}$ cups	
Celery, minced	$\frac{1}{4}$ cup	$1\frac{1}{2}$ cups	
Tabasco	$\frac{1}{4}$ tsp.	$1\frac{1}{2}$ tsp.	
Garlic powder	$\frac{1}{4}$ tsp.	$1\frac{1}{2}$ tsp.	
Celery salt	$\frac{1}{4}$ tsp.	$1\frac{1}{2}$ tsp.	
Salt	to taste	to taste	
Cayenne	to taste	to taste	

SPECIAL HANDLING FOR BUFFETS: *Offer with assorted shrimp, oysters, or other shellfish; also serve it with sliced raw vegetables and crackers.*

Cocktail Mushrooms

INGREDIENTS	TEST QUANTITY: 8	SERVICE QUANTITY: 50	METHOD
Chicken, poached, minced	1 cup	1½ qt.	Combine well. Adjust seasoning.
Pecans, chopped	¼ cup	1½ cups	
Curry powder	2 tbsp.	¾ cup	
Cognac	1 oz.	¾ cup	
MSG	1 tsp.	2 tbsp.	
Mayonnaise	1 tsp.	2 tbsp.	
Mustard, Dijon type	½ tsp.	1 tbsp.	
Salt	to taste	to taste	
Black pepper	to taste	to taste	
Lime juice, fresh, strained	to taste	to taste	
Mushroom caps (medium), wiped	2 doz.	12 doz.	Place on buttered sheet pan(s) and portion mixture in shallow mounds.
Bacon, fried, crumbled	2 tbsp.	¾ cup	Combine and sprinkle over. Bake in 350°F oven until well heated, about 10 minutes.
Parsley, chopped	2 tbsp.	¾ cup	

SPECIAL HANDLING FOR BUFFET SERVICE: *Serve warm from shallow insert pans set over single heating unit. Keep covered. Offer as an Italian antipasto or a Spanish tapas, on a Swedish smorgasbord, or simply as another signature item on your daily buffet.*

Cocktail Turnovers

INGREDIENTS	TEST QUANTITY: 8	SERVICE QUANTITY: 50	METHOD
Bleu cheese	$\frac{1}{2}$ lb.	3 lb.	Mash cheese and combine with other ingredients.
Green olives, chopped	$\frac{1}{4}$ cup	$1\frac{1}{2}$ cups	
Butter, soft, unsalted	$\frac{1}{4}$ lb.	$1\frac{1}{2}$ lb.	
Egg yolks	2	12	
Cognac	1 oz.	$\frac{3}{4}$ cup	
Pepper, black, crushed	$\frac{1}{2}$ tsp.	1 tbsp.	
Scallions (greens and whites), chopped	2 tbsp.	$\frac{3}{4}$ cup	
Garlic, minced	$\frac{1}{2}$ tsp.	1 tbsp.	
Heavy cream	as needed	as needed	Drizzle into paste, mixing well; the mixture should remain fairly thick, to hold its shape.
White wine	as needed	as needed	
Puff pastry dough	1 lb.	6 lb.	Roll $\frac{1}{8}$-in. thick. Cut into 3-in. squares.
Egg wash	as needed	as needed	Brush edges of squares. Spoon 1 tsp. of mixture into center of each square. Fold one corner over to another, forming triangle. Seal the edges. Brush with egg wash for glaze. Bake in upper third of 425°F oven for 15 minutes, or until lightly golden.

SPECIAL HANDLING FOR BUFFET SERVICE: *Serve from heated tray or from shallow insert pan over single heating unit. Do not cover or shells will soften. By substituting Stilton cheese for the specified bleu, a British flavor is achieved, making these ideal for tea-time buffets. Add chopped pistachios to the cheese mixture.*

Empanadas (Argentine beef hors d'oeuvres)

INGREDIENTS	TEST QUANTITY: 8	SERVICE QUANTITY: 50	METHOD
Onion (large), chopped	1	2 lb.	Sauté until soft.
Celery, minced	$\frac{1}{4}$ cup	$1\frac{1}{2}$ cups	
Garlic, minced	1 clove	6 cloves	
Olive oil, hot	2 tbsp.	$\frac{3}{4}$ cup	
Beef chuck roast, ground	$\frac{1}{2}$ lb.	3 lb.	Combine and add to pan. Cook until beef is browned; adjust seasonings; cool.
Raisins, chopped	$\frac{1}{4}$ cup	$1\frac{1}{2}$ cups	
Almonds, slivered	$\frac{1}{4}$ cup	$1\frac{1}{2}$ cups	
Tomato (medium), peeled, seeded, chopped	1	2 lb.	
Cilantro, chopped	1 tsp.	2 tbsp.	
Olives, stuffed, chopped	4	$\frac{1}{2}$ cup	
Olives, ripe, chopped	4	$\frac{1}{2}$ cup	
Egg, hard boiled, chopped	1	6	
Cumin, ground	$\frac{1}{4}$ tsp.	$1\frac{1}{2}$ tsp.	
Chili powder	1 tbsp.	$\frac{1}{3}$ cup	
Cayenne, ground	1 tsp.	2 tbsp.	
Flour, all purpose	1 tsp.	2 tbsp.	
Sugar	$\frac{1}{2}$ tsp.	1 tbsp.	
Salt	to taste	to taste	
Pepper	to taste	to taste	
Pie dough circles, 4-in. diam.	8	50	Arrange on work surface.
Water	1 tbsp.	$\frac{1}{3}$ cup	Combine and brush over pastries. Portion mixture on pastry circles. Fold in half and crimp edges—first up, then down, then up—to give a fluted effect. Make a tiny slit in each so steam can escape. Place on buttered sheet pan(s) and bake in 375°F oven until golden, approximately 30 minutes. Keep warm during service.
Egg(s), lightly beaten	1	6	
Chimichurri sauce	see Recipe Index	see Recipe Index	Offer for a light condiment.

SPECIAL HANDLING FOR BUFFET SERVICE: *Serve from trays or shallow insert pans set over a single heating unit. Do not cover or the pastry shells will soften. These can be offered in a number of themes, including a South American buffet or a Spanish tapas appetizer assortment. See recipe for Pate Brisee, page 316.*

Greek "Bourekakia" Rolls (spiced lamb in phyllo)

INGREDIENTS	TEST QUANTITY: 8	SERVICE QUANTITY: 50	METHOD
Olive oil, hot	2 tbsp.	$\frac{3}{4}$ cup	Sauté until soft.
Onion, chopped	$\frac{1}{3}$ cup	2 cups	
Celery, minced	$\frac{1}{4}$ cup	$1\frac{1}{2}$ cups	
Garlic, minced	1 tsp.	2 tbsp.	
Ground lamb	$\frac{1}{2}$ lb.	3 lb.	Add. Sauté until well browned.
Red wine, dry	2 tbsp.	$\frac{3}{4}$ cup	Add. Deglaze. Scrape pan well.
Cognac	1 tbsp.	$\frac{1}{3}$ cup	
Raisins, golden	$\frac{1}{2}$ cup	3 cups	Add. Simmer 1 minute. Adjust seasoning.
Pine nuts	1 tbsp.	$\frac{1}{3}$ cup	
Curry powder	$\frac{1}{2}$ tsp.	1 tbsp.	
Cinnamon	$\frac{1}{4}$ tsp.	$1\frac{1}{2}$ tsp.	
Allspice	$\frac{1}{4}$ tsp.	$1\frac{1}{2}$ tsp.	
Salt	$\frac{1}{2}$ tsp.	1 tbsp.	
Pepper	$\frac{1}{2}$ tsp.	1 tbsp.	
Phyllo sheets (commercial)	$\frac{1}{4}$ lb.	$1\frac{1}{2}$ lb.	Cut into 4 × 6-in. sheets. Cover with a towel.
Butter, melted	as needed	as needed	Brush on sheets. Place 4-in. side in front of you. Spoon 1 tsp. of mixture in middle of lower edge. Fold lower edge over. Fold sides over this. Roll up into small cylinder. Brush with butter. Bake at 450°F until golden, about 15 minutes. Offer warm.

SPECIAL HANDLING FOR BUFFET SERVICE: *Serve warm from heated tray or from shallow insert pan set over a single heating unit. Do not cover or the pastry will soften. Boureka-kia are ideal members of a raki table buffet or Spanish tapas and can be filled with chopped vegetables or cheese as well as meat.*

Greek-Style Stuffed Mussels

INGREDIENTS	TEST QUANTITY: 8	SERVICE QUANTITY: 50	METHOD
Mussels, scrubbed	24	12 doz.	Place in pot. Cover. Steam until mussels open.
Water	$\frac{3}{4}$ cup	1 qt. $+ \frac{1}{2}$ cup	Discard any mussels that do not open.
White wine	$\frac{3}{4}$ cup	1 qt. $+ \frac{1}{2}$ cup	Remove from shells. Reserve mussels. Reserve
Lemon juice	1 tbsp.	$\frac{1}{3}$ cup	half the shells and the cooking liquid.
Parsley, chopped	$\frac{1}{4}$ cup	$1\frac{1}{2}$ cups	
Salt	to taste	to taste	
Garlic, minced	$\frac{1}{2}$ tsp.	1 tbsp.	
Olive oil, hot	$\frac{1}{4}$ cup	$1\frac{1}{2}$ cups	Sauté until soft.
Onions, minced	$\frac{1}{2}$ lb.	3 lb.	
Rice, long grain, raw	$\frac{1}{2}$ cup	3 cups	Add to pan. Cover. Simmer for 15 minutes.
Reserved cooking liquid	1 cup	$1\frac{1}{2}$ qt.	Remove bay leaf.
Bay leaf	1	3	
Allspice	1 tsp.	2 tbsp.	Add. Combine. Cover. Simmer until rice is
Cinnamon	$\frac{1}{4}$ tsp.	$1\frac{1}{2}$ tsp.	cooked. Place mussels in scrubbed half shell.
Almonds, chopped	$\frac{1}{3}$ cup	2 cups	Spoon mixture over. *Serve with lemon wedges.*
Lemon peel, grated	$\frac{1}{2}$ tsp.	1 tbsp.	
Parsley, chopped	1 tbsp.	$\frac{1}{3}$ cup	
Pepper	to taste	to taste	

SPECIAL HANDLING FOR BUFFET SERVICE: *Serve very warm from shallow insert pan set over dual heating units. Keep covered as much as possible to maintain optimum heat level. In addition to cocktail hour presentation, these mussels are appropriate for raki table and Middle Eastern maza assortments.*

Happy-Hour Chile con Queso

INGREDIENTS	TEST QUANTITY: 8	SERVICE QUANTITY: 50	METHOD
Butter, melted	2 tbsp.	$\frac{3}{4}$ cup	Combine in sauce pan. Cook for 5 minutes.
Flour, all purpose	2 tbsp.	$\frac{3}{4}$ cup	
Heavy cream or half-and-half	1 cup	$1\frac{1}{2}$ qt.	Add gradually. Simmer for several minutes. Reserve.
Tomatoes, canned, chopped, drained	1 cup	$1\frac{1}{2}$ qt.	Combine in sauce pan and simmer to reduce liquid. Reduce heat to low.
Garlic, minced	1 clove	1 tbsp.	
Salt	$\frac{1}{2}$ tsp.	1 tbsp.	
Pepper	$\frac{1}{4}$ tsp.	$1\frac{1}{2}$ tsp.	
Green chilis, canned, mild, chopped	$\frac{1}{2}$ cup	3 cups	Add with reserved cream sauce. Combine well.
Monterey Jack cheese, grated	2 cups	$1\frac{1}{2}$ lb.	Add gradually, stirring well to combine. Keep warm.

SPECIAL HANDLING FOR BUFFET SERVICE: *Serve bubbly warm in chafer or shallow half-sized insert pans set over single or dual heating units. Stir often and keep covered to maintain correct consistency. Offer with tortilla chips or fresh cut vegetables as a cocktail hour or lunchtime appetizer. Adjust piquancy with chopped hot chilis.*

Hawaiian "Cho Cho" (marinated beef or chicken strips)

INGREDIENTS	TEST QUANTITY: 8	SERVICE QUANTITY: 50	METHOD
Flank steak (or chicken breasts) trimmed, sliced into $\frac{1}{8}$-in. thick slices	$1\frac{1}{2}$ lb.	9 lb.	Place on 8-in. long bamboo skewers, interlacing like ribbon. Reserve.
Soy sauce, mild	$1\frac{1}{4}$ cups	$7\frac{1}{2}$ cups	Combine; bring to boil. Cook until dissolved.
Brown sugar, dark	1 cup	3 lb.	
Ginger, minced	2 tbsp.	$\frac{3}{4}$ cup	
Cinnamon	$\frac{1}{4}$ tsp.	$1\frac{1}{2}$ tsp.	
Oyster sauce (commercial)	$1\frac{1}{2}$ tbsp.	$\frac{1}{2}$ cup	
Bean paste (commercial), sweet	$1\frac{1}{2}$ tbsp.	$\frac{1}{2}$ cup	
Molasses	$1\frac{1}{2}$ tbsp.	$\frac{1}{2}$ cup	
Horseradish, grated	$\frac{1}{2}$ tsp.	1 tbsp.	
Sherry, dry	$1\frac{1}{2}$ tbsp.	$\frac{1}{2}$ cup	
Cornstarch	1 tbsp.	$\frac{1}{3}$ cup	Dissolve well. Add to pan and blend. Simmer for 3 minutes. Remove from heat.
Beer or "sake"	2 tbsp.	$\frac{3}{4}$ cup	
Plum wine	$1\frac{1}{2}$ tbsp.	$\frac{1}{2}$ cup	Add. Brush sauce onto reserved beef strips. Broil for 2 minutes. Brush with sauce again and broil again as desired.

SPECIAL HANDLING FOR BUFFET SERVICE: *Serve very warm from heated tray or shallow insert pan set over dual heating units. Arrange skewers attractively with "handles" pointing toward outside edges of container. Pour basting sauce over meat and offer as Hawaiian* pu pu *during a luau, rijsttafel, or any Polynesian/Asian occasion.*

Hot Bacon Spread 'n Dip

INGREDIENTS	TEST QUANTITY: 8	SERVICE QUANTITY: 50	METHOD
Cream cheese	6 oz.	$2\frac{1}{4}$ lb.	Blend well.
Milk	2 tbsp.	$\frac{3}{4}$ cup	
Onion, chopped	2 tbsp.	$\frac{3}{4}$ cup	Add. Stir well. Place in small ovenproof
Bacon, fried, crumbled	$\frac{1}{2}$ lb.	3 lb.	containers. Bake at 375°F until hot and bub-
Horseradish	$\frac{1}{2}$ tsp.	1 tbsp.	bly, about 15 minutes. Serve hot.

SPECIAL HANDLING FOR BUFFETS: *Serve hot from small bain maries or appropriate shallow insert pan(s). Keep covered as much as possible to maintain optimum tempera-ture. Garnish with crumbled fried bacon. Serve with assorted raw vegetables and crackers.*

Hunan Chicken Wings

INGREDIENTS	TEST QUANTITY: 8	SERVICE QUANTITY: 50	METHOD
Chicken wings, whole or split	3 lb.	18 lb.	Combine. Marinate for at least 30 minutes.
Horseradish, grated	$\frac{1}{2}$ tsp.	1 tbsp.	
Ginger root, grated	1 tbsp.	$\frac{1}{3}$ cup	
Sherry, dry	1 tbsp.	$\frac{1}{3}$ cup	
Soy sauce, mild	2 tbsp.	$\frac{3}{4}$ cup	
Cilantro, chopped	1 tsp.	2 tbsp.	
Peanut oil, hot	$\frac{1}{4}$ cup	$1\frac{1}{2}$ cups	Stir-fry for 30 seconds. Add the chicken mixture. Stir-fry for 2 minutes. (Can do this step in batches. Keep oil very hot.)
Scallions (greens and whites), chopped	2	12	
Red pepper, crushed	$\frac{1}{2}$ tsp.	1 tbsp.	
Ginger, grated	$\frac{1}{2}$ tsp.	1 tbsp.	
Chicken stock	$\frac{1}{4}$ cup	$1\frac{1}{2}$ cups	Combine well. Add to chicken. Simmer just until chicken is tender.
White wine	$\frac{1}{4}$ cup	$1\frac{1}{2}$ cups	
Soy sauce	1 tbsp.	$\frac{1}{3}$ cup	
Rice wine vinegar	2 tbsp.	$\frac{3}{4}$ cup	
Honey	1 tbsp.	$\frac{1}{3}$ cup	
Sesame oil, Oriental	$\frac{1}{2}$ tsp.	1 tbsp.	
Salt	$\frac{1}{2}$ tsp.	1 tbsp.	
Star anise, ground	$\frac{1}{4}$ tsp.	$1\frac{1}{2}$ tsp.	
Sherry, dry	$\frac{1}{4}$ cup	$1\frac{1}{2}$ cups	Combine and add to pot. Simmer until thickened.
Cornstarch	1 tbsp.	$\frac{1}{3}$ cup	

SPECIAL HANDLING FOR BUFFET SERVICE: *Serve very warm from shallow insert pan set over dual heating units. Keep covered as much as possible to maintain optimum heat level. This dish can double as an entree item when offered with steamed rice and a variety or Oriental side dishes. Serve with sauce poured over or on the side for dipping.*

Japanese "Picnic Box" Clams

INGREDIENT	TEST QUANTITY: 8	SERVICE QUANTITY: 50	METHOD
Sake	$\frac{1}{4}$ cup	$1\frac{1}{2}$ cups	Combine. Simmer for 2 minutes.
Ginger, minced	1 tsp.	2 tbsp.	
Sugar	3 tbsp.	1 cup	
Littleneck clams, shucked	2 dozen	12 dozen	
Soy sauce, Japanese	3 tbsp.	1 cup + 2 tbsp.	Add; simmer for 1 minute. Remove clams
"Wasabe" or horseradish	$\frac{1}{4}$ tsp.	$1\frac{1}{2}$ tsp.	and reduce liquid to a syrup. Return clams
Sake	1 oz.	$\frac{3}{4}$ cup	and cook only until they are glazed. Transfer
Salt	to taste	to taste	to a bowl and chill. Serve cold.

SPECIAL HANDLING FOR BUFFET SERVICE: *Serve chilled from service tray or shallow insert pans. These are examples of Japanese zensai (appetizers). A unique addition to a clambake or oyster roast, these chilled shellfish can be served as an hors d'oeuvre or entree.*

Javanese Lamb Ribs

INGREDIENTS	TEST QUANTITY: 8	SERVICE QUANTITY: 50	METHOD
Peanut oil, hot	$\frac{1}{4}$ cup	$1\frac{1}{2}$ cups	Stir-fry for 2 minutes to sear.
Lamb ribs, split	4 lb.	24 lb.	
Water	1 qt.	$1\frac{1}{2}$ gal.	Add. Cover and simmer until ribs are tender.
Soy sauce	3 tbsp.	1 cup + 2 tbsp.	Combine well. Add to pot. Increase heat and
Sherry	$\frac{1}{4}$ cup	$1\frac{1}{2}$ cups	simmer until mixture becomes somewhat
Bean sauce (commercial), sweet	$\frac{1}{4}$ cup	$1\frac{1}{2}$ cups	thickened. Strain out ribs. Reduce sauce as
Rice wine vinegar	3 tbsp.	1 cup + 2 tbsp.	desired. Offer as a dipping sauce.
Sugar	1 tbsp.	$\frac{1}{3}$ cup	
Scallions (greens and whites), minced	$\frac{1}{4}$ cup	$1\frac{1}{2}$ cups	
Ginger root, grated	$1\frac{1}{2}$ tbsp.	$\frac{1}{2}$ cup	
Garlic, minced	2 tsp.	$\frac{1}{4}$ cup	
Cornstarch	1 tbsp.	$\frac{1}{3}$ cup	

SPECIAL HANDLING FOR BUFFET SERVICE: *Serve warm from heated tray or shallow insert pan set over single heating unit. Keep covered as much as possible to maintain optimum heat level. Serve with any rijsttafel, maza, or raki table assortment or as a variation on the ribs-with-cocktails theme.*

Kentucky Country Ham Pâté

INGREDIENTS	TEST QUANTITY: 8	SERVICE QUANTITY: 50	METHOD
Country ham, ground, very cold	$1\frac{1}{2}$ lb.	9 lb.	Combine in food processor and process until puréed.
Eggs, slightly beaten	2	12	Add; blend well.
Heavy cream, chilled	2 tbsp.	$\frac{3}{4}$ cup	Add; blend well. Place mixture in chilled bowl.
White wine, chilled	2 tbsp.	$\frac{3}{4}$ cup	
Sausage links ⎫ Fatback ⎪ Hard salami ⎬ finely chopped Olives, black ⎪ Olives, green ⎭ Sage, ground Nutmeg Pepper	$\frac{1}{2}$ lb. $\frac{1}{4}$ cup $\frac{1}{4}$ lb. 2 tbsp. 2 tbsp. 1 tbsp. $\frac{1}{2}$ tbsp. 1 tsp.	3 lb. $\frac{3}{4}$ lb. $1\frac{1}{2}$ lb. $\frac{3}{4}$ cup $\frac{3}{4}$ cup $\frac{1}{3}$ cup 3 tbsp. 2 tbsp.	Combine well. Add to ham mixture. Chill for 1 hour. Place in loaf pan(s) to fill within $\frac{1}{2}$ in. of top. Place in bain marie and bake at 375°F until internal temperature of 150°F, about 1 hour. Chill for 24 hours.

SPECIAL HANDLING FOR BUFFETS: *Serve chilled from garnished platter(s). Offer with apple rings filled with puréed cranberry sauce.*

Mexi-Cali Meatballs

INGREDIENTS	TEST QUANTITY: 8	SERVICE QUANTITY: 50	METHOD
Saltines	12	$\frac{3}{4}$ lb.	Combine until crackers are soft. Reserve.
Salt	1 tsp.	2 tbsp.	
Chili powder	$1\frac{1}{2}$ tsp.	3 tbsp.	
Red pepper, ground	$\frac{1}{4}$ tsp.	$1\frac{1}{2}$ tsp.	
Milk	2 tbsp.	$\frac{3}{4}$ cup	
Egg, beaten	1	6	
Olive oil, hot	1 tbsp.	$\frac{1}{3}$ cup	Sauté until soft.
Onions, minced	1 tbsp.	$\frac{1}{3}$ cup	
Green pepper, minced	1 tbsp.	$\frac{1}{3}$ cup	
Ground beef	1 lb.	6 lb.	Add with onions to cracker mixture and form into small balls. Place in one layer in baking pan(s). Bake uncovered in 400°F oven until browned, turning as necessary. Remove from oven and drain. Keep warm.
Butter, unsalted, melted	1 tbsp.	$\frac{1}{3}$ cup	Sauté until soft.
Garlic, minced	$\frac{1}{2}$ tsp.	1 tbsp.	
Onion, minced	$\frac{1}{4}$ cup	$1\frac{1}{2}$ cups	
Celery, minced	$\frac{1}{4}$ cup	$1\frac{1}{2}$ cups	
Flour, all purpose	$1\frac{1}{2}$ tbsp.	$\frac{1}{2}$ cup + 1 tbsp.	Add; stir in well.
Beef broth, heated	$2\frac{1}{2}$ cups	$3\frac{3}{4}$ qt.	Add gradually, stirring.
Tomato sauce	$\frac{3}{4}$ cup	$4\frac{1}{2}$ cups	Add. Simmer until blended and thickened. Add meatballs and continue to simmer until meat is cooked, about 10 minutes.
Salt	$\frac{1}{4}$ tsp.	$1\frac{1}{2}$ tsp.	
Pepper	to taste	to taste	
Chili powder	1 tsp.	2 tbsp.	
Cumin, ground	$\frac{1}{2}$ tsp.	1 tbsp.	

SPECIAL HANDLING FOR BUFFET SERVICE: *Serve very warm from shallow insert set over dual heating units. Offer as part of a "South of the Border" or "Tex-Mex" buffet or with any of a number of South American themes. Offer small wheat or corn tortillas to dip up some of the zesty sauce.*

Nut and Herb Rolled Olives

INGREDIENTS	TEST QUANTITY: 8	SERVICE QUANTITY: 50	METHOD
Nuts, toasted, ground coarsely	3 tbsp.	1 cup + 2 tbsp.	Mix together. Reserve.
Rosemary, fresh, chopped	1½ tbsp.	½ cup + 1 tbsp.	
Dill, fresh, chopped	1½ tbsp.	½ cup + 1 tbsp.	
Egg white(s)	1	6	Beat slightly. Reserve.
Jumbo California black ripe olives, pitted	16	100	Dip in egg white and then into nut mixture.

SPECIAL HANDLING FOR BUFFETS: *Serve chilled from garnished platter. Offer as part of a Middle Eastern buffet, a raki table assortment, or Spanish tapas buffet.*

Olives Pesto

INGREDIENTS	TEST QUANTITY: 8	SERVICE QUANTITY: 50	METHOD
Pesto sauce, commercial	$\frac{1}{3}$ cup	2 cups	Combine until very smooth.
Ricotta cheese	3 tbsp.	1 cup + 2 tbsp.	
Colossal California black ripe olives, pitted	16	100	Slice off bottom so olives will stand. Stuff with mixture.

SPECIAL HANDLING FOR BUFFETS: *Serve chilled from garnished platter. Offer as an Italian antipasto or in a Spanish tapas buffet. Combine some blanched anchovy with cheese and pesto.*

Olives Royale

INGREDIENTS	TEST QUANTITY: 8	SERVICE QUANTITY: 50	METHOD
Pimiento slices (or) water chestnut pieces	16	100	Stuff pieces into olives.
Colossal California black ripe olives, pitted	16	100	
Bacon slices	8	50	Cut in half and wrap around olives. Secure with toothpicks. Broil 1 to 2 minutes, or until bacon is crisp.

SPECIAL HANDLING FOR BUFFETS: *Serve very warm from shallow insert pan(s) set over dual heating units. Keep covered. Offer as part of a Spanish tapas buffet or "California cocktail hour."*

Oriental Shellfish Wontons

INGREDIENTS	TEST QUANTITY: 8	SERVICE QUANTITY: 50	METHOD
Peanut oil	2 tbsp.	$\frac{3}{4}$ cup	Heat.
Parsley, chopped	$1\frac{1}{2}$ tsp.	3 tbsp.	Stir fry for 30 seconds.
Scallions (greens and whites), finely chopped	$1\frac{1}{2}$ tsp.	3 tbsp.	
Carrots, minced	1 tsp.	2 tbsp.	
Pork, lean, ground	$\frac{1}{4}$ cup	$1\frac{1}{2}$ cups	Add; stir until meat turns gray.
Beef, lean, ground	$\frac{1}{4}$ cup	$1\frac{1}{2}$ cups	
Crab meat, picked and chopped	$\frac{1}{2}$ cup	3 cups	Add; stir for 1 minute.
Scallops, chopped	$\frac{1}{2}$ cup	3 cups	
Shrimp pieces, chopped finely	$\frac{1}{2}$ cup	3 cups	
Ginger, grated	$\frac{1}{2}$ tsp.	1 tbsp.	
Soy sauce	1 tbsp.	$\frac{1}{3}$ cup	
Rice wine vinegar	1 tsp.	2 tbsp.	
Sherry, dry	1 tbsp.	$\frac{1}{3}$ cup	
Sugar	$\frac{1}{2}$ tsp.	1 tbsp.	
Salt	$\frac{1}{4}$ tsp.	$1\frac{1}{2}$ tsp.	
Pepper	to taste	to taste	
Cornstarch	1 tsp.	2 tbsp.	Dissolve well; add. Reduce heat and stir until mixture is blended. Remove from heat. Chill.
Water	2 tsp.	$\frac{1}{4}$ cup	
Sesame oil, Oriental	1 tsp.	2 tbsp.	
Wonton wrappers (commercial)	16	100	Place each wrapper with one corner down; moisten edges. Portion 1 tbsp. of the mixture into center. Fold bottom corner to top; press edges. Moisten one side corner; twist and press to other side corner.
Peanut oil	as needed	as needed	Heat oil in wok to 375°F. Fry wontons until browned, approximately 2 minutes. Reserve and reheat at 450°F.

SPECIAL HANDLING FOR BUFFET SERVICE: *Serve from warmed tray or from shallow insert pan set over single heating unit. Do not cover or shells will soften. Offer with various condiments such as hot mustard, soy sauce, rice wine vinegar, sweet-sour sauce, or plum sauce. This is a great cocktail tidbit that can be prepared ahead, kept frozen, and deep fried straight from the freezer for later service.*

Pot Stickers (Chinese fried dumplings)

INGREDIENTS	TEST QUANTITY: 8	SERVICE QUANTITY: 50	METHOD
Flour, all purpose	2 cups	3 lb.	Combine in bowl. Cover and let rest for 30 minutes. Knead well, until dough is soft and elastic. Scale into nut-sized balls. Roll each ball into a 3-inch circle. Cover and chill until needed.
Salt	½ tsp.	1 tbsp.	
Water, cold	½ cup	3 cups	
White wine, cold	½ cup	3 cups	
Shrimp, peeled, minced	½ lb.	3 lb.	Combine well. Chill. Portion into center of wrappers. Wet edges and bring together on top of filling, forming a flat bottom. Crimp top edge together four or five times. Put finished dumplings on sheet pan(s) dusted with cornstarch. Cover and chill until ready to cook.
Pork, ground lean	¼ lb.	1½ lb.	
Carrots, grated	½ cup	3 cups	
Chinese cabbage, blanched, shredded	2 cups	3 lb.	
Radish, grated	1 tbsp.	⅓ cup	
Scallions (greens and whites), minced	2 tbsp.	¾ cup	
Horseradish, grated	½ tsp.	1 tbsp.	
Ginger root, grated	1½ tsp.	3 tbsp.	
Soy sauce, mild	1½ tsp.	3 tbsp.	
Salt	to taste	to taste	
Sherry, dry	1 tsp.	2 tbsp.	
Rice wine vinegar	1 tbsp.	⅓ cup	
Cornstarch	1 tsp.	2 tbsp.	
Sesame oil, Oriental	½ tsp.	1 tbsp.	
Peanut oil	2 tbsp.	¾ cup	Heat as needed in heavy wok or skillet. Turn off heat. Arrange single layer of dumplings, flat side down, into wok or pan. Turn heat to low. Cover and cook for 5 minutes. (These can be cooked in batches.)
Chicken stock	¼ cup	1½ cups	Add to pan. Cover and steam for 5 minutes.
Chicken stock	2 tbsp.	¾ cup	Add. Cover and cook until moisture is gone.

SPECIAL HANDLING FOR BUFFET SERVICE: *Serve very warm from heated tray or shallow insert pan set over dual heating units. These tasty dumplings will take some practice to master, but it will be worth the time to learn. Prepare as close to service as possible to obtain best results. Serve with soy sauce and rice wine vinegar as dipping sauces.*

Ripe Olive Nut Spread

INGREDIENTS	TEST QUANTITY: 8	SERVICE QUANTITY: 50	METHOD
California black ripe olives, chopped	$1\frac{1}{2}$ cups	9 cups	Chop finely in food processor.
Walnuts, chopped, toasted lightly	$\frac{1}{2}$ cup	3 cups	
Mayonnaise	2 tbsp.	$\frac{3}{4}$ cup	Mix in well.
Thyme or tarragon, fresh	$\frac{1}{4}$ tsp.	$1\frac{1}{2}$ tsp.	Season to taste.
Pepper	to taste	to taste	
White bread slices, trimmed	8	50	Lay out on table and roll with pin. Spread about 2 tbsp. of mixture on each slice. Roll up tightly and chill with plastic wrap. Slice into four pieces each on the diagonal.
California black ripe olives, wedges	as needed	as needed	Garnish as desired.

SPECIAL HANDLING FOR BUFFETS: *Serve chilled from garnished silver platter(s). Offer with cocktail assortment or as part of a Spanish tapas buffet.*

Saté of Ginger Pork

INGREDIENTS	TEST QUANTITY: 8	SERVICE QUANTITY: 50	METHOD
Pork tenderloin, $\frac{1}{2}$-in. slices	2 lb.	12 lb.	Combine all ingredients. Marinate for 4 hours. Remove pork from marinade and place on skewers. Put skewers on rack over a pan of water and roast at 375°F until dark and crispy, about 15 minutes. Turn often and baste with marinade.
Salt	$\frac{1}{4}$ tsp.	$1\frac{1}{2}$ tsp.	
Pepper	to taste	to taste	
Ginger root, grated	1 tbsp.	$\frac{1}{3}$ cup	
Ginger, powdered	1 tsp.	2 tbsp.	
Coriander, ground	1 tbsp.	$\frac{1}{3}$ cup	
Dry mustard	$\frac{1}{4}$ tsp.	$1\frac{1}{2}$ tsp.	
Cumin seed	1 tbsp.	$\frac{1}{3}$ cup	
Allspice	1 tsp.	2 tbsp.	
Olive oil	1 tbsp.	$\frac{1}{3}$ cup	Add to marinade and bring to a simmer. Cool. Strain and offer as a condiment.
Scallions (greens and whites), chopped	$\frac{1}{2}$ cup	3 cups	
Honey, light	1 tbsp.	$\frac{1}{3}$ cup	
Horseradish	2 tbsp.	$\frac{3}{4}$ cup	
Soy sauce, mild	$\frac{1}{4}$ cup	$1\frac{1}{2}$ cups	
Sake	$\frac{1}{4}$ cup	$1\frac{1}{2}$ cups	
Peanut butter, creamy	$\frac{1}{2}$ cup	3 cups	
MSG	1 tsp.	2 tbsp.	
Lime juice, strained	1 tbsp.	$\frac{1}{3}$ cup	

SPECIAL HANDLING FOR BUFFET SERVICE: *Serve warmed from heated tray or shallow insert pans over dual heating units. Keep covered as much as possible. From elegant cocktails to sit-down luaus or Indonesian or Tahitian buffets, these South Pacific favorites should be served with their marinade as a dipping sauce.*

Shanghai Shrimp in Shells

INGREDIENTS	TEST QUANTITY: 8	SERVICE QUANTITY: 50	METHOD
Peanut oil	$\frac{1}{3}$ cup	2 cups	Add to hot wok or skillet. Heat 30 seconds.
Shrimp, large unpeeled, washed, legs removed	2 lb.	12 lb.	Add. Stir-fry for 30 seconds.
Sherry, dry	$\frac{1}{4}$ cup	$1\frac{1}{2}$ cups	Add. Toss and stir over moderate heat for 5 minutes, or until shrimp are firm. Do not overcook.
Honey	$\frac{1}{4}$ cup	$1\frac{1}{2}$ cups	
Sesame oil, Oriental	$\frac{1}{2}$ tsp.	1 tbsp.	
Soy sauce	$\frac{1}{4}$ cup	$1\frac{1}{2}$ cups	
Scallions (greens and whites), chopped	$\frac{1}{4}$ cup	$1\frac{1}{2}$ cups	
Ginger root, grated	1 tbsp.	$\frac{1}{3}$ cup	
Garlic, minced	2 cloves	12 cloves	
White wine	$\frac{1}{2}$ cup	3 cups	
Parsley, chopped	1 tbsp.	$\frac{1}{3}$ cup	Toss into mixture before service.
Scallions, minced	2 tbsp.	$\frac{3}{4}$ cup	

SPECIAL HANDLING FOR BUFFET SERVICE: *Serve very warm from shallow insert pan set over dual heating units. Keep covered as much as possible to maintain optimum heating level. These can be a bit drippy, so offer your guests plenty of napkins. These will be popular items on your appetizer buffet, so plan (and price) accordingly.*

Shrimp Rounds

INGREDIENTS	TEST QUANTITY: 8	SERVICE QUANTITY: 50	METHOD
Shrimp, boiled, peeled	1 lb.	6 lb.	Marinate for 3 hours. Pass through fine disc
Rum, light	$\frac{1}{4}$ cup	$1\frac{1}{2}$ cups	of meat grinder.
Sherry, dry	1 tbsp.	$\frac{1}{3}$ cup	
Butter, soft	$\frac{1}{4}$ cup	$1\frac{1}{2}$ cups	Combine. Add to shrimp. Mix well.
Shallots, minced	1 tsp.	2 tbsp.	
Horseradish, grated	$\frac{1}{4}$ tsp.	$1\frac{1}{2}$ tsp.	
Dry mustard	$\frac{1}{4}$ tsp.	$1\frac{1}{2}$ tsp.	
Lemon juice	$\frac{1}{2}$ tbsp.	3 tbsp.	
Salt	to taste	to taste	
Pepper	to taste	to taste	
Tabasco	to taste	to taste	
Toast circles or crackers	as needed	as needed	Spread with shrimp mixture.
Scallions (greens and whites), chopped	1 tsp.	2 tbsp.	Sprinkle over. Chill well.

SPECIAL HANDLING FOR BUFFET SERVICE: *Serve chilled from garnished tray. Ideal as canapés or simply as cocktail tidbits, Shrimp Rounds offer a solution to leftover cocktail shrimp.*

Clockwise from top: **Florida Vegetable Salad, Indian Cucumbers with Turmeric, "Fire and Ice" Piquant Onions, Mustard Cole Slaw.**
(American Spice Trade Association, Florida Fruit and Vegetable Association and the Florida Tomato Exchange.)

Spanish Orange and Onion Salad.
(California Olive Industry.)

Clockwise from left: **Ripe Olive Nut Spread, Olive Cheese Balls, Olives Royale, Nut and Herb Rolled Olives.**
Center: **Olives Pesto.**
(California Olive Industry.)

Top: Szechuan Pork with Peanuts.
Bottom: Brazilian Bass with Peanuts.
(Peanut Advisory Board.)

Hot Bacon Spread.
(Oscar Mayer, Inc.)

Harvest Vegetable Medley.
(Florida Department
of Citrus.)

Upper left: Palm Beach Chicken and Pasta Salad.
Upper right: Winter Citrus Salad with Yogurt
Dressing. **On plate:** Grapefruit Seafood Salad.
(Florida Department of Citrus.)

Miniature Lamb Tartlets.
(American Sheep Producers Council, Inc.)

Top left: Dirty Rice. **Bottom right:**
Lamb Chops in Orange Sauce.
(American Sheep Producers Council, Inc.)

**Kentucky Country Ham Paté.
(Ocean Spray Cranberries, Inc.)**

**Mexican-Style Baked Pollock with Olives.
(Alaska Seafood Marketing Institute and Sunkist
Growers, Inc.)**

**Spanish Casserole de Mariscos.
(Alaska Seafood Marketing Institute —
Whitefish Division, and Sunkist
Growers, Inc.)**

Red Bean Soup.
(Beans of the West and
Sunkist Growers, Inc.)

Escabeche of Pacific Pollock.
(Alaska Seafood Marketing Institute
and Sunkist Growers, Inc.)

Garden Salad with
Grapes and Chives.
(Beans of the West and
Sunkist Growers, Inc.)

Turkey Salad with Grapes and Pecans.
(California Table Grape Commission.)

Great Northern Bean Salad.
(Beans of the West and Sunkist Growers, Inc.)

Szechuan
Flank Steak.
(California Beef
Council.)

Clockwise from left: **Potato Salad with Green Beans, Dutch Potato Salad, Turkish Potato Salad. (The Potato Board.)**

Golden Baklava. (California Raisin Advisory Board.)

Braised Quail with Walnuts and Oranges. (California Prune Board and the Walnut Marketing Board.)

Top: Jamaican Spiced Pork Roast.
Bottom: Scandinavian Pork Roast.
(National Livestock and Meat Board.)

Kentucky Spareribs with Whiskey.
(National Livestock and Meat Board.)

Spiced Lamb Tarts

INGREDIENTS	TEST QUANTITY: 8	SERVICE QUANTITY: 50	METHOD
Olive oil, hot	½ cup	3 cups	Sauté until golden.
Onions, chopped	½ lb.	3 lb.	
Garlic, minced	½ tsp.	1 tbsp.	
Lamb, cooked, minced	1 lb.	6 lb.	Add; mix well. Simmer to heat.
Raisins, golden	½ cup	3 cups	
Pine nuts	½ cup	3 cups	
Almonds, chopped	½ cup	3 cups	
Tomato paste	2 tbsp.	¾ cup	
Parsley, chopped	½ cup	3 cups	Add. Stir to combine.
Rosemary, dried	¼ tsp.	1½ tsp.	
Tart shells, miniature	8	50	Fill with mixture.
Onions, chopped, fried	1 cup	1½ qt.	Sprinkle over tops.
Parsley, chopped	¼ cup	1½ cups	

SPECIAL HANDLING FOR BUFFET SERVICE: *Serve on heated trays or from shallow insert pan set over a single heating unit. Do not cover or shells will soften. Offer with dessert or salad forks. An alternate service idea calls for folding the tart shells over the filling into a half-moon shape and proceeding with baking. In either case, Spiced Lamb Tarts will be ideal on American, Middle Eastern, New Zealand, or Spanish buffets as well as on your own version of the classic Indonesian rijsttafel.*

Stuffed Mussels

INGREDIENTS	TEST QUANTITY: 8	SERVICE QUANTITY: 50	METHOD
Butter, melted	$\frac{1}{2}$ cup	3 cups	Sauté until tender.
Onion, minced	$\frac{1}{2}$ cup	3 cups	
Red bell pepper, minced	$\frac{1}{2}$ cup	3 cups	
Celery, minced	$\frac{1}{2}$ cup	3 cups	
Scallions (greens only), minced	1 tbsp.	$\frac{1}{3}$ cup	
Mussels, shucked, chopped (reserve shells)	1 pt.	3 qt.	Add to vegetables. Cook just until firm. Scrub and reserve shells.
Dill, dried	$\frac{1}{4}$ tsp.	$1\frac{1}{2}$ tsp.	Combine and add to mixture. Spoon into mussels shells. Place on sheet pan(s).
Red pepper, crushed	$\frac{1}{2}$ tsp.	1 tbsp.	
Mustard, Dijon type	$1\frac{1}{2}$ tbsp.	$\frac{1}{2}$ cup + 1 tbsp.	
Bread crumbs, fine, fresh	2 cups	$1\frac{1}{2}$ lb.	
Cayenne	$\frac{1}{4}$ tsp.	$1\frac{1}{2}$ tsp.	
Lemon juice	of 1	of 6	
Parmesan cheese, grated	$\frac{1}{2}$ cup	3 cups	Sprinkle over. Bake at 375°F until golden and crisp, about 5 minutes.

SPECIAL HANDLING FOR BUFFET SERVICE: *Serve very warm from heated tray or shallow insert pan set over dual heating units. Offer as part of a Spanish tapas assortment or as a savory tidbit to get your clambake (American or even a Chilean* curanto) *off to a good start.*

Swedish Meatballs

INGREDIENTS	TEST QUANTITY: 8	SERVICE QUANTITY: 50	METHOD
Beef, ground twice	1 lb.	6 lb.	Combine and work until smooth. Form into small balls.
Pork, ground twice	$\frac{1}{4}$ lb.	$1\frac{1}{2}$ lb.	
Instant potato flakes	$\frac{3}{4}$ cup	$4\frac{1}{2}$ cups	
Salt	$\frac{1}{4}$ tsp.	$1\frac{1}{2}$ tsp.	
White pepper	$\frac{1}{8}$ tsp.	$\frac{3}{4}$ tsp.	
Allspice, ground	$\frac{1}{8}$ tsp.	$\frac{3}{4}$ tsp.	
Egg, beaten well	1	6	
Onion, grated	1 tbsp.	$\frac{1}{3}$ cup	
Light cream	$\frac{1}{2}$ cup	3 cups	
Water	3 tbsp.	1 cup $+$ 2 tbsp.	
Butter, soft	1 tbsp.	$\frac{1}{3}$ cup	
Butter	2 tbsp.	$\frac{3}{4}$ cup	Heat in skillet and brown all the meatballs completely. Remove with a slotted spoon to drain on paper.
Peanut oil	2 tbsp.	$\frac{3}{4}$ cup	
Flour, all purpose	2 tbsp.	$\frac{3}{4}$ cup	Add to skillet off the heat. Work together to combine mixture. Simmer 5 minutes.
Beef stock	2 cups	3 qt.	Add gradually, whisking. Cook for 5 minutes or more over moderate heat. Add meatballs. Simmer until cooked.
Light cream	$\frac{1}{2}$ cup	3 cups	

SPECIAL HANDLING FOR BUFFET SERVICE: *Serve well warmed in shallow insert pans over dual heating units. Natural members of a smorgasbord display, these meatballs can be used at brunchtime or lunchtime as an alternative entree for buffet service.*

Zesty Crab Meat Hors d'Oeuvres

INGREDIENTS	TEST QUANTITY: 8	SERVICE QUANTITY: 50	METHOD
Crab meat, flaked	1 lb.	6 lb.	Combine.
Olive oil	$\frac{1}{4}$ cup	$1\frac{1}{2}$ cups	
Salt	$\frac{1}{2}$ tsp.	1 tbsp.	
Mayonnaise	1 tbsp.	$\frac{1}{3}$ cup	
Prepared mustard	1 tsp.	2 tbsp.	
Celery, chopped	1 tbsp.	$\frac{1}{3}$ cup	
Green pepper, minced	2 tbsp.	$\frac{3}{4}$ cup	
Scallions (greens and whites), minced	1 tbsp.	$\frac{1}{3}$ cup	
Garlic, minced	$\frac{1}{2}$ tsp.	1 tbsp.	
Hot pepper sauce	to taste	to taste	
Bread crumbs, soft	$\frac{1}{2}$ cup	3 cups	
Egg yolks, beaten	2	1 dozen	Add. Chill. Form into small balls.
Vegetable oil	as needed	as needed	Fry in 375°F oil until golden. Serve with a favorite zesty mustard sauce.

SPECIAL HANDLING FOR BUFFET SERVICE: *Serve from heated tray or shallow insert pans over single heating unit. Do not cover, or hors d'oeuvres will become soggy. Substitute chopped cooked shrimp or scallops and experience profitable use of second-time-around food use. Serve dipping sauce on the side.*

Review Questions

1. Describe the meaning of dim sum, citing four examples.

2. Name five examples of Greek mezes.

3. Define satés, indicating their origin.

4. If Italian crudités are offered, what is a common accompanying sauce?

5. Differentiate sashimi from sushi and wasabe.

6. Where might one encounter lion's milk?

Four

Salads: A Time For All Seasons

Chronicles of Persian kings, which record the service of lettuce salads in the sixth century B.C., provide a 3000-year precedent for buffets of today, where salad dishes are often the first to be encountered, and the first to make impressions. Salads should be highly regarded by buffet planners, who might well follow a maxim of the late French chef Fernand Point: "The best of chefs are those that use the products of the season." Even in an age when market shelves almost always brim with great diversity, peak seasonality of salad produce offers buying and serving guides to enhance buffet appeal.

An organization dedicated to the service of fresh produce in this country is the United Fresh Fruit and Vegetable Association. From offices in the nation's capital, the UFFVA distributes helpful information, including a season-by-season guide to products that form our salad buffets. Fruit and vegetable salads are more beautiful and more profitable when their ingredients are served in season.

THE FRUITS

Apples. Many varieties make it impossible to specify a season. Varieties noted for raw eating and salads include Gravenstein, Jonathan, Delicious, Cortland, McIntosh, Stayman, Winesap, and York.

Apricots. Several varieties are from California, including Royal, Moorpark, and Tilton; all are high in vitamin A and low in calories (51 per three medium). Availability is May through August, with the peak in June and July.

Avocados. Avocados are low in sodium, high in the B vitamin groups; the fat is highly polyunsaturated. California varieties are available all year, with a December to May peak. Florida avocados are available from July to February, with a November peak.

Bananas. This low-salt, low-fat fruit is available all year. Almost always served uncooked, bananas' nutrients shine through. Use some citrus juice to prevent enzymatic browning.

Blackberries. Low-sodium, low-calorie blackberries are available fresh May through August, with midseason peak in July.

Blueberries. Low-sodium, low-calorie blueberries have a May through September season and July peak. Many varieties are grown in New Jersey, Michigan, North Carolina and Maine.

Cantaloupes. Cantaloupes are high in vitamins A and C and low in calories (60 per half). They are at their best from April to October, with a June to August peak.

Cherries. Sweet varieties provide moderate amounts of vitamin C. Many varieties are available, including Bing, Lambert, Royal Ann, Schmidt, and Windsor. Season runs from May to August, with a June and July peak.

Cranberries. Available fresh September through February, cranberries peak in October through December; frozen berries are always available.

Figs. Fresh from California, several varieties are Kadota, Black Mission, and Calimyrnas. The season is June through October.

Grapefruit. All are high in vitamin C; the pink varieties offer added vitamin A. Grapefruit is available all year, from Texas, California, Florida, and Arizona; availability is lowest in the summer months.

Grapes. Grapes are low in sodium, with a moderate profile of vitamins and minerals. Many varieties of table grapes are available in various seasons, but generally July through December with an October and November peak is the norm.

Honeydews. Low in calories (50 per 150 g), honeydews are available all year, but they are generally most abundant in July through October, with August and September peak, and lowest in November through January.

Limes. Low in sodium, high in vitamin C, limes are available all year. They peak in June and July and also in August and September; less availability exists otherwise.

Lemons. Lemons are an all-purpose source of vitamin C. They are available from California and Florida all year; their peak is in May through August.

Mangoes. High in vitamins A and C, mangoes are available May through August with a June peak.

Nectarines. High in vitamins A and C, nectarines are available domestically from early spring through September, with a July and August peak.

Oranges. For this vitamin C leader, seasons vary by growing area. In Florida, varieties and growing seasons are Early Florida, September to April; Temples, December to April; and Valencias, February to July. In California, varieties and growing seasons are California Navels, November through June; and Valencias, March through December. In Texas, the season is October through May. And in Arizona, the season is November through June. Generally, oranges are most available December through April and least available July through September.

Papayas. High in vitamin C and low in calories (40 per 100 g), these Hawaiian fruits are available in the peak months of May and June.

Peaches. High in vitamin A and minerals, low in calories (40 per medium), peaches are available from several areas, but peak supplies are available from late May to October, the highest being June through August.

Pears. Pears are high in B vitamins and have a moderate calory count (100 per medium.) They are available from many areas, so the season is long; primary period is August through November, and June is lowest.

Persian Melon. High in vitamins A and C, Persian melons are available generally from June through October, with an August and September peak.

Persimmons. Relatively high in vitamin A, autumn seasonality offers holiday possibilities. Availability is October through January, with a November peak.

Pineapples. With moderate calories (75 per cup) and vitamin C, availability is all year, but it is highest in March through June and lowest in August through November.

Plums. Several varieties are high in vitamins A and C, and low in sodium. Plums are available from late May through October, with foreign supplies in other periods.

Pomegranates. This autumn fruit is available from September to December, with a peak in October and November.

Raspberries. Raspberries are characterized by very low sodium, and 1 cup offers 50% RDA of vitamin C. Short seasonal peak occurs in June and July; smaller amounts are available in August through November.

Rhubarb. Rhubarb is available all year through hothouse distribution, but the season for fresh is February through June, with an April–May peak.

Strawberries. Low-salt and low-calorie (55 per cup), strawberries are available from April through July, with a peak in May. Low supplies exist in October through March.

Tangelos. Tangelos are a cross between the tangerine and the grapefruit. Their season is from October through January, with a peak in November and December.

Tangerines. This low-calorie (35 per medium) fruit is available from November through March, with a peak in December.

Watermelon. Watermelons are very low in sodium and calories (50 per cup). Season is from April to September, with summer peak in June to August.

THE VEGETABLES

Artichokes. Calories increase with time after harvest and range from 8 to 44 per 100 g. Artichokes are available all year, with an April and May peak and low levels in July and August.

Asparagus. Asparagus is very low in sodium and calories (35 per cup); this vegetable is high in vitamins A and C. Availability is increasing, but generally it is from March through June with an April and May peak.

Beets. Low-calorie (50 per cup) beets are available all year, with economical peaks in June through September; lowest supply is in December and January. Cook in an acid liquid to maintain bright red color, especially when water is hard.

Broccoli. This low-calorie (40 per cup) source of vitamins A and C is available all year, with October to April peaks and June to August lows.

Brussels Sprouts. High in vitamin C, low in calories (50 per cup), brussels sprouts are available in September through March, with a peak in October through December.

Cabbage. As rich in vitamin C as orange juice, outer leaves of the cabbage are especially high in nutrients. Cabbage is available all year.

Carrots. The established leader in vitamin A and low in calories (less than 50 per cup), carrots are available all year long.

Cauliflower. High in vitamin C and minerals, cauliflower is available all year, with a peak from September through November.

Celery. Celery is very low in calories (30 per cup) and has moderate levels of vitamins A and C. It is available all year.

Chinese Cabbage. This vegetable is very low in calories (16 per cooked cup); it is high in vitamin C. It is available all year, with lowest supplies March through May.

Corn. Corn contains very little sodium (trace amounts) and moderate amounts of vitamins A and C. In the northern United States, the season runs from May through September; a Florida crop is available in winter months, lowest supplies recorded in October through April.

Cucumbers. Very low in calories (20 per cup) and high in vitamin C, cucumbers are available all year, with summer peak in June and July; they are least abundant in December through March.

Eggplant. Very low in sodium, eggplants are available all year, but they peak in August and September.

Endive/Escarole/Chicory. These lettuces are very low in calories (20 per 100 g). Because of widespread growth, they are available almost all year, although cost will decrease in summer months.

Green Beans. Green beans are very low in calories (30 per cup) and high in vitamin C. Available all year, their peak is May through October.

Kohlrabi. Kohlrabi is high in vitamin C and low in calories (30 per 100 g). It is available all year, but its main supply is in June through October with a June peak.

Kumquats. This novelty fruit brightens holiday buffets and is available November to February.

Leeks. Leeks, a moderate source of vitamins and minerals, are available year-round, mostly from October to May and less in June through August.

Lettuce. Several varieties provide moderate vitamin C, while Boston and Bibb offer high iron and low calories (60 per head). Most varieties are available all year, depending on growth areas.

Mushrooms. Low in calories (17 per 100 g) and moderate in iron, mushrooms are available all year, but with a general high in October through April and low from July through September.

Okra. High in vitamins A and C and low in calories (30 per 100 g), okra is available all year, with seasonal high in June through August and a low period from November through April.

Onions. Many varieties offer low calories (35 per 100 g) and moderate vitamins and minerals. Onions are available all year.

Parsley. Parsley is high in vitamins A and C and iron and is available all year, with peak in May and June.

Peas. This moderate source for vitamin C is available all year in larger markets, but generally in February through July elsewhere; availability is lowest in November and December.

Peppers. Peppers are very low in calories (16 per medium) and are a good source of vitamins A and C. They are available all year, peaking in July through October.

Potatoes. Surprisingly high in vitamins C and D and iron, potatoes are available all year, with no detectable peaks or lows.

Radishes. Low in calories, high in iron and vitamin C, radishes are available all year, with peak season of May through July.

Spinach. Spinach is very high in iron and vitamin A, with all-year availability, but greatest abundance in autumn and lowest availability in summer.

Squash. Extremely low in sodium and high in vitamin A, winter squash (hard shell) is available August through March, peaking in October to December. Summer varieties (soft shell) are available all year, peaking May to July.

Swiss Chard. Swiss chard is high in iron and vitamins C and A and is available from spring to winter, with peak from June through October.

Tomatoes. High in vitamins A and C and minerals and low in calories (50 per cup), tomatoes are available year-round. Florida is a major winter supplier; the national peak is May through August.

Watercress. Watercress is high in iron and vitamin A. Its peak season is March through May, but it is available in shorter supply all year.

CALORIES AND PROTEIN CONTENT OF FRUITS AND VEGETABLES

Product (fresh)	Calories per 100 g	Protein per 100 g	Edible Portion after Trim (%)
FRUITS			
Apples	56	0.2	78
Apricots	51	1.0	93
Avocados			
California	171	2.1	68 to 75
Florida	128	2.2	60 to 70
Bananas	85	1.1	65
Blackberries	58	1.2	96
Cantaloupes	30	0.7	51
Cherries			
Sour	58	1.2	87
Sweet	70	1.3	90
Cranberries			
Raw	46	0.4	95
Sweetened	178	0.2	
Figs			
Raw	8	1.2	99
Dried	274	4.3	
Grapefruit	38 to 44	0.5	52
Grapes	68	0.6 to 1.3	89 to 96
Honeydews	33	0.8	46
Limes	28	0.7	57
Juice	26	0.3	47
Mangoes	66	0.7	69
Nectarines	64	0.6	85
Oranges			
California	51	1.2	75
Florida	47	0.7	75
Papayas	39	0.6	73
Peaches	38	0.6	76
Pears	61	0.7	78
Persimmon			
Domestic	127	0.8	82
Japanese	77	0.7	82
Pineapple	52	0.4	52
Plums			
Damson	66	0.5	94
Hybrid	48	0.5	94
Prune	75	0.8	94
Pomegranate	63	0.5	64

CALORIES AND PROTEIN CONTENT OF FRUITS AND VEGETABLES (Continued)

Product (fresh)	Calories per 100 g	Protein per 100 g	Edible Portion after Trim (%)
Rhubarb, no greens			
Raw	16	0.6	86
Sweetened	141	0.5	86
Strawberries	37	0.7	85
Tangerines	46	0.8	72
Watermelon	26	0.5	52
VEGETABLES			
Artichokes			
Fresh	9	2.9	40
Stored	47	2.9	40
Asparagus	26	2.5	53
Beets, no greens	43	1.6	67
Broccoli	32	3.6	78
Brussels sprouts	45	4.9	70 to 90
Cabbage	24	1.3	80
Carrots, no greens			
Raw	42	1.1	78
Cooked	31	0.9	78
Cauliflower			
Raw	27	2.7	92
Cooked	22	2.3	92
Cucumbers			
Pared	14	0.6	84
Not pared	15	0.9	95
Eggplant			
Raw	25	1.2	97
Cooked	19	1.0	97
Endive	20	1.7	86
Green beans	32	1.9	88
Kohlrabi			
Raw	29	2.0	63
Cooked	24	1.7	63
Leeks	52	2.2	44
Lettuce	13 to 18	0.9 to 1.3	90
Mushrooms	28	2.7	81
Okra			
Raw	36	2.4	86
Cooked	29	2.0	86

CALORIES AND PROTEIN CONTENT OF FRUITS AND VEGETABLES *(Continued)*

Product (fresh)	Calories per 100 g	Protein per 100 g	Edible Portion after Trim (%)
Onions			
Raw	38	1.5	90
Cooked	29	1.2	90
Scallions	36	1.5	96
Parsley	44	3.6	95
Peas, edible pod			
Raw	53	3.4	94
Cooked	43	2.9	94
Peas, other			
Raw	84	6.3	38
Cooked	71	5.4	38
Peppers, hot	37	1.3	73
Peppers, sweet	22	1.2	82
Potatoes			
Baked	93	2.6	80
Boiled	76	2.6	80
French fried	274	4.3	80
Mashed	94	2.1	80
Radishes	17	1.0	92
Spinach			
Raw	26	3.2	72
Cooked	23	3.0	72
Squash, summer			
Raw	19	1.1	95
Cooked	14	0.9	95
Squash, winter			
Boiled	38	1.1	75 to 85
Baked	63	1.8	75 to 85
Swiss chard			
Raw	25	2.4	92
Cooked	18	1.8	92
Tomatoes, peeled			
Raw	22	1.1	82
Cooked	26	1.3	82
Watercress	19	2.2	92

Source: United States Department of Agriculture.

60

Antipasto Mushrooms in Garlic Oil

INGREDIENTS	TEST QUANTITY: 8	SERVICE QUANTITY: 50	METHOD
Olive oil	$\frac{2}{3}$ cup	1 qt.	Combine and bring to a boil.
White wine	$\frac{1}{2}$ cup	3 cups	Reduce heat and simmer 15 minutes.
Lemon juice	of 2	2 cups	Strain into another pot.
Lemon peel, grated	$\frac{1}{2}$ tsp.	1 tbsp.	
Bay leaf	1	4	
Parsley, chopped	1 tbsp.	$\frac{1}{3}$ cup	
Garlic, crushed	2 cloves	12 cloves	
Red pepper, crushed	$\frac{1}{4}$ tsp.	$1\frac{1}{2}$ tsp.	
Peppercorns, black	6	1 tbsp.	
Salt	$\frac{1}{2}$ tsp.	1 tbsp.	
Mushrooms, small, whole, wiped	1 lb.	6 lb.	Add to pot; simmer just until tender. Cool in sauce. Chill. Drain and serve with cheese and meats.

SPECIAL HANDLING FOR BUFFETS: *Serve chilled from shallow insert pan(s) or from garnished platters. Replenish as often as necessary to maintain optimum presentation.*

Offer as part of an antipasto buffet or stuffed inside lemon-laced avocado halves.

Artichokes with Mustard Sauce

INGREDIENTS	TEST QUANTITY: 8	SERVICE QUANTITY: 50	METHOD
Artichokes	2	12	Remove and trim leaves; put in pot.
Water, boiling, salted	to cover	to cover	Pour over; simmer until leaves are tender.
Lemon juice, strained	1 tbsp.	$\frac{1}{3}$ cup	Drain and reserve.
Mayonnaise	1 cup	$1\frac{1}{2}$ qt.	Combine in bowl. Place in the center of
White wine	2 tbsp.	$\frac{3}{4}$ cup	service trays(s); surround with spirals of
Mustard, Dijon type	2 tbsp.	$\frac{3}{4}$ cup	artichoke leaves.
Worcestershire sauce	$\frac{1}{2}$ tsp.	1 tbsp.	
Light cream	2 tbsp.	$\frac{3}{4}$ cup	
Orange juice	1 tbsp.	$\frac{1}{3}$ cup	
Egg, hard cooked, chopped	1	6	
Parsley, chopped	1 tbsp.	$\frac{1}{3}$ cup	
Capers, chopped	1 tbsp.	$\frac{1}{3}$ cup	
Mustard, dry	$\frac{1}{2}$ tbsp.	3 tbsp.	
Salt	to taste	to taste	

SPECIAL HANDLING FOR BUFFETS: *Serve chilled from shallow insert pan(s) or from garnished platters. Replenish as often as necessary to maintain optimum presentation. Add finely diced celery and red onions. Sprinkle with chopped parsley and garnish with lemon wedges.*

Austrian Mixed Cabbage Salad

INGREDIENTS	TEST QUANTITY: 8	SERVICE QUANTITY: 50	METHOD
White cabbage, shredded	3 cups	$4\frac{1}{2}$ lb.	Combine well.
Red cabbage, shredded	3 cups	$4\frac{1}{2}$ lb.	
Radish, grated	2 tbsp.	$\frac{3}{4}$ cup	
Apples, peeled, cored, diced	$1\frac{1}{2}$ cups	2 lb.	Add. Toss well.
Cider vinegar	$1\frac{1}{2}$ tbsp.	$\frac{1}{2}$ cup + 1 tbsp.	Combine to dissolve. Add to mixture until
Sugar	$\frac{3}{4}$ tsp.	$1\frac{1}{2}$ tbsp.	well combined.
Cinnamon	$\frac{1}{8}$ tsp.	$\frac{3}{4}$ tsp.	
French dressing	$\frac{1}{2}$ cup	3 cups	Add. Toss to combine. Chill for several hours.
White wine	$\frac{1}{4}$ cup	$1\frac{1}{2}$ cups	
Black pepper, ground	$\frac{1}{2}$ tsp.	1 tbsp.	

SPECIAL HANDLING FOR BUFFETS: *Serve chilled from shallow insert pan(s) or from garnished platters. Replenish as often as necessary to maintain optimum presentation. Add raisins or grated carrots and radishes.*

Avocado Salad with Olives and Bacon

INGREDIENTS	TEST QUANTITY: 8	SERVICE QUANTITY: 50	METHOD
California avocado, ripe, firm, diced	1 lb.	6 lb.	Toss to coat well.
Lime juice, strained	$\frac{1}{2}$ tbsp.	3 tbsp.	
Tomatoes (medium), peeled, diced	2	3 lb.	Add. Mix well.
Onion, minced	$\frac{1}{4}$ cup	$1\frac{1}{2}$ cups	
Celery, minced	$\frac{1}{4}$ cup	$1\frac{1}{2}$ cups	
Chili pepper, minced	to taste	to taste	
Garlic minced	$\frac{1}{2}$ tsp.	1 tbsp.	
Olives, green, pimiento-stuffed, sliced	2 tbsp.	$\frac{3}{4}$ cup	
Cilantro, minced	1 tsp.	2 tbsp.	
Lime peel, grated	$\frac{1}{2}$ tsp.	1 tbsp.	Combine well. Add to mixture until well coated. Place in service piece.
Olive oil	2 tbsp.	$\frac{3}{4}$ cup	
Red wine vinegar	$\frac{1}{2}$ tbsp.	3 tbsp.	
Salt	$\frac{1}{2}$ tsp.	1 tbsp.	
Pepper	$\frac{1}{4}$ tsp.	$1\frac{1}{2}$ tsp.	
Cumin, ground	$\frac{1}{4}$ tsp.	$1\frac{1}{2}$ tsp.	
Chili powder	$\frac{1}{4}$ tsp.	$1\frac{1}{2}$ tsp.	
Bacon, fried, crumbled	$\frac{1}{4}$ cup	$1\frac{1}{2}$ cups	Sprinkle over top.
Cheddar cheese, grated	$\frac{1}{4}$ cup	$1\frac{1}{2}$ cups	

SPECIAL HANDLING FOR BUFFETS: *Serve chilled from shallow insert pan(s) or from garnished platters. Replenish as often as necessary to maintain optimum presentation. Substitute California sliced ripe black olives for green.*

Chicken and Pasta Salad

INGREDIENTS	TEST QUANTITY: 8	SERVICE QUANTITY: 50	METHOD
White wine vinegar	2 tbsp.	$\frac{3}{4}$ cup	Blend together.
Mustard, Dijon type	$\frac{1}{2}$ tsp.	1 tbsp.	
Garlic, minced	1 clove	6 cloves	
Oregano, dried	$\frac{1}{2}$ tsp.	1 tbsp.	
Salt	to taste	to taste	
White pepper, ground	to taste	to taste	
Cayenne	to taste	to taste	
Peanut oil	$\frac{1}{4}$ cup	$1\frac{1}{2}$ cups	Blend in gradually. Chill.
Chicken breasts (medium), boned	2	12	Bring to simmer. Cover. Cook until done,
Chicken stock	to cover	to cover	about 15 minutes. Remove chicken and cut
Sherry, dry	1 tbsp.	$\frac{1}{3}$ cup	into strips. Reserve.
Macaroni, raw	$1\frac{1}{2}$ cups	2 lb.	Cook until done. Drain. Combine with chicken.
Boiling water	to cover well	to cover well	
Salt	as desired	as desired	
Peas, cooked	1 cup	$1\frac{1}{2}$ qt.	Add to chicken and pasta with the reserved
Pimiento, diced	$\frac{1}{4}$ cup	$1\frac{1}{2}$ cups	dressing. Toss well. Place in service piece(s).
Orange juice, strained	$\frac{1}{3}$ cup	2 cups	

SPECIAL HANDLING FOR BUFFETS: *Serve very warm from shallow insert pan(s) set over dual heating units. Keep covered. Add sections of orange and chunks of cheddar cheese before service.*

Chilled Noodles with Chicken and Ginger

INGREDIENTS	TEST QUANTITY: 8	SERVICE QUANTITY: 50	METHOD
Chicken stock, boiling	1 cup	$1\frac{1}{2}$ qt.	Blanch for 2 minutes.
Broccoli flowerets	2 cups	3 qt.	
Asparagus, peeled, sliced	2 cups	3 qt.	Add. Blanch additional minute. Drain. Shock in ice water to stop cooking and set color.
Spinach, raw, thinly sliced	1 cup	$1\frac{1}{2}$ qt.	Combine well and add to vegetables. Toss to combine well. Chill.
Chicken breast, minced, cooked	1 cup	$1\frac{1}{2}$ qt.	
Vermicelli, cooked, drained	1 lb.	6 lb.	
Soy sauce, mild	2 tbsp.	$\frac{3}{4}$ cup	
Red pepper, crushed	$\frac{1}{2}$ tsp.	1 tbsp.	
Sherry, dry	1 tbsp.	2 tbsp.	
Sesame oil, Oriental	$\frac{1}{2}$ tsp.	1 tbsp.	
Salt	to taste	to taste	
Pepper, black, crushed	to taste	to taste	
Scallions (greens and whites), minced	as needed	as needed	Sprinkle over. Serve chilled.

SPECIAL HANDLING FOR BUFFETS: *Serve chilled from shallow insert pan(s) or from garnished platters. Replenish as often as necessary to maintain optimum presentation.*

Place on Bibb lettuce leaves or in the middle of finely chopped raw spinach.

Chilled Sweet and Sour Red Onions

INGREDIENTS	TEST QUANTITY: 8	SERVICE QUANTITY: 50	METHOD
Peanut oil	$\frac{1}{4}$ cup	$1\frac{1}{2}$ cups	Add to heated pan(s) or wok; heat on high for 30 seconds.
Scallions (greens only), minced	1 tbsp.	$\frac{1}{3}$ cup	Add; press into oil. Remove from oil.
Garlic, peeled, crushed	2 cloves	12 cloves	
Ginger, grated	1 tsp.	2 tbsp.	
Red onions, peeled, sliced $\frac{1}{2}$-in. thick	2 lb.	12 lb.	Separate individual rings. Add to hot oil. Toss quickly until onions are coated and slightly translucent.
Sugar	$\frac{1}{4}$ tsp.	$1\frac{1}{2}$ tsp.	Add; toss.
Salt	$\frac{1}{2}$ tsp.	1 tbsp.	
Red pepper, crushed	$\frac{1}{4}$ tsp.	$1\frac{1}{2}$ tsp.	
Soy sauce, mild	2 tbsp.	$\frac{3}{4}$ cup	Combine well; add; stir briskly. Pour into bowl, let rest. When cool, chill completely.
Cider vinegar	$\frac{1}{4}$ cup	$1\frac{1}{2}$ cups	
Sherry, dry	1 tbsp.	$\frac{1}{3}$ cup	
Sugar	$\frac{1}{4}$ cup	$1\frac{1}{2}$ cups	

SPECIAL HANDLING FOR BUFFETS: *Serve chilled from shallow insert pan(s) or from garnished platters. Replenish as often as necessary to maintain optimum presentation. Serve as a condiment for roasted beef or lamb.*

Chinese "Hot and Cold" Cucumbers

INGREDIENTS	TEST QUANTITY: 8	SERVICE QUANTITY: 50	METHOD
Peanut oil, hot	$\frac{1}{4}$ cup	$1\frac{1}{2}$ cups	Sauté until garlic is golden.
Garlic, minced	2 cloves	12 cloves	
Scallions (greens only), minced	1 tsp.	2 tbsp.	
Red pepper, crushed	$\frac{1}{2}$ tsp.	1 tbsp.	
Cucumbers, seeded, sliced thinly lengthwise	$1\frac{1}{2}$ lb.	9 lb.	Add to hot oil; swirl until the skin turns brilliant green.
Soy sauce, mild	1 tbsp.	$\frac{1}{3}$ cup	Add; stir briskly until sugar is dissolved.
Ginger, powdered	$\frac{1}{2}$ tsp.	1 tbsp.	
Sugar	2 tbsp.	$\frac{3}{4}$ cup	
Salt	$\frac{1}{2}$ tsp.	1 tbsp.	
Distilled vinegar, white	1 oz.	6 oz.	Sprinkle over. Chill completely.

SPECIAL HANDLING FOR BUFFETS: *Serve chilled from shallow insert pan(s) or from garnished platters. Replenish as often as necessary to maintain optimum presentation. Do not add vinegar until shortly before service. Serve as a buffet accompaniment for roasted lamb.*

Danish Potato Salad

INGREDIENTS	TEST QUANTITY: 8	SERVICE QUANTITY: 50	METHOD
Peanut oil	2 tbsp.	$\frac{3}{4}$ cup	Combine. Stir until dissolved.
White wine	2 tbsp.	$\frac{3}{4}$ cup	
Tarragon vinegar	2 tbsp.	$\frac{3}{4}$ cup	
Salt	$\frac{1}{2}$ tsp.	1 tbsp.	
Sugar	$\frac{1}{2}$ tsp.	1 tbsp.	
Dry mustard	$\frac{1}{4}$ tsp.	$1\frac{1}{2}$ tsp.	
Garlic, minced	$\frac{1}{4}$ tsp.	$1\frac{1}{2}$ tsp.	
Potatoes, red, peeled, cooked, diced	3 cups	8 lb.	Add. Toss to coat well. Chill for several hours.
Radishes, sliced	$\frac{1}{4}$ cup	$1\frac{1}{2}$ cups	Combine and toss in.
Scallions (greens and whites), chopped	$\frac{1}{4}$ cup	$1\frac{1}{2}$ cups	
Celery, minced	$\frac{1}{4}$ cup	$1\frac{1}{2}$ cups	
Mayonnaise	$\frac{1}{4}$ cup	$1\frac{1}{2}$ cups	Combine and fold in.
Mustard, Dijon-type	$\frac{1}{2}$ tsp.	1 tbsp.	
Dill leaves, dried	$\frac{1}{2}$ tsp.	1 tbsp.	

SPECIAL HANDLING FOR BUFFETS: *Serve chilled from shallow insert pan(s) or from garnished platters. Replenish as often as necessary to maintain optimum presentation. Add slivered toasted almonds or pecans.*

Dutch Potato Salad

INGREDIENTS	TEST QUANTITY: 8	SERVICE QUANTITY: 50	METHOD
Potatoes (medium), red, cooked, unpeeled, halved, and sliced	6	12 lb.	Combine, toss well.
Scallions (greens and whites), chopped	$\frac{1}{3}$ cup	2 cups	
Celery, minced	$\frac{1}{3}$ cup	2 cups	
Cucumbers, peeled, diced	$\frac{1}{2}$ cup	3 cups	
Green pepper, minced	1 tbsp.	$\frac{1}{3}$ cup	
Mayonnaise	$\frac{1}{3}$ cup	2 cups	Combine and blend well. Pour over potatoes and mix well.
Mustard, dry	$\frac{1}{2}$ tsp.	1 tbsp.	
Sour cream	$\frac{1}{3}$ cup	2 cups	
Horseradish	2 tsp.	$\frac{1}{4}$ cup	
Worcestershire	1 tsp.	2 tbsp.	
White wine vinegar	4 tsp.	$\frac{1}{2}$ cup	
Salt	1 tsp.	2 tbsp.	
Sugar	$\frac{1}{4}$ tsp.	$1\frac{1}{2}$ tsp.	
Black pepper	$\frac{1}{8}$ tsp.	$\frac{3}{4}$ tsp.	
Caraway seeds	1 tsp.	2 tbsp.	

SPECIAL HANDLING FOR BUFFETS: *Serve chilled from shallow insert pan(s) or from garnished platters. Replenish as often as necessary to maintain optimum presentation. Add a touch of gin to dressing. Garnish with paprika.*

"Fire and Ice" Piquant Onions

INGREDIENTS	TEST QUANTITY: 8	SERVICE QUANTITY: 50	METHOD
Red onions (large), $\frac{1}{4}$-in. slice	2	12	Combine in large bowl(s).
Tomatoes (medium), cut in wedges	6	8 lb.	
Bell peppers (medium), julienned	1	6	
Cider vinegar	$\frac{3}{4}$ cup	1 qt. + 2 cups	Combine in saucepan; boil 1 min. While hot, pour over vegetables. Chill.
Water	$\frac{1}{4}$ cup	$1\frac{1}{2}$ cups	
Celery seed	$1\frac{1}{2}$ tsp.	3 tbsp.	
Mustard seed	$1\frac{1}{2}$ tsp.	3 tbsp.	
Red pepper, crushed	$\frac{1}{2}$ tsp.	1 tbsp.	
Salt	$\frac{1}{2}$ tsp.	1 tbsp.	
Sugar	1 tbsp.	$\frac{1}{3}$ cup	
Black pepper, ground	$\frac{1}{2}$ tsp.	1 tbsp.	

SPECIAL HANDLING FOR BUFFETS: *Serve chilled from shallow insert pan(s) or from garnished platters. Replenish as often as necessary to maintain optimum appearance. Serve with grilled meats and poultry.*

Florida Vegetable Salad

INGREDIENTS	TEST QUANTITY: 8	SERVICE QUANTITY: 50	METHOD
Florida vegetables:			
Tomatoes (medium), cut in chunks	2	3 lb.	Combine in large bowl(s).
Cucumbers, peeled, halved, thinly sliced	1 cup	6 cups	
Zucchini, thinly sliced, quartered lengthwise	1 cup	6 cups	
Corn kernels	$\frac{1}{2}$ cup	3 cups	
Vegetable oil	$\frac{1}{4}$ cup	$1\frac{1}{2}$ cups	Whip to combine well. Pour over vegetables.
Lemon juice, fresh	2 tbsp.	$\frac{3}{4}$ cup	Cover and chill well.
Salt	$\frac{1}{4}$ tsp.	$1\frac{1}{2}$ tsp.	
Onion powder	$\frac{1}{4}$ tsp.	$1\frac{1}{2}$ tsp.	
Dill weed	$\frac{1}{4}$ tsp.	$1\frac{1}{2}$ tsp.	
Lemon peel, grated	$\frac{1}{4}$ tsp.	$1\frac{1}{2}$ tsp.	
Black pepper, ground	$\frac{1}{8}$ tsp.	$\frac{3}{4}$ tsp.	

SPECIAL HANDLING FOR BUFFETS: *Serve chilled from shallow insert pan(s) or from garnished bowls. Replenish as often as necessary to maintain optimum presentation. Serve with some Florida citrus chunks to add a fruity zest.*

Garden Salad with Capers and Chives

INGREDIENTS	TEST QUANTITY: 8	SERVICE QUANTITY: 50	METHOD
Celery, diced	½ cup	3 cups	Combine well.
Carrots, cooked, diced	½ cup	3 cups	
Peas, blanched	½ cup	3 cups	
Green beans, cooked, sliced	½ cup	3 cups	
Lima beans, cooked	½ cup	3 cups	
Kidney beans, cooked	½ cup	3 cups	
Cucumber, peeled, diced	½ cup	3 cups	
Red onion, diced	¼ cup	1½ cups	
Green pepper, diced	¼ cup	1½ cups	
Capers, chopped	½ tbsp.	3 tbsp.	
Chives, snipped	½ tbsp.	3 tbsp.	
French dressing	½ cup	3 cups	Combine. Add to vegetables. Chill for several
Sweet pickles, diced	½ tbsp.	3 tbsp.	hours. Drain off any excess liquid.
Parsley, chopped	½ tbsp.	3 tbsp.	
Mayonnaise	½ cup	3 cups	Combine well. Add to mixture. Toss to
Pimiento, minced	1 tbsp.	⅓ cup	combine well.

SPECIAL HANDLING FOR BUFFETS: *Serve from chilled deep bowls. Replenish as often as necessary to maintain optimum presentation. Garnish with sliced California ripe olives and California avocados.*

Grapefruit Seafood Salad

INGREDIENTS	TEST QUANTITY: 8	SERVICE QUANTITY: 50	METHOD
Peanut oil, hot	1 tbsp.	$\frac{1}{3}$ cup	Sauté until golden.
Garlic, minced	1 clove	6 cloves	
Green beans, 1-in. pieces	$\frac{1}{2}$ lb.	3 lb.	Add. Stir-fry until tender, about 5 minutes. Remove to bowl with slotted spoon.
Scallops, sliced	$\frac{1}{2}$ lb.	3 lb.	Add to same hot pan as beans were cooked in. Stir-fry 3 minutes. Remove and reserve.
Grapefruit juice, strained	$\frac{1}{4}$ cup	$1\frac{1}{2}$ cups	Combine in pan. Reduce by half. Add reserved beans and scallops. Heat through. Transfer to service piece(s).
White wine vinegar	$1\frac{1}{2}$ tbsp.	$\frac{1}{2}$ cup + 1 tbsp.	
Fennel seeds, crushed	$\frac{1}{4}$ tsp.	$1\frac{1}{2}$ tsp.	
Salt	to taste	to taste	
Grapefruit sections	$\frac{1}{2}$ lb.	3 lb.	Distribute over top.

SPECIAL HANDLING FOR BUFFETS: *Serve very warm from shallow insert pan(s) set over dual heating units. Keep covered. Sprinkle in some toasted almonds or pecans. Add some sweetened cranberries for color.*

Great Northern Bean Salad

INGREDIENTS	TEST QUANTITY: 8	SERVICE QUANTITY: 50	METHOD
Great Northern beans	2 cups	6 lb.	Bring to slow boil. Cover. Remove from heat. Let stand 1 hour. Drain.
Water	to cover	to cover	
Salt	1 tbsp.	$\frac{1}{3}$ cup	Add to beans. Bring to simmer. Simmer until beans are just tender, about $1\frac{1}{2}$ hours. Drain. Place in bowl.
Water	to cover	to cover	
Peanut oil	$\frac{2}{3}$ cup	1 qt.	Combine. Add to hot beans. Toss. Chill overnight. Drain.
White wine vinegar	$\frac{1}{3}$ cup	2 cups	
Cider vinegar	$\frac{1}{3}$ cup	2 cups	
Water	$\frac{1}{2}$ cup	3 cups	
Sugar	1 tsp.	2 tbsp.	
Salt	to taste	to taste	
Onion, minced	$\frac{3}{4}$ cup	$4\frac{1}{2}$ cups	Combine. Add to beans. Toss.
Bacon, chopped, crisp	$1\frac{1}{2}$ cups	2 qt.	
Parsley, chopped	$\frac{1}{4}$ cup	$1\frac{1}{2}$ cups	
Vinaigrette dressing	1 cup	$1\frac{1}{2}$ qt.	Add. Toss. Chill.

SPECIAL HANDLING FOR BUFFETS: *Serve from chilled bowls lined with desired variety of lettuce. Add some sour cream to dressing. Sprinkle with paprika.*

Green Bean Salad

INGREDIENTS	TEST QUANTITY: 8	SERVICE QUANTITY: 50	METHOD
Olive oil	1 cup	$1\frac{1}{2}$ qt.	Whip thoroughly.
White wine vinegar	$\frac{1}{4}$ cup	$1\frac{1}{2}$ cups	
Mustard, Dijon type	$\frac{1}{2}$ tbsp.	3 tbsp.	
Salt	to taste	to taste	
Black pepper	to taste	to taste	
Cayenne	to taste	to taste	
Marjoram, dried	to taste	to taste	
Green beans (trimmed whole) steamed, warm	1 lb.	6 lb.	Add while beans are warm. Combine well. Chill for service.
Onion, thinly sliced	$\frac{3}{4}$ cup	2 lb.	
Celery, bias sliced, thin	$\frac{1}{2}$ cup	3 cups	
Garlic, minced	$\frac{1}{2}$ tsp.	1 tbsp.	
Scallions (greens only), chopped	1 tbsp.	$\frac{1}{3}$ cup	
Parsley, chopped	2 tbsp.	$\frac{3}{4}$ cup	
Tarragon	$\frac{1}{2}$ tsp.	1 tbsp.	

SPECIAL HANDLING FOR BUFFETS: *Serve warm from shallow insert pan set over single heating unit. Keep covered. Sprinkle with toasted almonds, crumbled bacon, or crumbled fried onions.*

Grilled Pepper Salad with Scallions

INGREDIENTS	TEST QUANTITY: 8	SERVICE QUANTITY: 50	METHOD
Green bell peppers, large	3	3 lb.	Rotate over or under broiler until skin darkens. Rub skin off with towel. Cut in half. Discard seeds and veins. Cut into strips. Place in stainless steel bowl(s).
Red bell peppers, large	3	3 lb.	
Olive oil	$\frac{1}{2}$ cup	3 cups	Combine until dissolved. Pour over peppers.
Lemon juice	$\frac{1}{3}$ cup	2 cups	
Dry sherry	1 tbsp.	$\frac{1}{3}$ cup	
Sugar	1 tsp.	2 tbsp.	
Salt	$\frac{1}{2}$ tsp.	1 tbsp.	
Black pepper	$\frac{1}{4}$ tsp.	$1\frac{1}{2}$ tsp.	
Capers, small	$\frac{1}{4}$ cup	$1\frac{1}{2}$ cups	Combine. Add. Mix well. Chill for several hours.
Scallions (greens and whites), chopped	3 tbsp.	1 cup + 1 tbsp.	
Garlic, minced	$\frac{1}{2}$ tsp.	1 tbsp.	
Parsley, chopped	1 tsp.	2 tbsp.	
Oregano, dried	$\frac{1}{4}$ tsp.	$1\frac{1}{2}$ tsp.	
Pepper	$\frac{1}{2}$ tsp.	1 tbsp.	
Tomatoes, peeled, sliced	3	6 lb.	Arrange around edge of peppers.
Mediterranean olives, pitted	1 cup	$1\frac{1}{2}$ qt.	Sprinkle over salad.

SPECIAL HANDLING FOR BUFFETS: *Serve chilled from shallow insert pan(s) or from garnished platters. Replenish as often as necessary to maintain optimum presentation.*

Serve as part of antipasto buffet. See comments for Antipasto Mushrooms.

Hot Cole Slaw

INGREDIENTS	TEST QUANTITY: 8	SERVICE QUANTITY: 50	METHOD
Bacon, chopped	1 cup	6 cups	Sauté until crisp. Strain off the bacon, leaving drippings in pan.
Onions, minced	$\frac{1}{2}$ cup	3 cups	Sauté in bacon drippings until soft.
Brown sugar	$\frac{1}{4}$ cup	$1\frac{1}{2}$ cups	Combine. Add to skillet. Heat.
Celery seed	$\frac{1}{2}$ tsp.	1 tbsp.	
Dry mustard	$\frac{1}{2}$ tsp.	1 tbsp.	
Salt	$\frac{1}{2}$ tsp.	1 tbsp.	
Black pepper	$\frac{1}{4}$ tsp.	$1\frac{1}{2}$ tsp.	
Red wine vinegar	$\frac{1}{4}$ cup	$1\frac{1}{2}$ cups	
Cabbage, shredded	1 lb.	6 lb.	Add to skillet. Toss to coat and heat thoroughly.
Carrots, shredded	$\frac{1}{2}$ cup	3 cups	

SPECIAL HANDLING FOR BUFFETS: *Serve warm from shallow insert pan held over single heating unit. Keep covered.* *Season with mustard or poppy seeds.*

Indian Cucumbers with Turmeric

INGREDIENTS	TEST QUANTITY: 8	SERVICE QUANTITY: 50	METHOD
Cucumbers, peeled, seeded, halved lengthwise	1 lb.	6 lb.	Cut in quarters, lengthwise; cut into 2-in. slices.
Salt	1 tbsp.	$\frac{1}{3}$ cup	Sprinkle over. Refrigerate for several hours. Drain and rinse many times. Reserve.
Onions, instant, minced	$\frac{1}{4}$ cup	$1\frac{1}{2}$ cups	Combine and let stand for 10 minutes.
Garlic, instant, minced	$\frac{1}{2}$ tsp.	1 tbsp.	
Water	$\frac{1}{3}$ cup	2 cups	
Peanut oil, hot	2 tbsp.	$\frac{3}{4}$ cup	Sauté hydrated onion and garlic.
Turmeric	$\frac{1}{2}$ tbsp.	3 tbsp.	Add; stir well until dissolved.
Curry powder	1 tsp.	2 tbsp.	
Salt	to taste	to taste	
Sugar	$\frac{1}{2}$ tbsp.	3 tbsp.	
Ginger, ground	$\frac{1}{2}$ tbsp.	3 tbsp.	
Rice wine vinegar	$\frac{1}{2}$ cup	3 cups	Add; simmer 15 minutes.
Water	$\frac{1}{4}$ cup	$1\frac{1}{2}$ cups	
Red pepper, ground	to taste	to taste	Add. Pour over drained cucumbers. Refrigerate overnight. Adjust flavors.
Soy sauce	1 tsp.	2 tbsp.	
Brown sugar, light	1 tbsp.	$\frac{1}{3}$ cup	
Peanut butter	2 tbsp.	$\frac{3}{4}$ cup	
Chicken stock	$\frac{1}{4}$ cup	$1\frac{1}{2}$ cups	

SPECIAL HANDLING FOR BUFFETS: *Serve chilled from shallow insert pan(s) or from garnished platters. Replenish as often as necessary to maintain optimum presentation. Offer with chutneys or as a condiment for curry dishes.*

Marinated Broccoli Salad

INGREDIENTS	TEST QUANTITY: 8	SERVICE QUANTITY: 50	METHOD
Broccoli flowerets, trimmed	1½ lb.	9 lb.	Blanch. Shock in ice water. Place in shallow
Boiling water	to cover	to cover	pan(s). Cover. Keep warm.
Sugar	1 tbsp.	6 tbsp.	
Olive oil	½ cup	3 cups	Combine thoroughly. Pour over broccoli
Sesame oil, Oriental	½ tsp.	1 tbsp.	while vegetable is still warm. Marinate at
Mustard, Dijon type	½ tsp.	1 tbsp.	least 2 hours. Serve at room temperature.
Lemon juice, strained	3 tbsp.	1 cup + 2 tbsp.	
Celery, minced	¼ cup	1½ cups	
Garlic, minced	1 tsp.	2 tbsp.	
Worcestershire	1 tsp.	2 tbsp.	
Parsley, chopped	1 tbsp.	6 tbsp.	
Garlic, minced	½ tsp.	1 tbsp.	
Red pepper, crushed	1 tsp.	2 tbsp.	
Salt	½ tsp.	1 tbsp.	
Pepper	½ tsp.	1 tbsp.	

SPECIAL HANDLING FOR BUFFETS: *Serve chilled or at room temperature from shallow insert pan(s) or from garnished platters. Replenish as often as necessary to maintain optimum presentation. Offers as an antipasto or at a Spanish tapas buffet.*

Mustard Cole Slaw

INGREDIENTS	TEST QUANTITY: 8	SERVICE QUANTITY: 50	METHOD
Mustard, powdered	½ tbsp.	3 tbsp.	Combine well with whip.
White wine	2 tbsp.	¾ cup	
Water, warm	2 tbsp.	¾ cup	
Olive oil	½ cup	3 cups	Add gradually.
White wine	½ tbsp.	3 tbsp.	Add. Adjust seasoning.
Lemon juice	1 tbsp.	⅓ cup	
Caraway seed	½ tbsp.	3 tbsp.	
Salt	½ tbsp.	3 tbsp.	
White pepper, ground	¼ tsp.	1½ tsp.	
Tabasco	to taste	to taste	
Cabbage, thinly shredded	1 lb.	6 lb.	Add. Toss well. Chill.
Celery, julienned	½ cup	3 cups	
Carrots, thinly shredded	½ lb.	3 lb.	
Scallions (greens and whites), minced	½ cup	3 cups	

SPECIAL HANDLING FOR BUFFETS: *Serve chilled from shallow insert pan(s) or from garnished platters. Replenish as often as necessary to maintain optimum presentation. Substitute beer for white wine. Season with red pepper.*

New Delhi Cucumber Salad

INGREDIENTS	TEST QUANTITY: 8	SERVICE QUANTITY: 50	METHOD
Cucumbers, peeled, grated	2 lb.	12 lb.	Toss well. Let rest for several hours. Rinse under cold running water. Press out liquid. Place in bowl.
Salt	$\frac{1}{4}$ cup	$1\frac{1}{2}$ cups	
Cider vinegar	2 tsp.	$\frac{1}{4}$ cup	Combine until well dissolved.
Dry sherry	1 tsp.	2 tbsp.	
Sugar	2 tsp.	$\frac{1}{4}$ cup	
Curry powder	2 tsp.	$\frac{1}{4}$ cup	
Cumin	$\frac{1}{2}$ tsp.	1 tbsp.	
Soy sauce	2 tsp.	$\frac{1}{4}$ cup	
Garlic powder	$\frac{1}{4}$ tsp.	$1\frac{1}{2}$ tsp.	
Peanut oil	2 tbsp.	$\frac{3}{4}$ cup	Combine and add to vinegar mixture. Add cucumbers. Toss well. Chill for several hours.
Sesame oil, Middle Eastern	2 tbsp.	$\frac{3}{4}$ cup	

SPECIAL HANDLING FOR BUFFETS: *See comments for* *Indian Cucumbers with Turmeric.*

Pasta Salad with Scallions and Ham

INGREDIENTS	TEST QUANTITY: 8	SERVICE QUANTITY: 50	METHOD
Mustard, Dijon type	1 tsp.	2 tbsp.	Combine in bowl. Whip to blend well.
Tarragon vinegar	1 tbsp.	$\frac{1}{3}$ cup	
Red wine vinegar	1 tbsp.	$\frac{1}{3}$ cup	
Rosemary, dried	$\frac{1}{4}$ tsp.	$1\frac{1}{2}$ tsp.	
Garlic, minced	$\frac{1}{2}$ tsp.	1 tbsp.	
Oregano, dried	$\frac{1}{4}$ tsp.	$1\frac{1}{2}$ tsp.	
Salt	$\frac{1}{4}$ tsp.	$1\frac{1}{2}$ tsp.	
Pepper	$\frac{1}{2}$ tsp.	1 tbsp.	
Paprika	$\frac{1}{4}$ tsp.	$1\frac{1}{2}$ tsp.	
Olive oil	2 tbsp.	$\frac{3}{4}$ cup	Combine and whip in.
Peanut oil	$\frac{1}{4}$ cup	$1\frac{1}{2}$ cups	
Worcestershire sauce	1 tsp.	2 tbsp.	
Water, boiling	1 tbsp.	$\frac{1}{3}$ cup	Add to mixture. Whip at high speed for 5 minutes. Place in large bowl(s).
Macaroni or tubetti, cooked	1 lb.	6 lb.	Add while still warm. Mix well.
Mayonnaise	$1\frac{1}{2}$ cups	2 qt. + 1 cup	Combine and mix in well. Chill for several hours.
Scallions (greens and whites), chopped	1 cup	$1\frac{1}{2}$ qt.	
Capers, drained	$\frac{1}{4}$ cup	$1\frac{1}{2}$ cups	
Ham, finely diced	1 cup	$1\frac{1}{2}$ qt.	
Salt	to taste	to taste	
Pepper	to taste	to taste	

SPECIAL HANDLING FOR BUFFETS: *Serve chilled from shallow insert pan(s) or from garnished platters. Replenish as often as necessary to maintain optimum presentation. Offer as an entree for luncheon buffets.*

Pickled Beets

INGREDIENTS	TEST QUANTITY: 8	SERVICE QUANTITY: 50	METHOD
Sliced beets, cooked	3 cups	6 lb.	Combine all ingredients. Marinate at least 36 hours. Serve in marinade or drain.
Beet juice	$\frac{1}{2}$ cup	3 cups	
Vinegar	$\frac{1}{2}$ cup	3 cups	
Sugar	$\frac{1}{2}$ cup	3 cups	
Salad oil	2 tbsp.	$\frac{3}{4}$ cup	
Water	2 tbsp.	$\frac{3}{4}$ cup	
Onion, thinly sliced	$\frac{1}{2}$ lb.	3 lb.	
Pickling spice	$\frac{3}{4}$ tsp.	$1\frac{1}{2}$ tbsp.	

SPECIAL HANDLING FOR BUFFETS: *Serve chilled from shallow insert pan(s) or from garnished platters. Replenish as often as necessary to maintain optimum presentation. Add peeled hard-cooked eggs and slice them for garnish. Offer as a condiment for grilled chicken and beef.*

Pickled Black-Eyed Peas

INGREDIENTS	TEST QUANTITY: 8	SERVICE QUANTITY: 50	METHOD
Black-eyed peas, drained	1 lb.	6 lb.	Combine in bowl.
Ham, cooked, minced	1 cup	1½ qt.	
Onion, sliced	1	2 lb.	
Celery, chopped	¼ cup	1½ cups	
Olive oil	½ cup	3 cups	Bring to a boil and pour over peas. Refrigerate several hours. Remove bay leaf(s).
Red wine vinegar	¼ cup	1½ cups	
Garlic, crushed	2 cloves	12 cloves	
Thyme, dried	¼ tsp.	1½ tsp.	
Salt	1 tsp.	2 tbsp.	
Bay leaf	1	4	
Black pepper	to taste	to taste	
Worcestershire sauce	1 tbsp.	⅓ cup	

SPECIAL HANDLING FOR BUFFETS: *Serve chilled from shallow insert pans(s) or from garnished platters. Replenish as often as necessary to maintain optimum presentation.*

Offer as a condiment for an American Southern buffet with creamed shellfish and corn muffins.

Potato Salad with Green Beans

INGREDIENTS	TEST QUANTITY: 8	SERVICE QUANTITY: 50	METHOD
New potatoes, cooked, quartered	1½ lb.	9 lb.	Toss while potatoes are warm. Let rest for 30 minutes. Drain and reserve any liquid.
Scallions (greens and whites), chopped	½ cup	3 cups	
White wine, dry	⅓ cup	2 cups	
Chicken stock	⅓ cup	2 cups	
Sherry, dry	1 tbsp.	⅓ cup	
Vinaigrette dressing	½ cup	3 cups	Combine with reserved liquid. Add to potatoes. Toss. Chill for several hours.
Mustard, Dijon type	½ tsp.	1 tbsp.	
Summer savory	¾ tsp.	1½ tbsp.	
Basil	¾ tsp.	1½ tbsp.	
Marjoram	¼ tsp.	1½ tsp.	
Paprika	¼ tsp.	1½ tsp.	
Green beans, sliced, steamed	1 lb.	6 lb.	Add to potatoes. Toss.
Salt	to taste	to taste	Adjust seasoning. Chill.
Pepper	to taste	to taste	

SPECIAL HANDLING FOR BUFFETS: *Serve chilled from insert pan(s) or from garnished platters. Replenish as often as necessary to maintain optimum presentation. Top with crumbled bacon and sprinkle with red wine vinegar.*

Scandinavian Beet Salad with Caraway

INGREDIENTS	TEST QUANTITY: 8	SERVICE QUANTITY: 50	METHOD
Olive oil	$\frac{1}{2}$ cup	3 cups	Combine well.
Red wine vinegar	$\frac{1}{4}$ cup	$1\frac{1}{2}$ cups	
Worcestershire	1 tsp.	2 tbsp.	
Water	$\frac{1}{4}$ cup	$1\frac{1}{2}$ cups	
White wine	$\frac{1}{4}$ cup	$1\frac{1}{2}$ cups	
Sugar	1 tsp.	2 tbsp.	
Caraway seeds	$1\frac{1}{2}$ tbsp.	$\frac{1}{2}$ cup + 1 tbsp.	
Onion, minced	1 cup	2 lb.	
Garlic, minced	$\frac{1}{2}$ tsp.	1 tbsp.	
Cloves, ground	1 tsp.	2 tbsp.	
Bay leaf	2	4	
Salt	to taste	to taste	
Pepper	to taste	to taste	
Beets, cooked, peeled, sliced	1 lb.	6 lb.	Add. Chill. Marinate for several hours. Remove bay leaf.
Orange peel, grated	1 tsp.	2 tbsp.	
Red onions, sliced	$\frac{1}{2}$ cup	3 cups	Garnish.

SPECIAL HANDLING FOR BUFFETS: *Serve chilled from shallow insert pan(s) or from garnished platters. Replenish as often as necessary to maintain optimum presentation.*

Serve on smorgasbord buffet or with an assortment of harvest specialties. Try to make fresh daily because vinegar is best when used fresh.

Shrimp Ceviche

INGREDIENTS	TEST QUANTITY: 8	SERVICE QUANTITY: 50	METHOD
Shrimp, shelled, small	$1\frac{1}{2}$ lb.	9 lb.	Combine and chill overnight.
Lime juice	1 cup	$1\frac{1}{2}$ qt.	
Lemon juice	$\frac{1}{2}$ cup	3 cups	
Scallions (greens and whites), chopped	$\frac{1}{4}$ cup	$1\frac{1}{2}$ cups	Combine and add; refrigerate until service. Drain.
Jalapeño peppers, seeded, sliced	1	6	
Green peppers, minced	2 tbsp.	$\frac{3}{4}$ cup	
Peanut oil	3 tbsp.	1 cup + 2 tbsp.	
Lime juice	1 tbsp.	$\frac{1}{3}$ cup	
Lime peel, grated	1 tsp.	2 tbsp.	
Parsley, chopped	$\frac{1}{4}$ cup	$1\frac{1}{2}$ cups	
Oregano	to taste	to taste	
Red pepper, crushed	to taste	to taste	
Salt	to taste	to taste	
Pepper	to taste	to taste	

SPECIAL HANDLING FOR BUFFETS: *Serve chilled from shallow insert pan(s) or from garnished platters. Replenish as often as necessary to maintain optimum presentation.*

Serve in California avocado half or on slices of ripe cantaloupe. Substitute scallops for shrimp.

Spanish Onion and Ripe Olive Salad

INGREDIENTS	TEST QUANTITY: 8	SERVICE QUANTITY: 50	METHOD
Red onions (medium), peeled, thinly sliced	1 lb.	6 lb.	Combine for 1 hour. Drain and dry.
Ice water	to cover	to cover	
Salt	to taste	to taste	
California ripe olives, chopped	1 cup	1½ qt.	Add to bowl. Toss to combine. Marinate for several hours. Toss well before service.
Peanut oil	½ cup	3 cups	
Soy sauce, mild	2 tbsp.	¾ cup	
Dry sherry	1 tbsp.	3 oz.	
Vinegar	1 tbsp.	3 oz.	
Black pepper	½ tsp.	1 tbsp.	
Parsley, chopped	2 tbsp.	¾ cup	

SPECIAL HANDLING FOR BUFFETS: *Serve chilled from shallow insert pan(s) or from garnished platters. Replenish as often as necessary to maintain optimum presentation.*

Serve with Mediterranean items or as a Spanish tapas appetizer. Substitute olive oil. Sprinkle with red pepper flakes.

Spanish Orange and Onion Salad

INGREDIENTS	TEST QUANTITY: 8	SERVICE QUANTITY: 50	METHOD
Red onions, sweet, sliced Salt	1 lb. 2 tbsp.	6 lb. $\frac{3}{4}$ cup	Toss well to separate rings. Let rest 30 minutes. Rinse under cold running water. Squeeze out excess liquid.
Oranges (medium), seedless, peeled	4	2 dozen	Slice thinly and arrange in bowl with alternate layers of onion rings.
Peanut oil Red wine vinegar Cayenne pepper Salt	$\frac{1}{4}$ cup $\frac{1}{4}$ cup $\frac{1}{4}$ tsp. $\frac{1}{2}$ tsp.	$1\frac{1}{2}$ cups $1\frac{1}{2}$ cups $1\frac{1}{2}$ tsp. 1 tbsp.	Combine well. Pour over oranges. Let stand for 2 hours.
California black ripe olives, sliced	1 cup	$1\frac{1}{2}$ qt.	Arrange on top to garnish.

SPECIAL HANDLING FOR BUFFETS: *See comments for*   *Spanish Onion and Ripe Olive Salad.*

Swiss Potato Salad

INGREDIENTS	TEST QUANTITY: 8	SERVICE QUANTITY: 50	METHOD
Potatoes, cooked, peeled, sliced	1½ lb.	9 lb.	Place in bowl while still warm.
Mayonnaise	½ cup	3 cups	Combine well. Pour over potatoes and toss gently but well.
Celery seed	¼ tsp.	1½ tsp.	
Salt	1 tsp.	2 tbsp.	
Dry mustard	½ tsp.	1 tbsp.	
Pepper	1 tsp.	2 tbsp.	
Prepared mustard	1 tbsp.	⅓ cup	
White wine vinegar	1 tbsp.	⅓ cup	
Tarragon, dried	pinch	¼ tsp.	
Peanut oil	2 tbsp.	¾ cup	
Swiss cheese, grated	¼ cup	1½ cups	Combine and sprinkle over. Keep warm for service with spicy meat dishes.
Chives, finely chopped	1 tbsp.	⅓ cup	
Bacon, fried, crumbled	⅓ lb.	2 lb.	

SPECIAL HANDLING FOR BUFFETS: *Serve chilled from shallow insert pan(s) or from garnished platters. Replenish as often as necessary to maintain optimum presentation. Season with poppy or mustard seeds. Toss in chopped cucumbers.*

Tabbouleh Salad

INGREDIENTS	TEST QUANTITY: 8	SERVICE QUANTITY: 50	METHOD
Cracked wheat (bulgar)	$\frac{1}{2}$ lb.	3 lb.	Soak for 30 minutes. Drain well.
Water	to cover	to cover	
Scallions (greens and whites), minced	$\frac{1}{3}$ cup	2 cups	Add each ingredient separately, tossing well after each addition.
Onion, white, minced	$1\frac{1}{2}$ cups	3 lb.	
Tomato, seeded, chopped	1 lb.	6 lb.	
Mint, chopped	1 tsp.	2 tbsp.	
Parsley, chopped	$\frac{1}{2}$ cup	3 cups	
Olive oil	$\frac{1}{4}$ cup	$1\frac{1}{2}$ cups	Combine well. Add to mixture. Toss gently but thoroughly.
Lemon juice, strained	$\frac{1}{4}$ cup	$1\frac{1}{2}$ cups	
Salt	to taste	to taste	
Black pepper	to taste	to taste	
Tomato, wedged, medium	2	12	Garnish.
Parsley, chopped	$\frac{1}{4}$ cup	$1\frac{1}{2}$ cups	

SPECIAL HANDLING FOR BUFFETS: *Serve chilled from shallow insert pan(s) or from garnished platters. Replenish as often as necessary to maintain optimum presentation. Serve in scooped-out lemon or lime halves or in California avocado halves. Garnish with twists of lemon.*

Turkey Salad with Grapes and Pecans

INGREDIENTS	TEST QUANTITY: 8	SERVICE QUANTITY: 50	METHOD
Turkey (mixed dark and white), cooked, diced	$1\frac{1}{2}$ cups	6 lb.	Combine in bowl.
Celery, diced	1 cup	$1\frac{1}{2}$ lb.	
Scallions (greens only), minced	1 tbsp.	$\frac{1}{3}$ cup	
White grapes, seedless	1 cup	2 lb.	
Pecans, chopped	$\frac{1}{4}$ cup	$1\frac{1}{2}$ cups	
Celery seed	$\frac{1}{4}$ tsp.	$1\frac{1}{2}$ tsp.	
Scallions (greens and whites), chopped	1 tbsp.	$\frac{1}{3}$ cup	Combine well. Add to turkey and toss to combine. Chill for several hours.
Chicken stock	$\frac{1}{4}$ cup	$1\frac{1}{2}$ cups	
White wine	2 tbsp.	$\frac{3}{4}$ cup	
Mayonnaise	$\frac{1}{3}$ cup	2 cups	
Mustard, Dijon type	$\frac{1}{2}$ tsp.	1 tbsp.	
Vinaigrette dressing	2 tbsp.	$\frac{3}{4}$ cup	

SPECIAL HANDLING FOR BUFFETS: *Serve chilled from shallow insert pan(s) or from garnished platters. Replenish as often as necessary to maintain optimum presentation.*

Make vinaigrette dressing with walnut oil. Serve in Bibb lettuce cups or California avocado halves or over papaya slices.

Turkish Potato Salad

INGREDIENTS	TEST QUANTITY: 8	SERVICE QUANTITY: 50	METHOD
Potatoes, cooked, peeled, sliced	2 lb.	12 lb.	Combine in bowl.
White wine vinegar	$\frac{1}{4}$ cup	$1\frac{1}{2}$ cups	
Dry sherry	1 tsp.	2 tbsp.	
Dry mustard	1 tsp.	2 tbsp.	Whip thoroughly.
Olive oil	$\frac{1}{4}$ cup	$1\frac{1}{2}$ cups	
Lemon juice, strained	2 tbsp.	$\frac{3}{4}$ cup	
Tabasco	$\frac{1}{4}$ tsp.	$1\frac{1}{2}$ tsp.	
Tomato, seeded, peeled, chopped	$\frac{1}{4}$ cup	$1\frac{1}{2}$ cups	Combine. Add to oil mixture. Pour over
Parsley, chopped	2 tbsp.	$\frac{3}{4}$ cup	potatoes. Toss gently.
Dill, chopped	1 tbsp.	$\frac{1}{3}$ cup	
Mint, dried, crumbled	$\frac{1}{4}$ tsp.	$1\frac{1}{2}$ tsp.	
Salt	to taste	to taste	
Black pepper	to taste	to taste	
Cayenne	to taste	to taste	
Red onions, halved, sliced	1 lb.	6 lb.	Combine in bowl. Rub well with hands. Rinse
Salt	1 tbsp.	$\frac{1}{3}$ cup	well under running water. Squeeze thoroughly. Add to potato mixture. Toss gently.
Black olives, sliced	$\frac{1}{3}$ cup	2 cups	Garnish.

SPECIAL HANDLING FOR BUFFETS: *Serve chilled from shallow insert pan(s) or from garnished platters. Replenish as often as necessary to maintain optimum presentation. Fold in desired amount of plain yogurt and chopped walnuts.*

Winter Citrus Salad with Yogurt Dressing

INGREDIENTS	TEST QUANTITY: 8	SERVICE QUANTITY: 50	METHOD
Yogurt	1 cup	1½ qt.	Combine well. Place in small service pieces. Reserve.
Mayonnaise	¼ cup	1½ cups	
Scallions (greens and whites), chopped	2 tbsp.	¾ cup	
Honey	1 tbsp.	⅓ cup	
Coriander, ground	½ tbsp.	3 tbsp.	
Ginger, ground	1 tsp.	2 tbsp.	
Salt	½ tsp.	1 tbsp.	
Broccoli, flowerets	¾ lb.	4½ lb.	Steam until done. Shock in cold water. Drain. Chill.
Carrots, thinly sliced	¾ cup	2 lb.	
Grapefruit juice, strained	½ cup	3 cups	Combine well. Stir into reserved broccoli and carrots. Warm over low heat. Transfer to service piece(s).
Chick peas, cooked, drained	1½ cups	4 lb.	
Raisins	⅓ cup	2 cups	
Walnuts, chopped	1 cup	1½ lb.	
Grapefruit sections	1 lb.	6 lb.	Distribute over salad. Keep warm for service, but try not to hold much longer than 30 minutes. Offer reserved yogurt dressing on the side.

SPECIAL HANDLING FOR BUFFET SERVICE: *Serve warm from shallow insert pan(s) set over dual heating units. Keep covered for service. Toss in some steamed cauliflower buds and slivered almonds.*

Review Questions

1. Name five varieties each of salad apples and cherries.

2. Where are the main supply sources of avocados?

3. What vegetable increases in calories when stored?

4. Name six fruits that begin with "P."

5. What vegetable is exceptionally high in vitamin A?

6. Give a nutritional profile of potatoes.

The service of soup is common to every country of this world. In some cooking styles—America's, for example—soup is served as a preliminary course to the entree; in others—Chinese, for one—soup is on the table at all times and actually serves the dual functions of food and beverage. Some soups are thin and light, some are more substantial, but all are qualified candidates for international buffet menus. Which of the following multinational soup and stew favorites can you use to increase the international level of your buffet service?

Australia. Bread and cheese soup combines layers of its namesakes with a rich vegetable stock in small crocks that are oven baked and sprinkled with wine before service.

Austria. Tyrolean soup is a hearty blend of dried split peas and vegetables, whose chicken stock base is thickened with a roux of flour and bacon fat.

Barbados. Callaloo is a Caribbean favorite that combines greens of the taro plant (called callaloo or Chinese spinach) with crab, coconut, chicken stock, and hot peppers.

Brazil. Vatapa is a tomato-rich blend of shrimp, whitefish, and coconut; peanuts, garlic, and chili peppers heighten the flavor. Serve this South American classic with steamed rice.

Bulgaria. Soupa sus topchetas is a version of meatball soup with a base of chicken and beef stocks bubbling with lean beef and rice meatballs; an egg-yogurt mixture is added before service.

Ceylon (now Sri Lanka). Mulligatawny is a variation of chicken soup that sparkles with cumin, coriander, cinnamon, and ginger; black peppercorns and coconut round out the flavor.

Chile. Caldillo de congria is a meal in a bowl, rich with whitefish that has been steamed with tomatoes, green peppers, and potatoes; lemon slices accompany this dish.

China. Swan la tong is the classic hot and sour soup in which bamboo shoots and Chinese mushrooms bolster a stock spirited with hot oil, vinegar, and plenty of pepper.

Colombia. Ajiaco bogotano is a creamy chicken soup with potatoes; cumin, bay leaf, and thyme provide the essence, while capers and thin avocado slices serve as garnish.

Denmark. Brunkalsuppe combines buttery, browned cabbage shreds with a touch of sugar in a strong beef stock; black pepper and allspice fill in the flavoring edges.

Dominican Republic. Sopa de frijoles is one version of the almost ubiquitous bean soup, in this case kidney beans, piquant with onion, garlic, chili, vinegar, and Tabasco.

England. Cock-a-leekie soup provides a clue in its name; chicken and leeks form its base, while beads of barley and bay leaf fill out the flavor of this cold-weather favorite.

Finland. Hernekeitto is a split pea soup that combines softened peas with salt pork and stew beef; this fairly thin soup is spiked with onion, mustard, and thyme.

France. Bouillabaisse is the Mediterranean classic combination of fish and shellfish, bound together by a hearty, tomato-rich stock with saffron and garlic; croutons serve as an accompaniment.

Germany. Kartoffelsuppe is a potato soup, rich with onions, leeks, and diced bacon, that is topped with toasted croutons; knockwurst and zesty mustard are served on the side.

Haiti. Soupe au giraumon is a chicken and vegetable soup that features squash, cabbage, and rice in an orange-laced broth; strands of pasta and vinegar add texture and tang.

Hungary. Meggykeszoce is a cold cherry soup that's a mouthful to pronounce, but also to savor; sour cherries are stewed and then mixed with their juice, sour cream, and sugar.

India. Dhansak is a hearty stew

brimming with cubes of lamb and several varieties of simmered dry beans; eggplant, tomatoes, onions, and spinach are vegetable standards.

Iraq. *Kubba shalgum* is a soup that combines turnips and onions in a tomato-laced broth; beef and lamb meatballs are added to the broth along with almonds and raisins.

Italy. *Minnestrone* is a hearty soup that parlays vegetables with dried beans and pasta in a tomato-rich beef or chicken stock; grated Parmesan is always offered on the side.

Jamaica. *Pepper pot* is a bittersweet soup based on the traditional meat stew. Although the stew does not have vegetables, the soup is punctuated with spinach and okra.

Japan. *Sumashi wan* is a clear soup (that can contain tofu and shrimp) that relies on the Japanese basic *ichiban dashi* stock of dried kelp and a packaged, dried, and flaked bonito.

Jordan. *Kufta* is a lemony chicken broth that contains lamb meatballs that are spiced with cinnamon, allspice, and parsley; beaten eggs are briskly stirred in off the heat.

Laos. *Kengphed* combines cubes of swordfish and potatoes in a stock made rich with coconut milk; sautéed garlic, onions, and pimiento join pepper as flavoring sources.

Lebanon. *Abass bi hamod* is a lentil soup, flavored with lemon, coriander, pepper, and cinnamon, that can be served hot or cold, depending on the season.

Luxembourg. *Potage jardiniere* is a version of rich vegetable soup that also contains lima beans and shelled peas; the mixture is puréed with butter and cream for service.

Madagascar. *Soupe à la Malgache* is another vegetable soup, based on a hearty stock obtained from veal bones; carrots, onions, potatoes, tomatoes, and turnips are common vegetable additions.

Mexico. *Sopa de lima* is a lime soup that often appears in the Yucatán region; lime juice heightens flavors of simmered chicken, onion, peppers, garlic, and other spices.

Netherlands. *Kippesoep met balletjes* finds chicken broth afloat with onions, carrots, and pork meatballs, called *balletjes.* Cumin, saffron, and mace are all optional spices.

Norway. *Spinatsuppe med ostebrod* is spinach soup, rich with egg yolk and cream, that is flavored with fennel and served with squares of grilled, cheese-topped bread.

Peru. *Chupe de camarones* is shrimp soup with corn that also profits from diced potatoes, onions, and tomatoes; chilis, garlic, and oregano provide some of the flavor punch.

Philippines. *Tinola* is the simple name for a sautéed chicken soup that sparkles with fresh ginger and onion; prior to service, shreds of fresh spinach are added for color.

Poland. *Chlodnik* is a chilled soup based on thinly sliced vegetables such as beets, cucumbers, radishes, and garlic; shrimp and yogurt are added to the base of beef stock.

Portugal. *Sopa a Portuguesa* is a national soup of fish and shrimp, combined in a stock flavored with oregano and basil; bread crumbs and egg yolk combine to thicken the mixture.

Russia. *Borscht* is the well-known Russian beet soup that combines the deep red vegetable with spices and yogurt in a rich stock; brown sugar and pepper are common additions.

South Africa. *Bootjisoep* is an amber bean soup, stoutly based on beef bones and salt pork; turnips, celery, onions, carrots, and tomatoes are common vegetable additions.

Spain. *Gazpacho* combines garden vegetables such as cucumbers, onions, peppers, and tomatoes in a spicy, cold tomato juice base; olive oil and garlic provide additional character.

Sudan. *Shorba* is a version of peanut soup that is based on a rich beef stock; cinnamon, cardamom, garlic, onion, and black peppercorns add their flavors to lemon and peanut butter.

Sweden. *Gronsakssoppa* is a version of vegetable soup that relies on chicken stock as a base for thin slices of carrots, leeks, and onions, all joined by diced cauliflower and potato.

Switzerland. *Weisse kartoffelsuppe* is a basic, thin potato soup that contains a quantity of onions; the vegetable or chicken base can be strengthened with leeks or carrots.

Thailand. *Tom yum gai* is another hot and sour soup, also based on chicken, but using soy sauce and lemon juice for half the dish's strength and crushed red pepper for the heat.

Tunisia. *Lablabi* is a chickpea soup that begins with simmered beans in a vegetable stock to which such spices as cumin, cayenne, and coriander are added.

Turkey. *Casik* translates to "turquoise," but the keys to this cold soup are yogurt, cucumbers, and mint; dill and a touch of vinegar help to fill in its unique flavor.

Uruguay. *Chupin de pescado* is a variation on the *bouillabaise* theme; shellfish and fin fish share space with olive oil, tomatoes, and vegetables, with a final touch of sherry.

Vietnam. *Mang tay nau cua* is a crab and asparagus soup that joins tender white spears of asparagus with picked-over crab meat to bolster a base of chicken stock, onions, and sliced scallion.

Bookbinder's Snapper Soup

INGREDIENTS	TEST QUANTITY: 8	SERVICE QUANTITY: 50	METHOD
Butter, melted	1 tbsp.	$\frac{1}{3}$ cup	Sauté until tender.
Onions, chopped	2 tbsp.	$\frac{3}{4}$ cup	
Celery, diced	$\frac{1}{4}$ cup	$1\frac{1}{2}$ cups	
Green pepper, diced	$\frac{1}{2}$ cup	1 lb.	
Fish stock	1 cup	$1\frac{1}{2}$ qt.	Add; simmer for 25 minutes.
Worcestershire sauce	1 tsp.	2 tbsp.	
Sherry, dry	$\frac{1}{4}$ cup	$1\frac{1}{2}$ cups	
Red snapper, cleaned, cubed	$\frac{1}{2}$ cup	3 cups	Add; cook 10 minutes.
Tomato sauce	1 cup	$1\frac{1}{2}$ qt.	Add; simmer for 5 minutes. Offer with an
Brown sauce	2 cups	3 qt.	additional 2 oz. of sherry for each serving.

SPECIAL HANDLING FOR BUFFETS: *Serve very warm from bain marie set over single heating unit. Stir often to maintain optimum service temperature. Keep covered as much as possible. Substitute fish variety according to lean/fat ratio* *(see pp. 165–166 for a detailed discussion of this ratio). Season with Tabasco or hot red pepper to taste. Bookbinder's Seafood House has been serving fine food in Philadelphia for many years.*

Burmese Cabbage Soup

INGREDIENTS	TEST QUANTITY: 8	SERVICE QUANTITY: 50	METHOD
Peanut oil, hot	3 tbsp.	1 cup + 1 tbsp.	Sauté for 5 minutes.
Onion, chopped	1 cup	3 lb.	
Celery, chopped	$\frac{1}{2}$ cup	3 cups	
Garlic, minced	3 cloves	1 head	
Ginger, grated	1 tsp.	2 tbsp.	
Cabbage, finely shredded	3 cups	$4\frac{1}{2}$ lb.	Add; sauté for 10 minutes.
Chili peppers, dried, minced	$\frac{1}{2}$ tsp.	1 tbsp.	Simmer over low heat. Adjust seasoning.
Hoisin sauce (commercial)	2 tsp.	$\frac{1}{4}$ cup	
Lemon juice	2 tsp.	$\frac{1}{4}$ cup	
Salt	2 tsp.	$\frac{1}{4}$ cup	
Black pepper	$\frac{1}{2}$ tsp.	1 tbsp.	
Tomatoes, peeled, seeded, chopped	2	3 lb.	
Beef stock, strong	1 qt.	$1\frac{1}{2}$ gal.	

SPECIAL HANDLING FOR BUFFETS: *Serve very warm from bain marie set over single heating unit. Stir often to maintain optimum service temperature. Keep covered as much as possible. Serve with crisply fried noodles or fried sliced wonton wrappers. Adjust flavor with chili-garlic paste.*

Cajun Crab Soup

INGREDIENTS	TEST QUANTITY: 8	SERVICE QUANTITY: 50	METHOD
Olive oil, hot	$\frac{1}{4}$ cup	$1\frac{1}{2}$ cups	Sauté for 2–3 minutes.
Scallions (greens and whites), chopped	1 cup	$1\frac{1}{2}$ qt.	
Carrots, small, sliced	2	1 lb.	
Green pepper, minced	$\frac{1}{3}$ cup	2 cups	
Onion, diced	$\frac{2}{3}$ cup	2 lb.	
Celery, diced	$\frac{2}{3}$ cup	1 lb.	
Garlic, crushed	$\frac{1}{2}$ tsp.	1 tbsp.	
Fish stock	1 qt.	$1\frac{1}{2}$ gal.	Add.
Crabs, blue, raw	2	12	Remove top shells and gills; cut crabs into quarters and add.
Tomatoes, diced	1 cup	3 lb.	Add; simmer for 30 minutes.
Parsley, chopped	$\frac{1}{4}$ cup	$1\frac{1}{2}$ cups	
Gumbo filé	$\frac{1}{4}$ tsp.	$1\frac{1}{2}$ tsp.	
Saffron, powdered	$\frac{1}{8}$ tsp.	$\frac{3}{4}$ tsp.	
Tabasco	$\frac{1}{4}$ tsp.	$1\frac{1}{2}$ tsp.	
Black pepper	$\frac{1}{4}$ tsp.	$1\frac{1}{2}$ tsp.	Adjust seasoning.
Salt	to taste	to taste	

SPECIAL HANDLING FOR BUFFETS: *Serve very warm from bain marie set over single heating unit. Stir often to maintain optimum service temperature. Keep covered as much as possible. Serve with small, crusty loaves. Adjust seasoning with filé powder (powdered sassafras) or cayenne pepper.*

California Clam Chowder

INGREDIENTS	TEST QUANTITY: 8	SERVICE QUANTITY: 50	METHOD
Olive oil, hot	2 tbsp.	$\frac{3}{4}$ cup	Sauté until soft.
Onion, chopped	$\frac{1}{3}$ cup	2 cups	
Celery, chopped	$\frac{1}{3}$ cup	2 cups	
Flour, all purpose	2 tbsp.	$\frac{3}{4}$ cup	Add; cook over low heat for 5 minutes.
Clam juice	2 cups	3 qt.	Add; simmer until thickened.
Celery, minced	$\frac{1}{3}$ cup	2 cups	Add; bring to boil. Simmer for 30 minutes.
Sweet red peppers, minced	$\frac{1}{2}$ cup	3 cups	
Carrots, minced	$\frac{1}{2}$ cup	3 cups	
Clams, canned, with juice	$\frac{1}{2}$ lb.	3 lb.	
Tomatoes, chopped	$\frac{1}{2}$ cup	3 cups	
Crushed red pepper	$\frac{1}{4}$ tsp.	$1\frac{1}{2}$ tsp.	
Potatoes, peeled, diced	$\frac{1}{2}$ lb.	3 lb.	Add; simmer 30 more minutes.
Thyme	$\frac{1}{4}$ tsp.	$1\frac{1}{2}$ tsp.	
Oregano	$\frac{1}{4}$ tsp.	$1\frac{1}{2}$ tsp.	
Salt	to taste	to taste	
Black pepper	to taste	to taste	
Milk, hot	1 cup	$1\frac{1}{2}$ qt.	Add; heat, but do not boil. Adjust seasoning.

SPECIAL HANDLING FOR BUFFETS: *Serve very warm from bain marie set over single heating unit. Stir often to maintain optimum service temperature. Keep covered as much as possible. Add slices of California black ripe olives. Season with fresh bay leaf or marjoram.*

Chilled Olive Soup

INGREDIENTS	TEST QUANTITY: 8	SERVICE QUANTITY: 50	METHOD
Chicken stock	3 cups	$4\frac{1}{2}$ qt.	Simmer for 20 minutes.
California black ripe olives, sliced	1 cup	4 lb.	
Onion, grated	1 tbsp.	$\frac{1}{3}$ cup	
Celery, minced	1 tbsp.	$\frac{1}{3}$ cup	
Garlic, minced	$\frac{1}{2}$ tsp.	1 tbsp.	
Eggs, beaten	2	12	Combine. Add slowly to olive mixture.
Light cream	2 cups	3 qt.	Simmer, but do not boil. Remove from heat.
Sour cream	$\frac{1}{2}$ cup	3 cups	Add. Adjust seasoning. Chill.
White wine	$\frac{1}{3}$ cup	2 cups	
Tabasco	to taste	to taste	
Worcestershire sauce	to taste	to taste	
Salt	to taste	to taste	
White pepper	to taste	to taste	

SPECIAL HANDLING FOR BUFFETS: *Serve chilled from ice-lined bowl, garnished with sliced ripe olives and side bowls of sour cream.*

Chilled Polish Clodnick (borscht) —La Bastille

INGREDIENTS	TEST QUANTITY: 8	SERVICE QUANTITY: 50	METHOD
Buttermilk	2 cups	3 qt.	Combine well.
Sour cream	$\frac{1}{2}$ cup	3 cups	
Cucumbers, diced	$\frac{1}{2}$ cup	3 cups	Combine well and add.
Beets, cooked, diced	$\frac{1}{4}$ cup	$1\frac{1}{2}$ cups	
Green pepper, minced	$\frac{1}{4}$ cup	$1\frac{1}{2}$ cups	
Carrots, grated	$\frac{1}{2}$ tbsp.	3 tbsp.	
Scallions (greens and whites), chopped	$\frac{1}{2}$ tbsp.	3 tbsp.	
Dill seed	$\frac{1}{2}$ tbsp.	3 tbsp.	Add; stir well. Cover well and chill for 24 hours.
Salt	$\frac{1}{2}$ tbsp.	3 tbsp.	
Tiny shrimp	$\frac{1}{4}$ cup	$1\frac{1}{2}$ cups	Offer as garnish.
Eggs, hard cooked, sliced or chopped	1	6	
Croutons, toasted	$\frac{1}{4}$ cup	$1\frac{1}{2}$ cups	

SPECIAL HANDLING FOR BUFFETS: *Serve chilled from ice-lined service bowl, garnished with julienne of beet* *and side bowls of sour cream.*

Coach House Black Bean Soup

INGREDIENTS	TEST QUANTITY: 8	SERVICE QUANTITY: 50	METHOD
Black beans, dried	$\frac{1}{2}$ lb.	3 lb.	Soak overnight. Drain.
Water	to cover	to cover	
Water	$5\frac{1}{2}$ cups	2 gal.	Combine and pour over beans; simmer for $1\frac{1}{2}$ hours.
Smoked ham rind and bone	as desired	3	
Scallions (greens and whites), chopped	1 bunch	6 bunches	
Bay leaves	1	4	
Salt	$\frac{3}{4}$ tsp.	$1\frac{1}{2}$ tbsp.	
Black pepper	$\frac{1}{4}$ tsp.	$1\frac{1}{2}$ tsp.	
Garlic	1 clove	6 cloves	
Butter	2 tbsp.	$\frac{3}{4}$ cup	Sauté until soft.
Onions, chopped	$\frac{1}{4}$ lb.	$1\frac{1}{2}$ lb.	
Celery, chopped	1 rib	6 ribs	
Flour, all purpose	2 tsp.	$\frac{1}{4}$ cup	Add to onion-celery mixture; stir in to blend. Cook 5 minutes. Add to bean mixture. Continue to simmer for 6 hours, adding boiling water so beans stay covered. Remove bones and rind. Force mixture through a fine sieve.
Beef stock	as needed	as needed	Add to adjust flavor.
Madeira	$\frac{1}{4}$ cup	$1\frac{1}{2}$ cups	Add immediately before service.

SPECIAL HANDLING FOR BUFFETS: *Serve very warm from bain marie set over single heating unit. Stir often to maintain optimum service temperature. Keep covered as much as possible. Offer with side bowls of sour cream. Garnish with lemon slice and lump of softened butter. The Coach House is a popular restaurant located in New York City's Greenwich Village.*

Corn Chowder

INGREDIENTS	TEST QUANTITY: 8	SERVICE QUANTITY: 50	METHOD
Water	$\frac{1}{2}$ cup	3 cups	Combine and simmer for 15 minutes.
Chicken stock	1 cup	$1\frac{1}{2}$ qt.	
Canned corn, drained	2 cups	6 lb.	
Thyme, dried	$\frac{1}{4}$ tsp.	$1\frac{1}{2}$ tsp.	
Butter, melted	2 tbsp.	$\frac{3}{4}$ cup	Sauté until soft. Add to corn.
Celery, minced	$\frac{1}{4}$ cup	$1\frac{1}{2}$ cups	
Red onion, minced	$\frac{1}{4}$ cup	$1\frac{1}{2}$ cups	
Green pepper, minced	$\frac{1}{4}$ cup	$1\frac{1}{2}$ cups	
Potatoes (boiling or red), peeled, diced, cooked	$\frac{3}{4}$ cup	$4\frac{1}{2}$ cups	Add to mixture. Purée in blender.
Milk, scalded	1 cup	$1\frac{1}{2}$ qt.	
Heavy cream	$\frac{1}{2}$ cup	3 cups	Add; simmer very gently.
Yogurt, plain	$\frac{1}{2}$ cup	3 cups	
Salt	$\frac{1}{2}$ tsp.	1 tbsp.	
Black pepper	$\frac{1}{8}$ tsp.	$\frac{3}{4}$ tsp.	
Cayenne or pepper sauce	to taste	to taste	

SPECIAL HANDLING FOR BUFFETS: *Serve very warm from bain marie set over single heating unit. Stir often to maintain optimum service temperature. Keep covered as much as possible. Substitute diced cooked sweet potatoes for regular; add diced red sweet pepper.*

Danish Cabbage Soup

INGREDIENTS	TEST QUANTITY: 8	SERVICE QUANTITY: 50	METHOD
Butter, melted	$\frac{1}{4}$ cup	$1\frac{1}{2}$ cups	Sauté until cabbage is completely coated and onions are soft.
Onion, minced	$\frac{1}{4}$ cup	$1\frac{1}{2}$ cups	
Cabbage, shredded	1 lb.	6 lb.	
Brown sugar	2 tsp.	$\frac{1}{4}$ cup	Sprinkle over. Sauté slowly until cabbage browns, about 30 minutes.
Beef stock, strong	3 cups	$4\frac{1}{2}$ qt.	Add; cover. Simmer until cabbage is tender.
Salt	to taste	to taste	
Black pepper	to taste	to taste	
Cinnamon	to taste	to taste	
Allspice	to taste	to taste	
Ginger	to taste	to taste	
Parsley, chopped	2 tsp.	$\frac{1}{4}$ cup	Add. Stir to combine.

SPECIAL HANDLING FOR BUFFETS: *Serve very warm from bain marie set over single heating unit. Stir often to maintain optimum service temperature. Keep covered as much as possible. Serve with small squares of Scandinavian flat breads.*

Indian Vichyssoise

INGREDIENTS	TEST QUANTITY: 8	SERVICE QUANTITY: 50	METHOD
Butter, melted	$\frac{1}{4}$ cup	$1\frac{1}{2}$ cups	Sweat slowly for 10 minutes.
Shallots, chopped	$\frac{1}{4}$ cup	$1\frac{1}{2}$ cups	
Scallions (greens and whites)	1 bunch	6 bunches	
Potatoes, peeled, thinly sliced	1 cup	3 lb.	Add. Simmer 10 minutes.
Chicken stock	1 qt.	$1\frac{1}{2}$ gal.	Add; cover. Simmer 45 minutes. Purée.
White wine	$\frac{1}{2}$ cup	3 cups	Return to pot(s).
Salt	to taste	to taste	
Black pepper	to taste	to taste	
Tabasco	to taste	to taste	
Cinnamon	$\frac{1}{8}$ tsp.	$\frac{3}{4}$ tsp.	Add. Simmer 5 minutes. Chill thoroughly.
Curry powder	$\frac{1}{2}$ tsp.	1 tbsp.	
Turmeric	$\frac{1}{8}$ tsp.	$\frac{3}{4}$ tsp.	
Light cream	$\frac{1}{2}$ cup	3 cups	
Yogurt	$\frac{1}{2}$ cup	3 cups	Stir in before service. Offer additional chives
Chives, chopped	$\frac{1}{2}$ tbsp.	3 tbsp.	for garnish.

SPECIAL HANDLING FOR BUFFETS: *Serve chilled from ice-lined bowl, garnished with chopped chives and toasted Indian* pappadam *wafers; wheat tortillas could be substituted. Season with a small touch of fenugreek.*

Islands Shrimp Soup

INGREDIENTS	TEST QUANTITY: 8	SERVICE QUANTITY: 50	METHOD
Shrimp, unpeeled, large	1 lb.	6 lb.	Combine all but shrimp in pot. Bring to boil.
Water	1 qt.	3 qt.	Add shrimp and bring to boil again. Boil 1–2
Lemon slices	of 1	of 6	minutes. Turn off heat. Hold in pot for 1
Onion, sliced	$\frac{1}{2}$ cup	3 cups	minute. Remove shrimp from heat. Plunge
Clove, whole	2	12	shrimp in cold water to stop cooking. Slice
Celery, sliced	1 rib	6 ribs	and reserve shrimp. Simmer stock for 1 hour.
Carrot, sliced	1	6	Strain stock and reserve.
Celery seed	$\frac{1}{4}$ tsp.	$1\frac{1}{2}$ tsp.	
Salt	$\frac{1}{2}$ tsp.	1 tbsp.	
Black peppercorns	$\frac{1}{2}$ tsp.	1 tbsp.	
Olive oil, hot	1 tbsp.	$\frac{1}{3}$ cup	Sauté over moderate heat until onion is soft.
Onion, minced	$\frac{1}{4}$ cup	$1\frac{1}{2}$ cups	
Celery, minced	$\frac{1}{4}$ cup	$1\frac{1}{2}$ cups	
Red bell pepper, minced	2 tbsp.	$\frac{3}{4}$ cup	
Garlic, minced	$\frac{1}{4}$ tsp.	$1\frac{1}{2}$ tsp.	
Ginger root, minced	$\frac{1}{4}$ tsp.	$1\frac{1}{2}$ tsp.	
Saffron	to taste	to taste	
Thyme	to taste	to taste	
Allspice, ground	to taste	to taste	
Light rum	$1\frac{1}{2}$ tbsp.	$\frac{1}{2}$ cup + 1 tbsp.	Add; deglaze and flame.
Dark rum	1 tsp.	1 oz.	
Flour, all purpose	1 tbsp.	$\frac{1}{3}$ cup	Add. Stir to combine. Cook for 5 minutes. Add reserved shrimp stock. Simmer 20 minutes. Add reserved shrimp.

SPECIAL HANDLING FOR BUFFETS: *Serve very warm from bain marie set over single heating unit. Stir often to maintain optimum service temperature. Keep covered as much as possible. Substitute conch meat for all or part of the shrimp. Substitute bulgar wheat for the rice.*

Manhattan Clam Chowder

INGREDIENTS	TEST QUANTITY: 8	SERVICE QUANTITY: 50	METHOD
Bacon, chopped	1 slice	6 slices	Sauté until golden.
Carrots, diced	$\frac{1}{2}$ cup	3 cups	Add; sauté for 5 minutes.
Celery, chopped	$\frac{1}{3}$ cup	2 cups	
Onion, chopped	$\frac{1}{3}$ cup	2 cups	
Green pepper, diced	$\frac{1}{4}$ cup	$1\frac{1}{2}$ cups	
Garlic, minced	1 clove	6 cloves	Add; sauté for 2 minutes.
Thyme, dried	$\frac{1}{4}$ tsp.	$1\frac{1}{2}$ tsp.	
Clam liquor and water	to yield 1 qt.	to yield $1\frac{1}{2}$ gal.	Add and simmer for 15 minutes.
Tomatoes, chopped	$\frac{1}{4}$ cup	$1\frac{1}{2}$ cups	
Clams, large, chopped	$\frac{1}{2}$ dozen	3 dozen	Add and simmer for 1 hour. Adjust seasoning.
Potatoes, peeled, diced	1 cup	3 lb.	
Salt	to taste	to taste	
Pepper	to taste	to taste	

SPECIAL HANDLING FOR BUFFETS: *Serve very warm from bain marie set over a single heating unit. Stir often to maintain optimum service temperature. Keep covered as much as possible. Substitute oysters for clams. Season with Tabasco or crushed hot red pepper. Serve with toasted garlic croutons.*

Mediterranean Pepper Soup

INGREDIENTS	TEST QUANTITY: 8	SERVICE QUANTITY: 50	METHOD
Smoked ham, $\frac{1}{4}$-in. dice	2 tbsp.	$\frac{3}{4}$ cup	Sauté until lightly browned.
Chorizo sausage, diced	2 tbsp.	$\frac{3}{4}$ cup	
Olive oil, hot	$\frac{1}{2}$ tbsp.	3 tbsp.	
Onions, diced	$\frac{1}{4}$ cup	$1\frac{1}{2}$ cups	Add; cook until tender.
Leeks (white only), sliced	$\frac{1}{4}$ cup	$1\frac{1}{2}$ cups	
Celery, diced	$\frac{1}{4}$ cup	$1\frac{1}{2}$ cups	
Bell peppers, diced	$\frac{1}{4}$ cup	$1\frac{1}{2}$ cups	Add; sauté until carrots are barely tender.
Carrots, minced	$\frac{1}{4}$ cup	$1\frac{1}{2}$ cups	
Garlic, crushed	1 clove	6 cloves	
Flour, all purpose	1 tbsp.	$\frac{1}{3}$ cup	Stir in for 1 minute; remove from heat.
Chicken stock	$\frac{1}{2}$ cup	3 cups	Add gradually; stir in well.
Beef stock	2 cups	3 qt.	
Saffron	pinch	to taste	Add; simmer 20 minutes. Adjust seasoning. Reserve until service.
Savory	to taste	to taste	
Oregano	to taste	to taste	
Salt	to taste	to taste	
Black pepper	to taste	to taste	
Crushed red pepper	to taste	to taste	

SPECIAL HANDLING FOR BUFFETS: *Serve very warm from bain marie set over single heating unit. Stir often to maintain optimum service temperature. Keep covered as much as possible. Serve with miniature pita loaves or toasted garlic croutons.*

Minestrone, Casa Grisanti (Louisville, Kentucky)

INGREDIENTS	TEST QUANTITY: 8	SERVICE QUANTITY: 50	METHOD
Olive oil, hot	1 tbsp.	$\frac{1}{3}$ cup	Sauté until golden brown.
Garlic, minced	1 tsp.	2 tbsp.	
Beef brisket, diced finely	$\frac{1}{4}$ cup	$1\frac{1}{2}$ cups	
Beef stock, strong	2 cups	3 qt.	Add; heat.
Leeks, chopped	2 tbsp.	$\frac{3}{4}$ cup	Add. Simmer for 30 minutes.
Cabbage, chopped	2 tbsp.	$\frac{3}{4}$ cup	
Potatoes, diced	$\frac{1}{4}$ cup	$1\frac{1}{2}$ cups	
Onion, red, diced	$\frac{1}{4}$ cup	$1\frac{1}{2}$ cups	
Celery, diced	2 tbsp.	$\frac{3}{4}$ cup	
Carrots, diced	$\frac{1}{4}$ cup	$1\frac{1}{2}$ cups	
Zucchini, cubed	$\frac{1}{4}$ cup	$1\frac{1}{2}$ cups	
Tomato, peeled, coarsely chopped	1	6	
Bay leaf	1	3	
Pinto beans, cooked	2 tbsp.	$\frac{3}{4}$ cup	Add. Simmer until pasta is cooked, about 15
Chickpeas, cooked	2 tbsp.	$\frac{3}{4}$ cup	minutes. Adjust seasoning with salt and
Tubetti (tubular pasta)	$\frac{1}{4}$ cup	$1\frac{1}{2}$ cups	pepper.

SPECIAL HANDLING FOR BUFFETS: *Serve very warm from bain marie set over a single heating unit. Stir often to maintain optimum service temperature. Keep covered as much as possible. Substitute other squash varieties for zucchini and season with anisette or other anise-based liqueur.*

Oyster Chowder New Orleans

INGREDIENTS	TEST QUANTITY: 8	SERVICE QUANTITY: 50	METHOD
White wine, dry	½ cup	3 cups	Combine ingredients in sauce pot with one-third of oyster liquid. (Reserve remaining liquid.) Simmer for 15 minutes. Strain the liquid and reserve.
Onion, minced	½ cup	3 cups	
Green pepper, minced	¼ cup	1½ cups	
Carrots, minced	1	6	
Celery, minced	1 rib	6 ribs	
Thyme, dried	¼ tsp.	1½ tsp.	
Oregano, dried	¼ tsp.	1½ tsp.	
Bay leaf	1	3	
Clove, whole	1	4	
Oyster liquor from oysters and water to yield	3 cups	4½ qt.	
Olive oil	¼ cup	1½ cups	Combine and simmer, stirring for 6 to 8 minutes. Cool. Heat remaining oyster liquid and blend well. Simmer 20 minutes. Add reserved mixture and stir.
Flour, all purpose	¼ cup	1½ cups	
Potatoes, peeled, diced	½ cup	3 cups	Add; cook until potatoes are tender, about 30 minutes.
Garlic, minced	¼ tsp.	1½ tsp.	
Celery, chopped	½ cup	3 cups	
Oysters, chopped	2 cups	3 qt.	Add; simmer 15 minutes.
Heavy cream	¼ cup	1¼ cups	Prior to service, add and adjust.
White pepper	¼ tsp.	1½ tsp.	
Salt	to taste	to taste	
Tabasco	to taste	to taste	

SPECIAL HANDLING FOR BUFFETS: *Serve very warm from bain marie set over single heating unit. Stir often to maintain optimum service temperature. Keep covered as much as possible. Substitute clams or shrimp for oysters. Add cooked steamed rice. Serve with buttered muffins or oyster crackers.*

Pennsylvania Corn Soup

INGREDIENTS	TEST QUANTITY: 8	SERVICE QUANTITY: 50	METHOD
Chicken broth	3 cups	$4\frac{1}{2}$ qt.	Combine; simmer 1 hour. Remove bay leaf.
Onion, minced	3 tbsp.	1 cup + 2 tbsp.	
Celery, minced	$\frac{1}{2}$ cup	$1\frac{1}{2}$ tsp.	
Sage, dried	$\frac{1}{4}$ tsp.	$1\frac{1}{2}$ tsp.	
Salt	$\frac{1}{4}$ tsp.	$1\frac{1}{2}$ tsp.	
Black pepper	to taste	to taste	
Bay leaf	1	3	
Turkey, cooked, diced	$\frac{1}{4}$ cup	$1\frac{1}{2}$ cups	Add; simmer until hot.
Egg noodles, cooked	$\frac{1}{3}$ cup	2 cups	
Corn, whole kernel, drained or frozen	1 cup	3 lb.	
Scallions (greens only), chopped	1 tbsp.	$\frac{1}{3}$ cup	Stir in before service.
Parsley, chopped	2 tsp.	$\frac{1}{4}$ cup	

SPECIAL HANDLING FOR BUFFETS: *Serve very warm from bain marie set over single heating unit. Stir often to maintain optimum service temperature. Keep covered as much as possible. Add sautéed green or red sweet pepper. Season with a touch of nutmeg.*

Potato Soup with Bacon and Cabbage

INGREDIENTS	TEST QUANTITY: 8	SERVICE QUANTITY: 50	METHOD
Water	1 qt.	$1\frac{1}{2}$ gal.	Combine in pot; bring to boil. Cook potatoes
Potatoes (boiling), peeled, quartered	1 cup	3 lb.	until tender. Remove and reserve. Reserve
Lean bacon	$\frac{1}{2}$ lb.	3 lb.	cooking liquid, but strain.
Leeks (white only), sliced	1 cup	$1\frac{1}{2}$ qt.	
Cabbage, coarsely sliced	$\frac{1}{2}$ lb.	3 lb.	Add to reserved liquid. Partially cover and
Juniper berries, crushed	$\frac{1}{4}$ tsp.	$1\frac{1}{2}$ tsp.	simmer for $1\frac{1}{2}$ to 2 hours. Discard parsley, bay
Peppercorns, crushed	2	12	leaf, cloves and onion. Return potatoes to soup.
Red pepper, crushed	to taste	to taste	
Bay leaf	1	3	
Parsley sprigs, tied	2	12	
Oregano	pinch	to taste	
Thyme	pinch	to taste	
Garlic, crushed	2 cloves	12 cloves	
Onions, whole	1	1 lb.	
Cloves, whole	2	12	
Carrots, peeled, diced	1	1 lb.	
Turnips, peeled, diced	1	1 lb.	
Celery ribs, diced	1	6	
Salt	to taste	to taste	Adjust seasoning.

SPECIAL HANDLING FOR BUFFETS: *Serve very warm from bain marie set over a single heating unit. Stir often to maintain optimum service temperature. Keep covered as much as possible. Add shredded cheddar cheese after cooking and stir well. Offer cheese and chopped parsley or scallions in side bowls.*

Red Bean Soup

INGREDIENTS	TEST QUANTITY: 8	SERVICE QUANTITY: 50	METHOD
Olive oil, hot	$\frac{1}{2}$ tbsp.	3 tbsp.	Sauté in large pot until soft.
Onion, chopped	2 tbsp.	$\frac{3}{4}$ cup	
Celery, chopped	1 tbsp.	$\frac{1}{3}$ cup	
Red kidney beans, dried	$\frac{1}{3}$ lb.	2 lb.	Add. Simmer until beans are cooked, about 3 hours. Remove bay leaves. Strain and press through a fine sieve back into a pot.
Water	1 qt.	$1\frac{1}{2}$ gal.	
Garlic, minced	1 clove	6 cloves	
Carrot, diced	$\frac{1}{4}$ cup	$1\frac{1}{2}$ cups	
Celery, chopped	$\frac{1}{4}$ cup	$1\frac{1}{2}$ cups	
Onion, chopped	$\frac{1}{4}$ cup	$1\frac{1}{2}$ cups	
Bay leaves	1	3	
Oregano, dried	to taste	to taste	
Thyme, dried	to taste	to taste	
Worcestershire sauce	$\frac{1}{2}$ tsp.	1 tbsp.	
Tabasco	$\frac{1}{4}$ tsp.	$1\frac{1}{2}$ tsp.	
Smoked ham, diced	$\frac{1}{3}$ lb.	2 lb.	Add. Simmer for 10 minutes.
Salt	to taste	to taste	
Black pepper	$\frac{1}{2}$ tsp.	1 tbsp.	
Water	as needed	as needed	
Red wine	1 oz.	$\frac{3}{4}$ cup	Sprinkle in before service.

SPECIAL HANDLING FOR BUFFETS: *Serve very warm from bain marie set over a single heating unit. Stir often to maintain optimum service temperature. Keep covered as much as possible. Offer with side bowls of chopped hard-cooked egg and sour cream.*

San Francisco Crab Soup

INGREDIENTS	TEST QUANTITY: 8	SERVICE QUANTITY: 50	METHOD
Butter, melted	2 tbsp.	$\frac{3}{4}$ cup	Sauté until tender.
Onion, chopped	$\frac{1}{2}$ cup	3 cups	
Celery, chopped	$\frac{1}{2}$ cup	3 cups	
Green pepper, chopped	$\frac{1}{2}$ cup	3 cups	
Scallions (greens and whites), chopped	1 cup	$1\frac{1}{2}$ qt.	
Fish stock	1 qt.	$1\frac{1}{2}$ gal.	Add; bring to boil; cover. Simmer for 10 minutes.
White wine	1 cup	$1\frac{1}{2}$ qt.	
Rice, uncooked	$\frac{1}{2}$ cup	3 cups	
Vermicelli, crushed	$\frac{1}{2}$ cup	3 cups	
Tomatoes, peeled, chopped	1 cup	3 lb.	Add; bring to boil. Simmer until rice and noodles are cooked.
Thyme, dried	$\frac{1}{4}$ tsp.	$1\frac{1}{2}$ tsp.	
Okra, sliced	$\frac{1}{4}$ lb.	$1\frac{1}{2}$ lb.	
Dungeness crab meat, cooked	1 cup	2 lb.	
Worcestershire sauce	1 tsp.	2 tbsp.	
Tabasco	$\frac{1}{4}$ tsp.	$1\frac{1}{2}$ tsp.	
Salt	to taste	to taste	Adjust seasoning.
Black pepper	to taste	to taste	
Parsley, chopped	as needed	as needed	
Scallions (greens only), minced	as needed	as needed	

SPECIAL HANDLING FOR BUFFETS: *Serve very warm from bain marie set over a single heating unit. Stir often to maintain optimum service temperature. Keep covered as much as possible. Substitute crab variety as needed. Sauté onion mixture in bacon fat instead of butter. Season with Tabasco or hot red pepper.*

Scotch Broth

INGREDIENTS	TEST QUANTITY: 8	SERVICE QUANTITY: 50	METHOD
Lamb neck or shoulder, diced	1 lb.	6 lb.	Combine; bring to a boil. Skim.
Water	1 qt.	1½ gal.	
White wine	1 cup	1½ qt.	
Barley	1 tbsp.	⅓ cup	Add to pot; simmer for 1 hour.
Salt	1 tsp.	2 tbsp.	
Black pepper	¼ tsp.	1½ tsp.	
Bay leaf	1	3	
Potatoes, red, peeled, diced	1 cup	1½ qt.	Add; partially cover; simmer for 1 hour.
Carrots, minced	¼ cup	1½ cups	Remove bay leaf. Bring back to simmer. Adjust flavor.
Turnips, minced	¼ cup	1½ cups	
Onions, minced	¼ cup	1½ cups	
Leeks (white only), minced	¼ cup	1½ cups	
Celery minced	¼ cup	1½ cups	
Scallions (greens only), chopped	1 tbsp.	⅓ cup	Mix in; serve.
Egg yolk, hard boiled, sieved	1 tbsp.	⅓ cup	

SPECIAL HANDLING FOR BUFFETS: *Serve very warm from bain marie set over a single heating unit. Stir often to maintain optimum service temperature. Keep covered as much as possible. Serve with slices of thick soda bread.*

Southern Peanut Soup

INGREDIENTS	TEST QUANTITY: 8	SERVICE QUANTITY: 50	METHOD
Butter, melted	2 tbsp.	$\frac{3}{4}$ cup	Sauté until tender.
Celery, minced	$\frac{1}{2}$ cup	3 cups	
Onion, minced	$\frac{1}{2}$ cup	3 cups	
Carrot, minced	$\frac{1}{2}$ cup	3 cups	
Flour, all purpose	$1\frac{1}{2}$ tbsp.	$\frac{2}{3}$ cup	Add; stir well. Cook 5 minutes.
White wine	$\frac{1}{4}$ cup	$1\frac{1}{2}$ cups	Add; bring to boil. Remove bay leaf. Remove from heat and purée.
Chicken stock	1 qt.	$1\frac{1}{2}$ gal.	
Bay leaf	1	3	
Thyme, dried	$\frac{1}{4}$ tsp.	$1\frac{1}{2}$ tsp.	
Peanut butter, creamy	1 cup	3 lb.	Add and combine well. Return to heat, but do not boil.
Cream	1 cup	$1\frac{1}{2}$ qt.	
Tabasco	$\frac{1}{4}$ tsp.	$1\frac{1}{2}$ tsp.	

SPECIAL HANDLING FOR BUFFETS: *Serve very warm from bain marie set over a single heating unit. Stir often to maintain optimum service temperature. Keep covered as much as possible. Serve with side bowls of peanuts and popped corn.*

Swiss Onion Soup

INGREDIENTS	TEST QUANTITY: 8	SERVICE QUANTITY: 50	METHOD
Butter, melted	$\frac{1}{2}$ cup	3 cups	Sauté until soft.
Onions, sliced	2 lb.	12 lb.	
Leek (white only), sliced	$\frac{1}{2}$ lb.	3 lb.	
Beef stock	6 cups	$2\frac{1}{4}$ gal.	Add; bring to a boil.
Dark beer	1 cup	$1\frac{1}{2}$ qt.	
Thyme	$\frac{1}{4}$ tsp.	$1\frac{1}{2}$ tsp.	Add; stir to combine well. Simmer at least 2
Celery salt	$\frac{3}{4}$ tsp.	$1\frac{1}{2}$ tbsp.	hours.
Mustard seeds	$\frac{1}{4}$ tsp.	$1\frac{1}{2}$ tsp.	
Salt	to taste	to taste	
Black pepper	to taste	to taste	

SPECIAL HANDLING FOR BUFFETS: *Serve very warm from bain marie set over a single heating unit. Stir often to maintain optimum service temperature. Keep covered as much as possible. Deglaze pot with white wine before adding beef stock. Serve with cheddar croutons.*

Tide Water Oyster Bisque

INGREDIENTS	TEST QUANTITY: 8	SERVICE QUANTITY: 50	METHOD
Oysters, shucked	2 cups	3 qt.	Drain and reserve all liquor. Reserve oysters.
Water	3 cups	4½ qt.	Add to oyster liquor. Simmer for 45 minutes. Let rest for 1 hour. Strain. Reserve stock.
Black peppercorns	½ tsp.	1 tbsp.	
Bay leaf	1	4	
Whole clove	1	6	
Onion, chopped	½ cup	3 cups	
Celery, chopped	¼ cup	1½ cups	
Carrot, chopped	½ cup	3 cups	
Butter, melted	¼ cup	1½ cups	Sauté until tender.
Onion, chopped	½ cup	3 cups	
Celery, chopped	¼ cup	1½ cups	
Green pepper, minced	2 tbsp.	¾ cup	
Flour, all purpose	2 tbsp.	¾ cup	Add and stir for 5 minutes. Add reserved stock and combine well. Stir until smooth.
Salt	¼ tsp.	1½ tsp.	Add; adjust seasoning. Simmer for 15 minutes.
White pepper	⅛ tsp.	¾ tsp.	
Hot pepper sauce	to taste	to taste	
Cream	1 cup	1½ qt.	Add with reserved oysters. Simmer slowly until oysters are just plump.
Worcestershire sauce	½ tsp.	1 tbsp.	
Sherry, dry	¼ cup	1½ cups	Add; stir to combine.
Parsley, chopped	2 tbsp.	¾ cup	
Butter, soft	as desired	as desired	

SPECIAL HANDLING FOR BUFFETS: *Serve very warm from bain marie set over a single heating unit. Stir often to maintain optimum service temperature. Keep covered as much as possible. Substitute clams for oysters. Serve with small biscuits seasoned with cheddar cheese. The tide waters in this country usually refer to that area of the East Coast that begins in the watery lands bounding the Chesapeake Bay in Virginia and extends through the shores of the Carolinas, both North and South, to a stretch of land just south of Savannah, Georgia.*

Tortilla Soup, The Mansion on Turtle Creek

INGREDIENTS	TEST QUANTITY: 8	SERVICE QUANTITY: 50	METHOD
Corn oil, hot	$\frac{1}{2}$ tbsp.	3 tbsp.	Sauté over moderate heat until onions are
Onion, chopped	$\frac{1}{2}$ cup	3 cups	translucent.
Garlic, minced	1 tbsp.	$\frac{1}{3}$ cup	
Tomato, seeded, chopped	$\frac{1}{2}$ cup	3 cups	
Chicken stock (or beef)	1 qt.	$1\frac{1}{2}$ gal.	Add; simmer 30 minutes.
Cumin, ground	$\frac{1}{2}$ tsp.	1 tbsp.	Add; simmer 5 minutes; adjust the seasoning.
White pepper, ground	to taste	to taste	Ladle into service pieces. Keep warm.

SPECIAL HANDLING FOR BUFFETS: *Serve very warm from bain marie set over a single heating unit. Stir often to maintain optimum service temperature. Keep covered as much as possible. Garnish with triangles of deep-fried corn tortillas.*

Offer with side bowls of sour cream and chipped California black ripe olives. The Mansion on Turtle Creek in Dallas, Texas, is well recognized throughout the United States for its creative cuisine.

Tyrolean Dumpling Soup

INGREDIENTS	TEST QUANTITY: 8	SERVICE QUANTITY: 50	METHOD
Butter, melted	1 tbsp.	$\frac{1}{3}$ cup	Sauté until soft.
Garlic, minced	$\frac{1}{2}$ tsp.	1 tbsp.	
Onion, minced	$\frac{1}{2}$ cup	3 cups	
Celery, minced	$\frac{1}{2}$ cup	3 cups	
Bacon, minced	$\frac{1}{4}$ cup	$1\frac{1}{2}$ cups	Add. Sauté until bacon is translucent.
Ham, smoked, minced	$\frac{1}{4}$ cup	$1\frac{1}{2}$ cups	
Bread crumbs, stale	1 lb.	6 lb.	Place in bowl. Add bacon mixture.
Milk	$\frac{3}{4}$ cup	1 qt.	Combine well. Add to mixture. Let rest for 1 hour. Then mix the mixture until it is well combined. Form mixture into small balls.
Egg, beaten	1	6	
Egg yolk, beaten	1	6	
Flour, all purpose	$\frac{1}{4}$ cup	$1\frac{1}{2}$ cups	
Oregano, dried	$\frac{1}{4}$ tsp.	$1\frac{1}{2}$ tsp.	
Scallions (greens and whites), minced	1 tbsp.	$\frac{1}{3}$ cup	
Mustard, Dijon type	$\frac{1}{2}$ tsp.	1 tbsp.	
Parsley, chopped	1 tbsp.	$\frac{1}{3}$ cup	
Worcestershire sauce	$\frac{1}{2}$ tsp.	1 tbsp.	
Salt	to taste	to taste	
Black pepper	to taste	to taste	
Water, boiling	as needed	as needed	Simmer dumplings until cooked, about 15 minutes.
Salt	to taste	to taste	
Beef broth	$1\frac{1}{2}$ qt.	$2\frac{1}{4}$ gal.	Pour into service piece. Place dumplings in.

SPECIAL HANDLING FOR BUFFETS: *Serve very warm from bain marie set over a single heating unit. Stir often to maintain optimum service temperature. Keep covered as much as possible. Add sautéed crumbled sausage to dumpling mixture. Season with fennel as desired.*

Review Questions

1. Describe a mulligatawny stew.

2. What seasonings highlight Danish cabbage soup?

3. Name two soups that are based on beets.

4. Describe Peruvian shrimp soup.

5. What is the cold Spanish vegetable soup called?

6. Name two ethnic bean soups.

Six

Meats: A Culinary Road Map

Meat in some form or other serves as the focal point of most buffets. One example is the glistening roast pig that is served at Hawaii's celebrated luaus. Roasted in a great *imu* pit or turned on a spit over glowing coals, crisp and juicy suckling pig is the main attraction of the traditional luau buffet. In other settings, it might not be pork, or even cooked out of doors, but meat is at the center of both plate and attention in displays of buffet cuisine. Meat serves as a guide through a myriad cooking styles, and to become familiar with meats of many countries is to be better prepared for global buffet cookery.

CHINA

The major meat in Chinese cuisine is pork, chiefly because of the fact that the Chinese economy cannot afford grazing lands for cattle or veal. Lamb is prized in parts of China — mainly in the northern areas, where Mohammedan Chinese do not eat pork at all. (Generally, most methods for Chinese pork cookery can be applied to beef.) The key is to build an understanding of the various regions that combine to make up Chinese cookery; within each region, specific ingredients, cooking methods, and flavoring agents produce signature foods.

Canton is a major culinary region and the one with the greatest exposure in this country; a reliance on bright colors, soy sauce, plum sauce, and fairly mild spices are trademarks. Stir-fried pork with vegetables, or *cha shu bok tsoi,* is an example of Cantonese cookery.

Shanghai represents Eastern Chinese cooking, and because it is a seaport, its cuisine relies less on meat than on fish. There is even more soy sauce flavoring in Shanghai cuisine, as well as a prevalence of sugar and scallions. Pork with cucumbers, *hwang gwa ro pien,* is a meat cookery procedure from this region.

Peking has long been the center of China's epicurean cooking and has developed a unique reliance on scallions, leeks, bean paste, and noodles (including pancakes) for its cooking. In addition to meat, duck is a regional favorite. The ever-popular *mu shoo* pork and Mongolian beef are classics of Peking cuisine.

Szechuan, along with Hunan, represents the really feisty cooking style of China. A reliance on anise pepper and hot oils contributes to a broad base of often-sizzling Oriental delights. Ginger and *hoisin* sauce are additional seasoning favorites. Twice-cooked pork, or *hwei gwo ro,* is a well-known Szechuan specialty.

ENGLAND

Beef, lamb, and pork predominate in British cooking, with every preparation method from broiling to boiling used along the way. The British share a special fancy for meat pies, such as the famous Cornish pasties, small meat and vegetable pastry packets that were originally taken into coal mines and heated over the miners' lanterns. Steak and kidney pie, and such other British game pies as venison and rabbit, are baked, then cooled, filled with aspic, and often served cold. Conversely, a Lancashire hot pot is a lamb stew served, as its name suggests, warm. Lamb chops and oxtails are two more British meat favorites, as are pig's feet and salted pork. When beef is roasted, it is often served with Yorkshire pudding, actually a popover; boiled beef is often accompanied by horseradish sauce. "Bully beef" is a nickname for what we in America serve as creamed chipped beef on toast or muffins.

FRANCE

French cuisine offers a diversity of meat classics. *Boeuf bourguignon* is rich with onions and red wine. Chateaubriand is that luxurious roasted tenderloin, often carved for two but a cut that can also be prepared for many. Tournedoes are individual mini-filets that can be prepared in many ways. Veal dishes are often braised, but chops can be served in a variety of presentations; Lyon-style, for example, includes parmesan cheese. Veal kidneys Lyonnaise are prepared with cream and cognac. Pork is prevalent in many regions; a well-known version is *noisette de porc aux pruneaux,* or sauteed pork chops with prunes. *Choucroute garni* comprises various sausages as well as sauerkraut. *Jambon,* or ham, is a national favorite especially when served chilled *en persille,* with pork jelly and parsley.

GERMANY

Typified by the great pork buffet-on-a-platter *schlacht platte,* German cuisine is centered on meats. Pork is used, either smoked or fresh, for preparations of spareribs as well as for a vast array of sausages. Other pork presentations include *bayerisher linsentopf,* which is smoked pork with lentils (similar to French *cassoulet*), and *jaegerschnitzel,* a fried pork filet with mushrooms. Beef is more often than not stewed in German cuisine and is almost invariably marinated, as in *sauerbraten.* Cuts of beef are often sliced thinly, then pounded and filled before they are rolled and secured with a pick; these *rouladen* are then browned and braised until tender. Ground beef or veal often find their ways into meatballs or *hackbraten,* a version of meatloaf that is sometimes fried. Game such as venison and rabbit (including the famous *hassenpfeffer*) are also key items on a German meat menu.

GREECE

Lamb is the prevalent meat in Greek cuisine, and a classic preparation is the spit-roasted version served in conjunction with the Easter celebration; suckling pigs are also spit roasted, often first stuffed with a mixture of feta cheese and the Greek flavoring favorites, lemon, parsley, and oregano. Most meat dishes, however, are cubed and either stewed or braised with a variety of vegetables; beef and rabbit occasionally join lamb as the meat of choice. Often ground and mixed with seasonings, meat is then wrapped in grape leaves for the famous Greek *dolmades;* when ground and mixed with layers of eggplant, moussaka is the prized result. A general term for Greek stew, *stefado* refers to the highly seasoned combinations of cubed lamb, beef, or rabbit, redolent of cinnamon, garlic, tomato, parsley, onions, and oregano. All cuts of meat can be used in creative Greek stews or casseroles.

HUNGARY

Another country with a yen for pork over other meat types, Hungary has also developed some unique and ingenious procedures for curing and using bacon; according to chroniclers of this Middle European nation, there are more than 20 varieties, each having an inherent flavor quality. Paprika and garlic are just two of the seasonings used to attain the desired flavor. Lamb is low on Hungarian popularity charts, with the exception of residents of the Great Plains, or Little Cumania; in this area, lamb is often combined with spinach or with scallion greens. Beef cookery takes several forms, including the Hungarian version of the ubiquitous rouladen, called *legenysult.* An Hungarian favorite known as *rostelyos* refers to a family of dishes that combine thinly sliced sautéed beef with a variety of vegetables; cream, paprika, and tomato seem to be commonly recurring ingredients. Of course *gulyas* or goulash is a Hungarian classic, as are *borju porkholt* and *sertes porkholt,* two variations of the pork stew theme.

ITALY

One of the more regionally diverse of the world's culinary centers, Italy offers a variety of cooking methods for beef, veal, pork, and lamb. Beef from Tuscany and the Bologna area, pork from Umbria, and the famous Roman spit-roasted lamb preparation *abbacchio al forno* are world renowned; Parma ham and the bologna-like *mortadella* are other classics. When veal is on the menu, *vitello* is the Italian word; beef is *manzo,* as in the dish *pizzaiola di manzo,* a version of tomato-rich, sauced fried steak; and a dish of pork chops in white wine is *costolette di maiale alla modense.* When meat is fried on Italian menus, it is said to be *fritto;* if it is braised, it is *brasato;* when it is boiled, as beef often is, the preparation is *bollito.* Thinly pounded, stuffed and rolled meat dishes (like the German rouladen) are called *bracioli.* Not willing to pass up favored meat loaf, Italian cooks will grind up beef and pork for *polpettone;* a version of shish kebab on an Italian buffet would be called *arrostino annegato,* or skewered, braised veal. Flavoring principles will vary by region, but the use of beef, pork, lamb, and veal is an Italian hallmark.

JAPAN

The role of meat is not as significant in Japanese cuisine as it is in some others, due in large measure to the limited quantity available to cook. A method that is worthy of note, though, is the procedure known as *nimono,* in which a clear broth is used to poach thin slices of valued beef; the same procedure can be used with chicken and fish. Beef is also grilled in a skillet and served with a condiment of soy sauce and lime juice. In either case, the meat is sliced thinly enough so that the outside and inside cook evenly. When beef is combined with vegetables in a one-dish cooking method, the term *nabemono* applies; when marinated before charcoal grilling, the more familiar term *teriyaki* is encountered. Pork is less expensive than beef and is commonly served with shredded cabbage.

MEXICO

Because it is split almost its entire length by mountains, Mexico exhibits a diversity of cooking styles. Whereas herds of Sonoran beef are inherent to the northern plains, other sections such as Jalisco and the eastern Yucatán rely more heavily on pork. A Mexican version of the Hawaiian luau spit-roasted pig is the *cochinita pibil,* a suckling cooked in the Yucatán manner in a *pib* or pit oven; *guiso de puerco* is a more common pork stew. In any case, regional chilis and even chocolate (in the famous *mole* procedure) are used for flavoring. Mexican cooking uses a lot of charcoal grilling for pork, beef, and *cabrito* or goat; lamb makes a suitable domestic substitute. When a method calls for ground beef, the Mexican cook is more apt to poach the meat and then shred it, rather than grind it as we are known to do. Lemon and limes are used to flavor grilled meats; stews are heavily seasoned with oregano and cilantro.

GET ON THE "BALL"!

Although every country has developed unique ways in which to cook available meats, there are common methods that crop up throughout. One category that threads through the kitchens of many nations is meatballs, which appear in some way or other throughout global cookery and have a rightful place at almost any buffet (see Appetizers.) In addition to well-known Swedish meatballs in cream sauce, a Thai version made with pork is called *ma ho;* and East Indian beef meatballs, called *nargisi koftas,* are seasoned with cloves, pepper, and mace before being wrapped around hard-cooked eggs. Dutch *balletjes* are made from curried veal; *kadin budu* are Turkish beef, formed into oval shapes and poached and fried. As with so much of meat cookery, the limits are vast, and the possibilities almost without dimension.

Argentinian Rolled Beef

INGREDIENTS	TEST QUANTITY: 8	SERVICE QUANTITY: 50	METHOD
Flank steak, 1½ lb.	2	12	Rub meat with oil, mustard and spices on all surfaces. Pound flat and lay out on work surface.
Olive oil	¼ cup	1½ cups	
Mustard, Dijon type	1 tsp.	2 tbsp.	
Salt	to taste	to taste	
Black pepper	to taste	to taste	
Crushed red pepper	½ tsp.	1 tbsp.	
Onions, minced	½ cup	3 cups	Combine and divide among steaks. Roll and tie securely. Brown all surfaces well in hot sauté pan(s). Remove meat and place in baking pan(s). Reserve hot oil in pan(s).
Carrots, julienned	2 cups	3 lb.	
Cilantro	2 tsp.	¼ cup	
Celery, julienned	1 cup	1½ lb.	
Parsley, chopped	1 tbsp.	⅓ cup	
Scallions (greens and whites), chopped	½ cup	3 cups	
Onions, minced	2 cups	4 lb.	Add to sauté pans. Sauté until soft. Distribute around meat.
Celery, minced	1 cup	1½ qt.	
Garlic, minced	1 tsp.	1½ tbsp.	
Carrots, julienned	½ cup	3 cups	
Beef stock	2 cups	3 qt.	Pour into pan. Bring to a simmer. Cover. Place in 350°F oven and braise until meat is tender, about 1½ or 2 hours. Slice meat into ¾-in. slices. Arrange in service piece(s).
Parsley	2 tbsp.	¾ cup	Sprinkle over.

SPECIAL HANDLING FOR BUFFETS: *Serve very warm from shallow insert pan(s) set over dual heating units. Keep covered. Offer with Chimichurri Sauce (see Recipe Index) and plenty of sliced boiled new potatoes. A corn relish seasoned with crushed cumin would make a nice condiment.*

Beef Curry

INGREDIENTS	TEST QUANTITY: 8	SERVICE QUANTITY: 50	METHOD
Flank steak, sliced $1 \times \frac{1}{2} \times \frac{1}{8}$ in.	1 lb.	6 lb.	Dissolve dry ingredients with wine and oil.
Sugar	1 tsp.	2 tbsp.	Stir until meat is well coated. Chill until
Cornstarch	2 tbsp.	$\frac{3}{4}$ cup	ready to proceed.
White wine	2 tbsp.	$\frac{3}{4}$ cup	
Olive oil	2 tbsp.	$\frac{3}{4}$ cup	
Peanut oil, hot	$\frac{1}{3}$ cup	2 cups	
Garlic, minced	1–2 tbsp.	$\frac{1}{3}$ cup	Sauté quickly.
Ginger, grated	$\frac{1}{2}$–1 tsp.	1–2 tbsp.	
Onion, minced	1–2 cups	3 qt.	Add; toss for 30 seconds.
Apple, peeled, cored, diced	$\frac{1}{2}$–1 cup	3 cups	
Curry powder	1–2 tbsp.	$\frac{1}{3}$ cup	Add; stir quickly.
Turmeric	$\frac{1}{8}$–$\frac{1}{4}$ tsp.	$\frac{3}{4}$ tsp.	
Celery, sliced diagonally	2 cups–1 qt.	3 lb.	Add; stir to coat.
Carrots, sliced diagonally	2 cups–1 qt.	4 lb.	
Leeks (white only), sliced	$\frac{1}{2}$–1 cup	3 cups	
Sherry, dry	$\frac{1}{2}$–1 tsp.	1 tbsp.	Add; stir.
Soy sauce	2 tbsp.–$\frac{1}{4}$ cup	$\frac{3}{4}$ cup	
Sugar	$\frac{1}{2}$–1 tbsp.	3 tbsp.	
Water	2 cups–1 qt.	3 qts.	Add, stir, and cover. Cook 5 minutes at a gentle simmer. Add reserved meat, cover; cook 2 minutes. Turn heat to high; uncover; toss until sauce glazes. Pour into service piece(s).

SPECIAL HANDLING FOR BUFFETS: *Serve very warm from shallow insert pan(s) set over dual heating units. Keep covered. Offer with side bowls of typical curry condiments: coconut, chopped scallions, toasted almonds, chutney, sliced pappadams (Indian peppery wafers), and steamed white rice.*

Belgian-Style Braised Beef

INGREDIENTS	TEST QUANTITY: 8	SERVICE QUANTITY: 50	METHOD
Beef, lean boneless chuck	3 lb.	18 lb.	Slice beef in $2 \times 4 \times \frac{1}{2}$-in. strips and sear. Remove from pan and reduce heat. Reserve pan.
Olive oil, hot	$\frac{1}{4}$ cup	$1\frac{1}{2}$ cups	
Carrots, sliced	2 cups	4 lbs.	Add to pan and cook 10 minutes.
Onions, sliced	2 lb.	12 lb.	
Celery, sliced	2 cups	3 lb.	
Thyme, dried	$\frac{1}{4}$ tsp.	$1\frac{1}{2}$ tsp.	Add and stir to combine well. Put half the meat in roasting pan and cover with half the onion mixture. Season to taste. Repeat with rest of meat and onions.
Salt	to taste	to taste	
Pepper	to taste	to taste	
Garlic, crushed	6 cloves	$\frac{1}{4}$ cup	
Beef stock or broth	1 cup	$1\frac{1}{2}$ qt.	Add to pan used to sear beef; bring to a boil and scrape bottom. Pour over meat and onions.
Red wine	$\frac{1}{2}$ cup	3 cups	
Beer	to cover	to cover	Pour over meat to barely cover.
Brown sugar, light	2 tbsp.	$\frac{3}{4}$ cup	Add to pan. Bring to simmer on top of stove; cover. Put in 325°F oven and maintain bare simmer until meat is fork tender. Remove bouquet garni and drain and reserve all liquid from pan. Remove all fat.
Bouquet garni, in cheesecloth:			
Parsley	6 sprigs	1 bunch	
Bay leaf	1	6	
Thyme	1 tsp.	2 tbsp.	
Oregano	$\frac{1}{2}$ tsp.	1 tbsp.	
Peppercorns	8	2 tbsp.	
Cornstarch	$1\frac{1}{2}$ tbsp.	$\frac{1}{2}$ cup + 1 tbsp.	Combine well. Add to liquid and simmer for 5 minutes. Adjust seasoning. Arrange meat in serving pieces and pour sauce over.
Red wine vinegar	2 tbsp.	$\frac{3}{4}$ cup	
Cinnamon	$\frac{1}{4}$ tsp.	$1\frac{1}{2}$ tsp.	
Nutmeg	$\frac{1}{8}$ tsp.	$\frac{3}{4}$ tsp.	

SPECIAL HANDLING FOR BUFFETS: *Serve very warm from shallow insert pan(s) set over dual heating units. Keep covered. Offer with potato gnocchi or dumplings, green vege-tables, and red cabbage. Serve with chilled bottles of Pilsner-type beer.*

Boned Lamb with Garlic Sauce

INGREDIENTS	TEST QUANTITY: 8	SERVICE QUANTITY: 50	METHOD
Leg of lamb, boned	3 lb.	18 lb.	Lay meat out flat and season. Tie lamb into roll.
Mustard, Dijon type	1 tsp.	2 tbsp.	
Salt	1 tsp.	2 tbsp.	
Black pepper	$\frac{1}{2}$ tsp.	1 tbsp.	
Garlic, minced	$\frac{1}{2}$ tsp.	1 tbsp.	
Thyme	$\frac{1}{2}$ tsp.	1 tbsp.	
Rosemary	$\frac{1}{2}$ tsp.	1 tbsp.	
Olive oil, heated	$\frac{1}{4}$ cup	$1\frac{1}{2}$ cups	Brown lamb on all sides.
Onion, sliced	$\frac{1}{2}$ cup	3 cups	Add with lamb to roasting pan(s). Roast at
Carrots, chopped	$\frac{1}{2}$ cup	3 cups	375°F until desired doneness. Remove lamb
Celery, chopped	$\frac{1}{4}$ cup	$1\frac{1}{2}$ cups	and keep warm. Skim off any fat. Place
Garlic, peeled	2 cloves	$\frac{1}{2}$ head	pan(s) over medium heat. Remove bay leaf.
Bay leaf	1	3	
Lamb bones, broken	from leg	from legs	
White wine, dry	$\frac{1}{4}$ cup	$1\frac{1}{2}$ cups	Add; reduce by half. Remove bones and
Red wine, dry	$\frac{1}{4}$ cup	$1\frac{1}{2}$ cups	strain sauce. Adjust seasoning.
Water	1 qt.	$1\frac{1}{2}$ gal.	
Black peppercorns	$\frac{1}{4}$ tsp.	$1\frac{1}{2}$ tsp.	
Rosemary	$\frac{1}{8}$ tsp.	$\frac{3}{4}$ tsp.	

SPECIAL HANDLING FOR BUFFETS: *Serve very warm from shallow insert pan(s) set over dual heating units. Keep covered. Try adding some rosemary to the roasting bones for flavor. Offer with sautéed or grilled onions.*

Braised Veal with Dumplings

INGREDIENTS	TEST QUANTITY: 8	SERVICE QUANTITY: 50	METHOD
Butter, melted	2 tbsp.	$\frac{3}{4}$ cup	Sauté until golden.
Olive oil, hot	2 tbsp.	$\frac{3}{4}$ cup	
Onions, chopped	1 lb.	6 lb.	
Celery, chopped	1 cup	$1\frac{1}{2}$ lb.	
Veal leg, boneless, 1-inch cubes	3 lb.	18 lb.	Toss and add. Sauté until brown.
Hungarian paprika, hot	2 tbsp.	$\frac{3}{4}$ cup	
Salt	1 tsp.	2 tbsp.	
Black pepper	$\frac{1}{2}$ tsp.	1 tbsp.	
Brandy	$\frac{1}{4}$ cup	$1\frac{1}{2}$ cups	Add, deglaze, and flame.
Tomato, peeled, chopped	$\frac{1}{2}$ cup	3 cups	Add, cover, and simmer 45 minutes.
Green pepper, diced	$\frac{1}{2}$ cup	3 cups	
Onion, diced	1 cup	$1\frac{1}{2}$ lb.	
Beef stock	$\frac{1}{2}$ cup	3 cups	
Thyme, dried	$\frac{1}{4}$ tsp.	$1\frac{1}{2}$ tsp.	
Oregano, dried	$\frac{1}{4}$ tsp.	$1\frac{1}{2}$ tsp.	
Flour, all purpose, sifted	$1\frac{1}{2}$ cups	9 cups	Combine well.
Baking powder	2 tsp.	$\frac{1}{4}$ cup	
Salt	$\frac{1}{2}$ tsp.	1 tbsp.	
Parsley, chopped	2 tbsp.	$\frac{3}{4}$ cup	
Rosemary	$\frac{1}{2}$ tsp.	1 tbsp.	
Oregano	$\frac{1}{2}$ tsp.	1 tbsp.	
Lard or shortening, very cold	3 tbsp.	1 cup + 2 tbsp.	Work in until mealy.
Onion, minced	1 tsp.	2 tbsp.	Add until mixture is thick. Form into dumplings and spoon onto the simmering goulash. Cover and continue to cook until veal is tender and dumplings are done, about 15 minutes.
Celery, minced	1 tsp.	2 tbsp.	
Milk	$\frac{3}{4}$ cup (or as needed)	$1\frac{1}{2}$ qt. (or as needed)	
Capers	2 tbsp.	$\frac{3}{4}$ cup	Combine and stir in carefully.
Scallions (whites only), chopped	1 tsp.	2 tbsp.	
Sour cream	2 cups	3 qt.	
Worcestershire sauce	$\frac{1}{2}$ tsp.	1 tbsp.	
Salt	to taste	to taste	
Black pepper	to taste	to taste	

SPECIAL HANDLING FOR BUFFETS: *Serve very warm from shallow insert pan(s) set over dual heating units. Keep covered. Offer with buttered noodles with poppy seeds or with gratin of brussels sprouts. Try adding caraway seeds to dumpling mixture.*

Charcoal Roasted Boneless Lamb

INGREDIENTS	TEST QUANTITY: 8	SERVICE QUANTITY: 50	METHOD
Olive oil	1 cup	$1\frac{1}{2}$ qt.	Combine in roasting pan(s).
Red wine	$\frac{1}{3}$ cup	2 cups	
Lemon juice, strained	3 tbsp.	1 cup + 2 tbsp.	
Onion, sliced	1	$1\frac{1}{2}$ lb.	
Celery, sliced	$\frac{1}{2}$ cup	3 cups	
Carrots, sliced	$\frac{1}{3}$ cup	2 cups	
Garlic, crushed	4 cloves	$1\frac{1}{2}$ heads	
Thyme, dried	$\frac{1}{2}$ tsp.	1 tbsp.	
Rosemary	1 tbsp.	$\frac{1}{3}$ cup	
Bay leaf	1	3	
Dry mustard	1 tbsp.	$\frac{1}{3}$ cup	
Salt	1 tsp.	2 tbsp.	
Pepper	1 tsp.	2 tbsp.	
Lamb leg, boneless, butterflied	3 lb.	18 lb.	Insert metal skewers from one side to the other in 4-in. intervals. Place lamb in marinade. Marinate for 6 hours, turning often. Remove from marinade and wipe dry. Place lamb on broiler. Brush with marinade. Broil until cooked to desired doneness.

SPECIAL HANDLING FOR BUFFETS: *Serve very warm from shallow insert pan(s) set over dual heating units. Keep covered. Serve with grilled onion halves filled with a purée of spinach or with sautéed julienne of potato, seasoned with rosemary and olive oil.*

Chinese Spareribs

INGREDIENTS	TEST QUANTITY: 8	SERVICE QUANTITY: 50	METHOD
Soy sauce, mild	$\frac{1}{2}$ cup	3 cups	Combine well. Place in deep hotel pan(s).
Bean paste (commercial), sweet	2 tsp.	$\frac{1}{4}$ cup	
Hoisin sauce (commercial)	$\frac{1}{2}$ cup	3 cups	
Sherry, dry	1 oz.	$\frac{3}{4}$ cup	
Brown sugar, light	1 tsp.	2 tbsp.	
Tomato sauce	1 tbsp.	$\frac{1}{3}$ cup	
Orange juice	1 tbsp.	$\frac{1}{3}$ cup	
Beer	$\frac{1}{4}$ cup	$1\frac{1}{2}$ cups	
Honey	1 tsp.	2 tbsp.	
Ginger, grated	1 tsp.	2 tbsp.	
Garlic, minced	1 tsp.	2 tbsp.	
Mustard, dry	1 tsp.	2 tbsp.	
Black pepper, ground	to taste	to taste	
Anise pepper, ground	to taste	to taste	
Spareribs	4 lb.	24 lb.	Trim neatly; separate from rack(s) if desired. Place in marinade and turn regularly for several hours. Place on racks over pan(s) of water and roast at 375°F for 45 minutes. Finish under broiler to desired doneness. Separate now if not before; place in service piece(s).

SPECIAL HANDLING FOR BUFFETS: *Serve very warm from shallow insert pan(s) set over dual heating units. Keep covered. Offer with hot mustard sauce or prepared plum sauce.*

Curried Leg of Lamb

INGREDIENTS	TEST QUANTITY: 8	SERVICE QUANTITY: 50	METHOD
Butter, melted	$\frac{1}{2}$ cup	$1\frac{1}{2}$ lb.	Sauté in nonaluminum pot(s) until onions and apples are tender.
Onions, chopped	$\frac{1}{2}$ lb.	3 lb.	
Apples, cooking, cored, chopped	$\frac{1}{2}$ lb.	3 lb.	
Ham, diced	$\frac{1}{4}$ lb.	$1\frac{1}{2}$ lb.	
Curry powder	$1\frac{1}{2}$ tbsp.	$\frac{1}{2}$ cup + 1 tbsp.	Add; cook and stir 5 minutes. Reserve.
Garam masala (see Recipe Index)	$1\frac{1}{2}$ tbsp.	$\frac{1}{2}$ cup + 1 tbsp.	
Mustard, dry	$\frac{1}{2}$ tsp.	1 tbsp.	
Olive oil, hot	$\frac{1}{2}$ cup	3 cups	Sauté until lightly browned. Add to mixture.
Leg of lamb, boneless, small chunks	$2\frac{1}{2}$ lb.	15 lb.	
Tomatoes, chopped	1 × #2 can	6 × #2 cans	Add; mix well.
Raisins, golden	1 cup	2 lb.	
Banana, firm, sliced	1 cup	2 lb.	
Red pepper flakes	$\frac{1}{2}$ tsp.	1 tbsp.	
Water	if needed	if needed	Add, if needed, to cover by 1 in. Partly cover pot and simmer slowly until lamb is tender, approximately 2 hours.
Lemon juice	to taste	to taste	Add; adjust seasonings.
Salt	to taste	to taste	
Pepper	to taste	to taste	

SPECIAL HANDLING FOR BUFFETS: *Serve very warm from shallow insert pan(s) set over dual heating units. Keep covered. Accompany with steamed rice and assorted chopped condiments, including peanuts, scallions, chutney, and toasted coconut.*

Flank Steak with Onions and Pineapple

INGREDIENTS	TEST QUANTITY: 8	SERVICE QUANTITY: 50	METHOD
Flank steak, julienned 1 × $\frac{1}{8}$ × $\frac{1}{8}$ in.	3 lb.	18 lb.	Place in bowl(s).
Soy sauce, mild	2 tbsp.	$\frac{3}{4}$ cup	Combine until dissolved; pour over meat. Chill and marinate at least 1 hour. Drain and reserve meat.
Beer	$\frac{1}{2}$ cup	3 cups	
Sugar	1 tsp.	$1\frac{1}{2}$ tbsp.	
Plum jam	$\frac{1}{2}$ cup	3 cups	
Cornstarch	2 tbsp.	$\frac{3}{4}$ cup	
Peanut oil	2 tbsp.	$\frac{3}{4}$ cup	
Peanut oil	$\frac{1}{3}$ cup	2 cups	Add to hot pan(s) or wok; heat on high for 30 seconds.
Onions, julienned	3 cups	6 lb.	Add; stir-fry quickly until onions are translucent.
Carrots, julienned	1 cup	$1\frac{1}{2}$ qt.	
Salt	$\frac{1}{2}$ tsp.	1 tbsp.	Add, stir, and transfer mixture to bowl(s). Wipe out pan(s) or wok and reheat to high heat.
Brown sugar	1 tsp.	2 tbsp.	
Peanut oil	$\frac{3}{4}$ cup	1 qt.	Add to hot pan(s); heat until hot.
Garlic, peeled, crushed	4 cloves	1 head	Add; press into oil. Add drained marinated meat. Toss and stir for 30 seconds. Add reserved vegetables; toss to blend. (This can/should be done in batches.)
Ginger, grated	1 tsp.	2 tbsp.	
Soy sauce	$\frac{1}{3}$ cup	2 cups	Combine in advance to dissolve; add to pan(s) or wok. Stir until sauce is smooth and thickened.
Sherry, dry	$\frac{1}{4}$ cup	$1\frac{1}{2}$ cups	
Brown sugar, light	3 tbsp.	1 cup + 2 tbsp.	
Pineapple, canned, diced, drained	2 cups	3 qt.	
Cornstarch	$\frac{1}{4}$ cup	$1\frac{1}{2}$ cups	
White wine	$\frac{2}{3}$ cup	1 qt.	
Water	$\frac{2}{3}$ cup	1 qt.	
Sesame oil, Oriental	3 tbsp.	1 cup + 2 tbsp.	

SPECIAL HANDLING FOR BUFFETS: *Serve very warm from shallow insert pan(s) set over dual heating units. Keep covered. Add diced water chestnuts and bamboo shoots with drained pineapple.*

Garam Masala (Indian spice mixture)

INGREDIENTS	TEST QUANTITY: 8	SERVICE QUANTITY: 50	METHOD
Cardamom seeds	$\frac{1}{2}$ cup		Combine all ingredients in spice grinder or mortar and pestle; process to a fine powder.
Cinnamon sticks	4 × 4 in.		
Cloves, whole	$2\frac{1}{2}$ tbsp.	Repeat procedure	—Note: Spice assortment can be varied as desired.
Black peppercorns, whole	$2\frac{1}{2}$ tbsp.		
Nutmeg, ground	$1\frac{1}{2}$ tbsp.		

SPECIAL HANDLING FOR BUFFETS: *Make up spice mixture   regularly. Keep tightly covered in cool area.*

Grilled Lamb Kebabs

INGREDIENTS	TEST QUANTITY: 8	SERVICE QUANTITY: 50	METHOD
Leg of lamb, boneless, 1-in. cubes	$2\frac{1}{2}$ lb.	15 lb.	Combine to coat well. Marinate for at least 6 hours. Place cubes on skewers. Grill over/under high heat until done. Place skewers on service piece(s).
Cumin powder	1 tsp.	2 tbsp.	
Garlic, crushed	1 tsp.	2 tbsp.	
Salt	1 tsp.	2 tbsp.	
Black pepper	$\frac{1}{2}$ tsp.	1 tbsp.	
Mustard, dry	$\frac{1}{2}$ tsp.	1 tbsp.	
Turmeric, ground	$\frac{1}{2}$ tsp.	1 tbsp.	
Yogurt, plain	$\frac{1}{3}$ cup	2 cups	
Scallions (greens and whites), minced	$\frac{1}{4}$ cup	$1\frac{1}{2}$ cups	
Cilantro (or parsley), chopped	2 tbsp.	$\frac{3}{4}$ cup	
Bay leaf	1	3	
Ginger root, grated	1 tbsp.	$\frac{1}{3}$ cup	
Cucumber, grated	2 tbsp.	$\frac{3}{4}$ cup	

SPECIAL HANDLING FOR BUFFETS: *Serve very warm from shallow insert pan(s) set over dual heating units. Keep covered. Offer with timbales of rice flavored with turmeric or saffron.*

Hungarian Goulash

INGREDIENTS	TEST QUANTITY: 8	SERVICE QUANTITY: 50	METHOD
Olive oil, hot	$\frac{1}{4}$ cup	$1\frac{1}{2}$ cups	Sauté until tender.
Onions, sliced	2 lb.	12 lb.	
Celery, sliced	1 cup	$1\frac{1}{2}$ lb.	
Beef, lean, 1-in. cubes	3 lb.	18 lb.	Add; sauté until nicely browned.
Flour, all purpose	$\frac{1}{4}$ cup	$1\frac{1}{2}$ cups	Add; stir to combine.
Beef stock	2 cups	3 qt.	Add to cover.
Red wine	1 cup	$1\frac{1}{2}$ qt.	
Water	as needed	as needed	
Salt	1 tbsp.	$\frac{1}{3}$ cup	Add; cover and bring to a simmer.
Black pepper	$\frac{1}{2}$ tsp.	1 tbsp.	
Bay leaf	1	3	
Hungarian paprika	2 tbsp.	$\frac{3}{4}$ cup	Add; simmer until tender. Remove bay leaf.

SPECIAL HANDLING FOR BUFFETS: *Serve very warm from shallow insert pan(s) set over dual heating units. Keep covered. Flavor with sliced cucumbers, a julienne of lemon zest, or a scant amount of tomato purée. Serve with fried potato cakes, gnocchi, spaetzle, or dumplings.*

Jamaican Spiced Pork Roast

INGREDIENTS	TEST QUANTITY: 8	SERVICE QUANTITY: 50	METHOD
Pork loin, center cut	3 lb.	18 lb.	Score diagonally on top; rub with olive oil. Place in roasting pan(s). Roast at 350°F until golden. Skim off fat. Reserve meat and pan drippings.
Olive oil	$\frac{1}{2}$ cup	3 cups	
Brown sugar, light	$\frac{1}{2}$ cup	3 cups	Blend to a smooth paste. Rub on top surface of pork roast. Put roast(s) back in pan(s).
Dark rum	1 tbsp.	3 oz.	
Sherry, dry	$\frac{1}{4}$ cup	$1\frac{1}{2}$ cups	
Garlic, minced	1 tsp.	2 tbsp.	
Ginger, minced	1 tsp.	2 tbsp.	
Horseradish, grated	$\frac{1}{2}$ tsp.	1 tbsp.	
Cloves, ground	$\frac{1}{4}$ tsp.	$1\frac{1}{2}$ tsp.	
Bay leaf, crushed	1	4	
Salt	$\frac{1}{2}$ tsp.	1 tbsp.	
Pepper	$\frac{1}{4}$ tsp.	$1\frac{1}{2}$ tsp.	
Red pepper, crushed	$\frac{1}{4}$ tsp.	$1\frac{1}{2}$ tsp.	
Chicken stock	1 cup	$1\frac{1}{2}$ qt.	Pour into roasting pan(s) and roast pork until done. Remove roast(s) and reserve. Bring pan juices to simmer.
Light rum, heated	1 oz.	$\frac{3}{4}$ cup	Add, flame, and swirl to extinguish.
Lime juice, fresh, strained	$1\frac{1}{2}$ tbsp.	$\frac{1}{2}$ cup + 1 tbsp.	When flames die out, add. Reserve.
Cornstarch	1 tsp.	2 tbsp.	Dissolve and add to simmering pan sauce. Stir constantly as sauce thickens. Add reserved lime juice and rum. Pour sauce around sliced pork roast.
Sherry, dry	$\frac{1}{2}$ tbsp.	3 tbsp.	

SPECIAL HANDLING FOR BUFFETS: *Serve very warm from shallow insert pan(s) set over dual heating units. Keep covered. Offer with slices of oven-roasted potatoes and fried bananas or plantains.*

Kentucky Spareribs with Whiskey

INGREDIENTS	TEST QUANTITY: 8	SERVICE QUANTITY: 50	METHOD
Soy sauce, mild	$\frac{1}{2}$ cup	3 cups	Combine.
Molasses	$\frac{1}{4}$ cup	$1\frac{1}{2}$ cups	
Mustard, Dijon type	$\frac{1}{3}$ cup	2 cups	
Bourbon whiskey	$\frac{3}{4}$ cup	$4\frac{1}{2}$ cups	
Orange juice, strained	$\frac{1}{2}$ cup	3 cups	
Onion, minced	1 cup	2 lb.	
Celery, minced	1 cup	2 lb.	
Garlic, crushed	2 cloves	12 cloves	
Lemon peel, grated	$\frac{1}{2}$ tsp.	1 tbsp.	
Worcestershire sauce	1 tsp.	2 tbsp.	
Tabasco	$\frac{1}{2}$ tsp.	1 tbsp.	
Spareribs, trimmed	4 lb.	24 lb.	Add to marinade. Cover. Chill overnight. Drain. Grill over/under high heat to desired doneness. Slice individual ribs.

SPECIAL HANDLING FOR BUFFETS: *Serve very warm from shallow insert pan(s) set over dual heating units. Keep covered. Offer this as part of an All America buffet or as a celebration of "spirited" cooking. Serve with sautéed baby vegetables and Louisiana dirty rice.*

Lamb Chops in Orange Sauce

INGREDIENTS	TEST QUANTITY: 8	SERVICE QUANTITY: 50	METHOD
Peanut oil, hot	3 tbsp.	1 cup + 2 tbsp.	Sauté seasoned chops until browned. Transfer to roasting pan(s). Discard any fat.
Lamb chops, 1 in. thick	8	50	
Salt	1 tsp.	2 tbsp.	
Black pepper	$\frac{1}{2}$ tsp.	1 tbsp.	
White wine	$\frac{1}{4}$ cup	$1\frac{1}{2}$ cups	Deglaze and scrape pan. Bring to a boil and remove from heat.
Red wine vinegar	2 tbsp.	$\frac{3}{4}$ cup	
Orange juice, fresh, strained	1 cup	$1\frac{1}{2}$ qt.	Stir into vinegar; combine well. Pour over lamb chops. Bake at 325°F until chops are fork tender. Place on service piece(s).
Brown sugar, light	$\frac{1}{2}$ cup	3 cups	
Lemon rind, grated	1 tsp.	2 tbsp.	
Lemon juice, fresh, strained	1 tbsp.	$\frac{1}{3}$ cup	
Rum	1 tbsp.	$\frac{1}{3}$ cup	
Ginger, ground	$\frac{1}{2}$ tsp.	1 tbsp.	
Nutmeg, ground	$\frac{1}{4}$ tsp.	$1\frac{1}{2}$ tsp.	
Mandarin orange segments	as needed	as needed	Garnish and serve.

SPECIAL HANDLING FOR BUFFETS: *Serve very warm from shallow insert pan(s) set over dual heating units. Keep covered. Offer with corn fritters and steamed green vegetables; macerate mandarin orange slices in orange brandy before adding.*

Lamb Grilled with Onions

INGREDIENTS	TEST QUANTITY: 8	SERVICE QUANTITY: 50	METHOD
Lamb leg, boneless, trimmed well	$2\frac{1}{2}$ lb.	15 lb.	Butterfly until uniformly thick. Insert skewers crosswise so lamb will keep its shape.
Yellow onions, small, peeled	8	50	Prick with fork and place in baking pan with lamb.
Peanut oil	1 cup	$1\frac{1}{2}$ qt.	Combine well; pour over lamb and onions so everything is covered. Refrigerate for 12 hours. To prepare, grill onions and lamb separately until onions are soft and lamb is cooked as desired. Slice lamb on the bias.
Red wine	2 cups	3 qt.	
Shallots, chopped	$\frac{1}{4}$ cup	$1\frac{1}{2}$ cups	
Garlic, crushed	6 cloves	2 heads	
Black pepper, coarse	2 tsp.	$\frac{1}{4}$ cup	
Mustard, Dijon type	1 tsp.	2 tbsp.	
Salt	2 tsp.	$\frac{1}{4}$ cup	
Lemon juice	of 1	$1\frac{1}{2}$ cups	
Rosemary, dried	1 tsp.	2 tbsp.	
Basil, dried	$\frac{1}{2}$ tsp.	1 tbsp.	

SPECIAL HANDLING FOR BUFFETS: *Serve very warm from shallow insert pan(s) set over dual heating units. Keep covered. Season marinade mixture with rosemary or with juniper berries and gin. Offer with oven-roasted potatoes and sautéed squash.*

Lamb Meatballs Madeira

INGREDIENTS	TEST QUANTITY: 8	SERVICE QUANTITY: 50	METHOD
Ground lamb	2 lb.	12 lb.	Combine and shape into small balls.
Eggs, beaten	2	12	
Almonds, chopped	$\frac{1}{4}$ cup	$1\frac{1}{2}$ cups	
Parsley, chopped	$\frac{1}{2}$ cup	3 cups	
Bread crumbs	$\frac{2}{3}$ cup	4 cups	
Salt	1 tsp.	2 tbsp.	
Black pepper	$\frac{1}{2}$ tsp.	1 tbsp.	
Rosemary	1 tsp.	2 tbsp.	
Garlic, minced	$\frac{1}{2}$ tsp.	1 tbsp.	
Chives, chopped	$\frac{1}{4}$ cup	$1\frac{1}{2}$ cups	
Scallions (greens and whites), chopped	$\frac{1}{4}$ cup	$1\frac{1}{2}$ cups	
Olive oil, hot	$\frac{1}{4}$ cup	$1\frac{1}{2}$ cups	Sauté meatballs until browned. Drain fat.
Madeira	1 cup	$1\frac{1}{2}$ qts.	Add; combine well. Cover and simmer for 20
Chicken stock	1 cup	$1\frac{1}{2}$ qts.	minutes; stir. Pour into service piece(s).
Paprika	2 tsp.	$\frac{1}{4}$ cup	
Lemon slices	as needed	as needed	Garnish.

SPECIAL HANDLING FOR BUFFETS: *Serve very warm from shallow insert pan(s) set over dual heating units. Keep covered. Offer with buttered noodles or rice pilaf flavored with slivered toasted almonds.*

Maple Glazed Pork

INGREDIENTS	TEST QUANTITY: 8	SERVICE QUANTITY: 50	METHOD
Pork shoulder, boneless	3 lb.	18 lb.	Cut into 6 × 3 × 2-in. strips; place in shallow pan(s).
Sherry, dry	2 cups	3 qt.	Add to pork; mix well. Cover securely. Place on rack in larger pan(s) over water; cover. Set over moderate heat, and simmer $2\frac{1}{2}$ hours. Transfer pork to cutting board; cut into cubes. Discard cinnamon, anise, and tangerine peel. Reduce liquid by half over high heat. Add pork cubes. Stir to coat.
Maple syrup	1 cup	$1\frac{1}{2}$ qt.	
Scallions (greens and whites), chopped	3	2 cups	
Orange juice	$\frac{1}{2}$ cup	3 cups	
Cinnamon sticks	4	10	
Nutmeg	$\frac{1}{4}$ tsp.	$1\frac{1}{2}$ tsp.	
Star anise peppers	6	1 tbsp.	
Tangerine peel, dried (commercial)	2 strips	12	
Ginger, ground	$1\frac{1}{2}$ tsp.	3 tbsp.	
Black pepper, ground	$\frac{1}{2}$ tsp.	1 tbsp.	

SPECIAL HANDLING FOR BUFFETS: *Serve very warm from shallow insert pan(s) set over dual heating units. Keep covered. Toss in some diced crystallized ginger or add some chopped thick-cut sautéed bacon before cooking.*

Marinated Lamb Kebabs

INGREDIENTS	TEST QUANTITY: 8	SERVICE QUANTITY: 50	METHOD
Red wine vinegar	1 tbsp.	$\frac{1}{3}$ cup	Combine and blend until garlic is well combined.
Thyme	1 tsp.	2 tbsp.	
Rosemary	1 tsp.	2 tbsp.	
Oregano	$\frac{1}{2}$ tsp.	1 tbsp.	
Bay leaf	2	6	
Black pepper, ground	$\frac{1}{2}$ tsp.	1 tbsp.	
Garlic, minced	2 tsp.	$\frac{1}{4}$ cup	
Mustard, Dijon type	1 tsp.	2 tbsp.	
Parsley, chopped	$\frac{1}{4}$ cup	$1\frac{1}{2}$ cups	Add.
Scallions (greens and whites), chopped	1 tbsp.	$\frac{1}{3}$ cup	
Olive oil	$\frac{2}{3}$ cup	1 qt.	Add slowly, whipping constantly.
Leg of lamb, boneless, 1-inch cubes	3 lb.	18 lb.	Alternate on skewers into desired portions. Place in hotel pan(s) and pour in marinade; marinate at room temperature for several hours; turn regularly. Remove from marinade.
Red peppers, cut in wedges	$\frac{1}{2}$ lb.	3 lb.	
Onions, peeled, cut in wedges	1 lb.	6 lb.	
Salt	to taste	to taste	Season to taste and broil over/under high heat, turning often, to desired doneness.
Black pepper	to taste	to taste	

SPECIAL HANDLING FOR BUFFETS: *Serve very warm from shallow insert pan(s) set over dual heating units. Keep covered. See comments for Indonesian Lamb Saté.*

Olde English Corned Beef, The Plaza

INGREDIENTS	TEST QUANTITY: 8	SERVICE QUANTITY: 50	METHOD
Corned beef Water, cold	3 lb. to cover	18 lb. to cover	Place over high heat. Bring to rapid boil and cook for 5 minutes, skimming well. Lower heat; cover and simmer until meat is tender. Let meat cool in liquid, then drain. Trim away as much fat as possible. Place meat on rack(s) in roasting pan(s).
Whole cloves	1 tbsp. (or less, to taste)	$\frac{1}{3}$ cup	Stud meat on all surfaces. Roast at 350°F for 15 minutes.
Horseradish Chili sauce Mustard, dry Cider vinegar Butter Brown sugar, light	1 tsp. $\frac{1}{4}$ cup 1 tsp. $\frac{1}{4}$ cup 2 tbsp. $\frac{1}{3}$ cup	2 tbsp. $1\frac{1}{2}$ cups 2 tbsp. $1\frac{1}{2}$ cups $\frac{3}{4}$ cup 2 cups	Combine and simmer for 5 minutes. Brush over meat and continue to roast until well glazed. Let rest 20 minutes before carving.

SPECIAL HANDLING FOR BUFFETS: *Serve very warm from shallow insert pan(s) set over dual heating units. Keep covered. Offer with mustard sauce or piquant horseradish.*

The Plaza is the renowned hotel that stands on the southern edge of New York City's Central Park.

Osso Buco alla Milanese (braised veal shanks)

INGREDIENTS	TEST QUANTITY: 8	SERVICE QUANTITY: 50	METHOD
Veal shank sliced crosswise, 1 to 2 in.	8	50	Season and dredge shank slices.
Flour, all purpose	$\frac{1}{4}$ cup	$1\frac{1}{2}$ cups	
Salt	1 tsp.	2 tbsp.	
Black pepper	$\frac{1}{4}$ tsp.	$1\frac{1}{2}$ tsp.	
Olive oil, hot	$\frac{1}{2}$ cup	3 cups	Sauté until veal is golden and onions are soft.
Onions, minced	1 cup	$1\frac{1}{2}$ qt.	
White wine, dry	$\frac{1}{2}$ cup	3 cups	Add. Deglaze. Reduce until almost dry.
Beef stock, strong	1 cup	$1\frac{1}{2}$ qt.	Add. Cover. Simmer gently until veal is very tender. Remove bay leaf. Ladle juices over veal during cooking. Place in service piece(s).
Tomatoes, chopped	2 cups	6 lb.	
Lemon juice, strained	1 tbsp.	$\frac{1}{3}$ cup	
Bay leaf	1	3	
Parsley, chopped	$\frac{1}{2}$ cup	3 cups	Combine and divide among veal slices.
Lemon rind, grated	1 tbsp.	of 4	

SPECIAL HANDLING FOR BUFFETS: *Serve very warm from shallow insert pan(s) set over dual heating units. Keep covered. Offer with risotto, rice, or buttered noodles and steamed green vegetables.*

Pepper Beef

INGREDIENTS	TEST QUANTITY: 8	SERVICE QUANTITY: 50	METHOD
Soy sauce, mild	$1\frac{1}{2}$ tbsp.	$\frac{1}{2}$ cup	Combine until dissolved.
Cornstarch	2 tbsp.	$\frac{3}{4}$ cup	
Sherry, dry	1 tbsp.	$\frac{1}{3}$ cup	
Water	3 tbsp.	1 cup	
Black pepper	$\frac{1}{2}$ tsp.	1 tbsp.	
Peanut oil	2 tbsp.	$\frac{3}{4}$ cup	
Sesame oil, oriental	1 tsp.	2 tbsp.	
Flank steak, sliced $1 \times \frac{1}{4} \times \frac{1}{4}$ in.	3 lb.	18 lb.	Mix in until well coated; chill for at least 1 hour.
Garlic, minced	1 tsp.	2 tbsp.	
Peanut oil	1 qt.	as needed	Add to heated pan(s) or wok(s); heat to 350°F. Stir in reserved beef. Drain immediately. Reserve meat.
Peanut oil	$\frac{1}{2}$ cup	3 cups	Heat over low burner.
Red pepper, crushed	$\frac{1}{2}$ tsp.	1 tbsp.	Add; stir (strain if desired) until dark. Remove pepper if desired. Increase heat to medium.
Ginger, peeled, shredded	$\frac{1}{2}$ tbsp.	3 tbsp.	Add; stir. Increase heat to high.
Scallions (greens only), chopped	$\frac{1}{4}$ cup	$1\frac{1}{2}$ cups	Add; toss for 2 minutes. Add reserved beef; stir quickly.
Celery, $1\frac{1}{2}$-in. julienned	1 qt.	6 lb.	
Bamboo shoots, $1\frac{1}{2}$-in. julienned	2 cups	3 qt.	
Water chestnuts, chopped	$\frac{1}{2}$ cup	3 cups	
Soy sauce	$\frac{1}{2}$ cup	3 cups	Combine in advance; stir in to just coat.
Sherry, dry	$\frac{1}{4}$ cup	$1\frac{1}{2}$ cups	
Red wine vinegar	3 tbsp.	1 cup + 2 tbsp.	
Sugar	3 tbsp.	1 cup + 2 tbsp.	
Cornstarch	$1\frac{1}{2}$ tbsp.	$\frac{1}{2}$ cup + 1 tbsp.	
Water	3 tbsp.	1 cup + 2 tbsp.	
Sesame oil, Oriental	3 tbsp.	1 cup + 2 tbsp.	
Szechuan peppercorns, pan roasted until smoky, ground	2 tsp.	$\frac{1}{4}$ cup	Add; stir in quickly. Pour into service piece(s).

SPECIAL HANDLING FOR BUFFETS: *Serve very warm from shallow insert pan(s) set over dual heating units. Keep covered. Substitute sliced pork shoulder. Serve with steamed rice.*

Polish-Style Meatballs

INGREDIENTS	TEST QUANTITY: 8	SERVICE QUANTITY: 50	METHOD
Butter, melted	½ cup	3 cups	Sauté until soft. Place in large bowl(s).
Onion, minced	1 cup	3 lb.	
Celery, minced	½ cup	3 cups	
Ground beef	2 lb.	12 lb.	Add to bowl(s).
Parsley, chopped	½ cup	3 cups	
Egg yolks, beaten	2	1 dozen	
Bread slices, stale	4	1½ lb.	Soak well. Crumble and add to mixture.
Milk	⅔ cup	1 qt.	
Egg whites, beaten stiff	2	1 dozen	Add to mixture. Form into small meatballs.
Dill, fresh	1 tbsp.	⅓ cup	
Tarragon	½ tsp.	1 tbsp.	
Thyme	½ tsp.	1 tbsp.	
Red pepper, crushed	½ tsp.	1 tbsp.	
Salt	to taste	to taste	
Black pepper	to taste	to taste	
Flour, all purpose	as needed	as needed	Dredge meatballs. Shake off excess.
Olive oil, hot	½ cup	3 cups	Sauté meatballs until golden.
Cognac, warmed	1 oz.	¾ cup	Add. Deglaze. Flame.
Red wine	1 oz.	¾ cup	
Butter, melted	¼ cup	1½ cups	Sauté until golden. Add to meatballs.
Onions, chopped	1 cup	1½ qt.	
Garlic	1 tsp.	2 tbsp.	
Beef stock	½ cup	3 cups	Add. Stir in well. Simmer for 30 minutes.
Sour cream	1½ cups	2 qt. + 1 cup	
Chives, snipped	½ cup	3 cups	
Mushrooms, sliced	½ lb.	3 lb.	
Salt	to taste	to taste	
Black pepper	to taste	to taste	

SPECIAL HANDLING FOR BUFFETS: *Serve very warm from shallow insert pan(s) set over dual heating units. Keep covered. Offer with dumplings, buttered noodles, or Duchesse potatoes seasoned with almonds.*

Pork Almond Ding

INGREDIENTS	TEST QUANTITY: 8	SERVICE QUANTITY: 50	METHOD
Peanut oil	$\frac{1}{2}$ cup	3 cups	Add to heated pan(s) or wok; stir 30 seconds.
Onion, minced	$\frac{1}{4}$ cup	$1\frac{1}{2}$ cups	Add; stir for 30 seconds. Strain oil; return to pan(s).
Garlic, peeled, crushed	4 cloves	3 tbsp.	
Ginger, peeled, minced	$\frac{1}{2}$ tbsp.	3 tbsp.	
Celery, bias sliced	2 cups	3 lb.	Add to oil; stir briskly.
Bamboo shoots, canned, diced	1 lb.	6 lb.	
Carrots, julienned	1 cup	2 lb.	
Salt	1 tsp.	2 tbsp.	
Black pepper	$\frac{1}{2}$ tsp.	1 tbsp.	
Pork, cooked, $\frac{1}{4}$-in. diced	3 lb.	18 lb.	Add; stir briskly. This can/should be done in batches.
Sherry, dry	$\frac{1}{4}$ cup	$1\frac{1}{2}$ cups	
White wine	2 tbsp.	$\frac{3}{4}$ cup	
Water	1 cup	$1\frac{1}{2}$ qt.	Add; stir. Cover; cook 5 minutes.
Salt	$\frac{1}{2}$ tsp.	1 tbsp.	Combine until cornstarch is dissolved; add, stir quickly to coat. Pour into service piece(s).
Brown sugar, light	2 tsp.	$\frac{1}{4}$ cup	
Soy sauce, mild	$\frac{1}{4}$ cup	$1\frac{1}{2}$ cups	
Hoisin sauce (commercial)	3 tbsp.	1 cup + 2 tbsp.	
Cornstarch	$2\frac{1}{2}$ tbsp.	1 cup	
Water	$\frac{1}{2}$ cup	3 cups	
Sesame oil, Oriental	$1\frac{1}{2}$ tbsp.	$\frac{1}{2}$ cup + 1 tbsp.	

SPECIAL HANDLING FOR BUFFETS: *Serve very warm from shallow insert pan(s) set over dual heating units. Keep covered. Stir in a good amount of chopped almonds before serving with steamed rice and stir-fried vegetables.*

Pork and Apple Pie

INGREDIENTS	TEST QUANTITY: 8	SERVICE QUANTITY: 50	METHOD
Pork, ground	2 lb.	12 lb.	Mix together and spoon about one-third into buttered pan(s).
Celery salt	$\frac{1}{2}$ tsp.	1 tbsp.	
Garlic powder	$\frac{1}{2}$ tsp.	1 tbsp.	
Onions, minced	1 cup	$1\frac{1}{2}$ qt.	Combine well. Spoon small amount over pork.
Celery, minced	$\frac{1}{2}$ cup	3 cups	
Sage, crushed	$\frac{1}{2}$ tsp.	1 tbsp.	
Worcestershire sauce	1 tsp.	2 tbsp.	
Salt	$\frac{1}{2}$ tsp.	1 tbsp.	
Thyme, dried	$\frac{1}{4}$ tsp.	$1\frac{1}{2}$ tsp.	
Black pepper	to taste	to taste	
Cooking apples, peeled, cored, sliced $\frac{1}{4}$ in.	2	3 lb.	Toss in lemon juice. Place half of these on top. Then repeat layers of pork, onions, apples, and, finally, pork.
Lemon juice	1 tbsp.	$\frac{1}{3}$ cup	
White wine, dry	$\frac{1}{4}$ cup	$1\frac{1}{2}$ cups	Pour in. Bring to a boil. Then place in 325°F oven until a knife can pierce easily, about $1\frac{1}{2}$ hours.
Boiling potatoes, cooked, dried, mashed	1 lb.	6 lb.	Mash well, using enough milk to make a stiff purée.
Butter	2 tbsp.	$\frac{3}{4}$ cup	
Milk	as needed	as needed	
Mustard, dry	$\frac{1}{4}$ tsp.	$1\frac{1}{2}$ tsp.	
Salt	to taste	to taste	Adjust seasoning. When pork is done, spread potatoes on top.
Black pepper	to taste	to taste	
Butter, melted	1 tbsp.	$\frac{1}{3}$ cup	Brush on top. Bake in top part of 350°F oven until the potatoes start to brown, about 10 minutes. Then finish under the broiler until desired color is reached.

SPECIAL HANDLING FOR BUFFETS: *Serve very warm from shallow insert pan(s) set over dual heating units. Keep covered. Offer with cranberry or Cumberland sauce with steamed brussels sprouts.*

Pork Chops in Mustard Cream

INGREDIENTS	TEST QUANTITY: 8	SERVICE QUANTITY: 50	METHOD
Pork loin chops, 1 in. thick	8	50	Season pork chops. Sauté until golden brown. Transfer to shallow roasting pan(s). Pour off most fat.
Salt	to taste	to taste	
Black pepper	to taste	to taste	
Flour, all purpose	as needed	as needed	
Butter, melted	2 tbsp.	$\frac{3}{4}$ cup	
Olive oil, hot	3 tbsp.	1 cup	
Onions, sliced	1$\frac{1}{2}$ cups	3 lb.	Add to pan. Sauté until lightly browned.
Garlic, minced	1 tsp.	2 tbsp.	
Shallots, minced	1 tsp.	2 tbsp.	
White wine vinegar	3 tbsp.	1 cup + 2 tbsp.	Add; deglaze; scrape well. Reduce. Spoon over pork chops.
Sherry, dry	1 tsp.	2 tbsp.	
Bouquet garni:			Wrap in cheesecloth and mix in. Bring to a simmer, cover tightly, transfer to 325°F oven. Bake for 10 minutes, baste with juices; repeat. Turn chops over, bake until chops test done, about 10 minutes. Transfer chops to warming oven. Skim fat.
Parsley	2 sprigs	1 bunch	
Bay leaf	1	6	
Thyme	$\frac{1}{2}$ tsp.	1 tbsp.	
Marjoram	$\frac{1}{2}$ tsp.	1 tbsp.	
Cream	1 cup	1$\frac{1}{2}$ qt.	Add; simmer to reduce a bit. Remove from heat.
White wine	$\frac{1}{4}$ cup	1$\frac{1}{2}$ cups	
Mustard, Dijon type	1 tbsp.	$\frac{1}{3}$ cup	Add; adjust flavor. Place chops on service piece. Strain the sauce on and around.
Lemon juice	to taste	to taste	
Salt	to taste	to taste	
White pepper	to taste	to taste	

SPECIAL HANDLING FOR BUFFETS: *Serve very warm from shallow insert pan(s) set over dual heating units. Keep covered. Offer with baby carrots steamed with mint or green beans laced with marjoram.*

Pork Chops with Horseradish, à la Deutsch

INGREDIENTS	TEST QUANTITY: 8	SERVICE QUANTITY: 50	METHOD
Pork chops, loin	8	50	Season.
Salt	to taste	to taste	
Black pepper	to taste	to taste	
Cider vinegar	1 tbsp.	$\frac{1}{3}$ cup	Combine into a paste. Spread onto pork
Horseradish	$\frac{1}{2}$ cup	3 cups	chops. Chill for several hours.
Mustard, Dijon type	1 tsp.	2 tbsp.	
Butter, melted	$\frac{1}{4}$ cup	$1\frac{1}{2}$ cups	Sauté pork chops until golden on both sides.
Olive oil, hot	$\frac{1}{4}$ cup	$1\frac{1}{2}$ cups	Discard excess oil.
Beef stock	1 cup	$1\frac{1}{2}$ qt.	Add. Cover. Barely simmer until tender,
White wine	1 cup	$1\frac{1}{2}$ qt.	about 30 minutes. Strain sauce. Remove bay
Bay leaf	1	3	leaf.
Sour cream	$\frac{1}{4}$ cup	$1\frac{1}{2}$ cups	Combine and stir into sauce. Bring just to a
Egg yolk	1	6	simmer. Do not boil. Place chops in service piece(s). Pour sauce over.

SPECIAL HANDLING FOR BUFFETS: *Serve very warm from shallow insert pan(s) set over dual heating units. Keep covered. Offer with potato dumplings flavored with caraway and parsley.*

Savory Onion Entree Crêpes

INGREDIENTS	TEST QUANTITY: 8	SERVICE QUANTITY: 50	METHOD
Flour, all purpose	$1\frac{1}{4}$ cup	2 lb.	Sift together.
Salt	1 tsp.	2 tbsp.	
Black pepper	$\frac{1}{4}$ tsp.	$1\frac{1}{2}$ tsp.	
Onion, grated	2 tbsp.	$\frac{3}{4}$ cup	Combine; add; mix well.
Scallions (greens and whites), grated	1 tsp.	2 tbsp.	
Milk	$\frac{1}{2}$ cup	3 cups	
White wine	$\frac{1}{2}$ cup	3 cups	
Tabasco	$\frac{1}{8}$ tsp.	$\frac{3}{4}$ tsp.	
Eggs	2	12	Combine and add. Whip until mixture is smooth. Let rest for 1 hour. Make crêpes and reserve.
Egg yolks	2	12	
Butter, melted	1 tbsp.	$\frac{1}{3}$ cup	

SPECIAL HANDLING FOR BUFFETS: *Keep on hand for preparation of various entrees; these are especially good with cheese chicken and vegetable fillings.*

Scandinavian Lamb Shoulder

INGREDIENTS	TEST QUANTITY: 8	SERVICE QUANTITY: 50	METHOD
Butter, melted	¼ cup	1½ cups	Sauté to brown in large pot.
Lamb shoulder, boned, rolled	3 lb.	18 lb.	
Bay leaf	1	3	
Thyme	½ tsp.	1 tbsp.	
Rosemary	½ tsp.	1 tbsp.	
Red wine	½ cup	3 cups	Combine and add to pot. Cover and simmer until tender, about 3 hours. Remove lamb.
Lamb stock	1½ cups	2 qt.	
Flour, all purpose, sifted	¼ cup	1½ cups	
Red wine vinegar	¼ cup	1½ cups	Combine and add to pot. Put lamb back in pot. Cover and cook for 30 minutes more or as desired.
Dill, dry	1 tsp.	2 tbsp.	
Salt	1 tsp.	2 tbsp	
Black pepper	¼ tsp.	1½ tsp.	

SPECIAL HANDLING FOR BUFFETS: *Serve very warm from shallow insert pan(s) set over dual heating units. Keep covered. Garnish with fresh dill and serve with boiled new potatoes and steamed green beans.*

Scandinavian Pork Roast

INGREDIENTS	TEST QUANTITY: 8	SERVICE QUANTITY: 50	METHOD
Pork loin roast, boneless, butterflied	3 lb.	18 lb.	Season inside surface.
Onion, minced	$\frac{1}{2}$ cup	3 cups	
Ginger, ground	$\frac{1}{2}$ tsp.	1 tbsp.	
Cloves, ground	$\frac{1}{4}$ tsp.	$1\frac{1}{2}$ tsp.	
Mace, ground	$\frac{1}{8}$ tsp.	$\frac{3}{4}$ tsp.	
Mustard, dry	$\frac{1}{4}$ tsp.	$1\frac{1}{2}$ tsp.	
Salt	to taste	to taste	
Black pepper	to taste	to taste	
Prunes, pitted	12	2 lb.	Simmer for 20 minutes. Let rest for 30 minutes. Remove prunes and reserve liquid. Chop prunes and distribute over pork. Roll up from the long edge. Tie securely.
Orange rind, grated	1 tsp.	2 tbsp.	
Water	$1\frac{1}{2}$ cups	$2\frac{1}{4}$ qt.	
Orange brandy	1 oz.	$\frac{3}{4}$ cup	
Butter, clarified, hot	$\frac{1}{4}$ cup	$1\frac{1}{2}$ cups	In pan, brown roast on all sides.
Reserved cooking liquid	1 cup	$1\frac{1}{2}$ qt.	Add to pan. Bring to simmer. Pour into roasting pan. Roast at 350°F until meat tests done, about $1\frac{1}{2}$ hours. Remove roast. Keep warm and let rest 30 minutes. Skim off all fat.
Heavy cream	$\frac{1}{2}$ cup	3 cups	Combine. Add to pan juices. Simmer for 5 minutes, but do not boil.
Egg yolk	1	6	
Flour, all purpose	2 tbsp.	$\frac{3}{4}$ cup	
Cognac	1 oz.	$\frac{3}{4}$ cup	
Salt	to taste	to taste	Adjust seasoning.
Black pepper	to taste	to taste	

SPECIAL HANDLING FOR BUFFETS: *Serve very warm from shallow insert pan(s) set over dual heating units. Keep covered. Offer pan juices with $\frac{1}{2}$-in. slices of pork roast. Season cooking liquid with ground cardamom and proceed.*

Szechuan Flank Steak

INGREDIENTS	TEST QUANTITY: 8	SERVICE QUANTITY: 50	METHOD
Flank steak, sliced cross-grain, $\frac{1}{4}$-in. thick	3 lb.	18 lb.	Toss to mix well.
Red wine vinegar	2 tbsp.	$\frac{3}{4}$ cup	
Soy sauce	$\frac{1}{4}$ cup	$1\frac{1}{2}$ cups	
Cornstarch	1 tbsp.	$\frac{1}{3}$ cup	
Peanut oil	2 tbsp.	$\frac{3}{4}$ cup	
Sesame oil	1 tsp.	2 tbsp.	
Peanut oil, hot	1 cup	$1\frac{1}{2}$ qt.	Heat in wok or skillet. Add meat. Stir-fry for 2 minutes. Remove meat from oil. Reserve meat and reheat oil.
Asparagus, blanched, sliced	2 cups	6 lb.	Combine and add to hot oil. Stir-fry for 1 minute. Return reserved meat, and stir-fry an additional minute.
Broccoli flowerets, small	1 cup	6 cups	
Scallions (greens and whites), chopped	$\frac{1}{2}$ cup	3 cups	
Bok choy, bias sliced	1 cup	6 cups	
Ginger root, grated	1 tbsp.	$\frac{1}{3}$ cup	
Garlic, minced	2 tsp.	$\frac{1}{4}$ cup	
Red bell peppers, sliced	1 cup	2 lb.	
Soy sauce	2 tbsp.	$\frac{3}{4}$ cup	Combine well. Add to mixture. Simmer and toss until thickened.
Salt	to taste	to taste	
Sherry, dry	2 tbsp.	$\frac{3}{4}$ cup	
Rice wine vinegar	$\frac{1}{4}$ cup	$1\frac{1}{2}$ cups	
Honey	2 tbsp.	$\frac{3}{4}$ cup	
Cornstarch	3 tbsp.	1 cup + 2 tbsp.	
White wine	$\frac{1}{2}$ cup	3 cups	
Water	1 cup	$1\frac{1}{2}$ pt.	

SPECIAL HANDLING FOR BUFFETS: *Serve very warm from shallow insert pan(s) set over dual heating units. Keep covered. Season with Oriental sesame oil and serve with steamed rice and green vegetables. Garnish with chopped peanuts.*

Szechuan Pork with Peanuts

INGREDIENTS	TEST QUANTITY: 8	SERVICE QUANTITY: 50	METHOD
Cornstarch	2 tbsp.	$\frac{3}{4}$ cup	Combine until dissolved.
Soy sauce	2 tbsp.	$\frac{3}{4}$ cup	
Sherry, dry	1 tbsp.	$\frac{1}{3}$ cup	
Peanut oil	2 tbsp.	$\frac{3}{4}$ cup	
Sesame oil	1 tsp.	2 tbsp.	
Pork loin or butt, boneless, $\frac{1}{4}$-in. diced	3 lb.	18 lb.	Add to mixture; stir until well coated. Chill and marinate at least 30 minutes.
Water, boiling	2 qt.	3 gal.	Add pork; stir to separate cubes. Cook 1 minute after boil returns. Drain and reserve.
Peanut oil	$\frac{1}{4}$ cup	$1\frac{1}{2}$ cups	Add to heated pan(s) or wok. Heat for 30 seconds. Lower heat.
Chili peppers, dried	4	$\frac{1}{4}$ cup	Add; toss until darkened. Remove if desired.
Ginger root, peeled, minced	$\frac{1}{2}$ tbsp.	3 tbsp.	Add; stir-fry. Increase heat to high. Add pork; stir-fry rapidly.
Onion, minced	1 tbsp.	$\frac{1}{3}$ cup	
Celery, minced	1 tbsp.	$\frac{1}{3}$ cup	
Cornstarch	2 tsp.	$\frac{1}{4}$ cup	Combine until dissolved. Pour over pork; stir well. Pour into service piece(s).
Orange juice, strained	2 tbsp.	$\frac{3}{4}$ cup	
Sherry, dry	2 tbsp.	$\frac{3}{4}$ cup	
Soy sauce, mild	3 tbsp.	1 cup	
Red wine vinegar	$1\frac{1}{2}$ tbsp.	$\frac{1}{2}$ cup	
Brown sugar, light	1 tbsp.	$\frac{1}{3}$ cup	
Salt	$\frac{1}{2}$ tsp.	1 tbsp.	
Szechuan pepper, ground	$\frac{1}{4}$ tsp.	$1\frac{1}{2}$ tsp.	
Sesame oil, Oriental	1 tbsp.	$\frac{1}{3}$ cup	
Peanuts, salted	1 cup	2 lb.	Add; stir in before service.

SPECIAL HANDLING FOR BUFFETS: *Serve very warm from shallow insert pan(s) set over dual heating units. Keep covered. Offer with Mandarin pancakes or crêpes. Serve with steamed rice and green vegetables.*

Zesty Mustard Sauce

INGREDIENTS	TEST QUANTITY: 8	SERVICE QUANTITY: 50	METHOD
Mustard, dry	1 tsp.	2 tbsp.	Combine in top of bain marie.
Flour, all purpose	1 tsp.	2 tbsp.	
Cayenne	$\frac{1}{2}$ tsp.	1 tbsp.	
Salt	$\frac{1}{2}$ tsp.	1 tbsp.	
White pepper	$\frac{1}{4}$ tsp.	$1\frac{1}{2}$ tsp.	
Egg yolks, beaten	4	2 dozen	Add; combine well.
Worcestershire sauce	1 tsp.	2 tbsp.	
Milk, scalded	$1\frac{1}{2}$ cups	$2\frac{1}{4}$ qt.	Add; stir well. Cook until thick.
White wine	1 tbsp.	$\frac{1}{3}$ cup	Add. Serve hot.
Lemon juice	$\frac{1}{4}$ cup	$1\frac{1}{2}$ cups	

SPECIAL HANDLING FOR BUFFETS: *Offer as a condiment on the sandwich buffet or with corned beef, braised entrees, or with boiled ham and cabbage wedges or roast beef.*

Review Questions

1. What is bully beef?

2. Name five regions of Chinese cuisine.

3. What is the German version of a cassoulet?

4. What is the predominant meat in Greek cookery? Hungarian?

5. What is the unusual flavoring used in Mexican mole?

6. What is the Italian version of rouladen?

Seven

Seafood: Lean, Leaner, Leanest

A well-planned buffet is the perfect medium for seafood, where a spectacular variety of species and cooking methods can be presented. Buffets become very cosmopolitan when seafoods are featured performers. Regardless of the country or the region of the world being represented, seafood of some form always adds luster to a buffet.

Whatever the world of seafood has in store for us, we can begin our discussion with a description of a traditional buffet indigenous to our own Pacific Northwest: the "potlach." The potlach was a celebration offered by Indian chiefs for visitors from other villages. Games were played and gifts were given by the host to every guest. Everyone also shared in the food. Shellfish such as razor clams and geoducks ("gooey ducks") were arrayed in great profusion. Fruits in baskets rose toward the sky. At the center were mammoth salmon, split down their centers and splayed on rough-hewn boards. The great fish were angled to roast and sizzle over smoking, ashen-orange coals. Potlach celebrants savored bits and pieces of the succulent fish, just as modern diners are enticed by appetizing finger foods.

Fishing remains a prime activity from Washington State to the Alaska coast, though, recently, times have been hard for the hearty crews who trawl the Pacific Ocean for the fish and shellfish that fill our dinner tables. The shellfish catch has been spotty and prices often high, but with judicious selection of recipes, any buffet can offer some seafood magic.

Journeying west across the vast Pacific takes us to Japan, and to another buffet form, the sushi and sashimi bar. For sushi, delicate slivers of uncooked fish are wrapped in rice and then in seaweed, and arranged in a stunning array. In sashimi, soy sauce and piquant green horseradish serve to garnish deftly cut slices and cubes of tuna, tilefish, snapper, or bass. The art is in the carving; the art form is a version of buffet.

A hop over Asia prepares one for a visit to Mediterranean Spain. Castanets and guitar set the musical background from which appears a buffet in a pan, the splendor that deserves center ring: paella. Fluffed with saffron rice and dotted with peas, paella is a colorburst of langoustines, clams, shrimp, and mussels — all sharing space with chicken and sausage. Deck your tables with jugs and candles: paella is a buffet in itself.

Also, along the Mediterranean shore we enter the part of Marseille, whose seafood calling card is bouillabaisse. Like paella — a natural buffet — this hearty seafood stew is also an event. Though purists demand that native fishes be used, the key to bouillabaisse is *assortment,* in an aromatic red stock. Baskets of croutons and tubs of *rouille,* a tangy blend of garlic and peppers bound with oils to a mayon-naise thickness, are just about all you'll need to tempt guests with a taste of Marseille.

If shellfish tops purveyors' "Specials" charts, bring patrons back home to such Atlantic favorites as a New England clambake or an oyster roast of the tide waters of Virginia and the Carolinas. Travelers along the entire Eastern seaboard discover that one or another of these buffet standards fill the bill for East Coast dinners. Steamed potatoes, corn, and clams are a northern version; corn bread, red rice, and hot dogs mingle with oysters on a coastal Georgia buffet. Whether served from buckets or your everyday china, offer plenty of shellfish and some newspaper too, and then make room for the crowds!

"JACK SPRAT COULD EAT NO FAT . . ."

The world of seafood is a wide one indeed, but the confusing multitude of species found even in modest markets can be arranged into two distinguishing camps: whether the species is lean or fatty. In either case, fat percentages are functions not of surface layers but of inherent oils. A "lean" fish is one whose total body weight is composed of less than 4 percent of fat, whereas a "fat" variety naturally contains more. A key point to recall: even fish with a higher fat content are lower in fat than red meats.

The National Fisheries Institute offers the following fat/lean seafood categories. Fish within like categories can often be prepared in place of others for food-service buffet menus.

Less than 1 percent fat: blue crab, cod, cusk, Dungeness crab, grouper, Gulf shrimp, haddock, king crab, ling cod, pike, Quahog clams, rock fish, scallops, sole, weakfish.

One to 3 percent fat: croaker, hake, herring, monkfish, mussels, northern lobster, northern shrimp, ocean perch, other clams, oysters, pollock, sea bass, shark, smelt, snapper, snow crab, tilefish, whiting.

Three to 4 percent fat: bluefish, dolphin, flounder, ocean catfish, porgy, sea trout, striped bass.

Four to 6 percent fat: butterfish, chum, halibut, mullet, pompano, swordfish, tuna, whitefish.

Six to 10 percent fat: catfish, mackerel, salmon, shad, spiny lobster, trout, whitefish.

More than 10 percent fat: eel, lake trout, sablefish.

What does this mean to you?

As you become aware of lean/fat seafood combinations, you will discover that recipes for seasonally unavailable sea bass will work just as well with snapper or with sole. And your Mediterranean swordfish with ripe olives dish will do quite well when fresh tuna is offered as an alternative. Interspecies menu substitution can reduce not only the rigors, but also the costs, of buffet presentation.

THE COOKING METHODS

But once you have selected a variety, how should your kitchen prepare it? Just as there are vast numbers of species, so too is there a multiplicity of seafood cooking methods.

Poaching. Use with any type of fish. Bring cooking liquid (seasoned with wine, herbs, and vegetables) to a boil first. Liquid does not need to completely cover fish, but if it does not, fish should be covered with buttered foil. Wrap large pieces or whole fish in cheesecloth to prevent breakage. Lower heat to a bare simmer (150°F) as soon as liquid returns to boil. If you are going to serve the fish cold, let it cool in the liquid. Cook about 10 minutes per pound of fish.

Baking. Use with fatty fish, stuffed fish, or large cuts of lean or fat varieties. Place on hot rack or pan with skin side down. Baste frequently to prevent drying. Do not turn baking fish. Bake at temperatures in the 325°F to 350°F range; if you use a hotter oven, brush fish with oil or herb butter. You can also wrap fish in oiled parchment prior to baking; this process is called *en papillote.*

Broiling. Use this method with the fatter varieties. Always preheat the pan or rack. Place thinner portions closer to heat; place larger varieties farther from heat. Always place fatter species on a rack so the oils can drain. Dip lean or small fish in oil and flour before broiling to help keep in moisture. If fish is pre-broiled, finish in hot baking oven to retain moisture. Thaw frozen fish before broiling.

Pan Fry/Sauté. There *is* a difference between these two methods: milk is used with flour to form a batter in pan fry; only flour is used with sauté. Both call for the use of hot oil: a small amount with sauté, more with pan fry. Both are used ideally with lean fish; oilier fish varieties tend to become greasy. Batter should always be ice cold to prevent absorption of cooking oils. The fish should be placed in hot pan(s) with the firm side down; if one surface is not firm, then put fish into pan skin side down first. Fish prepared in this manner can be cooked well ahead of service if reheated in a dry oven; otherwise, never cover pan-fried or sautéed fish.

Deep Frying. Use with the leaner varieties too. Closely monitor oil temperature between 360°F and 380°F, depending on the size of portions: the smaller the fish, the higher the temperature. Peanut oil is an excellent choice, though rendered beef or pork fat will add distinctive flavor. Batter should be ice cold. Cooking oil must be returned to optimal temperature before each batch is cooked. All pieces in the fry basket should be completely immersed. Drain fried fish on paper after cooking. Never put salt on fried fish before service, as this will cause the surface to soften.

Regardless of cooking method chosen, fish should be cooked only until it exudes a slightly milky fluid from between its flakes when pierced and separated by a fork. Shellfish are cooked only until a firm texture is obtained. Moisture is always a concern, so sauces should be frequently spooned over seafood items. Proper holding temperatures help to maintain seafood quality.

Beer Crêpes for Seafood Fillings

INGREDIENTS	TEST QUANTITY: 8	SERVICE QUANTITY: 50	METHOD
Flour, all purpose	1 cup	$1\frac{1}{2}$ lb.	Sift together.
Cayenne	$\frac{1}{4}$ tsp.	$1\frac{1}{2}$ tsp.	
Salt	1 tsp.	2 tbsp.	
White pepper	$\frac{1}{4}$ tsp.	$1\frac{1}{2}$ tsp.	
Beer	1 cup	$1\frac{1}{2}$ qt.	Add; stir until smooth.
Eggs	2	12	Beat together and add.
Egg yolks	2	12	
Mustard, Dijon type	1 tsp.	2 tbsp.	
Sour cream	1 tbsp.	$\frac{1}{3}$ cup	Add; stir to blend. Let rest for 1 hour. Reserve for seafood and shellfish fillings.
Butter, melted	1 tbsp.	$\frac{1}{3}$ cup	
Parsley, chopped	1 tbsp.	$\frac{1}{3}$ cup	

SPECIAL HANDLING FOR BUFFETS: *Keep these on hand for various fish and shellfish entrees. Many times, what is left over in today's buffet can be tomorrow's crêpe star.*

Brazilian Bass with Peanuts

INGREDIENTS	TEST QUANTITY: 8	SERVICE QUANTITY: 50	METHOD
Olive oil, hot	$\frac{1}{4}$ cup	$1\frac{1}{2}$ cups	Season and sauté until golden. Remove and reserve fillets.
Sea bass fillets, 6 oz.	8	50	
Salt	to taste	to taste	
Pepper	to taste	to taste	
Red pepper, crushed	to taste	to taste	
Celery, minced	$\frac{1}{4}$ cup	$1\frac{1}{2}$ cups	Add to hot oil. Sauté until soft.
Onion, minced	$\frac{2}{3}$ cup	4 cups	
Green pepper, minced	$\frac{1}{3}$ cup	2 cups	
Italian tomatoes, drained, chopped	$\frac{3}{4}$ cup	$4\frac{1}{2}$ cups	Add; cover. Simmer 10 minutes.
Olives, green, stuffed, chopped	$\frac{1}{4}$ cup	$1\frac{1}{2}$ cups	
Hot pepper, fresh, chopped	1 tsp.	2 tbsp.	
Lemon peel, grated	1 tsp.	2 tbsp.	
Scallions, (greens and whites), minced	$\frac{1}{4}$ cup	$1\frac{1}{2}$ cups	Combine well. Add to mixture. Cover and simmer for 20 minutes. Strain well through fine sieve.
Peanuts, roasted, crumbled	$\frac{1}{3}$ cup	2 cups	
Clam juice	$\frac{1}{3}$ cup	2 cups	
Cilantro, chopped	1 tbsp.	$\frac{1}{3}$ cup	
Ginger root, grated	2 tsp.	$\frac{1}{4}$ cup	
Salt	to taste	to taste	
Black pepper	to taste	to taste	
Cornstarch	1 tbsp.	$\frac{1}{3}$ cup	Combine well. Add to strained sauce. Simmer until thickened. Place in service pieces. Pour the sauce around.
White wine	$\frac{1}{4}$ cup	$1\frac{1}{2}$ cups	
Sesame oil, Oriental oil	1 tbsp.	$\frac{1}{3}$ cup	
Peanuts, roasted, crumbled	$\frac{1}{4}$ cup	$1\frac{1}{2}$ cups	Sprinkle over.

SPECIAL HANDLING FOR BUFFETS: *Serve very warm from shallow insert pan(s) set over dual heating units. Keep covered. If small enough, prepare this item with whole fish.*

Burmese Shrimp and Mushroom Curry

INGREDIENTS	TEST QUANTITY: 8	SERVICE QUANTITY: 50	METHOD
Peanut oil, hot	$\frac{1}{2}$ cup	3 cups	Cover and cook until popping stops.
Mustard seed	1 tbsp.	$\frac{1}{3}$ cup	
Onions, large, chopped	3	4 lb.	Add; sauté until soft.
Celery, minced	$\frac{1}{2}$ cup	3 cups	
Garlic, minced	4 cloves	1 head	
Ginger, grated	1 tsp.	2 tbsp.	
Turmeric	4 tsp.	$\frac{1}{2}$ cup	Add; stir to blend for several minutes to
Coconut milk	1 tbsp.	$\frac{1}{3}$ cup	mingle flavors.
Chili powder	4 tsp.	$\frac{1}{2}$ cup	
Cumin, ground	$\frac{1}{4}$ tsp.	$1\frac{1}{2}$ tsp.	
Salt	to taste	to taste	
Mushrooms, quartered	2 lb.	12 lb.	Add, cover, and simmer until shrimp turn
Shrimp, peeled	2 lb.	12 lb.	pink, about 5 minutes. Do not overcook.
Zucchini, diced	1 cup	$1\frac{1}{2}$ qt.	
Chicken stock	1 pt.	3 qt.	
Lime juice	$\frac{1}{2}$ cup	3 cups	Add and adjust seasoning.

SPECIAL HANDLING FOR BUFFETS: *Serve very warm from shallow insert pan(s) set over dual heating units. Keep covered. Offer with traditional curry condiments.*

Caribbean-Style Red Snapper

INGREDIENTS	TEST QUANTITY: 8	SERVICE QUANTITY: 50	METHOD
Olive oil, hot	$\frac{1}{3}$ cup	2 cups	Simmer for 5 minutes.
Tomatoes, peeled, seeded, chopped	2 cups	6 lb.	
Parsley, chopped	$\frac{1}{4}$ cup	$1\frac{1}{2}$ cups	
Onion, minced	$1\frac{1}{2}$ cups	3 lb.	Combine and add. Simmer over high heat for 5 minutes. Reserve.
Celery, minced	$\frac{1}{2}$ cup	3 cups	
Garlic, minced	1 tbsp.	$\frac{1}{3}$ cup	
Ripe olives, sliced	$\frac{1}{2}$ cup	3 cups	
Orange rind, grated	2 tbsp.	$\frac{3}{4}$ cup	
Almonds, slivered	$\frac{1}{2}$ cup	3 cups	
Paprika, sweet	2 tbsp.	$\frac{3}{4}$ cup	
Sage	$\frac{1}{2}$ tsp.	1 tbsp.	
Cinnamon	$\frac{1}{4}$ tsp.	$1\frac{1}{2}$ tsp.	
Turmeric	$\frac{1}{2}$ tsp.	1 tbsp.	
Red pepper, crushed	$\frac{1}{2}$ tsp.	1 tbsp.	
Mace	to taste	to taste	
Nutmeg	to taste	to taste	
Salt	to taste	to taste	
Red snapper fillets, 6 oz.	8 lb.	50 lb.	Place in roasting pan(s). Season.
Salt	to taste	to taste	
Black pepper	to taste	to taste	
Green olives, stuffed, minced	$1\frac{1}{2}$ cups	2 qt.	Combine well. Spread on fillets. Pour reserved sauce over. Bake in 375°F oven for 20 minutes.
Scallions (greens and whites), minced	1 cup	6 cups	
Red bell peppers, grilled, skinned, julienned	1 cup	$1\frac{1}{2}$ qt.	
Capers	$\frac{1}{4}$ cup	$1\frac{1}{2}$ cups	

SPECIAL HANDLING FOR BUFFETS: *Serve very warm from shallow insert pan(s) set over dual heating units. Keep covered. Substitute fish varieties as appropriate.*

Chilled Mussels in Shell

INGREDIENTS	TEST QUANTITY: 8	SERVICE QUANTITY: 50	METHOD
Mussels, large, well brushed	4 doz.	25 doz.	Combine in pan; cover. Steam until open.
White wine	$\frac{1}{2}$ cup	3 cups	Remove from shells. Discard half of shells;
Parsley, chopped	$\frac{1}{4}$ cup	$1\frac{1}{2}$ cups	reserve half.
Celery, chopped	$\frac{1}{4}$ cup	$1\frac{1}{2}$ cups	
Garlic, chopped	1 tsp.	2 tbsp.	
Butter, melted	1 tbsp.	$\frac{1}{3}$ cup	
Black peppercorns	$\frac{1}{2}$ tsp.	1 tbsp.	
Olive oil	$\frac{1}{4}$ cup	$1\frac{1}{2}$ cups	Combine well in bowl(s); add mussels.
Dry vermouth	1 tbsp.	3 oz.	Marinate for 1 hour.
Raisins, chopped	$\frac{1}{4}$ cup	$1\frac{1}{2}$ cups	
Lemon juice	1 tbsp.	3 oz.	
Garlic, minced	1 tsp.	2 tbsp.	
Shallots, chopped	2 tbsp.	$\frac{3}{4}$ cup	
Parsley, chopped	3 tbsp.	$1\frac{1}{4}$ cups	
Tarragon, dried	$\frac{1}{2}$ tsp.	1 tbsp.	
Oregano, dried	$\frac{1}{2}$ tsp.	1 tbsp.	
White pepper	to taste	to taste	
Salt	to taste	to taste	
Mayonnaise	1 cup	$1\frac{1}{2}$ qt.	Combine; stir into mussels. Place a mussel in
Mustard, Dijon type	1 tbsp.	6 tbsp.	each shell.
Cayenne	$\frac{1}{2}$ tsp.	1 tbsp.	

SPECIAL HANDLING FOR BUFFETS: *Serve chilled on trays or platters. Garnish with parsley and lemon wedges wrapped in cheesecloth. Perfect for Spanish tapas or Italian antipasto.*

Clams "Jacqueline," René Verdon

INGREDIENTS	TEST QUANTITY: 8	SERVICE QUANTITY: 50	METHOD
Watercress, chopped	2 tbsp.	$\frac{3}{4}$ cup	Combine well.
Spinach, fresh, chopped	2 tbsp.	$\frac{3}{4}$ cup	
Parsley, chopped	2 tsp.	$\frac{1}{4}$ cup	
Lemon juice	2 tsp.	$\frac{1}{4}$ cup	
Pernod	2 tsp.	$\frac{1}{4}$ cup	
Butter, soft	$\frac{1}{2}$ lb.	3 lb.	
Salt	to taste	to taste	
Black pepper	to taste	to taste	
Clams, opened	2 doz.	12 doz.	Place on half shell on sheet pans lined with rock salt. Spoon mixture over each.
Bread crumbs, dried	as needed	as needed	Sprinkle over. Bake at 400°F until hot throughout, about 10 minutes.

SPECIAL HANDLING FOR BUFFETS: *Serve very warm from shallow insert pan(s) set over dual heating units. Keep covered. Substitute small oysters if desired. Season with a sprig of fresh thyme on each clam. René Verdon is chef at Le Trianon in San Francisco. He was also the Kennedy family's White House chef.*

Creamed Oysters

INGREDIENTS	TEST QUANTITY: 8	SERVICE QUANTITY: 50	METHOD
Oysters, tiny, shucked	2 pt.	6 qt.	Drain in sieve. Reserve liquor.
Butter, sweet	$\frac{1}{2}$ cup	3 cups	Combine in skillet. Heat. Stir until nutty brown.
Flour, all purpose	3 tbsp.	$1\frac{1}{4}$ cups	
Scallions (greens and whites), chopped	$\frac{1}{2}$ cup	3 cups	Combine. Add to roux. Cook until soft, about 20 minutes. Add oyster liquor. Mix well. Reserve.
Garlic, minced	1 tsp.	2 tbsp.	
Celery, minced	$\frac{1}{2}$ cup	3 cups	
Red sweet pepper, minced	$\frac{1}{2}$ cup	3 cups	
Bay leaf	1	4	
Thyme	to taste	to taste	
Salt	to taste	to taste	
Black pepper	to taste	to taste	
Butter, melted	2 tbsp.	$\frac{3}{4}$ cup	Sauté until almost dry.
Mushrooms, sliced	1 lb.	6 lb.	
Lemon juice, strained	1 tbsp.	3 oz.	Add to mushrooms. Pour into roux mixture. Cover. Simmer until thick.
Butter, melted	$\frac{1}{4}$ cup	$1\frac{1}{2}$ cups	Sauté reserved oysters just until they begin to curl. Pour into pan with other ingredients.
White wine	2 oz.	$1\frac{1}{2}$ cups	Add, stir, and adjust seasoning. Remove bay leaf(s).
Tabasco sauce	to taste	to taste	
Parsley, chopped	$\frac{1}{4}$ cup	$1\frac{1}{2}$ cups	Add, mix well, and pour into service piece(s).

SPECIAL HANDLING FOR BUFFETS: *Serve very warm from shallow insert pan(s) set over dual heating units. Keep covered. Offer with thin slices of toasted corn bread or individual corn pancakes.*

Creole Shrimp Stew

INGREDIENTS	TEST QUANTITY: 8	SERVICE QUANTITY: 50	METHOD
Flour, all purpose	¼ cup	1½ cups	Heat in skillet until golden brown.
Bacon fat, melted	¼ cup	1½ cups	
Onions, thinly sliced	3	5 lb.	Add; cook until tender, stirring.
Celery, sliced	½ cup	3 cups	
White wine	2 cups	3 qt.	Add; combine well.
Tomato purée	1 cup	1½ qt.	Add; simmer 10 minutes.
Garlic, minced	3 cloves	2 tbsp.	Add; simmer 10 minutes, adding water if needed.
Green pepper, minced	½ cup	3 cups	
Celery, minced	¼ cup	1½ cups	
Okra, sliced	½ cup	3 cups	
Lemon juice	1 tbsp.	3 oz.	
Worcestershire sauce	1 tsp.	2 tbsp.	
Water	2 cups	3 qt.	Add; combine well. Cover and let simmer for 30 minutes, stirring occasionally.
Salt	2 tsp.	¼ cup	
Cayenne	¼ tsp.	1½ tsp.	
Black pepper	¼ tsp.	1½ tsp.	
Shrimp, peeled	2 lb.	12 lb.	Add. Allow to barely simmer. Do not over-cook shrimp. Remove bay leaf(s).
Sherry, dry	¼ cup	1½ cups	
Avocado bottoms, sliced	2 cups	3 qt.	
Bay leaf	1	3	

SPECIAL HANDLING FOR BUFFETS: *Serve very warm from shallow insert pan(s) set over dual heating units. Keep covered. Offer with steamed rice. Substitute sliced sea scallops and reduce final cooking time by half.*

Deviled Clams

INGREDIENTS	TEST QUANTITY: 8	SERVICE QUANTITY: 50	METHOD
Bacon grease, melted	$\frac{1}{4}$ cup	$1\frac{1}{2}$ cups	Sauté slowly until tender.
Onion, chopped	$\frac{1}{4}$ cup	$1\frac{1}{2}$ cups	
Celery, chopped	2 ribs	1 bunch	
Green pepper, minced	2 tbsp.	1	
Garlic, minced	1 tsp.	2 tbsp.	
Clams, minced, drained	2 lb.	12 lb.	Add slowly, stirring.
Light cream	1 cup	$1\frac{1}{2}$ qt.	Add, stirring. Heat just to simmering. Remove from heat immediately. Cool slightly.
Egg yolks, beaten lightly	4	2 doz.	Beat in rapidly.
Chives, chopped	$\frac{1}{3}$ cup	2 cups	Add; combine well.
Scallions (greens only), chopped	1 tbsp.	$\frac{1}{3}$ cup	
Bread crumbs, toasted	as needed	as needed	Add to desired texture. Spoon into buttered ramekins or large clam shells. Bake at 375°F until golden.
Cayenne	as needed	as needed	
Parsley, chopped	$\frac{1}{4}$ cup	$1\frac{1}{2}$ cups	Sprinkle on top before service.

SPECIAL HANDLING FOR BUFFETS: *Serve very warm from shallow insert pan(s) set over dual heating units. Keep covered. Indoors or out, these would be perfect on a classic New England clambake buffet.*

Dominican Crab and Peppers

INGREDIENTS	TEST QUANTITY: 8	SERVICE QUANTITY: 50	METHOD
Olive oil, hot	$\frac{1}{4}$ cup	$1\frac{1}{2}$ cups	Sauté until soft, but not brown. Reserve.
Chili peppers, hot, minced	1 tbsp.	$\frac{1}{3}$ cup	(Note: Adjust quantity of chili pepper to taste.)
Onions, chopped	2	3 lb.	
Celery, minced	$\frac{1}{4}$ cup	$1\frac{1}{2}$ cups	
Green pepper, minced	$\frac{1}{2}$ cup	3 cups	
Carrots, minced	$\frac{1}{4}$ cup	$1\frac{1}{2}$ cups	
Garlic, minced	1 tbsp.	$\frac{1}{3}$ cup	
Ginger, grated	$\frac{1}{2}$ tsp.	1 tbsp.	
Tomatoes, peeled, seeded, chopped	1 qt.	12 lb.	Bring to boil over high heat. Stir constantly to reduce liquid almost completely. Do not burn. Reduce heat to very low. Remove bay leaf.
Tomato purée	$\frac{1}{3}$ cup	2 cups	
Sherry, dry	1 cup	$1\frac{1}{2}$ qt.	
Parsley, chopped	$\frac{1}{2}$ cup	3 cups	
Salt	$1\frac{1}{2}$ tsp.	3 tbsp.	
Black pepper	$\frac{1}{2}$ tsp.	1 tbsp.	
Bay leaf	1	3	
Crab meat, picked	2 lb.	12 lb.	Add with reserved vegetables and stir in carefully. Cook for 2 or 3 minutes. Pour into service piece(s).
Lime juice, strained	$\frac{1}{4}$ cup	$1\frac{1}{2}$ cups	Add and blend in gently.
Lemon rind, grated	$\frac{1}{2}$ tsp.	1 tbsp.	
Parsley, finely chopped	$\frac{1}{4}$ cup	$1\frac{1}{2}$ cups	

SPECIAL HANDLING FOR BUFFETS: *Serve very warm from shallow insert pan(s) set over dual heating units. Keep covered. Use leftover portions as crêpe filling for lunchtime buffets.*

Escabeche of Pacific Pollock

INGREDIENTS	TEST QUANTITY: 8	SERVICE QUANTITY: 50	METHOD
Pollock, boneless, 6 oz.	8	50	Combine; let rest 30 minutes. Drain and pat each piece dry.
Salt	$\frac{1}{4}$ cup	$1\frac{1}{2}$ cups	
Sugar	2 tbsp.	$\frac{3}{4}$ cup	
Water	2 cups	3 qt.	
White wine	2 cups	3 qt.	
Olive oil, hot	$\frac{1}{2}$ cup	3 cups	Sauté briefly.
Scallions (greens and whites), chopped	2 tbsp.	$\frac{3}{4}$ cup	
Garlic, chopped	2 cloves	3 tbsp.	
Red onion, minced	$\frac{1}{2}$ cup	3 cups	Add with fish in batches; sauté 15 minutes. Transfer to bowl(s).
Red bell pepper, minced	2	2 lb.	
Bay leaf	1	3	
Lemon juice	2 tbsp.	$\frac{3}{4}$ cup	Add to bowl(s); reserve.
Lime juice	2 tbsp.	$\frac{3}{4}$ cup	
Olive oil, hot	2 tbsp.	$\frac{3}{4}$ cup	Sauté until onion is tender.
Chili peppers, sliced	1	6	(Note: Adjust quantity of chili peppers to taste).
Red onion (large), sliced	1	$1\frac{1}{2}$ lb.	
White wine vinegar	$\frac{1}{2}$ cup	3 cups	Add to pan and simmer gently for 15 minutes, adding white wine as it is needed. Remove from heat and cool. Pour sauce over fish and stir very gently. Chill.
Oregano, dried	$\frac{3}{4}$ tsp.	$1\frac{1}{2}$ tbsp.	
Thyme, dried	$\frac{1}{2}$ tsp.	1 tbsp.	
Marjoram	$\frac{3}{4}$ tsp.	$1\frac{1}{2}$ tbsp.	
Cumin, ground	$\frac{1}{4}$ tsp.	$1\frac{1}{2}$ tsp.	
Cinnamon	$\frac{1}{4}$ tsp.	$1\frac{1}{2}$ tsp.	
Tabasco	$\frac{1}{4}$ tsp.	$1\frac{1}{2}$ tsp.	

SPECIAL HANDLING FOR BUFFETS: *Serve chilled. Present on Bibb lettuce or watercress with ripe olives, wedged egg, and cream sherry.*

Ginger Crab Crêpes "San Francisco"

INGREDIENTS	TEST QUANTITY: 8	SERVICE QUANTITY: 50	METHOD
Crab meat	1 lb.	6 lb.	Combine and marinate for 1 hour.
Mustard, dry	1 tsp.	2 tbsp.	
Ginger, minced	1 tsp.	2 tbsp.	
Scallions (greens only), chopped	1 tbsp.	$\frac{1}{3}$ cup	
Dry sherry	$1\frac{1}{2}$ oz.	1 cup	
Butter, hot	3 tbsp.	1 cup	Sauté until soft.
Peanut oil, hot	3 tbsp.	1 cup	
Garlic, minced	1 tsp.	2 tbsp.	
Onions (large), chopped	1	2 lb.	
Celery, chopped	$\frac{1}{4}$ cup	$1\frac{1}{2}$ cups	
Mushrooms, sliced	1 lb.	6 lb.	
Tabasco	$\frac{1}{4}$ tsp.	$1\frac{1}{2}$ tsp.	Season vegetable mixture and add to crab.
Salt	1 tsp.	2 tbsp.	
White pepper	to taste	to taste	
Butter, hot	3 tbsp.	1 cup	Cook about 5 minutes.
Peanut oil, hot	3 tbsp.	1 cup	
Flour	$\frac{1}{3}$ cup	2 cups	
Milk	$1\frac{1}{2}$ cups	$2\frac{1}{4}$ qt.	Add to roux gradually. Cook for 5 minutes.
Soy sauce	1 tbsp.	$\frac{1}{3}$ cup	Add; mix well. Combine with crab mixture and chill overnight.
Tabasco	to taste	to taste	
Mustard, dry	$\frac{1}{2}$ tsp.	1 tbsp.	
Nutmeg	$\frac{1}{2}$ tsp.	1 tbsp.	
Cinnamon	$\frac{1}{4}$ tsp.	$1\frac{1}{2}$ tsp.	
Parsley, chopped	3 tbsp.	1 cup	
Almonds, sliced	$\frac{1}{4}$ cup	$1\frac{1}{2}$ cups	
Beer crêpes (see Recipe Index)	16	100	Fill with 2 tbsp. of mixture. Roll and place seam down on sheet pan. Bake at 350°F for 20 minutes.

SPECIAL HANDLING FOR BUFFETS: *Serve very warm from shallow insert pan(s) set over dual heating units. Keep covered. Offer with side dishes of sour cream.*

Grilled Mussels with Garlic Butter

INGREDIENTS	TEST QUANTITY: 8	SERVICE QUANTITY: 50	METHOD
Butter, soft, whipped	$\frac{3}{4}$ cup	$2\frac{1}{4}$ lb.	Combine in bowl; mix well.
Mustard, Dijon type	1 tsp.	2 tbsp.	
Shallots, chopped	3 tbsp.	1 cup + 2 tbsp.	
Scallions (greens only), chopped	1 tbsp.	$\frac{1}{3}$ cup	
Garlic, crushed	3 cloves	2 tbsp.	
Almonds, ground	$\frac{1}{4}$ cup	$1\frac{1}{2}$ cups	
Parsley, chopped	$\frac{1}{4}$ cup	$1\frac{1}{2}$ cups	
Bread crumbs, fresh	$\frac{1}{2}$ cup	3 cups	
White wine	2 tbsp.	$\frac{3}{4}$ cup	
Sherry, dry	1 tbsp.	$\frac{1}{3}$ cup	
Tabasco	to taste	to taste	
Dill, dried	$\frac{1}{4}$ tsp.	$1\frac{1}{2}$ tsp.	
Salt	to taste	to taste	
White pepper	to taste	to taste	
Mussels, large, well brushed	4 dozen	24 dozen	Split with knife, discard half of shells. Portion $1\frac{1}{2}$ tbsp. of mixture onto each mussel. Broil until bubbly and golden.

SPECIAL HANDLING FOR BUFFETS: *Serve very warm from shallow insert pan(s) set over dual heating units. Keep covered. Substitute small oysters or clams. Add a dash of Worcestershire sauce and/or tarragon vinegar to taste.*

Hot 'n Cold Marinated Bluefish

INGREDIENTS	TEST QUANTITY: 8	SERVICE QUANTITY: 50	METHOD
Olive oil, hot	$\frac{1}{3}$ cup	2 cups	Sauté for 1 minute. Strain off pepper seeds.
Crushed red pepper	1 tsp.	2 tbsp.	Reserve oil.
Red onions, julienned	2 cups	4 lb.	Sauté in reserved hot oil until all vegetables
Carrots, thinly sliced	1 cup	1 lb.	are soft. Transfer the mixture to stainless
Celery, julienned	$\frac{1}{2}$ cup	3 cups	steel bowl(s).
Green pepper, julienned	1 cup	$1\frac{1}{2}$ lb.	
Red pepper, julienned	1 cup	$1\frac{1}{2}$ lb.	
Garlic, minced	1 tbsp.	$\frac{1}{3}$ cup	
Ginger, minced	1 tsp.	2 tbsp.	
Pimiento, cut in strips	$\frac{1}{4}$ cup	$1\frac{1}{2}$ cups	Add to mixture.
White wine, dry	$\frac{1}{2}$ cup	3 cups	
White wine vinegar	$\frac{1}{4}$ cup	$1\frac{1}{2}$ cups	
Sherry, dry	2 tbsp.	$\frac{3}{4}$ cup	
Salt	1 tsp.	2 tbsp.	
Black pepper	1 tsp.	2 tbsp.	
Bay leaf	1	6	
Thyme	$\frac{1}{2}$ tsp.	1 tbsp.	
Bluefish fillets, cooked, skinned, boned, 2-in. strips	2 lb.	12 lb.	Add to mixture. Arrange in one layer. Cover. Chill overnight. Remove bay leaf.
Green olives, sliced	$\frac{1}{4}$ cup	$1\frac{1}{2}$ cups	

SPECIAL HANDLING FOR BUFFETS: *Serve chilled on lettuce leaves, with marinade as sauce. Substitute an appropriate fattier fish variety. Before service, add some chopped cilantro or parsley.*

Lobster Savannah, Loch Ober

INGREDIENTS	TEST QUANTITY: 8	SERVICE QUANTITY: 50	METHOD
Butter, melted	$\frac{1}{4}$ cup	$1\frac{1}{2}$ cups	Sauté for 5 minutes.
Mushrooms, sliced	2 cups	3 lb.	
Green pepper, minced	1 cup	1 lb.	
Paprika, sweet	1 tbsp.	$\frac{1}{3}$ cup	Add; stir to combine.
Sherry, dry	$1\frac{1}{2}$ cups	$2\frac{1}{4}$ qt.	Add; deglaze. Simmer to reduce by half.
Salt	to taste	to taste	Adjust seasoning.
Black pepper	to taste	to taste	
Paprika	to taste	to taste	
Cream sauce, thick	1 qt.	$1\frac{1}{2}$ gal.	Add. Stir to combine well.
Mustard, dry	1 tsp.	2 tbsp.	
Lobster meat, cooked, chunks	3 lb.	18 lb.	Add. Combine well. Pour into buttered shallow pan(s).
Red peppers, grilled, diced	$\frac{1}{2}$ cup	3 cups	
Parmesan cheese, grated	1 cup	$1\frac{1}{2}$ lb.	Sprinkle over top. Bake at 375°F until golden and crisp.

SPECIAL HANDLING FOR BUFFETS: *Serve very warm from shallow insert pan(s) set over dual heating units. Keep covered. Season with nutmeg to taste. Substitute cooked crab or shrimp. Save unused portions for crêpe filling. Offer with individual puff pastry shells. Loch Ober is a popular Boston restaurant that has been serving this dish for decades.*

Louisiana Barbecued Trout

INGREDIENTS	TEST QUANTITY: 8	SERVICE QUANTITY: 50	METHOD
Olive oil, hot	$\frac{1}{4}$ cup	$1\frac{1}{2}$ cups	Sauté until tender.
Green pepper, minced	$\frac{1}{4}$ cup	$1\frac{1}{2}$ cups	
Onion (small), minced	2	3 lb.	
Beer	$\frac{1}{2}$ cup	3 cups	Add; simmer for 5 minutes.
Ketchup	1 cup	$1\frac{1}{2}$ qt.	
Lemon juice	$\frac{1}{3}$ cup	2 cups	
Chili sauce	1 cup	$1\frac{1}{2}$ qt.	
Worcestershire sauce	$\frac{1}{3}$ cup	2 cups	
Horseradish	1 tsp.	2 tbsp.	
Tabasco	$\frac{1}{2}$ tsp.	1 tbsp.	
Brown sugar, light	$\frac{1}{3}$ cup	2 cups	
Salt	$\frac{1}{2}$ tsp.	1 tbsp.	
Trout fillets, 6 oz., skinned	8	50	Place in buttered roasting pan(s). Pour sauce over. Bake in 350°F oven until the fish tests done.

SPECIAL HANDLING FOR BUFFETS: *Serve very warm from shallow insert pan(s) set over dual heating units. Keep covered. Offer with rice and the sauce formed while baking.*

Substitute appropriate fish. Season to taste with cayenne and/or dry mustard.

Madrasi Shrimp

INGREDIENTS	TEST QUANTITY: 8	SERVICE QUANTITY: 50	METHOD
Shrimp, peeled	$2\frac{1}{2}$ lb.	15 lb.	Marinate overnight. Drain and reserve.
Lemon juice	of 1	of 6	Remove ginger root.
Garlic, minced	1 clove	6 cloves	
Ginger root, sliced	1 slice	6 slices	
Scallions (greens and whites), chopped	$\frac{1}{2}$ cup	3 cups	
Peanut oil, hot	$\frac{1}{4}$ cup	$1\frac{1}{2}$ cups	Heat, covered, until popping stops.
Mustard seed	2 tbsp.	$\frac{3}{4}$ cup	
Onions, chopped	2	4 lb.	Add and sauté until onions are translucent.
Celery, chopped	$\frac{1}{4}$ cup	$1\frac{1}{2}$ cups	
Garlic, minced	1 tsp.	2 tbsp.	
White raisins	$\frac{1}{4}$ cup	$1\frac{1}{2}$ cups	
Ginger, grated	2 tbsp.	$\frac{3}{4}$ cup	
Curry powder	2 tbsp.	$\frac{3}{4}$ cup	
Cardamom, ground	$\frac{1}{2}$ tsp.	1 tbsp.	
Coriander, ground	$\frac{1}{2}$ tsp.	1 tbsp.	
Turmeric, ground	$\frac{1}{8}$ tsp.	$\frac{3}{4}$ tsp.	
Tabasco	$\frac{1}{2}$ tsp.	1 tbsp.	Add; mix thoroughly.
Soy sauce	1 tbsp.	$\frac{1}{3}$ cup	
Sugar	$1\frac{1}{2}$ tsp.	3 tbsp.	
Chicken stock	2 cups	3 qt.	Add with drained reserved shrimp. Stir to combine well and cook until shrimp turn pink, about 5 minutes.
Parsley, chopped	2 tbsp.	$\frac{3}{4}$ cup	Sprinkle over and serve.

SPECIAL HANDLING FOR BUFFETS: *Serve very warm from shallow insert pan(s) set over dual heating units. Keep covered. Top with toasted grated coconut and shredded green onions. Stir in toasted peanuts before placing in service piece(s).*

Mexican-Style Baked Pollock with Olives

INGREDIENTS	TEST QUANTITY: 8	SERVICE QUANTITY: 50	METHOD
Olive oil, hot	$\frac{1}{4}$ cup	$1\frac{1}{2}$ cups	Sauté until soft.
Celery, minced	$\frac{1}{4}$ cup	$1\frac{1}{2}$ cups	
Onions, minced	$\frac{1}{3}$ cup	2 cups	
Garlic, minced	1 clove	6 cloves	
Tomato, seeded, peeled, chopped	1 cup	$1\frac{1}{4}$ qt.	Add to onions. Simmer 5 minutes.
Olives, stuffed, sliced	1 cup	$1\frac{1}{4}$ qt.	
Pimiento, minced	$\frac{1}{2}$ cup	3 cups	
Cilantro or parsley	$1\frac{1}{2}$ tbsp.	$\frac{1}{2}$ cup	
Red pepper, crushed	$\frac{1}{2}$ tsp.	1 tbsp.	
Thyme, dried	$\frac{1}{2}$ tsp.	1 tbsp.	
Oregano, dried	$\frac{1}{2}$ tsp.	1 tbsp.	
Lime peel, grated	1 tsp.	2 tbsp.	
Cinnamon	$\frac{1}{8}$ tsp.	$\frac{3}{4}$ tsp.	
Orange juice, strained	$\frac{1}{3}$ cup	2 cups	Add. Simmer for 2 minutes.
Lemon juice, strained	2 tbsp.	$\frac{3}{4}$ cup	
Lime juice, strained	2 tbsp.	$\frac{3}{4}$ cup	
Salt	to taste	to taste	
Black pepper	to taste	to taste	
Pollock fillets, 6 oz.	8	50	Place in buttered baking pan(s). Pour sauce over and bake at 375°F until fish tests done, about 30 minutes. Baste with sauce. Place in service piece(s). Pour sauce over and around.

SPECIAL HANDLING FOR BUFFETS: *Serve very warm from shallow insert pan(s) set over dual heating units. Keep covered. Add toasted pine nuts or pistachios to sauce before service. Offer with small dishes of piquant tomato sauce and steamed tortilla wedges.*

Oyster Fritters

INGREDIENTS	TEST QUANTITY: 8	SERVICE QUANTITY: 50	METHOD
Flour, all purpose	1½ cups	2¼ lb.	Sift together.
Baking powder	1 tbsp.	6 tbsp.	
Salt	1 tsp.	2 tbsp.	
White pepper	¼ tsp.	1½ tsp.	
Paprika	½ tsp.	1 tbsp.	
Eggs, beaten	1	6	Add; combine well.
Oyster liquor	1¼ cups	7½ cups	Add; mix to desired thickness. Mixture
White wine	as needed	as needed	should be fairly thick.
Shallots, minced	¼ cup	1½ cups	Add; mix again.
Scallions (greens and whites), minced	⅓ cup	2 cups	
Celery, minced	¼ cup	1½ cups	
Parsley, chopped	2 tbsp.	¾ cup	
Oysters, chopped, drained	1 pt.	3 qt.	Add; mix well. Drop by spoons into 375°F oil.
Vegetable oil	as needed	as needed	Fry on both sides.

SPECIAL HANDLING FOR BUFFETS: *Serve very warm from shallow insert pan(s) set over dual heating units. Do not cover or salt; crispness will decrease. Offer with cocktail sauce, hot mustard, or herbed mayonnaise for dipping.*

Peppery Fried Oysters

INGREDIENTS	TEST QUANTITY: 8	SERVICE QUANTITY: 50	METHOD
Oysters, shucked	2 lb.	12 lb.	Combine in bowl; rub gently. Rinse under cold running water.
Salt	1 tsp.	2 tbsp.	
Boiling water	2 qt.	3 gal.	Blanch oysters for 20 seconds. Drain well.
White wine	1 cup	$1\frac{1}{2}$ qt.	
Black pepper, ground	$\frac{1}{2}$ tsp.	1 tbsp.	Toss oysters to season. Reserve.
Red pepper, crushed	$\frac{1}{8}$ tsp.	$\frac{3}{4}$ tsp.	
Ginger, ground	$\frac{1}{2}$ tsp.	1 tbsp.	
Cayenne	$\frac{1}{2}$ tsp.	1 tbsp.	
Flour, all purpose	1 cup	$1\frac{1}{4}$ lb.	Sift together.
Salt	1 tsp.	2 tbsp.	
Baking powder	$1\frac{1}{2}$ tsp.	3 tbsp.	
Paprika	$\frac{1}{2}$ tsp.	1 tbsp.	
Water	$\frac{2}{3}$ cup	4 cups	Add, stirring to blend.
Worcestershire sauce	1 tsp.	2 tbsp.	
Egg(s), beaten	1	6	Add; stir.
Peanut oil	1 tbsp.	$\frac{1}{3}$ cup	Add; stir. Let rest 30 minutes.
Peanut oil, hot	as needed	as needed	Heat to 375°F. Dip oysters in the batter; remove with spoon, removing excess batter. Fry until golden.

SPECIAL HANDLING FOR BUFFETS: *Serve very warm from shallow insert pan(s) set over dual heating units. Do not cover or salt; crispness will decrease. Sprinkle with Chinese pepper salt or lemon-pepper mixture. Offer with soy sauce and rice wine vinegar to sprinkle over.*

"Phoenix" Shrimp

INGREDIENTS	TEST QUANTITY: 8	SERVICE QUANTITY: 50	METHOD
Egg whites	4	2 doz.	Beat until just stiff.
Cornstarch	2 tbsp.	$\frac{3}{4}$ cup	
Flour, all purpose	1 tbsp.	6 tbsp.	
Shrimp, large, peeled, butterflied	3 lb.	18 lb.	Dip into mixture and fry in 350°F oil until golden. Drain on paper, and place in service piece(s).
Cornstarch	2 tsp.	$\frac{1}{4}$ cup	Combine well. Heat to simmer. Pour over shrimp before service.
Beer	2 tbsp.	$\frac{3}{4}$ cup	
Rice wine vinegar	3 tbsp.	1 cup + 2 tbsp.	
Sherry, dry	1 tbsp.	$\frac{1}{3}$ cup	
Sugar	3 tbsp.	1 cup + 2 tbsp.	
Hoisin sauce (commercial)	2 tbsp.	$\frac{3}{4}$ cup	
Soy sauce	2 tsp.	$\frac{1}{4}$ cup	
Garlic, minced	$\frac{1}{2}$ tsp.	1 tbsp.	
Ginger, grated	1 tsp.	2 tbsp.	
Scallions (greens and whites), minced	2 tbsp.	$\frac{3}{4}$ cup	
Salt	1 tsp.	2 tbsp.	
Red pepper, crushed	$\frac{1}{2}$ tsp.	1 tbsp.	

SPECIAL HANDLING FOR BUFFETS: *Serve very warm from shallow insert pan(s) set over dual heating units. Keep covered. Serve with steamed rice and stir-fried green vegetables. Marinate shrimp in dry sherry for 1 hour before preparation. Season to taste with plum sauce.*

Piquant Crab Crêpes

INGREDIENTS	TEST QUANTITY: 8	SERVICE QUANTITY: 50	METHOD
Crab meat, cooked	1 lb.	6 lb.	Combine in bain marie over simmering water. Stir until well heated, about 5 minutes.
Shallots, minced	2 tsp.	$\frac{1}{4}$ cup	
Scallions (greens and whites), chopped	1 tbsp.	$\frac{1}{3}$ cup	
Dry mustard	1 tsp.	2 tbsp.	
Horseradish	$\frac{1}{2}$ tsp.	1 tbsp.	
Salt	$\frac{1}{4}$ tsp.	$1\frac{1}{2}$ tsp.	
Black pepper	$\frac{1}{4}$ tsp.	$1\frac{1}{2}$ tsp.	
Lemon juice	of 2	of 12	
Worcestershire sauce	$\frac{1}{2}$ tsp.	1 tbsp.	
Cream sauce, thick	$\frac{2}{3}$ cup	1 qt.	
Parmesan cheese, grated	$\frac{1}{4}$ cup	$1\frac{1}{2}$ cups	
Sour cream	$\frac{1}{3}$ cup	2 cups	
Tabasco	$\frac{1}{4}$ tsp.	$1\frac{1}{2}$ tsp.	
Beer crêpes (see Recipe Index)	16	100	Lay out flat and spoon about 2 oz. of mixture onto each. Fold both sides over filling and place seam side down in buttered baking pan.
Bread crumbs, fine, fresh	1 cup	$1\frac{1}{2}$ qt.	Combine and sprinkle over crêpes. Bake at 400°F until tops are golden.
Peanut oil	2 tbsp.	$\frac{3}{4}$ cup	
Garlic, minced	2 cloves	4 tsp.	
Parsley, chopped	1 tbsp.	$\frac{1}{2}$ cup	
Chives, chopped	1 tbsp.	$\frac{1}{2}$ cup	
Parmesan cheese, grated	2 tbsp.	$\frac{3}{4}$ cup	

SPECIAL HANDLING FOR BUFFETS: *Serve very warm from shallow insert pan(s) set over dual heating units. Keep covered.*

These crêpes are perfect for brunch; try offering the filling in individual puff pastry shells too.

Public House Fish 'n Chips

INGREDIENTS	TEST QUANTITY: 8	SERVICE QUANTITY: 50	METHOD
Flour, all purpose	1½ cups	2 lb.	Mix together and stir until smooth. Let rest 30 minutes.
Paprika	1 tsp.	2 tbsp.	
Egg yolks	2	12	
Beer, dark	⅓ cup	2 cups	
Salt	¼ tsp.	1½ tsp.	
White pepper	¼ tsp.	1½ tsp.	
Milk	½ cup	3 cups	
White wine	½ cup	3 cups	
Peanut oil	as needed	as needed	Deep fry at 375°F. Keep warm on paper-lined sheet pans. Do not salt.
Baking potatoes, sliced ½ × ½-in. strips	3 lb.	18 lb.	
Egg whites	3	18	Whip until stiff. Fold into batter.
Cream of tartar	pinch	½ tsp.	
Fish: sole, cod, flounder	3 lb.	18 lb.	Cut into 3 × 5-in. pieces; pat dry. Dip into batter and then into hot oil. Fry until golden brown.

SPECIAL HANDLING FOR BUFFETS: *Serve very warm from shallow insert pan(s) set over dual heating units. Do not cover or salt; crispness will decrease. Serve with malt vinegar and plenty of thickly sliced French fries.*

Remoulade Sauce

INGREDIENTS	TEST QUANTITY: 8	SERVICE QUANTITY: 50	METHOD
Mustard, Creole style	$\frac{1}{4}$ cup	$1\frac{1}{2}$ cups	Combine in blender or food processor. Blend until well mixed. Chill for several hours.
Red wine vinegar	$\frac{1}{4}$ cup	$1\frac{1}{2}$ cups	
Chili sauce	2 tbsp.	$\frac{3}{4}$ cup	
Horseradish	2 tsp.	$\frac{1}{4}$ cup	
Dry mustard	1 tsp.	2 tbsp.	
Olive oil	$\frac{1}{2}$ cup	3 cups	
Capers, chopped	$\frac{1}{4}$ cup	$1\frac{1}{2}$ cups	
Egg yolks, hard cooked	2	12	
Celery, minced	1 rib	6 ribs	
Scallions (greens and whites), minced	2 tbsp.	$\frac{3}{4}$ cup	
Mayonnaise	2 tbsp.	$\frac{3}{4}$ cup	
Garlic powder	1 tsp.	2 tbsp.	
Salt	to taste	to taste	
Black pepper	to taste	to taste	
Cayenne	to taste	to taste	

SPECIAL HANDLING FOR BUFFETS: *Keep chilled during service. Offer with raw or cooked shellfish.*

Scallops and Shrimp in Brandy Cream

INGREDIENTS	TEST QUANTITY: 8	SERVICE QUANTITY: 50	METHOD
Butter, melted	2 tbsp.	$\frac{3}{4}$ cup	Sauté until soft.
Onion, minced	2 tbsp.	$\frac{3}{4}$ cup	
Celery, minced	1 tbsp.	$\frac{1}{3}$ cup	
Bay scallops	$1\frac{1}{2}$ lb.	9 lb.	Add; sweat for 3 minutes. Remove bay leaf.
Shrimp, small, peeled	$1\frac{1}{2}$ lb.	9 lb.	
Bay leaf	2	5	
White wine, dry	1 cup	$1\frac{1}{2}$ qt.	
Thyme, dry	$\frac{1}{2}$ tsp.	1 tbsp.	
Brandy	$\frac{1}{4}$ cup	$1\frac{1}{2}$ cups	Add; flame; simmer 1 minute. Drain and reserve sauce. Keep shellfish warm.
Butter, melted	$\frac{1}{4}$ cup	$1\frac{1}{2}$ cups	Sauté until soft.
Mushrooms, sliced	2 cups	2 lb.	
Scallions (whites only), chopped	$\frac{1}{2}$ cup	3 cups	
Flour, all purpose	$\frac{1}{2}$ cup	3 cups	Add to mushrooms. Cook 2 minutes. Add reserved sauce and cook until thickened.
Salt	1 tsp.	2 tbsp.	Add. Simmer for 10 minutes or until well seasoned.
White pepper	$\frac{1}{2}$ tsp.	1 tbsp.	
Paprika	$\frac{1}{4}$ tsp.	$1\frac{1}{2}$ tsp.	
Heavy cream	1 cup	$1\frac{1}{2}$ qt.	Combine and add to sauce. Stir over low heat until smooth and thickened. Add reserved shellfish and cook over low heat just until firm.
Egg yolks, beaten	4	2 dozen	
Worcestershire sauce	$\frac{1}{2}$ tsp.	1 tbsp.	
Tabasco	$\frac{1}{4}$ tsp.	$1\frac{1}{2}$ tsp.	
Parsley, chopped	2 tbsp.	$\frac{3}{4}$ cup	Add; adjust seasoning.
Lemon juice	2 tsp.	$\frac{1}{4}$ cup	

SPECIAL HANDLING FOR BUFFETS: *Serve very warm from shallow insert pan(s) set over dual heating units. Keep covered. Offer with individual puff pastry squares or in scallop shells lined with duchess potatoes. Season with nutmeg to taste.*

Sea Scallops in Cognac Cream

INGREDIENTS	TEST QUANTITY: 8	SERVICE QUANTITY: 50	METHOD
Butter, melted	2 tbsp.	$\frac{3}{4}$ cup	Sauté until vegetables are soft.
Carrots, julienned	$\frac{1}{4}$ cup	$1\frac{1}{2}$ cups	
Shallots, large, minced	2	3 tbsp.	
Celery, julienned	$\frac{1}{4}$ cup	$1\frac{1}{2}$ cups	
Saffron, powdered	$\frac{1}{4}$ tsp.	$1\frac{1}{2}$ tsp.	
White pepper	$\frac{1}{2}$ tsp.	1 tbsp.	
Sea scallops, sliced in half	$2\frac{1}{2}$ lb.	15 lb.	Pat dry and add. Stir to coat.
Tomatoes, large, peeled, seeded, chopped	2	3 lb.	Add; stir well, but gently.
Mushrooms, thinly sliced	1 lb.	6 lb.	
Celery seed	$\frac{1}{4}$ tsp.	$1\frac{1}{2}$ tsp.	
Cognac	$\frac{1}{4}$ cup	$1\frac{1}{2}$ cups	Add, stir, and cover. Simmer until scallops begin to firm. Remove scallops; cover and keep warm. Increase heat to high and cook until sauce begins to thicken.
Vermouth, dry	$\frac{1}{4}$ cup	$1\frac{1}{2}$ cups	
Heavy cream	1 pt.	3 qt.	Add; continue cooking rapidly until sauce reduces nicely.
Salt	to taste	to taste	Adjust seasoning. Return scallops to pan; warm. Place in service piece(s).
Black pepper	to taste	to taste	

SPECIAL HANDLING FOR BUFFETS: *Serve very warm from shallow insert pan(s) set over dual heating units. Keep covered. Season shallot mixture lightly with dried thyme; proceed. Offer with rectangles of golden puff pastry or seasoned bread sticks.*

Shrimp Fritters

INGREDIENTS	TEST QUANTITY: 8	SERVICE QUANTITY: 50	METHOD
Shrimp, medium, peeled, chopped very fine	2 lb.	12 lb.	Combine well.
Water chestnuts, ground well	4	2 dozen	
Scallion (white only), minced	1	6	
Garlic, minced	$\frac{1}{2}$ tsp.	1 tbsp.	
Salt	1 tsp.	2 tbsp.	
Sherry, dry	1 tbsp.	6 tbsp.	
Rice wine vinegar	1 tsp.	2 tbsp.	
Egg white, beaten to foam	1	6	Add. Stir until well blended.
Cream of tartar	pinch	$\frac{1}{8}$ tsp.	
Ginger, minced	2	12	Combine in bowl; press with spoon to extract juice. Strain into a small bowl, pressing hard.
Water	3 tbsp.	1 cup	
Red pepper, crushed	$\frac{1}{4}$ tsp.	$1\frac{1}{2}$ tsp.	
Cornstarch	3 tbsp.	1 cup + 2 tbsp.	Combine with ginger water; dissolve well. Pour over shrimp mixture; stir to combine well until mixture is smooth and fluffy. Pour onto a sheet pan.
Peanut oil	as needed	as needed	Lightly coat hands. Roll shrimp mixture into small balls. Chill.
Peanut oil	as needed	as needed	Heat to 325°F. Fry fritters until golden, constantly stirring with wooden spoon. Keep hot while others are cooking. DO NOT ALLOW TO CHILL.

SPECIAL HANDLING FOR BUFFETS: *Serve very warm from shallow insert pan(s) set over dual heating units. Do not cover or salt; crispness will decrease. Sprinkle with crushed Oriental pepper and offer with soy sauce and rice wine vinegar.*

Spanish Casserole de Mariscos (seafood stew)

INGREDIENTS	TEST QUANTITY: 8	SERVICE QUANTITY: 50	METHOD
Olive oil	$\frac{1}{4}$ cup	$1\frac{1}{2}$ cups	Heat until very hot.
Red snapper, large chunks	1 lb.	6 lb.	Season and dredge fish. Sauté in olive oil until golden.
Halibut, large chunks	1 lb.	6 lb.	
Flour, all purpose	as needed	as needed	
Salt	to taste	to taste	
Black pepper	to taste	to taste	
Cayenne	to taste	to taste	
Mussels, shelled	2 cups	3 qt.	Add to pan. Sauté just until firm.
Garlic	1 tsp.	2 tbsp.	
Brandy	$1\frac{1}{2}$ oz.	1 cup + 2 tbsp.	Add; deglaze; flame. Remove all seafood.
Onion, minced	1	2 lb.	Add to pan. Simmer until vegetables are tender.
Green pepper, diced	1	6	
Celery, minced	$\frac{1}{4}$ cup	$1\frac{1}{2}$ cups	
Garlic, minced	3 cloves	2 tbsp.	
Almonds, blanched, crumbled	3 tbsp.	1 cup	
Olives, ripe, sliced	$\frac{1}{4}$ cup	$1\frac{1}{2}$ cups	
Tomatoes, peeled, seeded, chopped	2	3 lb.	Add; adjust seasoning.
Salt	1 tsp.	2 tbsp.	
Black pepper	$\frac{1}{4}$ tsp.	$1\frac{1}{2}$ tsp.	
Clams, well scrubbed	1 qt.	$1\frac{1}{2}$ gal.	Add. Bring to boil on high heat. Cook until clams open. Return seafood to the pan; continue to cook until well heated.
White wine, dry	$\frac{1}{2}$ cup	3 cups	
Lemon juice, strained	1 tsp.	2 tbsp.	
Parsley, chopped	1 tbsp.	$\frac{1}{2}$ cup	Toss in before service.

SPECIAL HANDLING FOR BUFFETS: *Serve very warm from shallow insert pan(s) set over dual heating units. Keep covered. Sprinkle with grated lemon zest and slivers of toasted almonds.*

Szechuan Prawns

INGREDIENTS	TEST QUANTITY: 8	SERVICE QUANTITY: 50	METHOD
Peanut oil	$\frac{1}{3}$ cup	2 cups	Heat until very hot.
Prawns, or large shrimp, peeled	$2\frac{1}{2}$ lb.	15 lb.	Add; stir-fry for 2 minutes. This can/should be done in batches.
Garlic, minced	2 tsp.	$\frac{1}{4}$ cup	
Bok choy, shredded	1 cup	$1\frac{1}{2}$ qt.	
Ginger root, grated	2 tsp.	$\frac{1}{4}$ cup	
Scallions (greens and whites), chopped	$\frac{1}{2}$ cup	3 cups	
Green pepper, julienned	$\frac{1}{2}$ cup	3 cups	
Red pepper, crushed	to taste	to taste	
Sherry, dry	$\frac{1}{2}$ cup	3 cups	Combine to dissolve. Add to prawn mixture. Stir to blend well.
Tomato ketchup	$\frac{1}{4}$ cup	$1\frac{1}{2}$ cups	
Sugar	1 tsp.	2 tbsp.	
Cornstarch	4 tsp.	$\frac{1}{2}$ cup	Combine and add. Stir until thick. Cook until prawns are just firm but cooked.
Sesame oil	1 tsp.	2 tbsp.	
White wine	$\frac{1}{2}$ cup	3 cups	

SPECIAL HANDLING FOR BUFFETS: *Serve very warm from shallow insert pan(s) set over dual heating units. Keep covered. Season to taste with plum sauce. Offer with steamed rice and crisp-fried strips of egg roll wrapper.*

Warm Lemon Shrimp with Olive Oil

INGREDIENTS	TEST QUANTITY: 8	SERVICE QUANTITY: 50	METHOD
Shrimp, cooked, warm	2½ lb.	15 lb.	Peel and devein while still warm. Place in service piece(s).
Olive oil	1 cup	1½ qt.	Combine well. Pour over shrimp. Toss to coat well. Offer warm.
White wine	¼ cup	1½ cups	
Lemon juice, strained	2 tbsp.	¾ cup	
Worcestershire sauce	½ tsp.	1 tbsp.	
Mustard, Dijon type	1 tsp.	2 tbsp.	
Parsley, chopped	½ cup	3 cups	
Salt	to taste	to taste	
Black pepper	to taste	to taste	

SPECIAL HANDLING FOR BUFFETS: *Serve very warm from shallow insert pan(s) set over dual heating units. Keep covered. Offer unpeeled shrimp for do-it-yourself casual dining; pass finger bowls with warm towels and lemon slice.*

Review Questions

1. How do bouillabaisse and paella differ?

2. Are shrimp lean or fatty? Salmon? Lake trout?

3. Should frozen fish be thawed before broiling?

4. How is fish prepared en papillote?

5. Why should batter be ice cold when frying fish?

6. What types of fish sauté well?

Eight

Poultry: Birds of a Feather

Although Americans consider fried chicken and roast turkey decidedly native dishes, these and other poultry favorites enjoy worldwide exposure and appreciation; rare, indeed, is the country that cannot contribute recipes to a cookbook on poultry. Some ethnic dishes reach the table only after exposure to unique forms of cooking; others, after seasoning secrets have been applied. With culinary ingenuity, many of these poultry classics can take their places on your buffet tables.

CHICKEN

Chicken is the most common of the animal protein foods found in the world's kitchens. Whether pierced by bamboo splints to twirl above hot coals, held in circular pits to roast to a henna red, or framed by lacy pastry in a pie, chicken comes to table in a variety of garbs.

Belgium. One version of the famed soup called Waterzooi requires pieces of cut up, lemon-soaked chicken to be poached in wine and vegetables; once cooked and deboned, the chicken is returned to the thickened broth, which has been graced by a touch of clove.

Brazil. An ornate concoction inspired by Portuguese settlers, *cuscuz de galinha* takes chicken to decorative heights; corn-

meal and dozens of ingredients are combined with chicken and steamed in a garnished mold. When inverted for service, the ornate dish is enhanced with slices of ripe orange.

Greece. When a Greek cook decides to vary from the traditional stuffing of meats, nuts, and herbs, perhaps *kota kapama* will find its way to the table; a chicken casserole with macaroni and grated cheese, this cinnamon-laced Greek dish offers a unique way to serve a poultry favorite.

Hungary. World-renowned paprika flavors many Hungarian dishes, and *csirke paprikas* is a noted example. Golden brown pieces of sautéed chicken are combined with onions and garlic; then sour and heavy creams are added along with the namesake spice, and the simmered combination is served on a platter with noodles or dumplings.

India. The pit oven is called a tandoor and the chicken that comes out of it is called *tandoori murgh*; a brilliant red is derived from an orange dye, but this can be approximated in conventional kitchens with food coloring and a hot oven. The effect can be heightened if spicy flat bread *pappadams* are offered with the smoky chicken.

Japan. *Yakitori* is a cousin of shish kebab that includes sliced and ground

chicken grilled with scallions; teriyaki is a broiling method that includes a sweet glaze. In other methods, chicken is steamed, stewed, stir-fried, and cooked with eggs.

Philippines. If the chicken being carved offers no resistance to the knife, perhaps *rellenong manok* is on the menu. This boned and pork-stuffed dish combines ground meat, pickles, pimiento, and raisins with herbs and spices; when reformed, the chicken keeps its secret stuffing until ready for service.

Puerto Rico. Capers, green peppers, olives, and peas are just a quartet of the makings for *asopao*, a colorful chicken and rice stew from this island; onions and Parmesan cheese help the strong flavor base. The chicken for this traditional dish is rubbed with an herb paste (similar to pesto) and is browned in lard before being stewed in a vegetable/rice mixture.

Spain. The name might imply excessive indulgence, but *pollo borracho* (drunken chicken) is a stewed dish that brings white wine and almonds together with the bird; the French red wine version is *coq au vin*.

Tahiti. A preparation called *fafa* is named for a tropical tree from which leaves are taken to steam the chicken; prior to this step, the birds are sautéed in butter with a basting of vinegar and lime juice. Coconut milk is added, and the lot is steamed in banana leaves.

DUCK

We are fortunate to have access to a regular supply of Long Island duckling; although flavors are always tamed by domestication, this availability opens doors to some culinary specialties of other lands.

China. Each of China's culinary regions has a method for cooking duck. Peking duck, a crisp-skinned delight requiring preliminary drying steps before roasting, is served with scallions and Chinese pancakes. Shanghai duck is poached in soy sauce, sherry, sugar, and *hoisin* sauce prior to being glazed with the boiling broth. For Szechuan duck, the bird is steamed with seasoned salt before it is dried and dipped in hot oil; the crunchy duck is served with soy sauce and coriander. Cantonese duck is filled with a pungent marinade, sewn shut, scalded in sugar water, dried, roasted, and cut into small pieces.

Peru. One of the few Peruvian entrees not spiced with fiery *aji* (ah-HEE) peppers is *arroz con pato*, a variation of the well-known Spanish chicken classic. Duck for this South American dish is cut up and marinated in beer, cumin, and lemon juice; braised in the beer, the duck is accompanied by steamed rice with coriander and green peas.

Poland. Moving from plate to bowl, one can savor a favorite soup of Polish cooks, *czarnina*, a hearty concoction based on the stock and (peculiarly) the blood of a duck. Richly garnished with regionally cherished dumplings, this duck-based specialty also serves as a showcase for such typically Polish ingredients as cinnamon, mace, and vinegar; prunes are added to contribute a fruity, almost nutty, flavor. Another way cooks prepare *kaczka* is to braise it with onions, red cabbage, herbs, and wine.

GOOSE

Visions of the holidays usually accompany culinary conversations about geese, but in many countries this large, often menacing bird plays a year-round role in regional, and even national, cooking styles.

Czechoslovakia. No sage and bread crumbs will do in the Czech preparation of *pecena husa se zelim*, a sauerkraut-stuffed goose that bakes and bastes for hours. Drained and dried sauerkraut is combined with apples, onions, potatoes, caraway seeds, and pepper, and the mixture is cooked in goose fat prior to being stuffed into the waiting bird.

England. The Christmas goose is indelibly etched into English literature and custom; savory with its traditional sage and onion dressing, the roast bird graces the pages of Charles Dickens' novels and the tabletops of British families. (Other stuffings include apples with seasoned bread, ground veal with bacon, and ever-popular chestnuts with spicy ground sausage.) Another opportunity to proclaim tribute to English goose is September 29, Michaelmas Day, and the anniversary of a sixteenth-century English victory over the Spanish armada; Queen Elizabeth I, having celebrated with roast goose, is then said to have called for its service on succeeding anniversaries.

France. A true classic of goose preparation is *confit d'oie*, or *preserved goose*. Cut into small pieces and braised and sealed in its own rendered fat, *confit d'oie* is a necessary ingredient for cassoulet, the earthy, bean-laden casserole famous in various regions of France. Goose livers, or *foies d'oie*, are also known throughout the world to be standard-bearers of French cuisine.

Sweden. When roast goose arrives at Swedish tables, it carries both the name *stekt gas* and the flavors of nutmeg and sage; stuffed with fruits such as apples and prunes, the slow-roasted bird is carved and emptied of its cargo, which is served alongside.

TURKEY

An early (though ultimately unsuccessful) choice to be named our national bird, the turkey — our largest species of domestic poultry — has remained a culinary favorite within the 50 states and in foreign lands as well.

France. In the culinary musings of French gastronome Brillat-Savarin, turkey was deemed "one of the finest gifts of the New World to the Old." Since the seventeenth century, turkey (or *dindonneau*, as the French say) has received diverse culinary treatment. Boned and rolled into *ballottines* or galantines, turkey is seasoned, wrapped, and poached; roasted, it is often served with *chipolata* sausages or a chestnut stuffing. When brandy-soaked truffles are sliced and slipped under the bird's skin before roasting, *dindonneau truffe* is the elegant result.

Italy. Depending on regional preference, Italians prepare *tacchino* in a variety of ways. Cooks from Lambardy, at the very top of the "boot," use Parmesan cheese, chestnuts, and sausages in an aromatic stuffing; others from this region combine apples or pears with prunes and ground veal. A jaunt to the east brings the traveler to Veneto and a unique *melagrana* pomegranate sauce that is spooned over the roasting birds. Fans of sautéed veal *piccata* with lemon and capers will find sliced turkey breast to be a savory switch, especially when joined by a peppery creamed pasta such as *fetuccine all'Alfredo.*

Mexico. Especially dear to Yucatán cooks, turkey has joined major Mexican fiestas for centuries; its most classic presentation is *mole poblano de Guajolote* (turkey with mole in the pueblo style.) *Mole* (pronounced MO-lay) is a combination of spices, chilis, seeds, nuts, and herbs that are ground and heated on a griddle or in oil; it is not a chocolate sauce as some would care to think, though bitter chocolate is included. For the classic dish, turkeys are cut into pieces, browned in lard, braised in stock, and drained. Mole paste is added to the broth with a piece of bitter chocolate; turkey is placed in the pot, and the dish is served with sesame seeds and tamales.

Aromatic Steamed Chicken

INGREDIENTS	TEST QUANTITY: 8	SERVICE QUANTITY: 50	METHOD
Chicken, whole, 3 lb. each	2	12	Rub chicken thoroughly.
Sherry, dry	$\frac{1}{4}$ cup	$1\frac{1}{2}$ cups	
Mustard, dry	$\frac{1}{2}$ tsp.	1 tbsp.	
Salt	1 tbsp.	$\frac{1}{3}$ cup	
Scallions, whole	4	24	Divide among cavities. Refrigerate overnight.
Garlic, minced	1 tsp.	2 tbsp.	
Ginger, grated	2 tbsp.	$\frac{3}{4}$ cup	
Water	1 cup	$1\frac{1}{2}$ qt.	Place in pot. Place chickens on rack above. Cover and steam for 30 minutes. Turn heat off, but leave covered for 15 minutes more.
White wine	1 cup	$1\frac{1}{2}$ qt.	
Cinnamon, ground	$\frac{1}{2}$ tsp.	1 tbsp.	Combine well and place on sheet of foil in bottom of heavy pot. Put steamed chicken on rack above. Place over low heat and cover. Cook for 15 minutes. Remove from heat. Cut into small pieces.
Sesame seeds	1 tsp.	2 tbsp.	
Anise pepper pods	4	1 tbsp.	
Sugar	1 cup	3 lb.	
Honey	2 tbsp.	$\frac{3}{4}$ cup	
Molasses	2 tbsp.	$\frac{3}{4}$ cup	
Soy sauce	$\frac{1}{3}$ cup	2 cups	Combine and add to chicken. Toss well to coat. Serve warm or cold.
Sesame oil, Oriental	$\frac{1}{2}$ tsp.	1 tbsp.	
Hot pepper sauce	1 tsp.	2 tbsp.	
Mustard, dry	1 tsp.	2 tbsp.	

SPECIAL HANDLING FOR BUFFETS: *Serve very warm from shallow insert pan(s) set over dual heating units. Keep covered. Serve with an assortment of stir-fried vegetables and steamed rice. Place any excess sauce in small side bowls. Garnish with shredded scallions and carrots.*

Belgian Waterzooi

INGREDIENTS	TEST QUANTITY: 8	SERVICE QUANTITY: 50	METHOD
Chickens, whole, 3 lb. each	2	12	Rub thoroughly and sear carefully under broiler. Place in heavy, deep kettle(s).
Butter, soft	2 tbsp.	$\frac{3}{4}$ cup	
Garlic, minced	$\frac{1}{2}$ tsp.	1 tbsp.	
Celery, sliced	1 qt.	6 lb.	Add to kettle(s).
Leeks, sliced	4	2 dozen	
Carrot, diced	1	1 lb.	
Onion (small), chopped	3	6 lb.	
Cloves, whole	4	1 tbsp.	
Nutmeg, ground	$\frac{1}{8}$ tsp.	$\frac{3}{4}$ tsp.	
Bay leaf	1	4	
Thyme, dried	$\frac{1}{8}$ tsp.	$\frac{3}{4}$ tsp.	
Oregano, dried	$\frac{1}{8}$ tsp.	$\frac{3}{4}$ tsp.	
Nutmeg, ground	$\frac{1}{8}$ tsp.	$\frac{3}{4}$ tsp.	
Chicken stock	as needed	as needed	Add to the kettle to cover chicken. Bring to a boil; then cover and lower heat to a simmer until the chicken is tender, about 1 hour. Remove chicken and discard skin. Cut the chicken into small pieces and keep warm. Strain stock into a pot and simmer.
White wine	$\frac{1}{2}$ cup	3 cups	
Egg yolks	4	2 dozen	Combine and add small amount of heated stock. Then pour into the stock, but do not boil.
Heavy cream	$\frac{1}{4}$ cup	$1\frac{1}{2}$ cups	
Lemon juice, strained	of 1	of 6	Season.
Lemon rind, grated	$\frac{1}{2}$ tsp.	1 tbsp.	
Salt	to taste	to taste	
Black pepper	to taste	to taste	
Parsley, chopped	1 tbsp.	$\frac{1}{2}$ cup	

SPECIAL HANDLING FOR BUFFETS: *Serve very warm from round bain marie set over a single heating unit. Keep covered. Offer with toasted French-style bread. Adjust seasoning with a touch of cinnamon.*

Braised Chicken Wings

INGREDIENTS	TEST QUANTITY: 8	SERVICE QUANTITY: 50	METHOD
Chinese mushrooms, dried	6	36	Soak for 30 minutes. Drain. Cut mushrooms into quarters. Reserve.
Water	1 cup	$1\frac{1}{2}$ qt.	
Sherry, dry	2 tbsp.	$\frac{3}{4}$ cup	
Peanut oil, hot	3 tbsp.	1 cup	Sauté in very hot wok or skillet for 5 minutes. Remove and reserve wings. Keep warm.
Chicken wings, whole or split	4 lb.	24 lb.	
Garlic, minced	1 tsp.	2 tbsp.	
Bamboo shoots	$\frac{1}{2}$ cup	3 cups	Add to hot wok(s). Simmer for 25 minutes. Reserve.
Water chestnuts	$\frac{1}{2}$ cup	3 cups	
Soy sauce	1 tbsp.	$\frac{1}{3}$ cup	
Orange peel, grated	1 tsp.	2 tbsp.	
Ginger, grated	1 tsp.	2 tbsp.	
Anise pepper, ground	$\frac{1}{4}$ tsp.	$1\frac{1}{2}$ tsp.	
Salt	1 tsp.	2 tbsp.	
White wine	$\frac{1}{2}$ cup	3 cups	
Sesame oil, Oriental, heated	1 tbsp.	$\frac{1}{3}$ cup	Sauté briefly. Add to mixture, along with reserved mushrooms.
Scallions, chopped	2 tbsp.	$\frac{3}{4}$ cup	
Sherry, dry	2 tsp.	$\frac{1}{4}$ cup	Dissolve and add to mixture. Simmer for 10 minutes.
Brown sugar, light	1 tsp.	2 tbsp.	
Cornstarch	1 tsp.	2 tbsp.	Dissolve and add. Stir until thickened. Place chicken wings in service piece(s). Pour sauce over.
Sherry, dry	2 tbsp.	$\frac{1}{4}$ cup	

SPECIAL HANDLING FOR BUFFETS: *Serve very warm from shallow insert pan(s) set over dual heating units. Keep covered. Serve thick crêpes (or Mandarin pancakes) from side platter. Offer condiment bowls of plum sauce or sweet and sour.*

Braised Quail in Chardonnay

INGREDIENTS	TEST QUANTITY: 8	SERVICE QUANTITY: 50	METHOD
Olive oil, hot	¼ cup	1½ cups	Sauté until soft.
Scallions (greens and whites), chopped	½ cup	3 cups	
Carrots, diced	¾ cup	4½ cups	
Green pepper, minced	¼ cup	1½ cups	
Celery, minced	¼ cup	1½ cups	
Garlic, minced	1 tsp.	2 tbsp.	
Flour, all purpose	1 tbsp.	⅓ cup	Add. Stir in. Cook 5 minutes.
Chicken stock	1 cup	1½ qt.	Add. Stir until smooth. Strain well and reserve.
White wine	¼ cup	1½ cups	
Quail	8	50	Season quail inside and out.
Salt	to taste	to taste	
Black pepper	to taste	to taste	
Celery salt	to taste	to taste	
Butter, melted	1½ tbsp.	½ cup + 1 tbsp.	Brown quail carefully. Place in buttered roasting pan(s).
Chardonnay	1 cup	1½ qt.	Pour around quail. Roast at 350°F for 15 minutes. Spoon wine over quail frequently. Add strained sauce. Cover. Braise slowly until tender, about 30 minutes. Transfer quail to service piece(s).
Butter, melted	½ tbsp.	3 tbsp.	Sauté until golden. Spoon around quail. Pour sauce over mushrooms.
Mushrooms, sliced	1 cup	2 lb.	

SPECIAL HANDLING FOR BUFFETS: *Serve very warm from shallow insert pan(s) set over dual heating units. Keep covered. Place small amount of poultry or game pâté inside each quail; proceed. Offer with an assortment on baby vegetables and rissoto.*

Braised Quail with Walnuts and Oranges

INGREDIENTS	TEST QUANTITY: 8	SERVICE QUANTITY: 50	METHOD
Quail, split	8	50	Toss to coat well.
Salt	1 tsp.	2 tbsp.	
White pepper	$\frac{1}{4}$ tsp.	$1\frac{1}{2}$ tsp.	
Paprika	$\frac{1}{2}$ tsp.	1 tbsp.	
Flour, all purpose	$\frac{1}{2}$ cup	3 cups	
Olive oil, hot	2 tbsp.	$\frac{3}{4}$ cup	Sauté quail until golden brown. Remove from pan(s).
Peanut oil, hot	$\frac{1}{4}$ cup	$1\frac{1}{2}$ cups	
White wine	1 cup	$1\frac{1}{2}$ qt.	Add to pan(s). Deglaze. Bring to a boil. Lower heat. Add quail. Cover. Braise until quail test done, about 25 minutes. Place the quail on service piece(s) and cover.
Cognac	1 oz.	$\frac{3}{4}$ cup	
Cornstarch	2 tbsp.	$\frac{3}{4}$ cup	Combine well. Add to simmering sauce. Simmer and stir just until the mixture thickens.
Orange brandy	$\frac{1}{2}$ cup	3 cups	
Orange juice	$\frac{1}{4}$ cup	$1\frac{1}{2}$ cups	
Walnuts, chopped	$\frac{1}{2}$ cup	1 lb.	Add to sauce. Stir until heated. (See Handling notes below).
Mandarin orange slices, drained	$\frac{1}{2}$ cup	3 cups	
Orange rind, grated	1 tsp.	2 tbsp.	

SPECIAL HANDLING FOR BUFFETS: *Serve very warm from shallow insert pan(s) set over dual heating units. Keep covered. Place each quail in "nest" of thin cooked pasta; offer sauce on the side.*

Broiled Chicken Breasts with Walnuts

INGREDIENTS	TEST QUANTITY: 8	SERVICE QUANTITY: 50	METHOD
Walnut pieces	3 cups	5 lb.	Combine in food processor until the mixture is smooth.
Lime juice	$\frac{1}{3}$ cup	2 cups	
Orange juice	$\frac{1}{3}$ cup	2 cups	
Lemon juice	$\frac{1}{3}$ cup	2 cups	
Sherry, dry	1 tbsp.	$\frac{1}{3}$ cup	
Garlic, minced	2 tsp.	$\frac{1}{4}$ cup	
Scallions (greens and whites), chopped	$\frac{1}{2}$ cup	3 cups	
Chicken stock	$\frac{1}{4}$ cup	$1\frac{1}{2}$ cups	
Mustard, dry	$\frac{1}{2}$ tsp.	1 tbsp.	
Salt	to taste	to taste	
Black pepper	to taste	to taste	
Cayenne	to taste	to taste	
Yogurt	1 cup	$1\frac{1}{2}$ qt.	Combine and reserve.
Walnut mixture, from above	$\frac{1}{2}$ cup	3 cups	
Chicken breasts, skinned, small	8	50	Rub with walnut mixture on both sides. Chill for 4 hours. Grill on rack about 8 in. from heat for 10 minutes each side. Offer with remaining yogurt-walnut mixture.

SPECIAL HANDLING FOR BUFFETS: *Serve very warm from shallow insert pan(s) set over dual heating units. Keep covered. Offer with steamed rice or buttered noodles.*

California Lemon Quail

INGREDIENTS	TEST QUANTITY: 8	SERVICE QUANTITY: 50	METHOD
Quail	8	50	Season and dredge. Shake well.
Salt	1½ tsp.	3 tbsp.	
Black pepper	1 tsp.	2 tbsp.	
Paprika	½ tsp.	1 tbsp.	
Flour, all purpose	1 cup	1½ lb.	
Butter, melted	¼ cup	1½ cups	Combine in sauté pan. Sauté quail until golden. Remove to roasting pan and reserve.
Olive oil, hot	2 tbsp.	¾ cup	
Onions, minced	1 cup	2 lb.	Add; sauté until soft.
Celery, minced	½ cup	3 cups	
White wine, dry	¾ cup	1 qt.	Add; deglaze. Reduce for 1 minute. Add to reserved quail and juices. Cover and braise until birds test done, about 30 minutes. Place the quail in service pieces. Strain cooking liquids into sauce pan.
Water	¾ cup	1 qt.	
Orange brandy	1 tbsp.	⅓ cup	
Yogurt, plain	¾ cup	1 qt.	Add; simmer until slightly thick.
Lemon peel, blanched, julienned	¼ cup	1½ cups	Add; combine well.
Almonds, shivered	¼ cup	1½ cups	
Salt	to taste	to taste	Adjust seasoning. Pour over quail.
White pepper	to taste	to taste	

SPECIAL HANDLING FOR BUFFETS: *Serve very warm from shallow insert pan(s) set over dual heating units. Keep covered. After sautéeing quail, wrap each with a grape leaf; tie and proceed. Serve with pumpkin or squash purée and sautéed Spanish onions.*

Cantonese Chicken Curry

INGREDIENTS	TEST QUANTITY: 8	SERVICE QUANTITY: 50	METHOD
Milk	2 cups	3 qt.	Combine in pan. Simmer over low heat for 30 minutes. Strain and reserve liquid.
Sherry, dry	2 tbsp.	$\frac{3}{4}$ cup	
Coconut flakes, fresh	1 cup	1 lb.	
Peanut oil, hot	$\frac{1}{3}$ cup	2 cups	Sauté for 1 minute.
Celery, chopped	$\frac{1}{2}$ cup	3 cups	
Onion, chopped	$1\frac{1}{2}$ cups	3 lb.	
Garlic, minced	1 tsp.	2 tbsp.	
Ginger root, grated	1 tbsp.	$\frac{1}{3}$ cup	
Mushrooms, chopped	$\frac{1}{4}$ cup	$1\frac{1}{2}$ cups	
Curry powder	$1\frac{1}{2}$ tbsp.	$\frac{1}{2}$ cup	Add. Sauté 2 more minutes.
Turmeric	$\frac{1}{8}$ tsp.	$\frac{3}{4}$ tsp.	
Chicken stock	1 qt.	$1\frac{1}{2}$ gal.	Add. Bring to boil. Reduce heat. Simmer 5 minutes. Strain.
Salt	1 tbsp.	$\frac{1}{3}$ cup	
Chicken, 3 lb., cut up in small pieces	2	12	Add to strained stock. Simmer for 25 minutes.
Cornstarch	2 tbsp.	$\frac{3}{4}$ cup	Mix with reserved coconut milk. Add to chicken mixture to thicken. Simmer to adjust flavor.

SPECIAL HANDLING FOR BUFFETS: *Serve very warm from shallow insert pan(s) set over dual heating units. Keep covered. Offer with steamed rice and side bowls of desired curry condiments.*

Cashew Chicken Stir Fry

INGREDIENTS	TEST QUANTITY: 8	SERVICE QUANTITY: 50	METHOD
Chicken breasts, boned, diced	3 lb.	18 lb.	Combine well. Chill for 30 minutes.
Egg whites, beaten lightly	2	1 doz.	
Garlic, minced	$\frac{1}{2}$ tsp.	1 tbsp.	
Ginger, grated	1 tsp.	2 tbsp.	
Soy sauce	1 tbsp.	$\frac{1}{3}$ cup	
Sherry, dry	1 tbsp.	$\frac{1}{3}$ cup	
Rice wine vinegar	1 tsp.	2 tbsp.	
Sugar	1 tsp.	2 tbsp.	
Sesame oil, Oriental	1 tsp.	2 tbsp.	
Scallions (greens and whites), minced	1 tbsp.	$\frac{1}{3}$ cup	
Cornstarch	1 tbsp.	$\frac{1}{3}$ cup	
Peanut oil, hot	$\frac{1}{3}$ cup	2 cups	Heat very hot. Add chicken mixture and stir-fry for 3 minutes. This can/should be done in batches.
Peanut oil, hot	as needed	as needed	Deep fry at 375°F. Do not brown. Remove. Drain on paper. Add to chicken mixture. Toss well.
Cashews, whole, blanched	2 cups	4 lb.	

SPECIAL HANDLING FOR BUFFETS: *Serve very warm from shallow insert pan(s) set over dual heating units. Keep covered. Serve with stir-fried asparagus tips and cellophane noodles; sprinkle with crushed red pepper to taste.*

Chicken Braised with Green Peppercorns and Brandy

INGREDIENTS	TEST QUANTITY: 8	SERVICE QUANTITY: 50	METHOD
Chicken, cut up, 3 lb.	2	12	Sauté until golden. Remove chicken from pan and reserve.
Olive oil, hot	$\frac{1}{4}$ cup	$1\frac{1}{2}$ cups	
Onion, minced	$\frac{1}{2}$ cup	3 cups	
Scallions (greens and whites), chopped	$\frac{1}{2}$ cup	3 cups	Add to pan. Boil for 2 minutes. Return chicken pieces.
Green peppercorns, crushed	2 tbsp.	$\frac{3}{4}$ cup	
White wine vinegar	2 tbsp.	$\frac{3}{4}$ cup	
Thyme, dried	$\frac{1}{4}$ tsp.	$1\frac{1}{2}$ tsp.	
Brandy	2 tbsp.	$\frac{3}{4}$ cup	
White wine, dry	1 cup	$1\frac{1}{2}$ qt.	
Chicken stock	as needed	as needed	Add to cover chicken.
Salt	to taste	to taste	Season to taste. Cover and simmer for 30 minutes. Strain stock into saucepan and reduce for 5 minutes. Reserve.
Black pepper	to taste	to taste	
Butter, melted	$\frac{1}{4}$ lb.	$1\frac{1}{2}$ lb.	Combine in pan and cook slowly for 10 minutes. Add to reduced stock, whipping well.
Flour, all purpose, sifted	$\frac{1}{2}$ cup	3 cups	
Light cream	2 cups	3 qt.	Add; heat just to the simmer. Return the chicken pieces to the pot to heat thoroughly. Do not boil.
Egg yolk	1	6	

SPECIAL HANDLING FOR BUFFETS: *Serve very warm from shallow insert pan(s) set over dual heating units. Keep covered. Offer with buttered noodles with poppy seeds or spaetzle seasoned with a touch of nutmeg.*

Chicken Breasts with Garlic and Almonds

INGREDIENTS	TEST QUANTITY: 8	SERVICE QUANTITY: 50	METHOD
Almonds, ground	$\frac{1}{2}$ lb.	3 lb.	Combine. Cover. Let rest for at least 1 hour.
Onion, minced	1 tsp.	2 tbsp.	
Garlic, minced	1 tsp.	2 tbsp.	
Chardonnay	$1\frac{1}{2}$ cups	2 qt.	
White raisins	$\frac{1}{2}$ cup	3 cups	
Olive oil, hot	$\frac{1}{4}$ cup	$1\frac{1}{2}$ cups	Sauté until soft.
Onion, sliced	1	2 lb.	
Garlic, minced	1 clove	2 tsp.	
Mexican sausage, sliced	$\frac{1}{2}$ lb.	3 lb.	Add. Simmer for 5 minutes.
Cumin, ground	$\frac{1}{2}$ tsp.	1 tbsp.	
Chili powder	1 tsp.	2 tbsp.	
Cayenne	$\frac{1}{2}$ tsp.	1 tbsp.	
Oregano	$\frac{1}{2}$ tsp.	1 tbsp.	
Bay leaf	1	3	
Salt	to taste	to taste	
Black pepper	to taste	to taste	
Chicken breasts, boned, small	8	50	Add. Cover. Simmer for 10 minutes. Add reserved almond mixture. Simmer for 10 minutes. Remove bay leaf(s).

SPECIAL HANDLING FOR BUFFETS: *Serve very warm from shallow insert pan(s) set over dual heating units. Keep covered. Offer with side bowls of sliced jalapeño peppers, sour cream, and grated Monterey Jack cheese. This procedure can be used for crêpe filling if chicken is sliced after cooking.*

Chicken Breasts with Sesame Seeds

INGREDIENTS	TEST QUANTITY: 8	SERVICE QUANTITY: 50	METHOD
Chicken breasts, boned, small	8	50	Combine and marinate 2 hours. Remove chicken.
Soy sauce	$\frac{1}{4}$ cup	$1\frac{1}{2}$ cups	
Scallions (greens and whites), chopped	$\frac{1}{4}$ cup	$1\frac{1}{2}$ cups	
Ginger root, grated	2 tsp.	$\frac{1}{4}$ cup	
Sesame oil, Oriental	1 tsp.	2 tbsp.	
Lemon juice, strained	$\frac{1}{2}$ tsp.	1 tbsp.	
Red pepper, crushed	1 tsp.	2 tbsp.	
Black pepper	$\frac{1}{4}$ tsp.	$1\frac{1}{2}$ tsp.	
Sherry, dry	1 oz.	$\frac{3}{4}$ cup	
Rice wine vinegar	2 tbsp.	$\frac{3}{4}$ cup	
Sesame seeds	1 cup	$1\frac{1}{2}$ qt.	Roll chicken in seeds to coat. Place on sheet pan(s). Bake in 400°F oven until chicken tests done, about 20 minutes.

SPECIAL HANDLING FOR BUFFETS: *Serve very warm from shallow insert pan(s) set over dual heating units. Keep covered. Substitute wings for breasts and serve as an appetizer. Offer with steamed vegetables.*

Chicken Grilled with Mustard and Herbs

INGREDIENTS	TEST QUANTITY: 8	SERVICE QUANTITY: 50	METHOD
Broiler chickens, cut up	2	12	Brush chicken with oil. Broil close to burner for 5 minutes on each side, basting every 2 minutes. Drain off and reserve liquid.
Butter, melted	$\frac{1}{2}$ cup	3 cups	
Olive oil	2 tbsp.	$\frac{3}{4}$ cup	
Salt	to taste	to taste	Sprinkle lightly over chicken.
White pepper	to taste	to taste	
Cayenne	to taste	to taste	
Red wine vinegar	2 tbsp.	$\frac{3}{4}$ cup	Combine well. Add reserved liquids gradually, just to the point where mixture thickens. Reserve remaining liquid. Brush mixture on chicken.
Mustard, Dijon type	$\frac{1}{3}$ cup	2 cups	
Shallots, minced	3 tbsp.	1 cup	
Garlic, minced	$\frac{1}{2}$ tsp.	1 tbsp.	
Thyme	$\frac{1}{2}$ tsp.	1 tbsp.	
Cumin, ground	$\frac{1}{4}$ tsp.	$1\frac{1}{2}$ tsp.	
Cayenne pepper	to taste	to taste	
Bread crumbs, fresh	1 qt.	3 lb.	Put in bowl. Roll chicken in crumbs. Place chicken on rack, skin side down; drizzle with half reserved liquid. Broil at moderate heat until desired doneness; baste often.

SPECIAL HANDLING FOR BUFFETS: *Serve very warm from shallow insert pan(s) set over dual heating units. Keep covered. Offer with cheesey scalloped potatoes and barbecued pinto beans.*

Chicken with Paprika and Green Pepper

INGREDIENTS	TEST QUANTITY: 8	SERVICE QUANTITY: 50	METHOD
Olive oil, hot	$\frac{1}{4}$ cup	$1\frac{1}{2}$ cups	Sauté until golden brown.
Celery, sliced	1 cup	$1\frac{1}{2}$ qt.	
Onions, sliced	1 lb.	6 lb.	
Garlic, minced	1 tsp.	2 tbsp.	
Paprika sweet	2 tbsp.	$\frac{3}{4}$ cup	Combine. Add to vegetables. Stir to combine.
Oregano	$\frac{1}{2}$ tsp.	1 tbsp.	
Marjoram	1 tsp.	2 tbsp.	
White wine	$\frac{1}{2}$ cup	3 cups	
Beer, stale, heated	$1\frac{1}{2}$ cups	2 qt.	
Chicken, 3 lb., cut up	2	12	Add to mixture. Combine well. Cover.
Green pepper, sliced	1 cup	6 cups	Simmer until chicken is cooked as desired.
Tomato, chopped	1	6	Remove bay leaf.
Lemon peel, grated	1 tsp.	2 tbsp.	
Garlic, minced	1 clove	1 tbsp.	
Bay leaf	1	3	
Salt	to taste	to taste	
Black pepper	to taste	to taste	
Sour cream	2 cups	3 qt.	Temper with some sauce from chicken. Pour
Egg yolk	1	6	into chicken mixture and blend well.
Green pepper, minced	to taste	to taste	Sprinkle over the top.
Scallions (greens and whites), chopped	as needed	as needed	

SPECIAL HANDLING FOR BUFFETS: *Serve very warm from shallow insert pan(s) set over dual heating units. Keep covered. Offer with buttered noodles or spaetzle. Substitute boned turkey for chicken and offer in individual pastry shells.*

Chinese Hot Mustard Sauce

INGREDIENTS	TEST QUANTITY: 8	SERVICE QUANTITY: 50	METHOD
Mustard, dry	$\frac{1}{2}$ cup	3 cups	Combine; stir until well blended. Cover and
Water	$\frac{3}{4}$ cup	$4\frac{1}{2}$ cups	refrigerate for at least 1 hour. This is very
Rice wine vinegar	$\frac{1}{2}$ tbsp.	3 tbsp.	hot. Make it often.

SPECIAL HANDLING FOR BUFFETS: *This is a very hot sauce and should be made well in advance of service for flavor to develop. Offer on a Chinese or Indonesian buffet.*

Coq au Riesling (Alsatian chicken)

INGREDIENTS	TEST QUANTITY: 8	SERVICE QUANTITY: 50	METHOD
Butter, melted	$\frac{1}{3}$ cup	2 cups	Season and sauté chicken until golden.
Olive oil, hot	2 tbsp.	$\frac{3}{4}$ cup	
Chicken, 3 lb., cut up	2	12	
Onion, minced	$\frac{1}{2}$ cup	3 cups	
Salt	to taste	to taste	
Pepper	to taste	to taste	
Mustard, dry	to taste	to taste	
Shallots, minced	1 tsp.	2 tbsp.	Add. Sauté 2 minutes.
Garlic, minced	1 tsp.	2 tbsp.	
Cognac, warmed	2 oz.	$1\frac{1}{2}$ cups	Add. Flame. Deglaze.
Mushrooms, thinly sliced	1 cup	2 lb.	Add. Sauté briefly. Cover. Simmer until chicken is tender. Remove chicken and most fat.
Almonds, sliced, toasted	$\frac{1}{2}$ cup	3 cups	
Heavy cream	$\frac{1}{2}$ cup	3 cups	Add to pan. Deglaze. Simmer until sauce is thick and smooth.
Salt	to taste	to taste	Adjust seasoning. Pour over the reserved chicken.
Lemon peel, grated	$\frac{1}{2}$ tsp.	1 tbsp.	
White pepper	to taste	to taste	
Nutmeg	pinch	$\frac{1}{2}$ tsp.	

SPECIAL HANDLING FOR BUFFETS: *Serve very warm from shallow insert pan(s) set over dual heating units. Keep covered. Offer with buttered noodles and steamed green vegetables. Add sliced toasted almonds to the sauce before pouring over chicken.*

Cornish Hens with Bacon-Crab Stuffing

INGREDIENTS	TEST QUANTITY: 8	SERVICE QUANTITY: 50	METHOD
Bacon, chopped	1 cup	$1\frac{1}{2}$ qt.	Sauté until crisp. Drain. Reserve grease.
Shallots, chopped	$\frac{1}{2}$ cup	3 cups	Sauté in strained bacon grease. Strain. Reserve grease.
Scallions (greens and whites), chopped	$\frac{1}{4}$ cup	$1\frac{1}{2}$ cups	
Garlic, minced	$\frac{1}{2}$ tsp.	1 tbsp.	
Bread crumbs, stale, diced	3 cups	4 lb.	Add to hot grease. Sauté until golden brown. Combine with bacon and shallot mixture.
Black pepper	$\frac{1}{2}$ tsp.	1 tbsp.	
Paprika	$\frac{1}{2}$ tsp.	1 tbsp.	
Crab meat	$1\frac{1}{2}$ cups	2 lb.	Combine carefully and add to the bacon mixture.
Parsley, chopped	$\frac{1}{2}$ cup	3 cups	
Lemon juice	1 tbsp.	$\frac{1}{3}$ cup	
White wine	1 oz.	$\frac{3}{4}$ cup	
Eggs, beaten	2	1 dozen	
Thyme	$\frac{1}{2}$ tsp.	1 tbsp.	
Sage	$\frac{1}{4}$ tsp.	$1\frac{1}{2}$ tsp.	
Salt	to taste	to taste	
Black pepper	to taste	to taste	
Cornish hens, cleaned, dry	8	50	Season cavities. Spoon stuffing into cavities. Truss if desired. Roast in 350°F oven until tender and hens test done.
Salt	to taste	to taste	
Black pepper	to taste	to taste	

SPECIAL HANDLING FOR BUFFETS: *Serve very warm from shallow insert pan(s) set over dual heating units. Keep covered. Substitute quail for hens. Season stuffing with sage and add mushroom trimmings or chopped pecans.*

Cornish Hens with Brandy and Red Grapes

INGREDIENTS	TEST QUANTITY: 8	SERVICE QUANTITY: 50	METHOD
Butter, melted	¼ cup	1½ cups	Sauté until tender.
Onion, minced	1 cup	2 lb.	
Garlic, minced	1 tsp.	2 tbsp.	
Celery, minced	½ cup	3 cups	
Ginger, minced	½ tsp.	1 tbsp.	
Morel mushrooms, dried	2 oz.	¾ lb.	Soak until soft. Chop and add to mixture
Sherry, dry	1 tsp.	2 tbsp.	with liquid.
Cognac	2 oz.	1½ cups	
Bread crumbs, coarse, soft	3 cups	4 lb.	Combine. Add to mixture. Stir to combine
Parsley, chopped	⅔ cup	1 qt.	well. Reserve.
Walnuts, chopped	½ cup	3 cups	
Grapes, red, seedless	1 cup	2 lb.	
Lemon peel, blanched	1 tsp.	2 tbsp.	
Butter, melted	2 tbsp.	¾ cup	Sauté until golden.
Olive oil, hot	2 tbsp.	¾ cup	
Cornish hens	8	50	
Salt	to taste	to taste	Season cavities. Divide stuffing between hens.
Black pepper	to taste	to taste	Place in buttered baking pan(s).
Celery seed	to taste	to taste	
Thyme	to taste	to taste	
Cognac	2 oz.	1½ cups	Sprinkle over hens. Roast at 350°F until hens test done. Baste with juices. Remove hens and keep warm. Strain and reserve pan juices.
Cognac	2 oz.	1½ cups	Deglaze roasting pan. Flame. Add to reserved juices.
Grapes, red, seedless, split	1 lb.	6 lb.	Add to strained juices. Heat. Place hens on service piece(s). Pour sauce around.
Red wine vinegar	1 tbsp.	⅓ cup	
Salt	to taste	to taste	
Black pepper	to taste	to taste	

SPECIAL HANDLING FOR BUFFETS: *Serve very warm from shallow insert pan(s) set over dual heating units. Keep covered. Substitute quails for hens. Bard hens with bacon strips before roasting. Add chopped walnuts to stuffing.*

Cornish Hens with Sesame Oil

INGREDIENTS	TEST QUANTITY: 8	SERVICE QUANTITY: 50	METHOD
Lemon juice, fresh	$\frac{1}{3}$ cup	2 cups	Marinate at room temperature for no longer than 30 minutes. Drain and reserve marinade.
Garlic, minced	1 tsp.	2 tbsp.	
Soy sauce	$\frac{1}{2}$ cup	3 cups	
Ginger, grated	1 tsp.	2 tbsp.	
Sherry, dry	$\frac{1}{4}$ cup	$1\frac{1}{2}$ cups	
Rice wine vinegar	1 tbsp.	$\frac{1}{3}$ cup	
Sugar	1 tbsp.	$\frac{1}{3}$ cup	
Sesame oil, Oriental	1 tbsp.	$\frac{1}{3}$ cup	
Cornish hens, quartered	8	50	
Peanut oil	$\frac{1}{2}$ cup	3 cups	Add to heated pan(s) or wok; heat for 30 seconds. Add hens. Cook until seared. Add reserved marinade. Bring to a moderate simmer; cook until done. Arrange the pieces on service piece(s) and pour the sauce over.

SPECIAL HANDLING FOR BUFFETS: *Serve very warm from shallow insert pan(s) set over dual heating units. Keep covered. Serve with steamed rice and stir-fried mixed vegetables.*

Cornish Hens with Tangerines

INGREDIENTS	TEST QUANTITY: 8	SERVICE QUANTITY: 50	METHOD
Tangerines, peeled, halved	4	2 dozen	Divide fruit among hens. Season and truss.
Lemon peel, blanched	of 1	of 6	
Cornish hens	8	50	
Salt	to taste	to taste	
Black pepper	to taste	to taste	
Bacon fat, hot	$\frac{1}{4}$ cup	$1\frac{1}{2}$ cups	Brown hens. Remove to baking pans. Pour off fat.
Peanut oil, hot	2 tbsp.	$\frac{3}{4}$ cup	
Brandy	$\frac{1}{4}$ cup	$1\frac{1}{2}$ cups	Deglaze pan. Pour over hens.
Butter, hot	2 tbsp.	$\frac{3}{4}$ cup	Sauté.
Shallots, chopped	$\frac{1}{4}$ cup	$1\frac{1}{2}$ cups	
Garlic, minced	1 tsp.	2 tbsp.	
Mushrooms, sliced	$\frac{1}{2}$ lb.	3 lb.	Add; sauté for 3 minutes.
Walnut slices	$\frac{1}{2}$ cup	3 cups	
Lemon juice	1 tbsp.	$\frac{1}{3}$ cup	
Salt	1 tsp.	2 tbsp.	
White pepper	$\frac{1}{2}$ tsp.	1 tbsp.	
Madeira wine, dry	1 cup	$1\frac{1}{2}$ qt.	Add; bring to boil; remove.
Cornstarch	1 tsp.	2 tbsp.	Combine and add. Cook over high heat just until boiling. Pour on hens.
Water	1 tbsp.	$\frac{1}{3}$ cup	
Juniper berries, crushed (or gin)	20 (1 oz.)	$\frac{1}{3}$ cup ($\frac{3}{4}$ cup)	Add. Cover pot and roast at 400°F until hens test done. Remove hens from pot.
Salt	to taste	to taste	Adjust seasoning. Reduce sauce if desired.
Tangerine slices	as desired	as desired	Garnish.

SPECIAL HANDLING FOR BUFFETS: *Serve very warm from shallow insert pan(s) set over dual heating units. Keep covered. Serve as part of smorgasbord or Spanish tapas assortment.*

Country Captain

INGREDIENTS	TEST QUANTITY: 8	SERVICE QUANTITY: 50	METHOD
Olive oil, hot	$\frac{1}{4}$ cup	$1\frac{1}{2}$ cups	Sauté for 5 minutes.
Onion, minced	3	6 lb.	
Celery, minced	$\frac{1}{2}$ cup	3 cups	
Green pepper, minced	2	2 lb.	
Carrots, minced	$\frac{1}{2}$ cup	3 cups	
Garlic, minced	2 cloves	4 tsp.	
Tomatoes, chopped	1 × #10 can	6 × #10 cans	Add; stir to heat. Cook 3 minutes.
Corn, whole kernel	2 cups	3 qt.	
Curry powder	1 tbsp.	$\frac{1}{3}$ cup	Add; combine. Cook 10 minutes.
Thyme	2 tsp.	$\frac{1}{4}$ cup	
Salt	1 tsp.	2 tbsp.	
Black pepper	$\frac{1}{2}$ tsp.	1 tbsp.	
Sugar	2 tsp.	$\frac{1}{4}$ cup	
Red pepper, crushed	$\frac{1}{2}$ tsp.	1 tbsp.	
Banana, firm, sliced	2	12	
Chicken, 3 lb., poached, boned, large dice	2	12	Add.
Raisins	1 cup	3 lb.	Macerate for 30 minutes. Add.
Chicken stock	1 cup	$1\frac{1}{2}$ qt.	
Brandy	$\frac{1}{4}$ cup	$1\frac{1}{2}$ cups	
Almonds, blanched	1 cup	2 lb.	Add; heat well. Pour into service piece(s).
Peanuts	1 cup	2 lb.	Sprinkle over top.

SPECIAL HANDLING FOR BUFFETS: *Serve very warm from shallow insert pan(s) set over dual heating units. Keep covered. Serve as part of a Southern buffet with turnip greens and corn bread flavored with bacon crisps.*

Duck Breasts with Champagne and Cherries

INGREDIENTS	TEST QUANTITY: 8	SERVICE QUANTITY: 50	METHOD
Sour cherries, pitted	$\frac{1}{2}$ cup	3 cups	Combine. Let rest 1 hour. Drain and reserve liquid and cherries.
Lemon juice	1 tsp.	2 tbsp.	
Champagne	1 cup	$1\frac{1}{2}$ qt.	
Brandy	1 oz.	$\frac{3}{4}$ cup	
Mustard, Dijon type	1 tbsp.	$\frac{1}{3}$ cup	Rub with mustard and sauté in hot pan until skin is golden and meat is lightly pink. Pour off all fat.
Duck breasts (non-Long Island)	8	50	
Kirschwasser brandy	$\frac{1}{2}$ cup	3 cups	Pour over. Deglaze. Flame. Reduce to a thin glaze. Slice the breasts crosswise and place in service piece(s).
Beef stock, strong	2 tbsp.	$\frac{3}{4}$ cup	Add to sauté pan(s) with reserved liquid. Reduce to a thin glaze.
Red wine	2 tbsp.	$\frac{3}{4}$ cup	
Salt	to taste	to taste	Add with reserved cherries. Pour over duck slices.
Black pepper	to taste	to taste	

SPECIAL HANDLING FOR BUFFETS: *Serve very warm from shallow insert pan(s) set over dual heating units. Keep covered. Offer with timbales of fresh asparagus or purée of squash and sautéed tiny beans.*

Duck Breasts with Ginger Vinegar

INGREDIENTS	TEST QUANTITY: 8	SERVICE QUANTITY: 50	METHOD
Butter, melted	2 tbsp.	$\frac{3}{4}$ cup	Sweat for 3 minutes.
Ginger root, peeled, minced	$\frac{1}{2}$ cup	3 cups	
Bok choy, chopped	$\frac{1}{2}$ cup	3 cups	
Shallots, minced	2 tbsp.	$\frac{3}{4}$ cup	
Garlic, minced	$\frac{1}{2}$ tsp.	1 tbsp.	
White wine	$\frac{1}{2}$ cup	3 cups	Add; reduce to almost dry.
Duck stock	1 qt.	$1\frac{1}{2}$ gal.	Add; simmer 15 minutes. Skim as needed. Strain into another pot.
Bay leaf	1	3	
Thyme	$\frac{1}{2}$ tsp.	1 tbsp.	
Cornstarch	3 tbsp.	1 cup	Combine and add to sauce. Bring just to a boil and strain. Reserve.
White wine	$\frac{1}{3}$ cup	2 cups	
Red wine vinegar	$\frac{1}{2}$ cup	3 cups	Bring to a boil and simmer until it reaches caramel color. Remove from heat. Bring reserved sauce to a boil and add to vinegar mixture, stirring well. Simmer 1 minute.
Sugar	$\frac{1}{2}$ cup	3 cups	
Lemon juice	1 tbsp.	$\frac{1}{3}$ cup	Add; stir; reserve.
Lemon peel, grated	$\frac{1}{2}$ tsp.	1 tbsp.	
Duck breasts	8	50	Season.
Salt	to taste	to taste	
Black pepper	to taste	to taste	
Peanut oil, hot	as needed (minimal)	as needed	Heat in 450°F oven, add breasts, and roast to a medium rare. Slice on the bias and place in service piece. Ribbon with warmed reserved sauce.

SPECIAL HANDLING FOR BUFFETS: *Serve very warm from shallow insert pan(s) set over dual heating units. Keep covered. Sprinkle with blanched peanuts or almonds and garnish with shredded scallions. Offer small thin crêpes on the side.*

Duck Pâté, Alice Waters

INGREDIENTS	TEST QUANTITY: 8	SERVICE QUANTITY: 50	METHOD
Duckling, 5 lb.	1	6	Bone out duckling, reserving skin. Cut breasts
Cognac	$\frac{1}{3}$ cup	2 cups	into strips and place in marinade for at least
Shallot, minced	1	6	4 hours.
Truffle (optional), minced	1	6	
Salt	to taste	to taste	
Black pepper	to taste	to taste	
Salt pork, cubed	$\frac{1}{2}$ lb.	3 lb.	Process through fine grinder with boned,
Pork loin, lean, cubed	$\frac{1}{2}$ lb.	3 lb.	trimmed duck leg meat. Keep this mixture *very* cold.
Eggs, beaten	2	1 dozen	Combine and mix well with meats. Line
Garlic, minced	2 cloves	4 tsp.	terrine mold(s) with duck skin. Spoon
Ginger, powdered	$\frac{1}{4}$ tsp.	$1\frac{1}{2}$ tsp.	mixture into mold(s) to half full. Place mari-
Nutmeg, ground	$\frac{1}{4}$ tsp.	$1\frac{1}{2}$ tsp.	nated breast strips on top of forcemeat. Cover
Thyme, dried	$\frac{1}{2}$ tsp.	1 tbsp.	with remaining forcemeat. Pat down firmly.
Sage, rubbed	$\frac{1}{2}$ tsp.	1 tbsp.	
Black pepper, ground	$\frac{1}{2}$ tsp.	1 tbsp.	
Carrot, peeled, minced	1	1 lb.	
Pistachios, shelled, unsalted	$\frac{1}{2}$ cup	3 cups	
Bay leaves	3	18	Place on top of pâté(s). Bake in a water bath in 325°F oven until internal temperature is 150°F, about $1\frac{1}{2}$ hours. Let stand at room temperature for 4 hours. Weight down and chill for 6 hours.

SPECIAL HANDLING FOR BUFFETS: *Serve chilled from garnished platters or trays. Offer with assortment of breads and mustards, as well as tiny pickles called cornichons. Alice Waters has exerted a great influence on American cooking in the 1970s and 1980s through her restaurant interpretations and her writings. Her restaurant, Chez Panisse, is located in Berkeley, California.*

Grilled Cornish Hens with Madeira

INGREDIENTS	TEST QUANTITY: 8	SERVICE QUANTITY: 50	METHOD
Cornish hens, split	8	50	Toss to coat well. Place hens on rack over broiler pan(s).
Butter, melted	$\frac{1}{4}$ cup	$1\frac{1}{2}$ cups	
Mustard, Dijon type	1 tsp.	2 tbsp.	
Salt	1 tsp.	2 tbsp.	
Black pepper	$\frac{1}{2}$ tsp.	1 tbsp.	
Cayenne	$\frac{1}{2}$ tsp.	1 tbsp.	
Carrot, sliced	1 cup	$1\frac{1}{2}$ qt.	Place in broiler pan(s).
Celery, sliced	1 cup	$1\frac{1}{2}$ qt.	
Chicken stock	$\frac{1}{2}$ cup	3 cups	
White wine	$\frac{1}{4}$ cup	$1\frac{1}{2}$ cups	
Olive oil	$\frac{1}{2}$ cup	3 cups	Drizzle over hens. Broil under high heat, turning and basting, until birds test done. Place hens in service pieces and cover.
Madeira, dry	1 cup	$1\frac{1}{2}$ qt.	Deglaze pan(s). Scrape well.
Heavy cream	1 cup	$1\frac{1}{2}$ qt.	Combine and add to broiler pan(s). Place over moderate heat, stirring just until sauce begins to thicken. Adjust flavor, strain and pour around hens.
Egg yolk	1	6	

SPECIAL HANDLING FOR BUFFETS: *Serve very warm from shallow insert pan(s) set over dual heating units. Keep covered. Substitute quail and offer on a Spanish tapas appetizer buffet. Offer with thin cooked pasta or sautéed julienne of squash.*

Grilled Turkey with Mustard Butter

INGREDIENTS	TEST QUANTITY: 8	SERVICE QUANTITY: 50	METHOD
Butter, unsalted, soft	6 tbsp.	1 lb.	Combine well. Form into a tube in waxed paper. Chill.
Mustard, Dijon type	2 tbsp.	$\frac{3}{4}$ cup	
Shallots, minced	1	6	
Cilantro, fresh, chopped	1 tsp.	2 tbsp.	
Chive, chopped	1 tbsp.	$\frac{1}{3}$ cup	
Black pepper	to taste	to taste	
Turkey breast, boned, sliced in cutlets	2 lb.	12 lb.	Place between waxed paper or foil papers and pound to $\frac{1}{4}$ in. thick. Grill for 20 seconds, turn 90 degrees, and grill 20 seconds more.
Olive oil	as needed	as needed	Baste, turn over, and repeat procecure. Serve with slice of mustard butter.

SPECIAL HANDLING FOR BUFFETS: *Serve very warm from shallow insert pan(s) set over dual heating units. Keep covered. This dish should be prepared immediately prior to service. Offer with steamed green vegetables and roasted small potatoes.*

Indonesian Chicken Saté

INGREDIENTS	TEST QUANTITY: 8	SERVICE QUANTITY: 50	METHOD
Peanut butter, smooth	$\frac{1}{3}$ cup	2 cups	Combine and bring just to the boil. Remove from heat and whisk smooth. Cool and refrigerate overnight.
Chicken stock	$1\frac{1}{2}$ cups	2 qts. + 1 cup	
Sherry, dry	1 tbsp.	$\frac{1}{3}$ cup	
Soy sauce	2 tbsp.	$\frac{3}{4}$ cup	
Scallions (greens only), chopped	$\frac{1}{4}$ cup	$1\frac{1}{2}$ cups	
Honey	$\frac{1}{4}$ cup	$1\frac{1}{2}$ cups	
Coriander, ground	2 tbsp.	$\frac{3}{4}$ cup	
Garlic, minced	2 cloves	4 tsp.	
Ginger, minced	1 tsp.	2 tbsp.	
Crushed red pepper	$\frac{1}{4}$ tsp.	$1\frac{1}{2}$ tsp.	
Salt	to taste	to taste	
Black pepper	to taste	to taste	
Chicken breast, boned, skinned, sliced in crosswise strips	3 lb.	18 lb.	Marinate for 1 hour.
Garlic, minced	1 clove	2 tsp.	
Ginger, peeled, minced	1 tsp.	2 tbsp.	
Soy sauce	$\frac{1}{2}$ tbsp.	3 tbsp.	
Sherry, dry	1 tbsp.	$\frac{1}{3}$ cup	
Lemon juice	1 tbsp.	$\frac{1}{3}$ cup	
Rice wine vinegar	1 tbsp.	$\frac{1}{3}$ cup	
Butter, hot	2 tbsp.	$\frac{3}{4}$ cup	Sauté until tender. Add chicken and marinade and simmer until chicken is cooked. Add half the reserved sauce, simmer for 2 more minutes. Serve remaining sauce on the side.
Peanut oil, hot	1 tbsp.	$\frac{1}{3}$ cup	
Onions (medium), minced	2	4 lb.	
Celery, minced	$\frac{1}{2}$ cup	3 cups	
Garlic, minced	1 tsp.	2 tbsp.	

SPECIAL HANDLING FOR BUFFETS: *Serve very warm from shallow insert pan(s) set over dual heating units. Keep covered. Serve as part of a rijsttafel buffet with steamed rice and remaining saté sauce as a condiment.*

Lemon Chicken

INGREDIENTS	TEST QUANTITY: 8	SERVICE QUANTITY: 50	METHOD
Chicken breast, boned, skinned, sliced crosswise	3 lb.	18 lb.	Combine in bowl; toss.
Scallions (greens and whites), chopped	$\frac{1}{2}$ cup	3 cups	
Salt	1 tsp.	2 tbsp.	
Black pepper	$\frac{1}{2}$ tsp.	1 tbsp.	
Sherry, dry	1 oz.	$\frac{3}{4}$ cup	
Egg whites, barely beaten	2	12	Add; stir.
Cornstarch	$1\frac{1}{2}$ tbsp.	$\frac{1}{2}$ cup	Add; mix well.
Peanut oil	$1\frac{1}{2}$ tbsp.	$\frac{1}{2}$ cup	Add; mix well. Refrigerate for 1 hour.
Water, boiling	$1\frac{1}{2}$ qt.	$2\frac{1}{4}$ gal.	Combine in pot. Add chicken; stir well. As soon as outer surface of chicken turns white, remove and drain. Place in one layer in pans.
Oil	$1\frac{1}{2}$ tbsp.	$\frac{1}{2}$ cup	
Hoisin sauce (commercial)	$\frac{1}{4}$ cup	$1\frac{1}{2}$ cups	Combine well; pour over chicken. Place pan(s) on rack in larger pan; fill bottom with boiling water; cover. Steam over moderate heat for 25 or 30 minutes. Place in service piece; pour sauce over. Garnish with lemon slices.
Bean paste (commercial)	$1\frac{1}{2}$ tbsp.	$\frac{1}{2}$ cup + 1 tbsp.	
Garlic, minced	$\frac{1}{2}$ tsp.	1 tbsp.	
Soy sauce	2 tbsp.	$\frac{3}{4}$ cup	
White wine	2 tbsp.	$\frac{3}{4}$ cup	
Sherry, dry	2 tbsp.	$\frac{3}{4}$ cup	
Sugar	1 tbsp.	$\frac{1}{3}$ cup	
Cinnamon	$\frac{1}{4}$ tsp.	$1\frac{1}{2}$ tsp.	
Salt	$\frac{1}{2}$ tsp.	1 tbsp.	
Lemon juice	2 tbsp.	$\frac{3}{4}$ cup	
Tangerine, grated	1 tbsp.	$\frac{1}{3}$ cup	
Peanut oil	2 tbsp.	$\frac{3}{4}$ cup	

SPECIAL HANDLING FOR BUFFETS: *Serve very warm from shallow insert pan(s) set over dual heating units. Keep covered. Serve with steamed rice and stir-fried green vegetables.*

Peruvian-Style Duck

INGREDIENTS	TEST QUANTITY: 8	SERVICE QUANTITY: 50	METHOD
Ducks, 4 lb. each	2	13	Cut into 8 pieces each. Place in shallow pan(s).
Onions, minced	$\frac{1}{2}$ cup	3 cups	Combine well. Pour over ducks. Chill for several hours. Remove duck pieces and dry well.
Lemon juice, strained	$\frac{1}{2}$ cup	3 cups	
Lime juice, strained	$\frac{1}{2}$ cup	3 cups	
Orange juice, strained	$\frac{1}{2}$ cup	3 cups	
Cumin, ground	1 tsp.	2 tbsp.	
Garlic, minced	$\frac{1}{2}$ tsp.	1 tbsp.	
Cayenne pepper, ground	$\frac{1}{2}$ tsp.	1 tbsp.	
Coriander, ground	$\frac{1}{4}$ tsp.	$1\frac{1}{2}$ tsp.	
Turmeric	$\frac{1}{8}$ tps.	$\frac{3}{4}$ tsp.	
Salt	$\frac{1}{2}$ tsp.	1 tbsp.	
Black pepper	$\frac{1}{2}$ tsp.	1 tbsp.	
Olive oil	1 cup	$1\frac{1}{2}$ qt.	Heat in stainless steel pan(s). Add duck pieces in batches until all pieces are brown. Pour off all oil. Return all duck to pan.
Beer, light	$1\frac{1}{2}$ qt.	9 qt.	Add to marinade. Stir well. Bring to boil. Lower heat. Simmer until duck is tender. Remove duck and chill. Reduce liquid by at least half. Chill until all fat comes to surface. Remove. For service, heat remaining liquid and cook duck until hot.

SPECIAL HANDLING FOR BUFFETS: *Serve very warm from shallow insert pan(s) set over dual heating units. Keep covered. Offer this South American dish with green peas and yellow rice.*

Portuguese Chicken

INGREDIENTS	TEST QUANTITY: 8	SERVICE QUANTITY: 50	METHOD
Chicken, 3 lb., cut up	2	12	Dredge chicken and shake off the excess.
Flour	as needed	as needed	
Salt	to taste	to taste	
Black pepper	to taste	to taste	
Cayenne	to taste	to taste	
Butter, melted	3 tbsp.	1 cup	Sauté chicken until golden.
Olive oil, hot	3 tbsp.	1 cup	
Garlic, crushed	1 clove	6 cloves	Add; stir.
White wine, dry	½ cup	3 cups	
Chicken stock	1 cup	1½ qt.	
Chorizo sausage, sliced	½ lb.	3 lb.	Add; cover; simmer for 10 minutes.
Red onion, large, chopped	1	2 lb.	
Celery, chopped	½ cup	3 cups	
Green pepper, chopped	1	1 lb.	
Red pepper, chopped	1	1 lb.	
Almonds, slivered	½ cup	3 cups	
Parsley, chopped	1 tbsp.	½ cup	
Oregano, dried	¼ tsp.	1½ tsp.	
Basil, dried	½ tsp.	1 tbsp.	
Thyme, dried	⅛ tsp.	¾ tsp.	
Marjoram, dried	½ tsp.	1 tbsp.	
Chorizo sausage, diced	1 cup	1½ qt.	Add; simmer just until chicken is done.
Tomatoes, peeled, seeded, chopped	4	6 lb.	
Ripe olives, pitted	½ cup	3 cups	
Stuffed green olives	½ cup	3 cups	
Heavy cream	2 cups	3 qt.	Combine and add; bring just to a boil to thicken.
Egg yolk	1	6	

SPECIAL HANDLING FOR BUFFETS: *Serve very warm from shallow insert pan(s) set over dual heating units. Keep covered. Use all chicken wings and serve as part of a Spanish tapas buffet. Offer with steamed rice.*

Roasted Duckling with Natural Juices and Port

INGREDIENTS	TEST QUANTITY: 8	SERVICE QUANTITY: 50	METHOD
Duckling, cut into 8 pieces	2	12	Arrange pieces, skin side up, over vegetables; sprinkle on seasonings. Place in 425°F oven and reduce heat to 350°F. Roast until juices run slightly pink. Remove duck pieces and most fat.
Salt	1 tsp.	2 tbsp.	
Black pepper	½ tsp.	1 tbsp.	
Cayenne	¼ tsp.	1½ tsp.	
Thyme	½ tsp.	1 tbsp.	
Oregano	¼ tsp.	1½ tsp.	
Onion, sliced	2	3 lb.	
Carrot, sliced	2	2 lb.	
Celery, sliced	1 cup	1½ qt.	
Garlic, peeled, whole	2 cloves	4 tsp.	
Duck stock	1 qt.	1½ gal.	Add to roasting pan; place on high heat. Bring to a boil, scraping bottom of pan. Crush vegetables to release flavor. Reduce by half. Strain through fine sieve.
Port wine	½ cup	3 cups	
Red wine	¼ cup	1½ cups	
Butter	¼ cup	1½ cups	Add to sauce and swirl in. Pour over and around duck.
Red grapes, seedless	1 cup	1½ qt.	

SPECIAL HANDLING FOR BUFFETS: *Serve very warm from shallow insert pan(s) set over dual heating units. Keep covered. Serve with thin cooked pasta or gnocchi.*

Rum and Lime Fried Chicken

INGREDIENTS	TEST QUANTITY: 8	SERVICE QUANTITY: 50	METHOD
Dark rum, flamed	$\frac{1}{2}$ cup	3 cups	Combine after flame dies out. Pour into shallow pan(s).
Rice wine vinegar	1 tbsp.	$\frac{1}{3}$ cup	
Soy sauce, Japanese	$\frac{1}{2}$ cup	3 cups	
Lime rind, grated	$\frac{1}{2}$ tsp.	1 tbsp.	
Lime juice, fresh, strained	$\frac{1}{2}$ cup	3 cups	
Horseradish, grated	1 tsp.	2 tbsp.	
Fryer chickens, cut up into 12 to 16 small pieces	2	12	Add to marinade. Marinate at room temperature several hours.
Salt	1 tsp.	2 tbsp.	Combine and dredge chicken pieces. Fry in 375°F oil until well browned.
Black pepper	$\frac{1}{4}$ tsp.	$1\frac{1}{2}$ tsp.	
Ginger, ground	$\frac{1}{2}$ tsp.	1 tbsp.	
Flour, all purpose	2 cups	3 lb.	

SPECIAL HANDLING FOR BUFFETS: *Serve hot from shallow insert pan(s) set over dual heating units. Keep covered to maintain optimum temperature. Offer as part of a Caribbean buffet or use wings only and serve as a tasty hors d'oeuvre.*

Steamed Squab with Sesame Seeds

INGREDIENTS	TEST QUANTITY: 8	SERVICE QUANTITY: 50	METHOD
Squab, split, cleaned, flattened	8	50	Combine well in bowl. Marinate for 30 minutes.
Sherry, dry	1 tbsp.	$\frac{1}{3}$ cup	
Soy sauce	2 tbsp.	$\frac{3}{4}$ cup	
Rice wine vinegar	1 tsp.	2 tbsp.	
Ginger root, grated	1 tsp.	2 tbsp.	
Garlic, minced	$\frac{1}{2}$ tsp.	1 tbsp.	
Orange rind, julienned	1 tsp.	2 tbsp.	
Sugar	1 tsp.	2 tbsp.	
Anise pepper	$\frac{1}{2}$ tsp.	1 tbsp.	
Salt	1 tsp.	2 tbsp.	
Black pepper	$\frac{1}{2}$ tsp.	1 tbsp.	
Scallions, shredded	2	12	Place on steamer rack. Place the squab on top.
Bok choy, shredded	1 cup	$1\frac{1}{2}$ qt.	
Carrots, shredded	1 cup	$1\frac{1}{2}$ qt.	
Ginger root, slices	8	50	Place on top of squab. Pour the marinade into steamer and cover. Steam for 20 minutes. Cut squab into quarters. Arrange in service pieces. Sprinkle marinade over.
Sesame oil, hot	2 tbsp.	$\frac{3}{4}$ cup	Stir-fry for 30 seconds.
Anise pepper, crushed	$\frac{1}{2}$ tsp.	1 tbsp.	
Sesame seeds	2 tbsp.	$\frac{3}{4}$ cup	Add. Stir-fry 10 seconds. Sprinkle over squab.

SPECIAL HANDLING FOR BUFFETS: *Serve very warm from shallow insert pan(s) set over dual heating units. Keep covered. Offer as part of an Oriental buffet.*

Swiss-Style Fried Chicken Breasts

INGREDIENTS	TEST QUANTITY: 8	SERVICE QUANTITY: 50	METHOD
Flour, all purpose	1 cup	1½ lb.	Combine.
Mustard, dry	½ tsp.	1 tbsp.	
Nutmeg, ground	½ tsp.	1 tbsp.	
Allspice, ground	¼ tsp.	1½ tsp.	
Salt	1 tsp.	2 tbsp.	
White pepper	½ tsp.	1 tbsp.	
Paprika	½ tsp.	1 tbsp.	
Chicken breasts, boned, skinned, small	8	50	Dredge in flour mixture. Shake off excess.
Eggs, beaten	3	18	Dip chicken.
Peanut oil	1 cup	1½ qt.	
Bread crumbs, fine, stale	1½ cups	2 lb.	Combine. Dredge chicken. Shake off excess. Chill for 30 minutes.
Almonds, powdered	½ cup	3 cups	
Parsley, chopped	¼ cup	1½ cups	
Scallions (greens only), chopped	1 tbsp.	⅓ cup	
Swiss cheese, grated	½ cup	3 cups	
Lemon peel, grated	1 tsp.	2 tbsp.	
Butter, melted	½ cup	3 cups	Sauté breasts until golden on both sides.
Olive oil, hot	½ cup	3 cups	

SPECIAL HANDLING FOR BUFFETS: *Serve hot from shallow insert pan(s) set over dual heating units. Keep covered to maintain optimum temperature. Offer with Swiss potato salad or potato pancakes.*

Szechuan Spicy Chicken

INGREDIENTS	TEST QUANTITY: 8	SERVICE QUANTITY: 50	METHOD
Chicken breasts, boned, skinned	3 lb.	18 lb.	Flatten pieces; pound to tenderize. Cut into bite-size cubes.
Szechuan roasted pepper-salt	1 tsp.	2 tbsp.	Combine; stir into chicken pieces. Reserve.
Egg white(s), lightly beaten	1	6	
Cornstarch	1 tbsp.	$\frac{1}{3}$ cup	
Peanut oil	2 cups	3 qt.	Add to heated pan(s) or wok; heat to 375°F. Cook chicken 3 minutes. Pour into colander; drain.
Peanut oil	2 tbsp.	$\frac{3}{4}$ cup	Add to heated pan(s) or wok.
Chili peppers, dried	6	1 tbsp.	Add; cook until black. Remove from oil.
Ginger, peeled, minced	1 tbsp.	$\frac{1}{3}$ cup	Add along with chicken. Stir-fry for 10 seconds.
Scallion (greens and whites), chopped finely	1	6	
Garlic, minced	1 tsp.	2 tbsp.	
Sugar	1 tbsp.	$\frac{1}{3}$ cup	Add; stir until chicken is coated.
Salt	$\frac{1}{2}$ tsp.	1 tbsp.	
Cider vinegar	2 tbsp.	$\frac{3}{4}$ cup	
Orange juice	1 tbsp.	$\frac{1}{3}$ cup	
Soy sauce	2 tbsp.	$\frac{3}{4}$ cup	
Hoisin sauce (commercial)	1 tbsp.	$\frac{1}{3}$ cup	
Sherry, dry	1 tbsp.	$\frac{1}{3}$ cup	
Molasses	1 tbsp.	$\frac{1}{3}$ cup	
Sesame oil, Oriental	1 tbsp.	$\frac{1}{3}$ cup	Add; stir. Pour into service piece(s).

SPECIAL HANDLING FOR BUFFETS: *Serve warm from shallow insert pan(s) set over dual heating units. Keep covered to maintain optimum service temperature. Offer with steamed rice and stir-fried vegetables. Garnish with peanuts or Mandarin orange slices.*

Viennese Fried Chicken

INGREDIENTS	TEST QUANTITY: 8	SERVICE QUANTITY: 50	METHOD
Onion (medium), chopped	2	4 lb.	Combine thoroughly.
Celery, chopped	$\frac{1}{2}$ cup	3 cups	
Garlic, crushed	2 cloves	12 cloves	
Olive oil	$\frac{3}{4}$ cup	$4\frac{1}{2}$ cups	
White wine	$\frac{1}{2}$ cup	3 cups	
Salt	2 tsp.	$\frac{1}{4}$ cup	
Black pepper	$\frac{1}{2}$ tsp.	1 tbsp.	
Cayenne	$\frac{1}{4}$ tsp.	$1\frac{1}{2}$ tsp.	
Lemon juice	2 tbsp.	$\frac{3}{4}$ cup	
Sugar	1 tsp.	2 tbsp.	
Paprika	1 tsp.	2 tbsp.	
Chicken, 3 lb., cut up	2	12	Add; marinate for 3 hours. Drain and pat dry.
Bread crumbs, dried	2 cups	1 lb.	Combine; toss chicken in. Shake off excess.
Parsley, chopped	$\frac{1}{2}$ cup	3 cups	
Salt	2 tsp.	$\frac{1}{4}$ cup	
Black pepper	$\frac{1}{2}$ tsp.	1 tbsp.	
Eggs, beaten	2	1 dozen	Mix. Dip chicken pieces in, and then again in bread crumbs. Fry in 375°F oil until golden. Place on sheet pan(s) and bake in 375°F oven to desired doneness.
Peanut oil	$\frac{1}{2}$ cup	3 cups	
Water	$\frac{1}{4}$ cup	$1\frac{1}{2}$ cups	

SPECIAL HANDLING FOR BUFFETS: *Serve hot from shallow insert pan(s) set over dual heating units. Keep covered for optimum service temperature. Offer on Sunday brunch menu as an alternative to always popular Southern fried chicken. Try adding grated cheese and parsley to bread crumbs.*

Review Questions

1. Describe Belgian Waterzooi.

2. What are pappadams?

3. Name and describe four forms of Chinese duck preparation.

4. What form of goose is used in French cassoulet?

5. What is the French term for turkey? The Mexican?

6. What country features sauerkraut-stuffed goose?

Nine
Side Dishes:
Of Cabbages and Kings

Just as maps serve to orient the global traveler, so too does a basic knowledge of vegetables provide a blueprint for ethnic buffet cookery. Vegetables have taken some incredible journeys throughout the centuries, and to know their sources is to expand their profitable use. By cross-matching available vegetables with a spice, seafood, or meat of similar origin, you can create an environment for effective menu merchandising and creative buffet cooking.

Brussels Sprout. A relative newcomer on the vegetable scene, this is a true native of Europe. First encountered in literature in the late sixteenth century, the brussels sprout needs the long, cool growing season found in Northern Europe. It appears on French and English menus, but it has not gained a foothold throughout much more of the culinary world.

Cabbage. Origins in Mediterranean and Eastern Europe led to the distribution of cabbage through the rest of Europe after Celtic and later Roman invasions; evidence points to its presence in Britain in the third century B.C. Most early varieties were loose leafed, with the common hard-headed types not prevalent until the sixteenth century. Loose-leaf types appear in Oriental cuisines, though there is little reference to the hard-headed varieties. Red cabbage is first mentioned in late sixteenth-century England and exists in many European cooking methods. The crumpled, wavy Savoy variety comes from an Italian province and has been available since the mid-sixteenth century. Cabbage was introduced into the Americas by a French explorer who brought it to Canada during a 1542 expedition.

Carrot. Thought to originate in Afghanistan, carrots are found throughout Asia and Eastern Europe and were recorded in ancient Greek and Roman literature as important dietary constituents. By the thirteenth century, carrots were being cultivated in Germany and France as well as in China; by the sixteenth century, they were well developed throughout Europe. One of the first crops attempted by English settlers, carrots had been introduced to South America by sixteenth-century Spanish explorers. They appeared in Brazilian culinary references by the middle of the seventeenth century.

Celery. Long regarded as a medicinal plant only, celery first appeared as a culinary performer in early seventeenth-century France, where it was enjoyed with an oil dressing; in nineteenth-century Sweden, it was held as a valued winter cellar vegetable. Mentioned in the writings of Homer (850 B.C.), celery has been recorded throughout Asia and the Himalayan nations as well as in Mediterranean and Eastern European cookery. A relative of celery, parsley was once worn in garlands by the Romans, who used it as a flavoring agent as early as the fifth century B.C. Eating parsley was once thought to ward off intoxication.

Corn. Corn, the spine of Western Hemisphere cooking, derives from prehistoric times, but only recently (early nineteenth century) has it evolved into the sweet varieties we desire. Probably orginating from Peruvian wild grasses, each kernel was wrapped in an individual husk. Today football-shaped ears exist with kernels that exceed an inch in length. When corn is cooked with lima beans, another protein source, the resulting succotash is a life-sustaining combination in many Latin countries. Corn was introduced to Italy in the mid-seventeenth century, after which it became the grain of choice for polenta (cornmeal mush to Americans and *mamaglia Bucharest* to Hungarians), a staple in some of that country's regional cooking. Another form of cornmeal preparation, gnocchi, finds favor in Swiss and German kitchens, while scrapple is a version from the Pennsylvania Dutch. Corn finds its way, either as a vegetable or bread grain, onto the menus of fully half the world.

Cucumber. Originating in India and migrating with great favor throughout the Middle East, by the first century A.D. the cucumber has spread to Northern Africa and China; in the ninth century, it was recorded in France. Brazilian cultivation of the cucumber is first mentioned in the seventeenth century. Cucumbers are favored in Armenian and Greek cookery as well as in some Italian regions; Japanese and Chinese cooks prepare it extensively as well.

Eggplant. Once thought to possess aphrodisiac properties, eggplant is another native of India. Arabs probably were responsible for introducing some form of it to Europe in the early Middle Ages; many ancient languages have names for eggplant. It exists in many forms other than our familiar purple variety and is a staple in several ethnic cookery styles, including Japanese and Greek. A wide range of seasonings, from soy sauce to cinnamon, can be used to flavor eggplant.

Garlic. Related to the onion, the English name stems from Anglo-Saxon, but garlic was mentioned in the writings of Homer in the ninth century B.C. Chinese references begin in fifteenth century A.D., although actual use there probably predates 200 B.C. The Spanish introduced it to Mexico, and it spread from there in acceptance throughout the New World.

Lettuce. Known throughout the Eastern world by the sixth century B.C., lettuce grew in popularity from its native Asia to Persia and then into Greece and Rome; it has been popular in China since at least the fifth century. Early forms were loose leafed, while the compact types, as with cabbage, developed later. Forms of romaine appeared in Italy in the fifteenth century A.D. and were taken to France some time later. Columbus brought lettuce to the New World, where it flourished in both the North and South. Lettuce was one of the first crops attempted by American colonists.

Onion. Related to the lily family, onions originated in middle Asia and developed a strong heritage in ancient Egypt. Individual names exist in Sanskrit, Hebrew, Greek, and Latin; a broad-base variety is suggested. Forms that evolved in Japan more closely resemble the scallion. Romans developed an affinity for leeks, which by the middle of the eighteenth century were being cultivated in North America.

Potato. Prevalent in the cuisines of virtually every country of the world with the exceptions of most Oriental nations (in Japan, they are called *jagaimo*), potatoes first served a culinary purpose in the high Andes of Chile and Peru, where prehistoric gatherers took advantage of the drying powers of the sun and the thin atmosphere to dry the tubers for future use. Migration was initiated by the Spanish, and by the late fifteenth century, potatoes had been introduced to Europe; Irish farmers quickly adopted the potato and in turn brought it back to the New World, in New Hampshire, in 1719. By the middle of the nineteenth century, po-

tatoes were menu staples throughout Europe and the Americas.

Radish. Of prehistoric Chinese origin, and often cultivated to more than 100 pounds, the radish has been recorded in ancient Greek, middle Asian, and Egyptian literature. The Japanese white daikon has enjoyed increased popularity in the United States; some Indian varieties are cultivated for their seeds, while some Oriental varieties may grow as large as basketballs! White radishes can be seasoned with salt, soy sauce, sesame oil, and sugar for a simple Chinese presentation. The French often serve fresh radish slices atop buttered crusty bread, in a style similar to Scandinavian open-faced sandwiches, which also make good use of radishes.

Rice. Like corn—a grain, not a vegetable—rice is a menu staple in more global areas than virtually any other food known today. Origins are probably China and India, from where it was traded to Egypt and Greece, and then into Mediterranean Europe. First introduced to North America in the seventeenth century, rice has come to flourish in the Southeast and Southwest. Now marketed in long-, medium-, and short-grain white types, as well as untreated brown, rice can be prepared in countless ways to complement any buffet. The American wild rice is not rice at all; rather, it is the seed of a wild grass that is indigenous to the upper Great Lakes region.

Spinach. Unknown except in its native Persia before the first century A.D., spinach was introduced to China from Nepal in the fifth century A.D. The Moors are thought to have borne it to Spain from

North Africa about 1000 years ago. By the thirteenth century, it was well known in Europe, and within 100 years it was first mentioned in cookbooks. Japanese cooks often sprinkle it with a mild dried fish; Indian cookery calls for a similar treatment with pistachios.

Tomato.   A unique vegetable traveler, tomatoes originated in the Americas yet were not included in our cuisine until long after their sixteenth-century introduction to Europe. First records suggest a Peru-vian or Ecuadorian origin, with a north-ward migration to Mexico along with corn; the name stems from the Indian word *tomati*. Italians were the first Euro-peans to eat tomatoes; other countries grew them, but only as garden curiosities. By the end of the eighteenth century, to-matoes had taken their place in French cuisine, but it was well into the nine-teenth century before North American farmers began to grow what they had theretofore thought to be a poisonous plant. Tomatoes, whether red, yellow, or green, now appear on virtually every Eu-ropean and Middle European menu, as well as on those of North and South America.

This list of vegetables is merely a primer of some whose presence through-out the world suggests ethnic flair that can be added to your buffet menus. When seasoned in ways indigenous to certain countries and regions (see Spices and Herbs), vegetables are nutritious buffet offerings.

Apple Sauerkraut

INGREDIENTS	TEST QUANTITY: 8	SERVICE QUANTITY: 50	METHOD
Bacon, chopped	$\frac{1}{4}$ lb.	$1\frac{1}{2}$ lb.	Sauté until just crisp. Remove and drain. Reserve grease.
Onion, chopped	$\frac{3}{4}$ cup	$2\frac{1}{2}$ lb.	Sauté in reserved bacon grease until soft.
Celery, chopped	$\frac{1}{2}$ cup	3 cups	
Carrots, minced	$\frac{1}{2}$ cup	3 cups	
Sauerkraut, rinsed, drained	$1\frac{1}{2}$ lb.	9 lb.	Combine in pot with vegetables and reserved bacon. Bring to simmer. Transfer to baking pan(s). Cover. Bake at 325°F for 4 to 6 hours.
Apples, tart, cored, peeled, diced	1 cup	2 lb.	
White wine, dry	$\frac{1}{2}$ cup	3 cups	
Beer	$\frac{1}{2}$ cup	3 cups	
Chicken stock	$\frac{1}{2}$ cup	3 cups	
Juniper berries	6	1 tbsp.	
Bay leaf	1	3	
Thyme	$\frac{1}{2}$ tsp.	1 tbsp.	

SPECIAL HANDLING FOR BUFFETS: *Serve very warm from shallow insert pan(s) set over dual heating units. Keep covered. Season with caraway seeds or a touch of anise pepper.*

Asparagus Mousse

INGREDIENTS	TEST QUANTITY: 8	SERVICE QUANTITY: 50	METHOD
Asparagus, cooked, peeled, ½-in. slices	1 pt.	3 qt.	Divide into two equal amounts. Purée one batch, reserve the other.
Light cream	1 pt.	3 qt.	Add to half of purée; strain through sieve into bowl.
Eggs, lightly beaten	4	2 dozen	
Cheddar cheese, grated	¼ cup	1½ cups	
Nutmeg	½ tsp.	1 tbsp.	
Salt	to taste	to taste	
White pepper	to taste	to taste	
Tabasco	to taste	to taste	
Butter, melted	2 tbsp.	6 oz.	Add with reserved asparagus to mixture. Portion into lightly buttered half-cup ramekins. Place in hotel pan(s); add boiling water to one-half height of ramekins. Bake at 350°F until custards test for done, approximately 30 minutes. Serve immediately.

SPECIAL HANDLING FOR BUFFETS: *Serve very warm from shallow insert pan(s) set over dual heating units. Keep covered. This procedure can be applied to other vegetables and is especially good with squash. Season with a touch of ground red pepper or cayenne.*

Baked Acorn Squash

INGREDIENTS	TEST QUANTITY: 8	SERVICE QUANTITY: 50	METHOD
Acorn squash, small, halved, seeded	4	25	Trim and place in baking pan(s).
Brown sugar, light	$\frac{1}{2}$ cup	3 cups	Combine and distribute among the squash halves.
Orange rind, grated	1 tsp.	2 tbsp.	
Cinnamon, ground	1 tsp.	2 tbsp.	
Nutmeg, ground	$\frac{1}{2}$ tsp.	1 tbsp.	
Mace, ground	$\frac{1}{4}$ tsp.	$1\frac{1}{2}$ tsp.	
Cloves, ground	$\frac{1}{4}$ tsp.	$1\frac{1}{2}$ tsp.	
Salt	$\frac{1}{2}$ tsp.	1 tbsp.	
Black pepper	$\frac{1}{4}$ tsp.	$1\frac{1}{2}$ tsp.	
Butter, melted	$\frac{1}{2}$ cup	3 cups	
Maple syrup	$\frac{1}{2}$ cup	3 cups	Sprinkle over.
Honey	$\frac{1}{4}$ cup	$1\frac{1}{2}$ cups	
Bacon, sliced, chopped, browned	1 piece	$\frac{1}{4}$ lb.	Distribute among squash.
Sausage, lightly browned	1 cup	$1\frac{1}{2}$ qt.	
Water, boiling	as needed	as needed	Pour around to 1 in. deep. Bake at 350°F until squash is soft.

SPECIAL HANDLING FOR BUFFETS: *Serve very warm from shallow insert pan(s) set over dual heating units. Keep covered. Offer this as a brunch item, with browned sausage balls in each squash. Offer applesauce on the side.*

Braised Celery

INGREDIENTS	TEST QUANTITY: 8	SERVICE QUANTITY: 50	METHOD
Celery stalks, large, split, peeled, trimmed, halved	2 lb.	12 lb.	Season and place in buttered pan(s).
Shallots, minced	$\frac{1}{4}$ cup	$1\frac{1}{2}$ cups	
Salt	to taste	to taste	
Pepper	to taste	to taste	
Nutmeg, ground	to taste	to taste	
Chicken stock	2 cups	3 qt.	Pour over. Bring to a boil. Cover and transfer
White wine	$\frac{1}{2}$ cup	3 cups	to 350°F oven until tender. Drain off all
Bay leaf	1	3	liquid. Reduce by half. Remove bay leaf.
Butter, unsalted	$\frac{1}{4}$ cup	$1\frac{1}{2}$ cups	Swirl into simmering liquid.
Worcestershire sauce	1 tsp.	2 tbsp.	Combine and add. Place celery in service
Mustard, dry	$\frac{1}{2}$ tsp.	1 tbsp.	piece. Pour sauce over.
Almonds, toasted, chopped	1 tbsp.	$\frac{1}{3}$ cup	Sprinkle over before service.
Parsley, chopped	2 tbsp.	$\frac{3}{4}$ cup	

SPECIAL HANDLING FOR BUFFETS: *Serve very warm from shallow insert pan(s) set over dual heating units. Keep covered. Top with buttered crumbs from garlic or cheese bread.*

Braised Romaine

INGREDIENTS	TEST QUANTITY: 8	SERVICE QUANTITY: 50	METHOD
Romaine lettuce (small), halved	4	25	Trim as needed and wash carefully. Shake off excess water.
Water, boiling	as needed	as needed	Blanch lettuce for 2 minutes. Dry. Reserve.
White wine	$\frac{1}{2}$ cup	3 cups	
Bacon, chopped	$\frac{1}{2}$ lb.	3 lb.	Sauté until crisp. Drain off half the fat.
Garlic, minced	1 tsp.	2 tbsp.	Add to pan. Sauté until tender. Add lettuce.
Onion, minced	1 cup	2 lb.	
Celery, minced	$\frac{1}{2}$ cup	3 cups	
Tomatoes, peeled, seeded, chopped	$\frac{1}{2}$ cup	$1\frac{1}{2}$ lb.	
Parsley, chopped	1 tbsp.	$\frac{1}{3}$ cup	
Worcestershire sauce	$\frac{1}{2}$ tsp.	1 tbsp.	Season. Cover. Simmer slowly until lettuce is barely cooked.
Salt	to taste	to taste	
Black pepper	to taste	to taste	
Beef stock	as needed	as needed	Add if needed to prevent dryness. Spoon bacon, onion, and tomato over lettuce before service.

SPECIAL HANDLING FOR BUFFETS: *Serve very warm from shallow insert pan(s) set over dual heating units. Keep covered. Top with crumbled hard-cooked eggs and offer a small cruet of red wine vinegar for zest.*

Baked Cheese Gnocchi

INGREDIENTS	TEST QUANTITY: 8	SERVICE QUANTITY: 50	METHOD
Water	2 cups	3 qt.	Bring to boil.
Milk	1½ cups	2¼ qt.	
Salt	1 tsp.	2 tbsp.	
Nutmeg	¼ tsp.	1½ tsp.	
Cornmeal, yellow	1 cup	2 lb.	Stir in very gradually. Simmer until thick. Stir constantly. Remove from heat.
Butter, softened	¼ cup	1½ cups	Stir in. Pour a ¼-in. layer into sheet pan(s). Chill. Cut into 2-in. rounds. Place rounds on buttered sheet pan(s).
Parmesan cheese, grated	½ cup	3 cups	
Bacon, fried, crumbled	2 tbsp.	¾ cup	
Parsley, chopped	2 tbsp.	¾ cup	
Scallions (greens and whites), chopped	1 tbsp.	⅓ cup	
Eggs, beaten	3	1½ dozen	
Black pepper	½ tsp.	1 tbsp.	
Swiss cheese, grated	1½ cups	2¼ lb.	Place 1 tbsp. on each round.
Olive oil	¼ cup	1½ cups	Drizzle over top. Bake at 350°F until golden and crisp.

SPECIAL HANDLING FOR BUFFETS: *Serve very warm from shallow insert pan(s) set over dual heating units. Keep covered. Season the mixture with a touch of cinnamon; proceed.*

Brussels Sprouts Gratinée

INGREDIENTS	TEST QUANTITY: 8	SERVICE QUANTITY: 50	METHOD
Brussels sprouts, trimmed	2 lb.	12 lb.	Simmer until tender, about 10 minutes. Drain and reserve liquid. Refresh brussels sprouts in ice water; place in baking pan, base down.
Water, boiling	to cover	to cover	
Butter, melted	2 tbsp.	$\frac{3}{4}$ cup	Sauté for 3 minutes.
Scallions (greens and whites), chopped	$\frac{1}{2}$ cup	3 cups	
Garlic, minced	1 tsp.	2 tbsp.	
Flour, all purpose	1 tbsp.	6 tbsp.	Add and cook for 3 minutes.
Bacon, chopped	1 slice	$\frac{1}{4}$ lb.	Add and cook 3 minutes.
Smoked ham, chopped	1 tbsp.	$\frac{1}{3}$ cup	
Parsley, chopped	$\frac{1}{2}$ tbsp.	3 tbsp.	
Cooking water	$\frac{1}{2}$ cup	3 cups	Add; bring to boil. Stir until mixture is thick as cream. Pour over brussels sprouts.
White wine	$\frac{1}{2}$ cup	3 cups	
Salt	$\frac{1}{2}$ tsp.	1 tbsp.	
Nutmeg	$\frac{1}{8}$ tsp.	$\frac{3}{4}$ tsp.	
Black pepper	$\frac{1}{8}$ tsp.	$\frac{3}{4}$ tsp.	
Cheddar cheese, grated	$\frac{1}{2}$ cup	$\frac{3}{4}$ lb.	Sprinkle over.
Lemon rind, grated	1 tsp.	2 tbsp.	Sprinkle over. Bake at 325°F until golden brown.
Bread crumbs	$\frac{1}{4}$ cup	$1\frac{1}{2}$ cups	
Cayenne	$\frac{1}{4}$ tsp.	$1\frac{1}{2}$ tsp.	

SPECIAL HANDLING FOR BUFFETS: *Serve very warm from shallow insert pan(s) set over dual heating units. Keep covered. These could be served nicely in individual pastry cases or, if sliced thin, in a savory crêpe.*

Buttered Carrots with Orange

INGREDIENTS	TEST QUANTITY: 8	SERVICE QUANTITY: 50	METHOD
Carrots, peeled, sliced 2 × $\frac{1}{2}$ in.	2 lb.	12 lb.	Simmer until just tender. Drain.
Salt	to taste	to taste	
Black pepper	to taste	to taste	
Water, boiling	as needed	as needed	
Butter, melted	2 tbsp.	$\frac{3}{4}$ cup	Sauté with carrots until hot.
Ginger, grated	$\frac{1}{2}$ tsp.	1 tbsp.	
Orange juice, strained	$\frac{1}{4}$ cup	$1\frac{1}{2}$ cups	Add. Cook rapidly until carrots are almost dry.
Honey	1 tbsp.	$\frac{1}{3}$ cup	
Brown sugar, light	1 tsp.	2 tbsp.	
Cinnamon	$\frac{1}{8}$ tsp.	$\frac{3}{4}$ tsp.	
Salt	to taste	to taste	
White pepper	to taste	to taste	
Orange brandy	1 oz.	$\frac{3}{4}$ cup	Add. Deglaze. Flame.

SPECIAL HANDLING FOR BUFFETS: *Serve very warm from shallow insert pan(s) set over dual heating units. Keep covered. Serve with sliced roast beef or lamb, along with biscuits or popovers.*

Colcannon—St. Patrick's Potatoes

INGREDIENTS	TEST QUANTITY: 8	SERVICE QUANTITY: 50	METHOD
Cabbage, green, shredded	1 lb.	6 lb.	Boil for 10 minutes, uncovered. Drain. Remove bay leaf.
Bay leaf	1	3	
Water	to cover	to cover	
White wine	½ cup	3 cups	
Butter, melted	2 tbsp.	¾ cup	Sauté cabbage for 2 minutes. Cover and remove from heat. Reserve.
Russett potatoes, cooked, dried	2 lb.	12 lb.	Mash well.
Butter	2 tbsp.	¾ cup	
Mustard, dry	½ tsp.	1 tbsp.	
Milk, warm	1 cup	1½ qt.	Combine and add gradually. Purée should be thick.
Egg yolk	1	6	
Scallions (greens and whites), chopped	6	2 cups	Add to potatoes with cabbage; mix well. Adjust seasoning.
Ham, chopped	½ cup	3 cups	
Salt	1 tsp.	2 tbsp.	
Black pepper	½ tsp.	1½ tbsp.	
Parsley, chopped	2 tbsp.	¾ cup	

SPECIAL HANDLING FOR BUFFETS: *Serve very warm from shallow insert pan(s) set over dual heating units. Keep covered. This is ideal for St. Patrick's Day, with good beer and corned beef.*

Corn Pudding

INGREDIENTS	TEST QUANTITY: 8	SERVICE QUANTITY: 50	METHOD
Sugar	$\frac{1}{3}$ cup	2 cups	Combine in bowl.
Flour, all purpose	2 tbsp.	$\frac{3}{4}$ cup	
Salt	$\frac{1}{2}$ tsp.	1 tbsp.	
Baking powder	$\frac{1}{2}$ tsp.	1 tbsp.	
Paprika, hot	$\frac{1}{4}$ tsp.	$1\frac{1}{2}$ tsp.	
Eggs, well beaten	3	$1\frac{1}{2}$ dozen	Add gradually, one at a time.
Butter, melted	1 tbsp.	$\frac{1}{3}$ cup	Add.
Green pepper, minced	1 tbsp.	$\frac{1}{3}$ cup	
Red pepper, hot, crushed	to taste	to taste	
Almonds, slivered	$\frac{1}{2}$ cup	3 cups	
White corn, canned, drained	3 cups	9 lb.	Combine and add. Place in buttered pan(s) and bake at 350°F until done, about 45 minutes.
Light cream	1 cup	$1\frac{1}{2}$ qt.	
Cheddar cheese, grated	$\frac{1}{2}$ cup	3 cups	
Salt	to taste	to taste	
Black pepper	to taste	to taste	

SPECIAL HANDLING FOR BUFFETS: *Serve very warm from shallow insert pan(s) set over dual heating units. Keep covered. Top with crumbled, buttered cracker crumbs; season with pimiento or minced green pepper.*

Corn and Chili Dumplings

INGREDIENTS	TEST QUANTITY: 8	SERVICE QUANTITY: 50	METHOD
Water	2 cups	3 qt.	Combine. Bring to boil.
Salt	2 tsp.	$\frac{1}{4}$ cup	
Cornmeal, yellow	1 cup	2 lb.	Add slowly. Simmer until thick and smooth.
Green chilis, mild	$\frac{1}{2}$ cup	3 cups	Add to corn mixture. Reserve.
Jalopeño pepper, minced	to taste	to taste	
Monterrey Jack cheese, grated	$\frac{1}{2}$ cup	3 cups	
Bacon grease, strained	1 tbsp.	$\frac{1}{3}$ cup	Heat in sauté pan.
Olive oil	1 tbsp.	$\frac{1}{3}$ cup	
Onions, minced	2 tbsp.	$\frac{3}{4}$ cup	Add; sauté until soft. Add to the corn and
Celery, minced	1 tbsp.	$\frac{1}{3}$ cup	chili mixture. Combine well.
Green peppers, minced	2 tbsp.	$\frac{3}{4}$ cup	
Garlic, minced	1 tsp.	2 tbsp.	
Cumin, ground	$\frac{1}{2}$ tsp.	1 tbsp.	Combine and gradually add to mixture.
Flour, all purpose	1 cup	$1\frac{1}{2}$ lb.	
Salt	$\frac{1}{4}$ tsp.	$1\frac{1}{2}$ tsp.	
Black pepper	$\frac{1}{4}$ tsp.	$1\frac{1}{2}$ tsp.	
Cayenne	$\frac{1}{4}$ tsp.	$1\frac{1}{2}$ tsp.	
Baking powder	2 tsp.	$\frac{1}{4}$ cup	
Corn, drained	1 cup	3 lb.	Add; combine well.
Water, simmering	as needed	as needed	Spoon mixture into barely simmering water.
Salt	to taste	to taste	Cover and cook until done, about 10 minutes.

SPECIAL HANDLING FOR BUFFETS: *Serve very warm from shallow insert pan(s) set over dual heating units. Keep covered. Serve with chili (with or without meat) or beef stew.*

Creamed Corn with Grated Parmesan

INGREDIENTS	TEST QUANTITY: 8	SERVICE QUANTITY: 50	METHOD
Corn, whole kernel, frozen	2 lb.	12 lb.	Combine in saucepan and simmer for 5 minutes.
Banana peppers, diced	$\frac{1}{2}$ cup	3 cups	
Heavy cream	1 cup	$1\frac{1}{2}$ qt.	
Worcestershire sauce	$\frac{1}{4}$ tsp.	$1\frac{1}{2}$ tsp.	
Milk	1 cup	$1\frac{1}{2}$ qt.	
Brandy	1 tbsp.	$\frac{1}{3}$ cup	
Salt	1 tsp.	2 tbsp.	
MSG	$\frac{1}{4}$ tsp.	$1\frac{1}{2}$ tsp.	
White pepper	$\frac{1}{4}$ tsp.	$1\frac{1}{2}$ tsp.	
Tabasco	$\frac{1}{4}$ tsp.	$1\frac{1}{2}$ tsp.	
Butter, melted	2 tbsp.	$\frac{3}{4}$ cup	Combine and cook 5 minutes. Add to corn mixture. Stir to blend; remove from heat. Pour into service piece(s).
Flour, all purpose	2 tbsp.	$\frac{3}{4}$ cup	
Parmesan cheese, grated	$\frac{1}{2}$ cup	$\frac{3}{4}$ lb.	Sprinkle over the top. Place under broiler until golden.
Parsley, chopped	$\frac{1}{4}$ cup	$1\frac{1}{2}$ cups	

SPECIAL HANDLING FOR BUFFETS: *Serve very warm from shallow insert pan(s) set over dual heating units. Keep covered. Offer on a country buffet with griddle-fried steaks or roasted chicken.*

Creamed Spinach with Artichokes

INGREDIENTS	TEST QUANTITY: 8	SERVICE QUANTITY: 50	METHOD
Bacon, diced	$\frac{1}{2}$ cup	3 cups	Sauté until soft and bacon is browned.
Scallions, chopped	$\frac{2}{3}$ cup	1 qt.	
Garlic, minced	1 tsp.	2 tbsp.	
Spinach, cooked, squeezed	2 lb.	12 lb.	Chop spinach coarsely and add to scallions with egg whites.
Egg whites, chopped	$\frac{1}{2}$ cup	3 cups	
Yogurt, plain	2 cups	3 qt.	Combine. Add. Mix well. Pour into buttered pan(s).
Red wine vinegar	2 tbsp.	$\frac{3}{4}$ cup	
Button mushrooms, drained	$\frac{1}{2}$ cup	3 cups	
Parmesan cheese, grated	$\frac{1}{4}$ cup	$1\frac{1}{2}$ cups	
Almonds, slivered	$\frac{1}{4}$ cup	$1\frac{1}{2}$ cups	
Artichoke bottoms, chopped	1 cup	$1\frac{1}{2}$ qt.	
Water chestnuts, chopped	$\frac{1}{2}$ cup	3 cups	
Bread crumbs, fine, stale	$\frac{3}{4}$ cup	1 lb.	Combine. Sprinkle over top. Bake at 350°F for 30 minutes.
Bacon, sautéed, crumbled	$\frac{1}{4}$ cup	$1\frac{1}{2}$ cups	

SPECIAL HANDLING FOR BUFFETS: *Serve very warm from shallow insert pan(s) set over dual heating units. Keep covered. This would be appropriate on any Mediterranean buffet, especially if grilled swordfish or tuna is on the menu.*

Dutch Edam Potatoes

INGREDIENTS	TEST QUANTITY: 8	SERVICE QUANTITY: 50	METHOD
Potatoes, large, russet, sliced $\frac{1}{16}$ in. thick	3 lb.	18 lb.	Alternate in layers in hotel pan(s).
Butter	$\frac{1}{4}$ cup	$1\frac{1}{2}$ cups	
Edam cheese, grated	$\frac{1}{2}$ lb.	3 lb.	
Onion (large), minced	2	3 lb.	
Bacon, crumbled, sautéed	$\frac{1}{2}$ cup	3 cups	
Parsley, chopped	$\frac{1}{2}$ cup	3 cups	
Scallions (greens only), finely chopped	1 tbsp.	$\frac{1}{3}$ cup	
Salt	1 tsp.	2 tbsp.	
Black pepper	1 tsp.	2 tbsp.	
Fine herbes	1 tsp.	2 tbsp.	
Paprika	$\frac{1}{2}$ tsp.	1 tbsp.	
Cayenne	$\frac{1}{4}$ tsp.	$1\frac{1}{2}$ tsp.	
Sherry, dry	1 tbsp.	$\frac{1}{3}$ cup	Pour over mixture. Bake at 450°F for 10 minutes. Reduce to 350°F.
Light cream	$2\frac{1}{2}$ cups	$3\frac{3}{4}$ qt.	
Egg yolk	2	12	
Edam cheese, grated	$\frac{1}{4}$ cup	$1\frac{1}{2}$ cups	Sprinkle on. Continue baking until potatoes are tender.

SPECIAL HANDLING FOR BUFFETS: *Serve very warm from shallow insert pan(s) set over dual heating units. Keep covered. Add finely minced ham; proceed. Offer with veal or lamb dishes.*

German Mashed Potatoes with Pears

INGREDIENTS	TEST QUANTITY: 8	SERVICE QUANTITY: 50	METHOD
Pears, fresh, peeled, cored, sliced	1 lb.	6 lb.	Combine in sauce pan. Simmer until pears are tender. Drain. Reserve pears and poaching liquid.
White wine	½ cup	3 cups	
Brandy	¼ cup	1½ cups	
Water	½ cup	3 cups	
Vanilla extract	¼ tsp.	1½ tsp.	
Sugar	½ cup	3 cups	
Cinnamon, ground	1 tsp.	2 tbsp.	
Nutmeg, ground	¼ tsp.	1½ tsp.	
Cloves, ground	¼ tsp.	1½ tsp.	
Lemon rind, grated	½ tsp.	1 tbsp.	
Potatoes, cooked, mashed	1½ lb.	9 lb.	Combine. Adjust seasoning. Spoon half of mixture into shallow baking pan(s). Spoon pears over top.
Pecans, chopped	½ cup	3 cups	
Salt	1 tsp.	2 tbsp.	
White pepper	½ tsp.	1 tbsp.	
Mustard, dry	½ tsp.	1 tbsp.	
Pear liquid	2 tbsp.	¾ cup	Drizzle over. Cover with potatoes.
Bread crumbs, coarse, stale	2 cups	3 qt.	Toss to combine. Spread over top of potatoes. Bake at 350°F until golden and crunchy.
Butter, melted	¼ cup	1½ cups	

SPECIAL HANDLING FOR BUFFETS: *Serve very warm from shallow insert pan(s) set over dual heating units. Keep covered. Offer with sautéed or braised pork chops with red cabbage.*

German Potato Dumplings (Kartoffelklosse)

INGREDIENTS	TEST QUANTITY: 8	SERVICE QUANTITY: 50	METHOD
Potatoes (medium), cooked, riced	2 lb.	12 lb.	Combine. Beat until fluffy. Roll into small balls. Reserve.
Muenster cheese, grated	$\frac{1}{3}$ cup	2 cups	
Eggs, beaten	2	1 dozen	
Flour, all purpose	$\frac{1}{2}$ cup	3 cups	
Onion, grated	$\frac{1}{2}$ cup	3 cups	
Celery, minced	$\frac{1}{4}$ cup	$1\frac{1}{2}$ cups	
Parsley, chopped	1 tbsp.	$\frac{1}{3}$ cup	
Almond extract	1 drop	$\frac{1}{4}$ tsp.	
Nutmeg	$\frac{1}{4}$ tsp.	$1\frac{1}{2}$ tsp.	
Salt	1 tsp.	2 tbsp.	
Black pepper	$\frac{1}{2}$ tsp.	1 tbsp.	
Mustard, dry	$\frac{1}{4}$ tsp.	$1\frac{1}{2}$ tsp.	
Chicken stock	as needed	as needed	Bring to a boil and cook dumplings at low simmer until they float.

SPECIAL HANDLING FOR BUFFETS: *Serve very warm from shallow insert pan(s) set over dual heating units. Keep covered. Serve with roasted or braised beef or game.*

Gingered Green Beans

INGREDIENTS	TEST QUANTITY: 8	SERVICE QUANTITY: 50	METHOD
Peanut oil, hot	3 tbsp.	1 cup	Stir-fry. Do not brown. Remove garlic and ginger. Reserve oil.
Garlic, mashed	2 large cloves	2 tbsp.	
Ginger, fresh, peeled	3 thin slices	$\frac{1}{3}$ cup	
Green beans, trimmed, halved	2 lb.	12 lb.	Add to hot oil. Stir and toss until well colored and sugar has dissolved.
Scallions (greens and whites), chopped	$\frac{1}{2}$ cup	3 cups	
Sugar	1 tbsp.	$\frac{1}{3}$ cup	
Salt	to taste	to taste	Add. Turn heat to low; cover wok or pan; cook over medium heat until beans are just tender.
Chicken broth	$\frac{1}{3}$ cup	2 cups	
Sherry, dry	1 tsp.	2 tbsp.	
Tomatoes, chopped	$\frac{1}{2}$ cup	3 cups	
Almonds, slivered	$\frac{1}{4}$ cup	$1\frac{1}{2}$ cups	
Sesame oil, Oriental	1 tbsp.	$\frac{1}{3}$ cup	Pour over beans; toss well.

SPECIAL HANDLING FOR BUFFETS: *Serve very warm from shallow insert pan(s) set over dual heating units. Keep covered. These would be well served with many Chinese dishes or as part of an Indonesian Rijsttafel buffet. They can also be served at room temperature, or even chilled.*

Grated Buttered Carrots

INGREDIENTS	TEST QUANTITY: 8	SERVICE QUANTITY: 50	METHOD
Carrots, peeled, grated	2 lb.	12 lb.	Combine and toss. Place in pot and cover.
Raisins	$\frac{1}{2}$ cup	3 cups	Simmer until tender.
Peanut oil	1 tbsp.	$\frac{1}{3}$ cup	
Scallions (greens and whites), minced	1 tbsp.	$\frac{1}{3}$ cup	
Garlic, chopped	$\frac{1}{4}$ tsp.	$1\frac{1}{2}$ tsp.	
Honey	2 tbsp.	$\frac{3}{4}$ cup	
Salt	$\frac{1}{2}$ tsp.	1 tbsp.	
Pepper	$\frac{1}{8}$ tsp.	$\frac{3}{4}$ tsp.	
Water	1 tbsp.	$\frac{1}{3}$ cup	
Sherry, dry	1 tbsp.	$\frac{1}{3}$ cup	
Butter	4 tbsp.	$\frac{3}{4}$ lb.	Add; toss until melted.
Brown sugar	1 tbsp.	$\frac{1}{3}$ cup	

SPECIAL HANDLING FOR BUFFETS: *Serve very warm from shallow insert pan(s) set over dual heating units. Keep covered. A real quickie, these can save the day when a speedy buffet replacement dish is needed. Sprinkle with a little chopped ginger for some added zest.*

Green Beans with Red Sauce

INGREDIENTS	TEST QUANTITY: 8	SERVICE QUANTITY: 50	METHOD
Bacon grease, hot	1 tbsp.	$\frac{1}{3}$ cup	Sauté until soft.
Olive oil, hot	1 tbsp.	$\frac{1}{3}$ cup	
Onion, minced	$\frac{1}{3}$ cup	2 cups	
Garlic, minced	1 tsp.	2 tbsp.	
Scallions (greens only), minced	$\frac{1}{3}$ cup	2 cups	
Italian tomatoes, canned, drained, chopped	2 cups	3 qt.	Add. Simmer 5 minutes.
Sugar	1 tbsp.	$\frac{1}{3}$ cup	
Almonds, blanched, sliced	1 tbsp.	$\frac{1}{3}$ cup	Add. Simmer 5 minutes.
Cilantro (or parsley)	2 tsp.	$\frac{1}{4}$ cup	
Cumin, ground	$\frac{1}{4}$ tsp.	$1\frac{1}{2}$ tsp.	
Thyme, dried	$\frac{1}{4}$ tsp.	$1\frac{1}{2}$ tsp.	
Oregano, crushed	$\frac{1}{4}$ tsp.	$1\frac{1}{2}$ tsp.	
Basil, dried	$\frac{1}{4}$ tsp.	$1\frac{1}{2}$ tsp.	
Red pepper, crushed	$\frac{1}{2}$ tsp.	1 tbsp.	
Lemon rind, grated	$\frac{1}{4}$ tsp.	$1\frac{1}{2}$ tsp.	
Salt	to taste	to taste	
Black pepper	to taste	to taste	
Green beans, cooked, trimmed	2 lb.	12 lb.	Place in service piece(s). Pour sauce in straight line down middle of beans.

SPECIAL HANDLING FOR BUFFETS: *Serve very warm from shallow insert pan(s) set over dual heating units. Keep covered. A true holiday dish, this presents the traditional Christmas colors in a unique way. Offer with other holiday fare.*

Green Beans with Scallions and Bacon

INGREDIENTS	TEST QUANTITY: 8	SERVICE QUANTITY: 50	METHOD
Bacon, chopped	1 cup	3 lb.	Sauté until crisp. Strain off and reserve bacon, leaving drippings in the pan.
Scallions (greens and whites), chopped	1½ cups	3 lb.	Add to pan. Sauté until just soft.
Green pepper, minced	1 tbsp.	⅓ cup	
Red onions, minced	¼ cup	1½ cups	
Garlic, minced	1 tsp.	2 tbsp.	
Green beans, trimmed	2 lb.	12 lb.	Add to pan. Cover. Cook just until beans are bright green.
Sugar	1 tbsp.	⅓ cup	
White wine	1 oz.	¾ cup	
Red wine vinegar	1 tbsp.	⅓ cup	
Red pepper, crushed	½ tsp.	1 tbsp.	Add with reserved bacon. Simmer until beans are done. Toss well before service.
Salt	to taste	to taste	
Pepper	to taste	to taste	

SPECIAL HANDLING FOR BUFFETS: *Serve very warm from shallow insert pan(s) set over dual heating units. Keep covered. Season with dried marjoram and serve with German or Swiss dishes.*

Green Rice

INGREDIENTS	TEST QUANTITY: 8	SERVICE QUANTITY: 50	METHOD
Rice, raw	1 cup	3 lb.	Combine well; place in baking pan(s) and bake at 350°F until liquid is absorbed. Toss with a fork to combine.
Green pepper, minced	$\frac{1}{3}$ cup	2 cups	
Cilantro, chopped	1 tbsp.	$\frac{1}{3}$ cup	
Parsley, chopped	$\frac{1}{4}$ cup	$1\frac{1}{2}$ cups	
Scallions (greens and whites), minced	$\frac{1}{2}$ cup	3 cups	
Bacon grease, melted	2 tbsp.	$\frac{3}{4}$ cup	
Peanut oil	2 tbsp.	$\frac{3}{4}$ cup	
White wine	$\frac{1}{4}$ cup	$1\frac{1}{2}$ cups	
Worcestershire sauce	1 tbsp.	$\frac{1}{3}$ cup	
Salt	$\frac{1}{2}$ tsp.	1 tbsp.	
Black pepper	$\frac{1}{4}$ tsp.	$1\frac{1}{2}$ tsp.	
Tabasco	to taste	$\frac{3}{4}$ tsp.	
Chicken stock	2 cups	3 qt.	

SPECIAL HANDLING FOR BUFFETS: *Serve very warm from shallow insert pan(s) set over dual heating units. Keep covered. This is a Cajun classic, so it will do well with seafood, game, or chicken.*

Harvest Vegetable Medley

INGREDIENTS	TEST QUANTITY: 8	SERVICE QUANTITY: 50	METHOD
Zucchini, $\frac{1}{2}$-in. slices	1 lb.	6 lb.	Combine in appropriate hotel pan(s). Mix together well.
Rutabaga, peeled, diced	$\frac{1}{2}$ lb.	3 lb.	
Carrots, julienned	$\frac{1}{2}$ lb.	3 lb.	
Onion, diced	$\frac{1}{2}$ lb.	3 lb.	
Chicken stock	$1\frac{1}{2}$ cups	$2\frac{1}{4}$ qt.	
Orange juice concentrate, thawed, undiluted	$\frac{3}{4}$ cup	$4\frac{1}{2}$ cups	
Salt	1 tsp.	2 tbsp.	
Nutmeg, ground	$\frac{1}{2}$ tsp.	1 tbsp.	
Butter, clarified	$\frac{1}{3}$ cup	2 cups	Combine in bowl. Toss to combine. Sprinkle over vegetables. Bake at 350°F until vegetables are tender.
Bread crumbs, soft, whole wheat	3 cups	2 lb.	
Nutmeats, chopped	1 cup	6 cups	

SPECIAL HANDLING FOR BUFFETS: *Serve very warm from shallow insert pan(s) set over dual heating units. Keep covered. Add segments of citrus fruits or sautéed apples. Season with ginger to taste.*

Indonesian Eggplant "Rafts"

INGREDIENTS	TEST QUANTITY: 8	SERVICE QUANTITY: 50	METHOD
Water	$\frac{1}{2}$ cup	3 cups	Combine and purée to a paste.
White wine	$\frac{1}{2}$ cup	3 cups	
Onion, chopped	1 cup	2 lb.	
Celery, chopped	$\frac{1}{2}$ cup	3 cups	
Garlic, chopped	1 tbsp.	$\frac{1}{3}$ cup	
Ham, chopped	$\frac{1}{2}$ cup	3 cups	
Tomato, peeled, seeded, chopped	1 cup	3 lb.	
Peanuts, unsalted	$\frac{1}{2}$ cup	3 cups	
Sugar	1 tbsp.	$\frac{1}{3}$ cup	
Coconut, grated	1 tbsp.	$\frac{1}{3}$ cup	
Red pepper, crushed	2 tsp.	$\frac{1}{4}$ cup	
Salt	1 tsp.	2 tbsp.	
Black pepper	$\frac{1}{2}$ tsp.	1 tbsp.	
Parsley, chopped	1 tbsp.	$\frac{1}{3}$ cup	
Cilantro, chopped	1 tbsp.	$\frac{1}{3}$ cup	
Lime rind, grated	1 tsp.	2 tbsp.	
Olive oil	2 tbsp.	$\frac{3}{4}$ cup	Combine and heat. Add and simmer purée until mixture is thickened and dry.
Peanut oil	2 tbsp.	$\frac{3}{4}$ cup	
Eggplant, small, quartered	2	12	Wrap in foil. Bake at 400°F until tender. Unwrap and place on service piece. Portion warmed purée over each section.

SPECIAL HANDLING FOR BUFFETS: *Serve very warm from shallow insert pan(s) set over dual heating units. Keep covered. Another rijsttafel offering, they could also be served in a Mediterranean setting. Offer with boiled pasta and grilled chicken.*

Italian Bacon Dumplings

INGREDIENTS	TEST QUANTITY: 8	SERVICE QUANTITY: 50	METHOD
Bread, trimmed	4 slices	$1\frac{1}{2}$ lb.	Combine until totally absorbed.
Bacon fat, melted	6 tbsp.	$2\frac{1}{2}$ cups	
Flour, all purpose	$1\frac{1}{2}$ cups	9 cups	Combine. Add to bread mixture. Let rest for
Milk	1 cup	$1\frac{1}{2}$ qt.	30 minutes. Stir. Shape in walnut-sized
Parmesan cheese, grated	$\frac{1}{4}$ cup	$1\frac{1}{2}$ cups	dumplings.
Egg yolks, beaten	2	12	
Scallions (greens and whites), chopped	2 tbsp.	$\frac{3}{4}$ cup	
Bacon, sautéed, crumbled	1 tbsp.	$\frac{1}{3}$ cup	
Garlic, minced	1 tsp.	2 tbsp.	
Basil	$\frac{1}{2}$ tsp.	1 tbsp.	
Oregano	$\frac{1}{2}$ tsp.	1 tbsp.	
Parsley, chopped	$\frac{1}{2}$ tbsp.	3 tbsp.	
Tomato, drained, chopped	2 tbsp.	$\frac{3}{4}$ cup	
Salt	to taste	to taste	
Black pepper	to taste	to taste	
Chicken stock, simmering	1 qt.	as needed	Add dumplings. Simmer gently for a few
White wine	$\frac{1}{2}$ cup	3 cups	minutes, then cover until cooked, about 10 minutes.

SPECIAL HANDLING FOR BUFFETS: *Serve very warm from shallow insert pan(s) set over dual heating units. Keep covered. Offer these as an accompaniment to clear chicken soup or as a side dish on an Italian buffet.*

Mexican-Style Red Beans

INGREDIENTS	TEST QUANTITY: 8	SERVICE QUANTITY: 50	METHOD
Kidney beans, red, dried, rinsed	1 lb.	6 lb.	Combine. Bring to boil. Cover. Simmer over low heat until most liquid is evaporated.
Water, cold	1 qt.	1½ gal.	
Beer	1 cup	1½ qt.	
Onion, sliced	1	2 lb.	
Celery, chopped	½ cup	3 cups	
Bay leaf	1	4	
Cumin, ground	½ tsp.	1 tbsp.	
Oregano	1 tsp.	2 tbsp.	
Basil	½ tsp.	1 tbsp.	
Olive oil	2 tbsp.	¾ cup	
Ham hock	1	6	
Water, boiling	1 qt.	1½ gal.	Add. Cover. Simmer 1 hour. Remove bay leaf and ham hock. Dice meat and return to pot.
Salt	1 tbsp.	⅓ cup	Add. Cook until beans are very soft.
Black pepper	½ tsp.	1 tbsp.	
Olive oil, hot	2 tbsp.	¾ cup	Sauté until soft.
Onion, minced	¾ cup	2 lb.	
Celery, minced	¼ cup	1½ cups	
Green pepper, minced	¼ cup	1½ cups	
Garlic, minced	1 tsp.	1 tbsp.	
Tomato, peeled, seeded, chopped	1 cup	3 lb.	Combine with sautéed vegetables. Stir into beans. Simmer for 30 minutes.
Red onion, minced	¼ cup	1½ cups	
Jalapeño pepper, seeded, chopped	1 tbsp.	⅓ cup	
Scallions (greens and whites), chopped	½ cup	3 cups	
Lime juice, strained	¼ cup	1½ cups	
Salt	to taste	to taste	
Black pepper	to taste	to taste	
Cinnamon, ground	½ tsp.	1 tbsp.	
Cloves, ground	¼ tsp.	1½ tsp.	
Oregano, ground	¼ tsp.	1½ tsp.	

SPECIAL HANDLING FOR BUFFETS: *Serve very warm from shallow insert pan(s) set over dual heating units. Keep covered. Offer with buttered corn bread and braised lamb.*

Mexican-Style Rice

INGREDIENTS	TEST QUANTITY: 8	SERVICE QUANTITY: 50	METHOD
Peanut oil, hot	2 tbsp.	$\frac{3}{4}$ cup	Sauté until golden.
Rice, long grain, washed, dried	1 cup	3 lb.	
Tomatoes, peeled, seeded, chopped	1	2 lb.	Purée and add. Simmer until all moisture is evaporated.
Onion, minced	$\frac{1}{2}$ cup	3 cups	
Celery, minced	$\frac{1}{4}$ cup	$1\frac{1}{2}$ cups	
Garlic, minced	$\frac{1}{2}$ tsp.	1 tbsp.	
Pine nuts, toasted	$\frac{1}{4}$ cup	$1\frac{1}{2}$ cups	
Chicken stock, simmering	$1\frac{1}{2}$ cups	$2\frac{1}{2}$ qt.	Add. Bring to boil. Cover. Reduce heat. Bake at 350°F until rice is dry and fluffy. Toss with fork. Remove bay leaf.
Carrots, thinly sliced	$\frac{1}{2}$ cup	3 cups	
Oregano, dried	$\frac{1}{2}$ tsp.	1 tbsp.	
Peas, fresh	$\frac{1}{2}$ cup	3 cups	
Pimientos, minced	$\frac{1}{2}$ cup	3 cups	
Bay leaf	1	3	
Parsley, chopped	2 tsp.	$\frac{1}{4}$ cup	Sprinkle over before service.

SPECIAL HANDLING FOR BUFFETS: *Serve very warm from shallow insert pan(s) set over dual heating units. Keep covered. A good dish to have on hand when South of the* *Border fare is called for. Spark it up a bit with your favorite fresh or dried peppers.*

New Mexico Spiced Rice

INGREDIENTS	TEST QUANTITY: 8	SERVICE QUANTITY: 50	METHOD
Bacon grease, melted	2 tbsp.	$\frac{3}{4}$ cup	Sauté until soft.
Onion, minced	$\frac{3}{4}$ cup	$1\frac{1}{2}$ lb.	
Celery, minced	$\frac{1}{4}$ cup	$1\frac{1}{2}$ cups	
Garlic, minced	$\frac{1}{2}$ tsp.	1 tbsp.	
Red pepper, minced	$\frac{1}{4}$ cup	$1\frac{1}{2}$ cups	
Ginger, ground	$\frac{1}{4}$ tsp.	$1\frac{1}{2}$ tsp.	Add. Stir to combine.
Cinnamon, ground	$\frac{1}{8}$ tsp.	$\frac{3}{4}$ tsp.	
Coriander, ground	$\frac{1}{8}$ tsp.	$\frac{3}{4}$ tsp.	
Black pepper	$\frac{1}{8}$ tsp.	$\frac{3}{4}$ tsp.	
Salt	to taste	to taste	
Rice, long grain, raw	1 cup	3 lb.	Add. Sauté until golden.
Tomatoes, peeled, seeded, puréed	1 cup	3 lb.	Add. Cover and simmer until rice is cooked.
Parsley, chopped	$\frac{1}{4}$ cup	$1\frac{1}{2}$ cups	
Water, boiling	$1\frac{1}{4}$ cups	2 qt.	

SPECIAL HANDLING FOR BUFFETS: *Serve very warm from shallow insert pan(s) set over dual heating units. Keep covered. Offer with chili and blue cornmeal tortillas.*

Polynesian Sweet Potatoes

INGREDIENTS	TEST QUANTITY: 8	SERVICE QUANTITY: 50	METHOD
Sweet potatoes, cooked, peeled, mashed	2 lb.	12 lb.	Combine in bowl. Beat well.
Orange brandy	2 tbsp.	$\frac{3}{4}$ cup	
Lemon juice, strained	2 tbsp.	$\frac{3}{4}$ cup	
Orange juice, strained	1 tbsp.	$\frac{1}{3}$ cup	
Pineapple, canned, crushed, drained	$\frac{1}{2}$ cup	3 cups	
Coconut, grated	$\frac{1}{4}$ cup	$1\frac{1}{2}$ cups	
Almonds, slivered, toasted	$\frac{1}{2}$ cup	3 cups	
Salt	1 tsp.	2 tbsp.	
Cinnamon, ground	$\frac{1}{4}$ tsp.	$1\frac{1}{2}$ tsp.	
Ginger, ground	$\frac{1}{4}$ tsp.	$1\frac{1}{2}$ tsp.	
Butter, soft	$\frac{1}{4}$ lb.	$1\frac{1}{2}$ lb.	Beat in well.
Egg yolks, beaten	2	12	Add; beat well. Pour into buttered 2-qt. pan(s).
Coconut, grated	1 tbsp.	$\frac{1}{3}$ cup	Sprinkle on top. Bake at 325°F until done.

SPECIAL HANDLING FOR BUFFETS: *Serve very warm from shallow insert pan(s) set over dual heating units. Keep covered. Portions remaining after service can be formed into patties and chilled; dust with flour and sauté in hot butter for second service use.*

Potato-Almond Croquettes

INGREDIENTS	TEST QUANTITY: 8	SERVICE QUANTITY: 50	METHOD
Baking potatoes, peeled, diced, cooked, dry, hot	2 lb.	12 lb.	Combine slowly, beating well with each egg yolk addition. Place in pot on low heat.
Egg yolks	3	$1\frac{1}{2}$ dozen	
Salt	$\frac{1}{2}$ tsp.	1 tbsp.	
Black pepper	$\frac{1}{4}$ tsp.	$1\frac{1}{2}$ tsp.	
Butter, melted	$\frac{1}{4}$ cup	$1\frac{1}{2}$ cups	Add. Stir to combine. Remove from heat. Cool. Form into tube(s) and cut into 1-in. sections.
Mustard, dry	$\frac{1}{8}$ tsp.	$\frac{3}{4}$ tsp.	
Nutmeg	$\frac{1}{8}$ tsp.	$\frac{3}{4}$ tsp.	
Almonds, ground	1 tbsp.	$\frac{1}{3}$ cup	
Almond extract	4 drops	$\frac{1}{2}$ tsp.	
Parsley, chopped	1 tbsp.	$\frac{1}{3}$ cup	
Flour, all purpose	as needed	as needed	Dredge each piece lightly.
Eggs, beaten	1	6	Dip in each piece.
Peanut oil	$\frac{1}{4}$ cup	$1\frac{1}{2}$ cups	
Bread crumbs, dry, crumbled	2 cups	3 lb.	Dredge each piece and shake off excess. Fry in 375°F oil until hot and golden.
Almonds, crushed	$\frac{1}{2}$ cup	3 cups	
Parsley, chopped	$\frac{1}{4}$ cup	$1\frac{1}{2}$ cups	

SPECIAL HANDLING FOR BUFFETS: *Serve very warm from shallow insert pan(s) set over dual heating units. Keep covered. A French classic, these are wonderful with sliced lamb.*

Potato and Onion Gratin

INGREDIENTS	TEST QUANTITY: 8	SERVICE QUANTITY: 50	METHOD
Olive oil, hot	$\frac{1}{4}$ cup	$1\frac{1}{2}$ cups	Sauté over very low heat, covered, until soft, but crunchy, about 10 minutes. Remove from heat.
Bacon grease, strained	2 tbsp.	$\frac{3}{4}$ cup	
Red onions (medium), sliced	1 lb.	6 lb.	
Garlic, minced	1 tsp.	2 tbsp.	
Thyme, fresh	3 sprigs	$\frac{1}{4}$ cup	
Scallions (greens only), chopped	2 tbsp.	$\frac{3}{4}$ cup	
Red potatoes, peeled, sliced, rinsed several times	2 lb.	12 lb.	Arrange along the bottom of well-buttered pan(s). Season. Sprinkle with a layer of onions. Repeat and end with layer of potatoes.
Salt	to taste	to taste	
Black pepper	to taste	to taste	
Butter, unsalted, soft	2 tbsp.	$\frac{3}{4}$ cup	Spread on top. Bake at 425°F until nicely browned.
Bread crumbs, soft	1 cup	$1\frac{1}{2}$ qt.	

SPECIAL HANDLING FOR BUFFETS: *Serve very warm from shallow insert pan(s) set over dual heating units. Keep covered. Serve with grilled quail or other poultry.*

Potato-Cheese Croquettes

INGREDIENTS	TEST QUANTITY: 8	SERVICE QUANTITY: 50	METHOD
Baking potatoes, peeled, cooked, dried, riced	2 lb.	12 lb.	Combine in bowl(s).
Butter, soft	$\frac{1}{2}$ cup	3 cups	
Almond paste	1 tbsp.	$\frac{1}{3}$ cup	
Parmesan cheese, grated	$1\frac{1}{2}$ cup	$1\frac{1}{2}$ lb.	
Egg yolks, beaten	2	12	
Scallions (greens and whites), chopped	$\frac{1}{4}$ cup	$1\frac{1}{2}$ cups	
Parsley, chopped	$\frac{1}{2}$ cup	3 cups	
Salt	1 tsp.	2 tbsp.	
White pepper	$\frac{1}{2}$ tsp.	1 tbsp.	
Cayenne	$\frac{1}{4}$ tsp.	$1\frac{1}{2}$ tsp.	
Olive oil, hot	$\frac{1}{4}$ cup	$1\frac{1}{2}$ cups	Sauté until soft. Add to potato mixture. Cool.
Onion, minced	2 cup	6 lb.	Form into log shapes, about 2 in. long.
Green pepper, minced	$\frac{1}{2}$ cup	3 cups	
Celery, minced	$\frac{1}{2}$ cup	3 cups	
Flour, all purpose	as needed	as needed	Dredge the cylinders. Shake off the excess.
Egg, beaten	2	12	Dip cylinders in this mixture.
Water	1 cup	$1\frac{1}{2}$ qt.	
Oil	$\frac{1}{4}$ cup	$1\frac{1}{2}$ cups	
Bread crumbs, fine, fresh	1 lb.	6 lb.	Roll cylinders to coat.
Parsley, chopped	$\frac{1}{4}$ cup	$1\frac{1}{2}$ cups	
Vegetable oil, hot	as needed	as needed	Deep fry in 375°F oil until golden on all sides.

SPECIAL HANDLING FOR BUFFETS: *Serve very warm from shallow insert pan(s) set over dual heating units. Keep covered. Add some chopped fried bacon to the mixture; proceed.*

Potato Dumplings

INGREDIENTS	TEST QUANTITY: 8	SERVICE QUANTITY: 50	METHOD
Potato, peeled, raw, grated	1 lb.	6 lb.	Combine into small balls.
Onion, minced	1 cup	3 lb.	
Scallions (greens and whites), chopped	$\frac{1}{2}$ cup	3 cups	
Bacon, fried, crumbled, drained	$\frac{1}{2}$ lb.	3 lb.	
Croutons, fresh, fine	1 cup	6 cups	
Eggs, beaten	6	3 dozen	
Parsley, chopped	2 tsp.	$\frac{1}{4}$ cup	
Flour, all purpose	2 cups	3 lb.	
Mustard, dry	$\frac{1}{2}$ tsp.	1 tbsp.	
Salt	1 tsp.	2 tbsp.	
Black pepper	$\frac{1}{4}$ tsp.	$1\frac{1}{2}$ tsp.	
Thyme	$\frac{1}{4}$ tsp.	$1\frac{1}{2}$ tsp.	
Nutmeg	$\frac{1}{4}$ tsp.	$1\frac{1}{2}$ tsp.	
Cinnamon	$\frac{1}{8}$ tsp.	$\frac{3}{4}$ tsp.	
Water, boiling	as needed	as needed	Drop dumplings into water and cook until done, about 30 minutes. Remove with slotted spoon and drain.
Salt	to taste	to taste	

SPECIAL HANDLING FOR BUFFETS: *Serve very warm from shallow insert pan(s) set over dual heating units. Keep covered. Serve with German and Swiss dishes, especially veal and sausage.*

Potato Fritters with Chives and Mustard

INGREDIENTS	TEST QUANTITY: 8	SERVICE QUANTITY: 50	METHOD
Potatoes, peeled, cooked, riced, diced, cooled	2 lb.	12 lb.	Combine well. Chill for 1 hour. Form mixture into small balls.
Sour cream	$\frac{1}{3}$ cup	2 cups	
Parsley, chopped	2 tbsp.	$\frac{3}{4}$ cup	
Garlic, minced	$\frac{1}{2}$ tsp.	1 tbsp.	
Eggs, beaten	1	6	
Chive, minced	1 tbsp.	$\frac{1}{3}$ cup	
Bacon grease, strained	$1\frac{1}{2}$ tbsp.	$\frac{1}{2}$ cup + 1 tbsp.	
Dry mustard	$\frac{1}{2}$ tsp.	1 tbsp.	
Thyme, ground	$\frac{1}{4}$ tsp.	$1\frac{1}{2}$ tsp.	
Salt	to taste	to taste	
Black pepper	to taste	to taste	
Cayenne	to taste	to taste	
Flour, all purpose	as needed	as needed	Dredge balls in flour.
Vegetable oil, hot	as needed	as needed	Shake off excess. Deep fry in 375°F oil until golden, about 1 minute. Transfer to hot oven to warm completely.

SPECIAL HANDLING FOR BUFFETS: *Serve very warm from shallow insert pan(s) set over dual heating units. Keep covered. Offer with prime rib or other beef cut. Add a touch of horseradish to the mixture.*

Potato Kugel

INGREDIENTS	TEST QUANTITY: 8	SERVICE QUANTITY: 50	METHOD
Potatoes, raw, grated, squeezed	2 lb.	12 lb.	Combine. Toss well.
Onion, grated	$\frac{1}{2}$ lb.	3 lb.	
Carrot, grated	$\frac{1}{2}$ lb.	3 lb.	
Parsley, chopped	$\frac{1}{4}$ cup	$1\frac{1}{2}$ cups	
Flour, all purpose	1 cup	$1\frac{1}{2}$ lb.	
Almonds, ground	1 tbsp.	$\frac{1}{3}$ cup	
Eggs, beaten	4	2 dozen	
Raisins	$\frac{1}{2}$ cup	3 cups	
Salt	$1\frac{1}{2}$ tsp.	3 tbsp.	
Cinnamon	$\frac{1}{4}$ tsp.	$1\frac{1}{2}$ tsp.	
Nutmeg	$\frac{1}{4}$ tsp.	$1\frac{1}{2}$ tsp.	
Black pepper	$\frac{1}{2}$ tsp.	1 tbsp.	
Cayenne	$\frac{1}{4}$ tsp.	$1\frac{1}{2}$ tsp.	
Chicken fat, rendered	$\frac{1}{3}$ cup	2 cups	Heat. Add potato mixture. Sauté for 1 minute. Place in 375°F oven until kugel is golden.

SPECIAL HANDLING FOR BUFFETS: *Serve very warm from shallow insert pan(s) set over dual heating units. Keep covered. A variation of this dish is made with noodles.*

Potatoes Brabant, Commander's Palace

INGREDIENTS	TEST QUANTITY: 8	SERVICE QUANTITY: 50	METHOD
Potatoes, peeled, ½-in. dice	2 lb.	12 lb.	Deep fry in batches until golden. Drain well.
Vegetable oil, heated (360°F)	as needed	as needed	
Butter, heated	2 tbsp.	¾ cup	Sauté until onion and garlic soften. Add potatoes; toss.
Pimiento, diced	2 tbsp.	¾ cup	
Red onion, minced	1 tbsp.	⅓ cup	
Garlic, crushed and chopped	1 tbsp.	⅓ cup	
Parsley, chopped	1 tbsp.	⅓ cup	
Salt	to taste	to taste	Add; adjust seasoning. Toss until potatoes are warmed.
Black pepper	to taste	to taste	

SPECIAL HANDLING FOR BUFFETS: *Serve very warm from shallow insert pan(s) set over dual heating units. Keep covered. Excellent on the brunch menu with poached eggs and country ham. Commander's Palace has been a landmark New Orleans restaurant for years.*

Red Beets with Butter and Chives

INGREDIENTS	TEST QUANTITY: 8	SERVICE QUANTITY: 50	METHOD
Butter, melted	$\frac{1}{3}$ cup	2 cups	Sauté until soft.
Onion, minced	2 tbsp.	$\frac{3}{4}$ cup	
Garlic, minced	$\frac{1}{2}$ tsp.	1 tbsp.	
Celery, minced	1 tbsp.	$\frac{1}{3}$ cup	
Chives, minced	1 tbsp.	$\frac{1}{3}$ cup	Add. Stir in.
Parsley, chopped	1 tbsp.	$\frac{1}{3}$ cup	
Thyme, dried	$\frac{1}{4}$ tsp.	$1\frac{1}{2}$ tsp.	
Flour, all purpose	2 tsp.	$\frac{1}{4}$ cup	Add. Simmer for 3 minutes.
Beets, cooked, sliced	2 lb.	12 lb.	Add. Simmer until flavor is well adjusted.
Cider vinegar	2 tbsp.	$\frac{3}{4}$ cup	
Cognac	1 tbsp.	$\frac{1}{3}$ cup	
Salt	to taste	to taste	
Black pepper	to taste	to taste	
Caraway	to taste	to taste	

SPECIAL HANDLING FOR BUFFETS: *Serve very warm from shallow insert pan(s) set over dual heating units. Keep covered. Offer with other favorites on a smörgåsbord.*

Red Cabbage and Chestnuts with Wine

INGREDIENTS	TEST QUANTITY: 8	SERVICE QUANTITY: 50	METHOD
Bacon, sliced	$\frac{1}{4}$ lb.	$1\frac{1}{2}$ lb.	Blanch 10 minutes. Drain. Reserve bacon.
Water	to cover	to cover	
Butter, melted	3 tbsp.	1 cup	Cook slowly, covered, 10 minutes.
Carrots, thinly sliced	$\frac{1}{2}$ cup	3 cups	
Onions, sliced	1 cup	2 lb.	
Celery, sliced	$\frac{1}{2}$ cup	3 cups	
Salt	$\frac{1}{2}$ tsp.	1 tbsp.	
Black pepper	$\frac{1}{4}$ tsp.	$1\frac{1}{2}$ tsp.	
Red cabbage, cored, shredded	$1\frac{1}{2}$ lb.	9 lb.	Stir in to coat well; cover and cook slowly for 10 minutes. Stir in blanched bacon.
Apples, tart, diced	2 cups	3 lb.	Add; stir well. Bring to boil on moderate fire. Cover and place in 325°F oven for 3 hours; cook only at a gentle simmer.
Garlic, crushed	2 cloves	1 tbsp.	
Bay leaf, flaked	$\frac{1}{4}$ tsp.	$1\frac{1}{2}$ tsp.	
Nutmeg	$\frac{1}{8}$ tsp.	$\frac{3}{4}$ tsp.	
Cinnamon	$\frac{1}{8}$ tsp.	$\frac{3}{4}$ tsp.	
Juniper berries	$\frac{1}{2}$ tsp.	1 tbsp.	
Clove, ground	$\frac{1}{8}$ tsp.	$\frac{3}{4}$ tsp.	
Black pepper	$\frac{1}{8}$ tsp.	$\frac{3}{4}$ tsp.	
Salt	$\frac{1}{2}$ tsp.	1 tbsp.	
Red wine	1 pt.	3 qt.	
Beef stock	1 pt.	3 qt.	
Chestnuts, peeled, raw	2 cups	3 lb.	Add; cover; return to oven. Bake until chestnuts are tender and most liquid is absorbed.

SPECIAL HANDLING FOR BUFFETS: *Serve very warm from shallow insert pan(s) set over dual heating units. Keep covered. Wonderful with roast goose or duck, this dish can stand a touch of ginger.*

Red Cabbage with Apples

INGREDIENTS	TEST QUANTITY: 8	SERVICE QUANTITY: 50	METHOD
Red cabbage, shredded	2 lb.	12 lb.	Wash and drain; place in skillet or tilt brazier. Heat.
Butter, soft	$\frac{1}{4}$ cup	$1\frac{1}{2}$ cups	Add; cook over fairly high heat for 5 minutes.
Apples, tart, cored, diced	2 cups	3 lb.	
Orange peel, grated	$\frac{1}{2}$ tsp.	1 tbsp.	
Sugar, dark brown, packed	1 tbsp.	$\frac{1}{3}$ cup	
Brandy	1 tbsp.	$\frac{1}{3}$ cup	
Vinegar, red wine	$\frac{1}{4}$ cup	$1\frac{1}{2}$ cups	
Pecans, chopped	$\frac{1}{4}$ cup	$1\frac{1}{2}$ cups	
Bay leaf	1	3	Add; stir in; cover. Simmer for 1 hour; stir occasionally. Let rest several hours to blend flavors. Remove whole cloves and bay leaf. Reheat for service.
Cloves, whole	4	10	
Cinnamon	$\frac{1}{4}$ tsp.	$1\frac{1}{2}$ tsp.	
Nutmeg	to taste	to taste	
Salt	to taste	to taste	
Pepper	to taste	to taste	

SPECIAL HANDLING FOR BUFFETS: *Serve very warm from shallow insert pan(s) set over dual heating units. Keep covered. Serve this with steamed potatoes or dumplings and German sausages with mustard.*

Rice Pilaf

INGREDIENTS	TEST QUANTITY: 8	SERVICE QUANTITY: 50	METHOD
Butter, melted	$\frac{1}{4}$ cup	$\frac{3}{4}$ lb.	Sauté until soft.
Onion, minced	3 tbsp.	1 cup + 1 tbsp.	
Celery, minced	$\frac{1}{4}$ cup	$1\frac{1}{2}$ cups	
Garlic, minced	1 clove	6 cloves	
Rice, long grain	1 cup	3 lb.	Add; stir until well coated.
Pine nuts	$\frac{1}{4}$ cup	$1\frac{1}{2}$ cups	
Golden raisins	$\frac{1}{3}$ cup	2 cups	Stir in.
Chicken stock	2 cups	3 qt.	Pour over to cover by $\frac{3}{4}$ in. Bring to a boil over high heat. Transfer to hotel pan(s) and cover. Bake in 350°F oven until tender. Transfer to service dishes (if necessary).
White wine	$\frac{1}{4}$ cup	$1\frac{1}{2}$ cups	
Butter, soft, sliced	$\frac{1}{4}$ cup	$\frac{1}{4}$ cup	Add; adjust seasoning. Fluff with fork.
Parmesan cheese, grated	$\frac{3}{4}$ cup	$\frac{3}{4}$ lb.	
Parsley, chopped	as needed	as needed	Sprinkle on top before service.
Scallions (greens only), minced	as needed	as needed	
Pine nuts, toasted	as desired	as desired	

SPECIAL HANDLING FOR BUFFETS: *Serve very warm from shallow insert pan(s) set over dual heating units. Keep covered. This dish holds well for service if covered with a damp towel.*

Sautéed Onions

INGREDIENTS	TEST QUANTITY: 8	SERVICE QUANTITY: 50	METHOD
Olive oil, hot	$\frac{1}{4}$ cup	$1\frac{1}{2}$ cups	Sauté slowly until golden. Drain.
Bacon drippings, strained, melted	$\frac{1}{4}$ cup	$1\frac{1}{2}$ cups	
Onion, sliced, $\frac{1}{4}$ in.	$1\frac{1}{2}$ lb.	9 lb.	
Thyme, dried	$\frac{1}{4}$ tsp.	$1\frac{1}{2}$ tsp.	
Salt	2 tsp.	$\frac{1}{4}$ cup	Combine. Add to onions. Stir.
Black pepper	1 tsp.	2 tbsp.	
Flour, all purpose	1 tbsp.	6 tbsp.	
Paprika, hot	$\frac{1}{2}$ tsp.	1 tbsp.	
White wine vinegar	3 tbsp.	1 cup + 2 tbsp.	Add. Stir carefully but well.

SPECIAL HANDLING FOR BUFFETS: *Serve very warm from shallow insert pan(s) set over dual heating units. Keep covered. Serve with Scandinavian or German foods, especially mashed potatoes and pork.*

Scalloped Fresh Corn

INGREDIENTS	TEST QUANTITY: 8	SERVICE QUANTITY: 50	METHOD
Corn, fresh, scraped	1 qt.	12 lb.	Combine. Pour into buttered pan(s).
Pimiento, diced	$\frac{1}{4}$ cup	$1\frac{1}{2}$ cups	
Heavy cream	$2\frac{1}{4}$ cups	$3\frac{1}{2}$ qt.	
Eggs, beaten	6	3 dozen	
Cheddar cheese, grated	$\frac{1}{2}$ cup	3 cups	
Salt	1 tsp.	2 tbsp.	
White pepper	$\frac{1}{2}$ tsp.	1 tbsp.	
Cayenne	$\frac{1}{4}$ tsp.	$1\frac{1}{2}$ tsp.	
Bread crumbs, stale, fine	$1\frac{1}{2}$ cups	2 lb.	Toss in bowl. Sprinkle over corn mixture.
Parmesan cheese, grated	$\frac{1}{2}$ cup	3 cups	Bake at 325°F until top is crunchy and golden.
Butter, melted	2 tbsp.	$\frac{3}{4}$ cup	
Paprika	$\frac{1}{2}$ tsp.	1 tbsp.	
Scallions (greens only), minced	1 tbsp.	$\frac{1}{3}$ cup	
Parsley, chopped	1 tbsp.	$\frac{1}{3}$ cup	

SPECIAL HANDLING FOR BUFFETS: *Serve very warm from shallow insert pan(s) set over dual heating units. Keep covered. Offer on a barbecue with ribs or pork; also excellent with roasted pork or chicken.*

Scalloped Sweet Potatoes

INGREDIENTS	TEST QUANTITY: 8	SERVICE QUANTITY: 50	METHOD
Sweet potatoes, peeled	2 lb.	12 lb.	Slice thinly. Place in large pot(s).
Milk	$1\frac{1}{2}$ cups	$2\frac{1}{4}$ qt.	Add. Bring to simmer.
Cream	$\frac{1}{2}$ cup	3 cups	
Cognac	1 tbsp.	$\frac{1}{3}$ cup	
Salt	to taste	to taste	Adjust seasoning. Pour into buttered baking pan(s). Bake in 400°F oven for 20 minutes. Reduce heat to 350°F. Continue baking for 20 minutes.
Black pepper, ground	to taste	to taste	
Nutmeg	to taste	to taste	
Cinnamon	to taste	to taste	
Ginger	to taste	to taste	
Pecans, chopped	$\frac{1}{4}$ cup	$1\frac{1}{2}$ cups	Combine. Sprinkle on top. Bake until golden and potatoes are tender.
Brown sugar, light	$\frac{1}{2}$ cup	3 cups	
Orange peel, grated	$\frac{1}{2}$ tsp.	1 tbsp.	
Lemon peel, grated	$\frac{1}{2}$ tsp.	1 tbsp.	

SPECIAL HANDLING FOR BUFFETS: *Serve very warm from shallow insert pan(s) set over dual heating units. Keep covered. Add some toasted coconut to the topping; proceed.*

Spinach with Sesame Dressing

INGREDIENTS	TEST QUANTITY: 8	SERVICE QUANTITY: 50	METHOD
Spinach, fresh, cleaned	2 lb.	12 lb.	Plunge into water just until color is bright green. Remove and drain. Refresh in cold water. Squeeze out liquid; tear pieces in half; place in bowl(s); reserve.
Water, boiling, salted	as needed	as needed	
Red wine vinegar	$\frac{1}{4}$ cup	$1\frac{1}{2}$ cups	
Sesame seeds, toasted	$\frac{1}{2}$ cup	3 cups	Grind coarsely.
Sugar, extra fine	$\frac{1}{4}$ cup	$1\frac{1}{2}$ cups	Add to sesame seeds; grind until well combined.
Lemon rind, grated	$\frac{1}{4}$ tsp.	$1\frac{1}{2}$ tsp.	
Soy sauce	$\frac{1}{4}$ cup	$1\frac{1}{2}$ cups	Add; stir to a paste. Toss with reserved spinach leaves.
Ginger, grated	$\frac{1}{4}$ tsp.	$1\frac{1}{2}$ tsp.	

SPECIAL HANDLING FOR BUFFETS: *Serve very warm from shallow insert pan(s) set over dual heating units. Keep covered. Offer with Japanese dishes or in any other Oriental buffet. This dish should not rest too long, so refresh often.*

Stir-Fried Broccoli Flowerets

INGREDIENTS	TEST QUANTITY: 8	SERVICE QUANTITY: 50	METHOD
Peanut oil, hot	$\frac{1}{3}$ cup	2 cups	Sauté over moderate heat. Remove ginger slices.
Sesame oil, hot	$\frac{1}{2}$ tsp.	1 tbsp.	
Ginger, peeled	4 thin slices	$\frac{1}{2}$ cup	
Garlic, minced	$\frac{1}{2}$ tsp.	1 tbsp.	
Scallions (greens and whites), minced	1 tbsp.	$\frac{1}{3}$ cup	
Broccoli flowerets, small, trimmed, peeled	about 2 lb.	12 lb.	Add; toss quickly until broccoli turns bright green.
Salt	1 tbsp.	$\frac{1}{3}$ cup	Add; toss. Turn heat to high.
Sugar	1 tsp.	2 tbsp.	
Red pepper, crushed	$\frac{1}{4}$ tsp.	$1\frac{1}{2}$ tsp.	
Chicken stock or water	2 cups	3 qt.	Add; stir; cover. Cook 3 minutes. Remove cover; toss over high heat to desired doneness. Drain liquid.
Sherry, dry	1 tbsp.	$\frac{1}{3}$ cup	
Sesame oil, Oriental	1 tbsp.	$\frac{1}{3}$ cup	Pour over broccoli; toss. Serve hot, warm, or cold.

SPECIAL HANDLING FOR BUFFETS: *Serve very warm from shallow insert pan(s) set over dual heating units. Keep covered. This procedure can also be done with asparagus tips.*

Sweet and Sour Glazed Pearl Onions

INGREDIENTS	TEST QUANTITY: 8	SERVICE QUANTITY: 50	METHOD
Pearl onions, trimmed	2 lb.	12 lb.	With paring knife, make a small X-shaped incision in stem end.
Water, boiling	to cover	to cover	Boil onions for 5 minutes. Drain.
Salt	1 tsp.	2 tbsp.	
Butter, melted	$\frac{1}{2}$ cup	3 cups	Add drained onions. Sauté until tender.
Thyme, dried	$\frac{1}{4}$ tsp.	$1\frac{1}{2}$ tsp.	
Brown sugar, light	$\frac{1}{4}$ cup	$1\frac{1}{2}$ cups	Combine with onions. Stir to dissolve. Toss to evenly glaze the onions.
Honey	1 tbsp.	$\frac{1}{3}$ cup	
Salt	to taste	to taste	
Black pepper	$\frac{1}{4}$ tsp.	$1\frac{1}{2}$ tsp.	
Red wine vinegar	3 tbsp.	1 cup + 1 tbsp.	Add. Deglaze. Simmer until well heated.
Nutmeg	$\frac{1}{8}$ tsp.	$\frac{3}{4}$ tsp.	

SPECIAL HANDLING FOR BUFFETS: *Serve very warm from shallow insert pan(s) set over dual heating units. Keep covered. Perfect with grilled poultry. Add some toasted pine nuts or almonds.*

Sweet Potato Pudding

INGREDIENTS	TEST QUANTITY: 8	SERVICE QUANTITY: 50	METHOD
Sweet potatoes, cooked, peeled	2 lb.	12 lb.	Place in pan and crush. Stir over low heat
Orange peel, grated	$\frac{1}{2}$ tsp.	1 tbsp.	until fluffy and dry.
Cinnamon	$\frac{1}{4}$ tsp.	$1\frac{1}{2}$ tsp.	
Nutmeg	$\frac{1}{4}$ tsp.	$1\frac{1}{2}$ tsp.	
Egg yolks, whipped	6	3 dozen	Add; stir well. Beat until light. Chill. Then
Cognac	1 tbsp.	$\frac{1}{3}$ cup	pour into buttered molds or hotel pan(s).
Butter	$\frac{1}{4}$ cup	$1\frac{1}{2}$ cups	Bake in bain marie at 350°F until pudding(s)
Sour cream	$\frac{1}{4}$ cup	$1\frac{1}{2}$ cups	test done. Let rest 10 minutes before service.
Salt	to taste	to taste	
Sugar, granulated	1 tsp.	2 tbsp.	
Brown sugar, light	1 tbsp.	6 tbsp.	

SPECIAL HANDLING FOR BUFFETS: *Serve very warm from shallow insert pan(s) set over dual heating units. Keep covered. Season with ginger and cayenne pepper to taste.*

Sweet Potatoes with Pineapple and Dark Rum

INGREDIENTS	TEST QUANTITY: 8	SERVICE QUANTITY: 50	METHOD
Sweet potatoes, cooked, peeled, mashed	2 lb.	12 lb.	Combine until fluffy. Pour into buttered pan(s).
Butter, soft	$\frac{1}{4}$ cup	$1\frac{1}{2}$ cups	
Milk	$\frac{1}{3}$ cup	2 cups	
Egg yolk, beaten	1	6	
Cinnamon	$\frac{1}{2}$ tsp.	1 tbsp.	
Salt	$\frac{1}{2}$ tsp.	1 tbsp.	
Cayenne	$\frac{1}{4}$ tsp.	$1\frac{1}{2}$ tsp.	
Coconut, toasted	$\frac{1}{4}$ cup	$1\frac{1}{2}$ cups	
Almonds, sliced	$\frac{1}{4}$ cup	$1\frac{1}{2}$ cups	
Dark rum	$\frac{1}{4}$ cup	$1\frac{1}{2}$ cups	
Orange brandy	1 tbsp.	$\frac{1}{3}$ cup	
Pineapple, fresh, chopped	1 cup	3 lb.	
Pineapple juice	$\frac{1}{2}$ cup	3 cups	
Butter, sliced	$\frac{1}{4}$ cup	$1\frac{1}{2}$ cups	Sprinkle over top. Bake at 400°F until well heated and coconut is golden brown.
Orange rind, grated	2 tbsp.	$\frac{3}{4}$ cup	
Almonds, crushed	1 tbsp.	$\frac{1}{3}$ cup	
Coconut flakes	2 tbsp.	$\frac{3}{4}$ cup	

SPECIAL HANDLING FOR BUFFETS: *Serve very warm from shallow insert pan(s) set over dual heating units. Keep covered. Offer with roast pork dishes.*

Swiss Potatoes and Cream

INGREDIENTS	TEST QUANTITY: 8	SERVICE QUANTITY: 50	METHOD
Potatoes, peeled, diced	2 lb.	12 lb.	Arrange and season alternately in 2-qt. pan(s).
Gruyère cheese, grated	2 cups	3 lb.	
Onions, diced, sautéed	1 cup	2 lb.	
Parsley, chopped	$\frac{1}{4}$ cup	$1\frac{1}{2}$ cups	
Salt	1 tsp.	2 tbsp.	
Black pepper	1 tsp.	2 tbsp.	
Mustard, dry	$\frac{1}{4}$ tsp.	$1\frac{1}{2}$ tsp.	
Heavy cream	$\frac{3}{4}$ cup	$4\frac{1}{2}$ cups	Pour over potato mixture. Bake at 325°F until potatoes are cooked.
Egg yolk	1	6	
Scallions (greens and whites), chopped	1 tbsp.	$\frac{1}{3}$ cup	
Cayenne	$\frac{1}{2}$ tsp.	1 tbsp.	

SPECIAL HANDLING FOR BUFFETS: *Serve very warm from shallow insert pan(s) set over dual heating units. Keep covered. Add some crumbled bacon or browned sausage; proceed.*

Review Questions

1. Trace the flow of cabbage to North America.

2. What does parsley have to do with overimbibing?

3. Is garlic indigenous to the United States?

4. What is the origin of cucumber?

5. What is the Japanese word for white radish?

6. How did the potato get to Ireland?

Ten

Desserts: Sweet Dreams

Americans share a love of desserts with folk of many nations, though what we might call pie, others call tarts, and when we request cake, others call for torte. Dessert forms a theme that weaves through buffet fare of almost every ethnic cuisine. A strong working knowledge of dessert classics, beginning with some basic terms from several cooking styles, can help to build a creative buffet foundation.

Bavarian Cream. Egg yolks, sugar, and milk are cooked until thickened; this mixture is combined with unflavored gelatin and chilled. As the mixture solidifies, either whipped cream or a fruit mixture is added; the mixture is poured into large or individual molds and is chilled until firm. Lemon, chocolate, almond, raspberry, and various liqueurs are possible flavorings.

Butter Cream. In one of several versions, a heated sugar syrup is added to whipped egg yolks and then soft butter is whipped in. Flavorings such as coffee, chocolate, orange, or raspberry are just a beginning for this versatile cake filling mixture.

Charlotte. Charlottes are formed by lining molds with lady fingers and filling them with a flavored Bavarian cream. They can also be made hot by lining molds with bread slices and filling them with stewed or sautéed fruits such as apples. The charlotte is baked, unmolded, and served with a fruit sauce.

Crêpe. Flour, sugar, butter, and milk are combined into a thin batter that is cooked in hot pans; the resulting lace-thin pancakes can be filled with fruits and creams for quick and creative buffet desserts. When made ahead and frozen, crêpes are always ready for service. Blintzes and the Swedish *plattar* are treated in the same ways.

Flan. In addition to the version using pastry cream (see explanation), a flan is also a fruit and cream-filled open tart. A variation is the *clafouti*, a French cherry specialty.

French Meringue. Egg whites and sugar are whipped until mixture is stiff; it is then piped into desired shapes (such as shells) and baked at low temperatures. When baked, the crisp pastries can be filled with nut creams or fruits. Different shapes can be filled with various mixtures, including coffee and chocolate creams, and arranged in paper shells on buffet trays.

Fried Pastry. Flour, sugar, and shortening are combined with flavoring, rolled thin, and cut into shapes; they are then fried in hot oil and served with fruits, powdered sugar, or syrup. The Swiss call these desserts *struzeli* or fried cookies; in Mexican fare they are called *sopapillas.*

Cannoli is an Italian version where the dough is wrapped around a mold, fried, and then filled with pistachio cream, nuts, or cheese; when the cannoli dough is cut into strips and fried, the result is *frappe. Beignets* are a version popular in France and in New Orleans; *kokisters* are Dutch treats served with cinnamon syrup.

Fritters. Flour, milk, eggs, yeast, and even beer are combined into a semi-thick mixture; when allowed to rest, and combined with beaten egg whites, the mixture becomes light and smooth and it can be used to coat fruit slices before they are deep fried. The golden pieces are served with powdered sugar, whipped cream, or flavored syrups.

Gateau. French word for cake.

Genoise. This is the classic preparation that forms the base of countless buffet dessert creations. Eggs and sugar are whipped over hot water; flour and flavoring (such as cocoa powder) are folded in, clarified butter is added quickly, and the batter is poured into baking pans of any size or shape. When baked, genoise (or sponge cake) can be split into thin layers for use in small tortes or large layer cakes. Butter creams, fruits, and liqueurs of all descriptions can be used with this classic pastry preparation. When flavored with chocolate and cherry brandy, the mixture can be used to make the German classic Black Forest cake. A Hungarian classic is the Dobos torte, topped with carmelized wedges of thin genoise slices.

Italian Meringue. Egg whites are beaten until stiff and then a very hot sugar syrup is gradually added and the mixture whipped until very stiff. This can be flavored with cocoa powder and baked in much the same way as a soufflé, but this mixture will hold up for service much longer. It is also used in conjunction with hot pastry cream (see explanation) to form a light cream filling for *pâte à chou.*

Japonais Torte. A Swiss version of *Succes* batter (see explanation) is layered with many shells and filled and iced with flavored creams.

Jelly Roll. A batter of egg yolks, sugar, and flour is mixed with whipped egg whites and spread onto a lined pan. Once baked, the supple pastry can be cooled and rolled; it holds its shape in uses such as a yule log *(Bûche de Noël)*, jelly roll, or roll of virtually any preserve or cream filling. An English favorite includes a tart lemon curd filling, with a dusting of powdered sugar; a Mexican version might include anise as a flavoring agent. Once prepared, this pastry holds well for service.

Kuchen. German word for cake.

Ladyfingers. A simple combination of egg yolks, sugar, flour, and whipped egg whites forms this basic batter. Piped onto baking sheets, dusted with sugar and baked, these pastries are available for service with Bavarian creams and charlottes, fresh and stewed fruits, and various pastry creams.

Pastry Cream. Milk, egg yolks, and sugar are combined with flavoring (va-

nilla, orange, coffee, etc.) and cornstarch; the mixture is cooked until smooth and thick. When cool, the mixture can be used to fill cream puffs and éclairs, as well as crêpes and tarts; when used as a base for pastries, this cream can be topped with nuts and fruits. *Frangipane* is an Italian version that contains crushed macaroons. A Spanish flan is created by pouring pastry cream into a mold that has been partially filled with caramel; when baked and unmolded, the cream holds its shape.

Pâte à Chou. This classic cream puff pastry is formed when water, milk, sugar, and butter are heated and flour is stirred in quickly; the mixture is heated, cooled slightly, and then eggs are beaten in. The batter can be piped into shapes of all sizes; when baked, the mixture puffs up and holds its shape for fillings of all kinds. Cream puffs and éclairs are just two of the countless possibilities; *profiterole* is a term that applies to a miniature version, such as those that garnish a cream-filled St. Honore torte.

Phyllo. Sometimes spelled *filo*, this Middle Eastern (Turkish and Greek) pastry is paper thin and is available in packages of individual sheets. When brushed with butter, sprinkled with nuts, baked, and then drenched in syrup, the result is baklava, an ideal buffet dessert. *Baniza* is a Rumanian dessert that uses a phyllo-like dough with nuts and spices.

Pudding. A general term that applies to many mixtures, many of which are based on eggs and cream; the mixtures are poured into molds, covered, and then either baked or steamed. If cooked in large molds puddings are often unmolded onto service trays; if small molds are used

they can be plated individually for service. Bread, rice, and dried fruits are the base for many English puddings; almonds and milk are popular in Greek and Turkish puddings.

Puff Pastry. The classic French preparation calls for a flour and butter dough to be prepared and chilled. When rolled out into a rectangle, additional butter is placed over part of the surface; the remaining dough is folded over the butter and the whole is rolled out, folded, and allowed to rest. The rolling/folding/resting processes are repeated three or four times, finally resulting in a pastry that has incorporated approximately 1000 butter/pastry layers; when baked, these layers swell to dramatic heights. The pastry can be cut into any shape, and form the base for tarts, Napoleons, and wondrous French *millefeuille* (thousand leaves) pastry shells for fruits and creams.

Short Pastry. This is classic pie dough, a combination of shortening, flour, water, or milk; if desired, sugar can be added to the basic dough. After the ingredients are combined, the dough should rest overnight before rolling into shells for tarts and pies of any description.

Strudel. A German-Swiss pastry similar in thinness to phyllo, strudel pastry is used with fruit and nut fillings to form a delicate, flaky dessert. Individual strudels or slices from larger ones are popular buffet desserts. Hungarian strudel is called *retes.*

Succes Batter. Egg whites are whipped with sugar and then are combined with a mixture of warm milk, ground almonds, and powdered sugar.

The mixture is spread or piped into round shapes of any size and baked at a low temperature until dried. The batter can be formed on the baking sheets into small shells and baked to form the base for chocolate, creams, and fruits. If stored in sealed containers, succes shells can be on hand for continual use.

Swiss Meringue. Egg whites and sugar are combined over hot water and whipped until hot; continual whipping off the heat creates a very stiff mixture that can be piped into various shapes and sizes (mushrooms, snow figures, pumpkins) for use in decorating buffet platters and desserts; once baked until dry, the Swiss meringue pieces can be kept for several weeks, ever at the ready for buffet use.

Zabaglione. An Italian egg yolk and sugar mixture that is whipped over heat to a froth and flavored with Marsala wine; a specialty of the Piedmont area, it can be served with fruits or biscuits. A Hungarian variation on the wine cream theme is *borsodo*, a mixture of egg yolks, sugar, lemon, and Riesling; the French call their version *sabayon*.

Baked Apples in Brandy Sauce 1

INGREDIENTS	TEST QUANTITY: 8	SERVICE QUANTITY: 50	METHOD
Sugar	2 cups	6 lb.	Combine and boil for 5 minutes.
Water	1 cup	$1\frac{1}{2}$ qt.	
White wine	1 cup	$1\frac{1}{2}$ qt.	
Currant jelly	$\frac{1}{2}$ cup	3 cups	
Vanilla	1 tsp.	2 tbsp.	
Apple jelly	$\frac{1}{2}$ cup	3 cups	
Lemon rind, grated	$\frac{1}{2}$ tsp.	1 tbsp.	
Tart apples, cored, peeled	8	50	Drop into syrup. Simmer for 15 minutes. Place apples in roasting pan(s) and pour syrup over. Cover tightly and bake at 350°F until the apples are tender, about 15 minutes. Cool in pan(s). Transfer apples with slotted spoon to shallow insert pan(s). Ladle syrup over apples as desired.
Brandy	1 oz.	6 oz.	Pour over apples.
Heavy cream	$\frac{1}{2}$ cup	3 cups	Combine and beat until stiff.
Sugar	to taste	to taste	
Cinnamon	$\frac{1}{8}$ tsp.	$\frac{3}{4}$ tsp.	
Apple brandy	1 oz.	$\frac{3}{4}$ cup	Add to cream. Spoon on top of each apple.
Orange brandy	1 tbsp.	$\frac{1}{3}$ cup	
Pecans, chopped	$\frac{1}{4}$ cup	$1\frac{1}{2}$ cups	Sprinkle over apples.
Walnuts, chopped	$\frac{1}{4}$ cup	$1\frac{1}{2}$ cups	

SPECIAL HANDLING FOR BUFFETS: *Serve warm from shallow insert pan(s) set over single heating unit. Keep covered. Offer with small vanilla wafers and additional whipped cream if desired. Note: A similar procedure can be found in the Brunch chapter, page 331.*

Baked Pears

INGREDIENTS	TEST QUANTITY: 8	SERVICE QUANTITY: 50	METHOD
Corn syrup, light	$\frac{1}{3}$ cup	2 cups	Combine. Simmer for 3 minutes. Remove cinnamon stick(s).
White wine	$\frac{1}{3}$ cup	2 cups	
Brown sugar, light	$\frac{1}{3}$ cup	2 cups	
Cinnamon stick	1	6	
Vanilla extract	1 tsp.	2 tbsp.	
Orange extract	$\frac{1}{4}$ tsp.	$1\frac{1}{2}$ tsp.	
Pears (small), fresh, ripe, peeled	4	25	Cut in half. Coat with lemon juice. Place in buttered baking pan(s). Pour sugar mixture over. Cover. Bake at 375°F oven for 10 minutes. Uncover. Baste. Bake until done. Place pears in service piece(s). Reduce sauce until thick.
Lemon juice, strained	2 tsp.	$\frac{1}{4}$ cup	
Heavy cream	$\frac{1}{3}$ cup	2 cups	Add gradually to sauce. Spoon sauce over pears.
Almond extract	$\frac{1}{8}$ tsp.	$\frac{3}{4}$ tsp.	

SPECIAL HANDLING FOR BUFFETS: *Serve warm from shallow insert pan(s) set over single heating unit. Keep covered. Offer with unsweetened whipped cream and either chopped toasted pecans or crumbled macaroons.*

Brandy Rolls with Cognac Cream

INGREDIENTS	TEST QUANTITY: 8	SERVICE QUANTITY: 50	METHOD
Butter, melted	$\frac{1}{4}$ cup	$1\frac{1}{2}$ cups	Combine over heat until dissolved. Remove from heat.
Powdered sugar	$\frac{1}{4}$ cup	$1\frac{1}{2}$ cups	
Flour, all purpose	$\frac{1}{2}$ cup	3 cups	Stir into butter mixture. Stir until smooth. Drop by teaspoons onto buttered and floured sheet pan(s). Bake at 350°F until the wafers spread to 4 in. wide. Let cool a bit. Wrap around a buttered wooden spoon handle. Put each roll on rack to cool.
Almonds, powdered	1 tbsp.	$\frac{1}{3}$ cup	
Ginger, ground	$\frac{1}{2}$ tsp.	1 tbsp.	
Cinnamon, ground	$\frac{1}{8}$ tsp.	$\frac{3}{4}$ tsp.	
Nutmeg, ground	$\frac{1}{8}$ tsp.	$\frac{3}{4}$ tsp.	
Allspice, ground	$\frac{1}{8}$ tsp.	$\frac{3}{4}$ tsp.	
Corn syrup, light	$1\frac{1}{2}$ tbsp.	$\frac{1}{2}$ cup + 1 tbsp.	
Brown sugar, light	1 tbsp.	$\frac{1}{3}$ cup	
Molasses	$\frac{1}{2}$ tbsp.	3 tbsp.	
Orange brandy	$\frac{1}{4}$ cup	$1\frac{1}{2}$ cups	
Lemon peel, grated	1 tsp.	2 tbsp.	
Orange peel, grated	1 tsp.	2 tbsp.	
Heavy cream	2 cups	3 qt.	Whip until thick. Pipe into the cooled rolls.
Powdered sugar	$\frac{1}{4}$ cup	$1\frac{1}{2}$ cups	
Cognac	1 oz.	$\frac{3}{4}$ cup	
Orange extract	$\frac{1}{8}$ tsp.	$\frac{3}{4}$ tsp.	

SPECIAL HANDLING FOR BUFFETS: *Keep chilled until service. These make a perfect light dessert for a British brunch or breakfast or an after-theater coffee buffet. Serve with extra cream.*

Bread and Butter Pudding, The Coach House

INGREDIENTS	TEST QUANTITY: 8	SERVICE QUANTITY: 50	METHOD
French bread slices, thin	12	4 lb.	Spread with butter. Place in shallow pan(s), buttered side up.
Butter	$\frac{1}{4}$ cup	$1\frac{1}{2}$ cups	
Eggs, beaten	5	$2\frac{1}{2}$ dozen	Combine well.
Egg yolks	4	2 dozen	
Sugar	1 cup	3 lb.	
Salt	$\frac{1}{8}$ tsp.	$\frac{3}{4}$ tsp.	
Milk, scalded	1 qt.	$1\frac{1}{2}$ gal.	Combine well. Pour small amount into egg mixture; then pour that back into milk.
Heavy cream	1 cup	$1\frac{1}{2}$ qt.	
Vanilla extract	1 tsp.	2 tbsp.	Add. Stir well and pour over the bread slices. Bake in a 350°F oven until pudding tests for done, about 45 minutes.
Powdered sugar	$\frac{1}{3}$ cup	2 cups	Sprinkle over top. Broil until golden and bubbly.

SPECIAL HANDLING FOR BUFFETS: *Serve warm from shallow insert pan(s) set over single heating unit. Keep covered. Offer with a fresh berry purée. If desired, add some chopped pecans to the cream mixture or simply flavor with almond or walnut extract. The Coach House is a popular restaurant located in New York City's Greenwich Village.*

Caribbean Rum Custards

INGREDIENTS	TEST QUANTITY: 8	SERVICE QUANTITY: 50	METHOD
Cream, light	2 cups	3 qt.	Scald. Let cool to lukewarm.
Sugar	$\frac{1}{2}$ cup	3 cups	
Molasses	1 tbsp.	$\frac{1}{3}$ cup	
Egg yolks, beaten	6	3 dozen	Whip together until thick and lemony in color. Add warm cream mixture. Pour into ramekins. Cover each with foil. Place in baking pan(s). Fill halfway with boiling water. Bake at 325°F until custards test done, about 25 minutes.
Dark rum	$1\frac{1}{2}$ oz.	9 oz.	
Orange extract	$\frac{1}{8}$ tsp.	$\frac{3}{4}$ tsp.	

SPECIAL HANDLING FOR BUFFETS: *Serve warm or chilled. Offer with unsweetened whipped cream and a selection of tea cookies or cakes. These are wonderful with coffee or espresso.*

Chilled Citrus Mousse

INGREDIENTS	TEST QUANTITY: 8	SERVICE QUANTITY: 50	METHOD
Gelatin powder, unflavored	2 tsp.	$\frac{1}{4}$ cup	Dissolve well.
White wine, dry	1 tbsp.	$\frac{1}{3}$ cup	
Orange juice	1 tbsp.	$\frac{1}{3}$ cup	Combine over low heat with gelatin. Stir until
Lemon juice	$\frac{1}{3}$ cup	2 cups	gelatin dissolves completely.
Lemon peel, grated	1 tbsp.	$\frac{1}{3}$ cup	
Orange peel, grated	1 tbsp.	$\frac{1}{3}$ cup	
Egg yolks, beaten	3	$1\frac{1}{2}$ dozen	Beat until lemony in color. Stir into the
Orange brandy	1 tbsp.	$\frac{1}{3}$ cup	gelatin mixture. Reserve.
Sugar	3 tbsp.	1 cup + 2 tbsp.	
Egg whites, beaten slightly	3	$1\frac{1}{2}$ dozen	Beat until frothy.
Cream of tartar	pinch	$\frac{1}{4}$ tsp.	
Sugar	$\frac{1}{3}$ cup	2 cups	Add to whites. Beat until stiff.
Nutmeg, ground	$\frac{1}{8}$ tsp.	$\frac{3}{4}$ tsp.	
Heavy cream, whipped	1 cup	$1\frac{1}{2}$ qt.	Fold into egg yolk mixture. Then combine
Cinnamon	$\frac{1}{8}$ tsp.	$\frac{3}{4}$ tsp.	with the egg white mixture. Spoon into parfait glasses or pudding cups. Chill well.
Water, boiling	as needed	as needed	Blanch. Drain. Pat dry. Use to garnish each
Lemon peel, julienned	of 1	of 6	serving.
Orange peel, julienned	of 1	of 6	

SPECIAL HANDLING FOR BUFFETS: *Serve chilled. Wrap each parfait glass or cup with a band of aluminum foil; pour mousse up to top of band. Chill; remove band and serve.*

Chocolate Bread Pudding

INGREDIENTS	TEST QUANTITY: 8	SERVICE QUANTITY: 50	METHOD
Chocolate, semisweet	8 oz.	3 lb.	Combine. Heat over low fire. Stir until chocolate melts. Do not overheat.
Cognac or coffee liqueur	1 tbsp.	$\frac{1}{3}$ cup	
Butter	6 oz.	$2\frac{1}{4}$ lb.	
Milk	$1\frac{1}{3}$ cup	2 qt.	
Bread crumbs, fresh	1 qt.	3 lb.	Add. Heat for 5 minutes. Cool slightly.
Cinnamon	$\frac{1}{4}$ tsp.	$1\frac{1}{2}$ tsp.	
Sugar	1 cup	3 lb.	Combine. Add to tepid mixture.
Molasses	1 tbsp.	$\frac{1}{3}$ cup	
Egg yolks, beaten	4	2 dozen	
Vanilla	1 tsp.	2 tbsp.	
Orange extract	$\frac{1}{2}$ tsp.	1 tbsp.	
Lemon peel, grated	$\frac{1}{2}$ tsp.	1 tbsp.	
Egg whites, beaten stiff	4	2 dozen	Fold into mixture. Pour into buttered 2-qt. mold(s). Cover with buttered foil. Secure with string. Place in bain marie half filled with boiling water. Cover. Simmer for 2 hours. Unmold onto service piece(s).
Heavy cream	1 cup	$1\frac{1}{2}$ qt.	Whip until stiff. Offer with the pudding.
Powdered sugar	2 tbsp.	$\frac{3}{4}$ cup	
Coffee liqueur	1 oz.	$\frac{3}{4}$ cup	

SPECIAL HANDLING FOR BUFFETS: *Serve warm from shallow insert pan(s) set over single heating unit. Keep covered. Add orange or raspberry liqueur to egg yolk mixture. Offer with fresh berry purée.*

Chocolate Orange Custard

INGREDIENTS	TEST QUANTITY: 8	SERVICE QUANTITY: 50	METHOD
Milk, cold	$\frac{1}{2}$ cup	3 cups	Combine to dissolve.
Vanilla extract	$\frac{1}{2}$ tsp.	1 tbsp.	
Cocoa powder	3 tbsp.	4 oz.	
Cornstarch	3 tbsp.	6 oz.	
Cinnamon	$\frac{1}{4}$ tsp.	$1\frac{1}{2}$ tsp.	
Sugar	$\frac{1}{4}$ cup	$1\frac{1}{2}$ cups	Cream together until thick and lemony. Add to cocoa mixture.
Orange peel, grated	1 tsp.	2 tbsp.	
Eggs, beaten	2	1 dozen	
Milk, scalded	$2\frac{1}{2}$ cups	$3\frac{3}{4}$ qt.	Add gradually to cocoa mixture. Bring to a boil. Simmer barely for 5 minutes, stirring. Do not boil. Pour into individual glasses or cups.
Orange brandy	1 oz.	$\frac{3}{4}$ cup	
Coffee liqueur	1 tsp.	2 tbsp.	

SPECIAL HANDLING FOR BUFFETS: *Serve warm or chilled.* *Offer with unsweetened whipped cream.*
Add chopped nutmeats to mixture before pouring into cups.

Chocolate Rum Sauce

INGREDIENTS	TEST QUANTITY: 8	SERVICE QUANTITY: 50	METHOD
Heavy cream	$\frac{1}{2}$ cup	3 cups	Melt in bain marie.
Semisweet chocolate	10 squares	$3\frac{3}{4}$ lb.	
Unsweetened chocolate	2 squares	$\frac{3}{4}$ lb.	
Butter	2 tbsp.	$\frac{3}{4}$ cup	
Cinnamon, ground	$\frac{1}{4}$ tsp.	$1\frac{1}{2}$ tsp.	
Corn syrup, light	$\frac{2}{3}$ cup	1 qt.	Stir in until smooth.
Egg yolk	1	6	
Light cream	$\frac{1}{2}$ cup	3 cups	
Instant coffee granules	2 tbsp.	$\frac{3}{4}$ cup	Add; stir to blend.
Pecans, chopped	1 tbsp.	$\frac{1}{3}$ cup	
Dark rum	$\frac{1}{4}$ cup	$1\frac{1}{2}$ cups	Heat; flame; add to sauce. Offer with dessert
Orange brandy	$\frac{1}{4}$ cup	$1\frac{1}{2}$ cups	crêpes, pound cake, ice cream, or poached pears.

SPECIAL HANDLING FOR BUFFETS: *Keep on hand as a natural accompaniment for cold desserts or hot puddings.*

Citrus Meringue Tarts

INGREDIENTS	TEST QUANTITY: 8	SERVICE QUANTITY: 50	METHOD
Flour, all purpose	5 tbsp.	2 cups	Combine in bain marie over simmering water. Stir constantly until thickened, about 10 minutes. Remove from heat.
Sugar	$\frac{3}{4}$ cup	$2\frac{1}{4}$ lb.	
Salt	$\frac{1}{8}$ tsp.	$\frac{3}{4}$ tsp.	
Nutmeg	$\frac{1}{8}$ tsp.	$\frac{3}{4}$ tsp.	
Egg yolks, beaten	2	1 dozen	
Vanilla extract	$\frac{1}{2}$ tsp.	1 tbsp.	
Water	10 oz.	$7\frac{1}{2}$ cups	
Butter, soft	2 tbsp.	$\frac{3}{4}$ cup	Add to mixture. Combine well. Cool.
Orange brandy	1 tbsp.	$\frac{1}{3}$ cup	
Lemon juice, strained	2 tbsp.	$\frac{3}{4}$ cup	
Orange juice, strained	2 tbsp.	$\frac{3}{4}$ cup	
Lime juice, strained	1 tbsp.	$\frac{1}{3}$ cup	
Lemon rind	1 tsp.	2 tbsp.	
Orange rind	1 tsp.	2 tbsp.	
Tart shells	8	50	Spoon mixture into shells.
Egg whites, frothy	2	1 dozen	Combine and whip until stiff. Spoon over tarts. Bake at 350°F until golden.
Cream of tartar	pinch	$\frac{1}{8}$ tsp.	
Sugar	$\frac{1}{4}$ cup	$1\frac{1}{2}$ cups	
Orange brandy	1 tsp.	2 tbsp.	
Almonds, powdered	1 tbsp.	$\frac{1}{3}$ cup	

SPECIAL HANDLING FOR BUFFETS: *Serve warm from shallow insert pan(s) set over single heating unit or from service tray. If desired, sprinkle toasted coconut over meringue before baking.*

Custard Sauce

INGREDIENTS	TEST QUANTITY: 8	SERVICE QUANTITY: 50	METHOD
Milk, cold	$\frac{1}{2}$ cup	3 cups	Combine well and bring just to a boil.
Cornstarch	4 tsp.	$\frac{1}{2}$ cup	
Milk, hot	$2\frac{1}{2}$ cups	$3\frac{3}{4}$ qt.	Combine and add, stirring, until mixture thickens and returns to a boil. Remove from heat immediately.
Sugar	2 tbsp.	$\frac{3}{4}$ cup	
Egg yolks, lightly beaten	2	12	Combine with small amount of sauce. Stir well. Pour back into sauce and stir well, off the heat. Then bring back just to the simmer for 1 minute, stirring constantly. Remove from heat. Do not boil!
Vanilla extract	1 tsp.	2 tbsp.	Add; stir. Strain if necessary.

SPECIAL HANDLING FOR BUFFETS: *Serve chilled with bread puddings or baked fruits.*

Fruit-Stuffed Apples

INGREDIENTS	TEST QUANTITY: 8	SERVICE QUANTITY: 50	METHOD
Raisins, whole	½ cup	3 cups	Combine well.
Sugar	⅓ cup	2 cups	
Raisins, chopped	⅓ cup	2 cups	
Almonds, chopped finely	2 tbsp.	¾ cup	
Pecans, chopped finely	2 tbsp.	¾ cup	
Walnuts, chopped finely	2 tbsp.	¾ cup	
Lemon peel, grated	½ tsp.	1 tbsp.	
Bread crumbs, fine, stale	2 tbsp.	¾ cup	
Cinnamon	2 tsp.	¼ cup	
Nutmeg	½ tsp.	1 tbsp.	
Apples (small), peeled	8	50	Slice off tops. Reserve. Spoon out cavity around core. Spoon the reserved mixture into cavity.
Butter, soft	⅓ cup	2 cups	Combine and distribute on top of stuffing. Put tops back on. Place in buttered baking pan(s).
Orange brandy	1 tbsp.	⅓ cup	
Powdered sugar	1 tbsp.	⅓ cup	
Sugar	1 tbsp.	⅓ cup	Sprinkle over.
Butter, melted	2 tbsp.	¾ cup	
Almonds, powdered	1 tbsp.	⅓ cup	
White wine	1½ cups	9 cups	Pour into pan around apples. Cover with foil. Bake at 350°F until tender.

SPECIAL HANDLING FOR BUFFETS: *Serve warm from shallow insert pan(s) set over single heating unit. Keep covered. Offer with barely sweetened whipped cream or lemon-flavored pastry cream.*

Glazed "Ice" Oranges

INGREDIENTS	TEST QUANTITY: 8	SERVICE QUANTITY: 50	METHOD
Navel oranges	8	50	Peel off skin in strips; julienne strips about 2 in. long. Place strips in pan, cover with water, and blanch for 10 minutes. Drain; pat dry and place in bowl. Reserve oranges.
Orange brandy	1 oz.	$\frac{3}{4}$ cup	Pour over strips; reserve. Cut pith from
Cognac	1 tbsp.	$\frac{1}{3}$ cup	oranges, and trim one end so oranges will sit upright.
Sugar	2 cups	6 lb.	Combine; boil to 244°F. Add small amount to
Water	$\frac{2}{3}$ cup	1 qt.	peels, and spoon remaining over oranges.
Candied fruits, diced	$\frac{1}{2}$ cup	3 cups	Glaze oranges slowly with all the syrup.
Cinnamon	$\frac{1}{4}$ tsp.	$1\frac{1}{2}$ tsp.	

SPECIAL HANDLING FOR BUFFETS: *Serve chilled. Top with reserved shredded orange peel and candied violets. This is a fine dessert idea for an Italian buffet.*

Golden Baklava

INGREDIENTS	TEST QUANTITY: 8	SERVICE QUANTITY: 50	METHOD
Walnuts, finely chopped	$\frac{1}{4}$ lb.	$1\frac{1}{2}$ lb.	Combine. Mix well.
Pecans, finely chopped	$\frac{1}{4}$ lb.	$1\frac{1}{2}$ lb.	
Almonds, finely chopped	$\frac{1}{4}$ lb.	$1\frac{1}{2}$ lb.	
Raisins	$\frac{1}{4}$ lb.	$1\frac{1}{2}$ lb.	
Brown sugar, light	2 tsp.	$\frac{1}{4}$ cup	
Cinnamon	$\frac{1}{2}$ tsp.	1 tbsp.	
Nutmeg, ground	$\frac{1}{4}$ tsp.	$1\frac{1}{2}$ tsp.	
Clove, ground	pinch	$\frac{1}{2}$ tsp.	
Lemon peel, grated	$\frac{1}{2}$ tsp.	1 tbsp.	
Orange peel, grated	$\frac{1}{2}$ tsp.	1 tbsp.	
Phyllo sheets, 20 × 15 in. (commercial)	$\frac{1}{3}$ lb.	2 lb.	Remove four sheets, keeping remainder under damp towel.
Butter, melted	as needed	as needed	Brush each of the four sheets with butter. Stack sheets. Sprinkle with nut mixture. Roll up into tight cylinders. Cut into 2-in. slices. Place open end up on sheet pan(s). Repeat process.
Butter, melted	$\frac{1}{4}$ cup	$1\frac{1}{2}$ cups	Drizzle butter into open ends. Bake at 350°F for 10 minutes. Turn over each piece.
Butter, melted	$\frac{1}{4}$ cup	$1\frac{1}{2}$ cups	Repeat drizzling procedure. Bake at 350°F until golden, about 25 minutes.
Sugar	$\frac{2}{3}$ cup	2 lb.	Combine to dissolve. Bring to boil for 30 minutes. Strain. Cool. Pour into open ends of pastries.
Water	$\frac{1}{3}$ cup	2 cups	
Lemon juice, strained	1 tsp.	2 tbsp.	
Lemon peel, grated	1 tsp.	2 tbsp.	
Honey	3 tbsp.	1 cup + 2 tbsp.	
Cinnamon	to taste	to taste	

SPECIAL HANDLING FOR BUFFETS: *Serve warm from shallow insert pan(s) set over single heating unit. Keep covered. Perfect for Middle Eastern buffets. Offer with demitasse cups of Turkish or Greek coffee.*

Lemon Cookie Balls

INGREDIENTS	TEST QUANTITY: 8	SERVICE QUANTITY: 50	METHOD
Butter	$\frac{1}{4}$ cup	$1\frac{1}{2}$ cups	Combine well.
Shortening or lard	$\frac{1}{4}$ cup	$1\frac{1}{2}$ cups	
Almonds, ground	$\frac{1}{4}$ cup	$1\frac{1}{2}$ cups	
Sugar	$\frac{3}{4}$ cup	$2\frac{1}{4}$ lb.	
Eggs, beaten	1	6	
Lemon juice	2 tbsp.	$\frac{3}{4}$ cup	
Orange brandy	1 tbsp.	6 tbsp.	
Water	1 tbsp.	6 tbsp.	
Flour, all purpose, sifted	$1\frac{3}{4}$ cups	3 lb.	Combine well and work into mixture. Chill well. Form into small balls and bake at 400°F for 12 to 15 minutes.
Baking powder	$1\frac{1}{2}$ tsp.	3 tbsp.	
Salt	$\frac{1}{4}$ tsp.	$1\frac{1}{2}$ tsp.	
Lemon rind	1 tsp.	2 tbsp.	
Orange rind	1 tsp.	2 tbsp.	
Pecans, chopped	$\frac{1}{4}$ cup	$1\frac{1}{2}$ cups	
Walnuts, chopped	$\frac{1}{4}$ cup	$1\frac{1}{2}$ cups	
Powdered sugar	as needed	as needed	Roll balls in sugar.

SPECIAL HANDLING FOR BUFFETS: *Serve at room temperature from tray(s) lined with lemon leaves. Ideal for an afternoon tea or an after-theater buffet.*

Lemon Crème Roll

INGREDIENTS	TEST QUANTITY: 8	SERVICE QUANTITY: 50	METHOD
Sugar	$\frac{1}{3}$ cup	2 cups	Whip together until lemon yellow.
Eggs, beaten	4	2 dozen	
Flour, self-rising, sifted	$\frac{1}{2}$ cup	3 cups	Sift over mixture. Fold in. Butter and flour jelly roll pan(s). Line with parchment. Butter and flour again. Pour batter in. Bake at 400°F until golden brown, about 10 minutes. Invert onto parchment or towel.
Lemon peel, grated	1 tsp.	2 tbsp.	Combine and spread over cake(s).
Orange marmalade	$\frac{1}{2}$ cup	3 cups	
Cognac	1 tbsp.	$\frac{1}{3}$ cup	
Butter, sweet, melted	$\frac{1}{2}$ cup	3 cups	Combine and cook over very low heat until well thickened. Do not boil.
Sugar	1 cup	3 lb.	
Lemon juice, strained	1 cup	$1\frac{1}{2}$ qt.	
Egg yolks, beaten	8	4 dozen	
Cinnamon	$\frac{1}{4}$ tsp.	$1\frac{1}{2}$ tsp.	
Orange rind, grated	1 tbsp.	$\frac{1}{2}$ cup	Stir into lemon mixture. Spread over cake layer. Roll from the long side. Let rest for 1 hour.
Lemon rind, grated	1 tbsp.	$\frac{1}{2}$ cup	
Pecans, chopped	$\frac{1}{4}$ cup	$1\frac{1}{2}$ cups	
Walnuts, chopped	$\frac{1}{4}$ cup	$1\frac{1}{2}$ cups	
Powdered sugar	$\frac{1}{2}$ cup	3 cups	Sprinkle over. Chill.

SPECIAL HANDLING FOR BUFFETS: *Serve chilled from silver tray or platter.*

Lemon Nut Cookie Bars

INGREDIENTS	TEST QUANTITY: 8	SERVICE QUANTITY: 50	METHOD
Butter, soft	$\frac{1}{2}$ cup	3 cups	Cream together until fluffy and light.
Powdered sugar, sifted	$\frac{1}{4}$ cup	$1\frac{1}{2}$ cups	
Orange brandy	1 tbsp.	4 oz.	
Vanilla extract	$\frac{1}{2}$ tsp.	1 tbsp.	
Flour, all purpose	1 cup	$1\frac{1}{2}$ lb.	Combine. Add to egg mixture. Beat until well
Baking powder	$\frac{3}{4}$ tsp.	$1\frac{1}{2}$ tbsp.	combined. Pour into buttered shallow half-
Cinnamon	$\frac{1}{4}$ tsp.	$1\frac{1}{2}$ tsp.	size sheet pans. Bake at 350°F for 15 minutes.
Salt	pinch	$\frac{1}{4}$ tsp.	
Almonds, crumbled	$\frac{1}{2}$ cup	3 cups	
Pecans, crumbled	$\frac{1}{2}$ cup	3 cups	
Walnuts, crumbled	$\frac{1}{2}$ cup	3 cups	Combine and sprinkle over pastry.
Brown sugar, light	$\frac{1}{4}$ cup	$1\frac{1}{2}$ cups	
Sugar	$\frac{3}{4}$ cup	$4\frac{1}{2}$ cups	Combine. Pour into baked shell. Bake at
Flour, all purpose	2 tbsp.	$\frac{3}{4}$ cup	350°F until mixture is set, about 35 minutes.
Baking powder	$\frac{1}{2}$ tsp.	1 tbsp.	
Salt	pinch	$\frac{1}{4}$ tsp.	
Eggs, beaten	3	$1\frac{1}{2}$ dozen	
Lemon juice, strained	3 tbsp.	1 cup + 2 tbsp.	
Orange extract	$\frac{1}{2}$ tsp.	1 tbsp.	
Orange rind, grated	$\frac{1}{2}$ tsp.	1 tbsp.	
Lemon rind, grated	$\frac{1}{2}$ tsp.	1 tbsp.	
Powdered sugar, sifted	$\frac{1}{2}$ cup	3 cups	Sprinkle over while warm. Cut into service
Brown sugar, light	$\frac{1}{4}$ cup	$1\frac{1}{2}$ cups	portions.
Lemon rind, grated	1 tsp.	2 tbsp.	
Pecans, crumbled	2 tbsp.	$\frac{3}{4}$ cup	

SPECIAL HANDLING FOR BUFFETS: *Serve warm from shallow insert pan(s) set over single heating unit. Keep covered. Offer with cognac-laced whipped cream.*

Louisiana Bread Pudding

INGREDIENTS	TEST QUANTITY: 8	SERVICE QUANTITY: 50	METHOD
French bread, large chunks	12 oz.	4½ lb.	Combine in bowl until milk is absorbed. Pour off excess.
Cinnamon	½ tsp.	1 tbsp.	
Milk	1 qt.	1½ gal.	
Cognac	1 oz.	¾ cup	
Eggs, beaten	7	3½ dozen	Combine and whip until very thick. Pour over bread mixture. Mix well.
Sugar	1 cup	3 lb.	
Vanilla extract	1 tsp.	2 tbsp.	
Lemon extract	1 tsp.	2 tbsp.	
Pecans, chopped	½ cup	3 cups	Stir into mixture. Pour into buttered shallow pan(s). Place in bain marie and bake at 350°F until golden and custard tests done.
Raisins	½ cup	3 cups	
Nutmeg, ground	to taste	to taste	
Cinnamon, ground	to taste	to taste	
Ginger, ground	to taste	to taste	

SPECIAL HANDLING FOR BUFFETS: *Serve warm or chilled.   Offer with Whiskey Sauce (see Recipe Index).*

Louisiana French Silk Pie

INGREDIENTS	TEST QUANTITY: 8	SERVICE QUANTITY: 50	METHOD
Vanilla wafers, crumbled	1¼ cups	7½ cups	Combine. Press onto bottom and sides of 9-in. pie pan(s). Cool.
Pecans, ground	¼ cup	1½ cups	
Brown sugar, light	1½ tbsp.	½ cup + 1 tbsp.	
Butter, melted	6 tbsp.	1 lb. + ¼ cup	
Butter, soft	¾ cup	4½ cups	Whip together until creamy.
Sugar, extra fine	1 cup + 1 tbsp.	3 lb. + 6 tbsp.	
Chocolate, unsweetened	1½ oz.	9 oz.	Melt carefully in bain marie. Add to butter.
Vanilla extract	½ tbsp.	3 tbsp.	
Cognac	1 tbsp.	⅓ cup	
Eggs, beaten	2	12	Add gradually. Whip rapidly for 3 minutes.
Lemon peel, grated	1 tsp.	2 tbsp.	
Eggs, beaten	1	6	Add gradually. Whip for 2 more minutes. Divide mixture among reserved pie pans. Chill for several hours.
Heavy cream	½ cup	1 qt.	Whip until stiff. Divide over pies.
Powdered sugar	to taste	to taste	
Cognac	½ oz.	½ cup	
Chocolate, semisweet, grated	¼ cup	1½ cups	Sprinkle over cream.
Pecans, chopped	¼ cup	1½ cups	

SPECIAL HANDLING FOR BUFFETS: *Serve chilled. Add some orange brandy or cognac to custard mixture before filling pies.*

Maple Rice Pudding

INGREDIENTS	TEST QUANTITY: 8	SERVICE QUANTITY: 50	METHOD
Raisins	$\frac{1}{2}$ cup	3 cups	Macerate for several hours.
Dark rum	$\frac{1}{4}$ cup	$1\frac{1}{2}$ cups	
Rice, raw	$\frac{2}{3}$ cup	2 lb.	Cook just until tender. Drain. Return to pan.
Water, salted, boiling	to cover	to cover	
Heavy cream	$\frac{2}{3}$ cup	1 qt.	Add to rice; cook until cream is absorbed.
Lemon rind, grated	of 1	of 6	Remove pan from heat.
Cinnamon	$\frac{1}{4}$ tsp.	$1\frac{1}{2}$ tsp.	
Nutmeg	$\frac{1}{4}$ tsp.	$1\frac{1}{2}$ tsp.	
Heavy cream	$2\frac{1}{2}$ cups	3 qt. + 3 cups	Combine and add to rice mixture. Pour into
Pecans, chopped	$\frac{1}{2}$ cup	3 cups	buttered shallow pans and bake at 350°F
Maple syrup	$\frac{2}{3}$ cup	1 qt.	until firm and golden.
Raisin mixture	from above	from above	
Eggs, beaten	2	1 dozen	

SPECIAL HANDLING FOR BUFFETS: *Serve warm from shallow insert pan(s) set over single heating unit. Keep covered.*

Marmalade Pudding

INGREDIENTS	TEST QUANTITY: 8	SERVICE QUANTITY: 50	METHOD
Butter	$\frac{1}{4}$ cup	$\frac{3}{4}$ lb.	Cream together well.
Lemon peel, grated	$\frac{1}{2}$ tsp.	1 tbsp.	
Sugar	$\frac{2}{3}$ cup	2 lb.	
Eggs, beaten	2	1 dozen	Add; mix in.
Flour, all purpose	1 cup	$1\frac{1}{2}$ lb.	Sift together.
Baking powder	$1\frac{1}{2}$ tsp.	3 tbsp.	
Cloves, ground	$\frac{1}{4}$ tsp.	$1\frac{1}{2}$ tsp.	
Cinnamon, ground	$\frac{1}{2}$ tsp.	1 tbsp.	
Nutmeg, ground	$\frac{1}{4}$ tsp.	$1\frac{1}{2}$ tsp.	
Salt	$\frac{1}{4}$ tsp.	$1\frac{1}{2}$ tsp.	
Milk	$\frac{1}{4}$ cup	$1\frac{1}{2}$ cups	Combine and add to the egg mixture alter-
Water	$\frac{1}{4}$ cup	$1\frac{1}{2}$ cups	nately with dry ingredients. Mix until batter is smooth.
Vanilla extract	1 tsp.	2 tbsp.	Combine and add to batter.
Orange brandy	1 tbsp.	$\frac{1}{3}$ cup	
Orange peel, grated	1 tsp.	2 tbsp.	
Lemon peel, grated	$\frac{1}{2}$ tsp.	1 tbsp.	
Orange marmalade, bitter, melted	1 cup	$1\frac{1}{2}$ qt.	Pour into buttered loaf pan(s) and add batter.
Red currant jelly	$\frac{1}{4}$ cup	$1\frac{1}{2}$ cups	Bake in the middle of 350°F oven until it tests
Pecans, chopped	$\frac{1}{2}$ cup	3 cups	for done with an inserted skewer. Cool 10 minutes. Run a knife around edges and invert onto service piece.

SPECIAL HANDLING FOR BUFFETS: *Serve warm from shallow insert pan(s) set over single heating unit. Keep covered. This is a British favorite.*

Orange Caramel Cream with Pineapple

INGREDIENTS	TEST QUANTITY: 8	SERVICE QUANTITY: 50	METHOD
Sugar	2 cups	6 lb.	Combine in heavy saucepan. Simmer until mixture dissolves and turns a fairly dark brown. Immediately pour mixture into individual buttered pudding mold(s). Rotate to coat. Invert and allow to cool.
Water	1 cup	$1\frac{1}{2}$ qt.	
Condensed milk	2 cups	3 qt.	Combine well. Strain into the sugar-lined mold(s). Place in bain marie. Bake in 350°F oven until puddings test done. Let cool. Refrigerate overnight. Invert onto service piece(s).
Vanilla extract	$\frac{1}{2}$ tsp.	1 tbsp.	
Orange peel, grated	1 tbsp.	$\frac{1}{2}$ cup	
Pecans, chopped	$\frac{1}{4}$ cup	$1\frac{1}{2}$ cups	
Pineapple juice, strained	$1\frac{1}{2}$ cups	$2\frac{1}{4}$ qt.	
Ginger, ground	$\frac{1}{4}$ tsp.	$1\frac{1}{2}$ tsp.	
Sugar	$\frac{1}{4}$ cup	$1\frac{1}{2}$ cups	
Cinnamon	$\frac{1}{4}$ tsp.	$1\frac{1}{2}$ tsp.	
Orange brandy	2 tbsp.	$\frac{3}{4}$ cup	
Eggs	4	2 dozen	
Egg yolks	2	1 dozen	
Crushed pineapple	2 cups	3 qt.	Combine. Pour around individual puddings.
Coconut, toasted	$\frac{1}{2}$ cup	3 cups	

SPECIAL HANDLING FOR BUFFETS: *Serve chilled with side   dishes of orange sections, crushed pineapple, and nuts.*

Pâte Brisée for Tarts

INGREDIENTS	TEST QUANTITY: 8	SERVICE QUANTITY: 50	METHOD
Butter, chilled, chopped	$\frac{1}{4}$ lb.	$1\frac{1}{2}$ lb.	Work together until crumbly. Reserve.
Flour, all purpose	$1\frac{2}{3}$ cups	$2\frac{1}{2}$ lb.	
Salt	pinch	as desired	
Egg yolks	1	6	Mix well.
Ice water	2 tbsp.	$\frac{3}{4}$ cup	
White wine, ice cold	2 tbsp.	$\frac{3}{4}$ cup	
Peanut oil	1 tbsp.	$\frac{1}{3}$ cup	Add to egg mixture. Then toss with flour to form ball(s). Wrap and chill for 30 minutes. Roll out into 9-in. rounds.

SPECIAL HANDLING FOR BUFFETS: *If desired, roll out into rectangular shape and fit into half-sized sheet pans; proceed with desired recipe.*

Peach-Nut Crisp

INGREDIENTS	TEST QUANTITY: 8	SERVICE QUANTITY: 50	METHOD
Cling peaches, canned, sliced, drained	1½ lb.	9 lb.	Reserve peach syrup. Combine drained peaches with lemon and nut mixture; reserve.
Lemon juice	¼ cup	1½ cups	
Lemon peel, grated	½ tsp.	1 tbsp.	
Raisins	½ cup	3 cups	
Almonds, chopped	¼ cup	1½ cups	
Pecans, chopped	½ cup	3 cups	
Walnuts, chopped	¼ cup	1½ cups	
Peach syrup, from above, heated	2 cups	3 qt.	Combine well. Add to peaches. Pour into shallow pan(s).
Cognac	1 tbsp.	⅓ cup	
Cornstarch	2 tbsp.	¾ cup	
Clove, ground	⅛ tsp.	¾ tsp.	
Nutmeg	¼ tsp.	1½ tsp.	
Cinnamon	½ tsp.	1 tbsp.	
Brown sugar, light	1 cup	3 lb.	
Honey	2 tbsp.	¾ cup	
Vanilla extract	½ tsp.	1 tbsp.	
Butter, melted	1 cup	3 lb.	Combine well and distribute over mixture. Bake in 350°F oven until crisp and hot, about 1½ hours.
Flour, all purpose	2 cups	3 lb.	
Sugar	1 cup	3 lb.	

SPECIAL HANDLING FOR BUFFETS: *Serve warm or at room temperature. Offer with side dishes of crème fraiche or unsweetened whipped cream.*

Raisin Crème Pudding

INGREDIENTS	TEST QUANTITY: 8	SERVICE QUANTITY: 50	METHOD
Bread slices, thin, trimmed	6	2 lb.	Trim to fit $\frac{1}{3}$ of slices into bottom of buttered baking pan(s).
Dried currants	$\frac{1}{4}$ cup	$1\frac{1}{2}$ cups	Combine and distribute half over bread.
Candied fruit, chopped	$\frac{1}{4}$ cup	$1\frac{1}{2}$ cups	Cover with another third of bread, then fruit,
White raisins	$\frac{1}{4}$ cup	$1\frac{1}{2}$ cups	then bread.
Cinnamon	pinch	$\frac{1}{2}$ tsp.	
Nutmeg	pinch	$\frac{1}{2}$ tsp.	
Eggs, beaten	3	$1\frac{1}{2}$ dozen	Whip together and pour over bread. Let rest
Milk	$2\frac{1}{2}$ cups	$3\frac{3}{4}$ qt.	until all liquid is absorbed. Cover pudding
Vanilla extract	$\frac{1}{2}$ tsp.	1 tbsp.	with buttered foil and bake at 350°F for 30
Heavy cream	$\frac{1}{2}$ cup	3 cups	minutes. Remove foil and bake until top is
Brown sugar, light	2 tbsp.	$\frac{3}{4}$ cup	golden brown and crisp.
Nutmeg	to taste	to taste	
Cinnamon	to taste	to taste	

SPECIAL HANDLING FOR BUFFETS: *Serve warm from shallow insert pan(s) set over single heating unit. Keep covered.*

Spiced Apple Crisp

INGREDIENTS	TEST QUANTITY: 8	SERVICE QUANTITY: 50	METHOD
Dried currants	1 cup	2 lb.	Combine. Let rest for 10 minutes. Drain.
Dark rum	1 tbsp.	$\frac{1}{3}$ cup	
Cognac	1 tbsp.	$\frac{1}{3}$ cup	
Water, boiling	to cover	to cover	
Apples, Golden Delicious, pared, cored, coarsely chopped	1 lb.	6 lb.	Toss and combine with currants. Arrange in buttered shallow pan.
Lemon juice, strained	1 tbsp.	$\frac{1}{3}$ cup	
Walnuts, chopped	$\frac{1}{4}$ cup	$1\frac{1}{2}$ cups	Combine well until mixture reaches mealy appearance. Sprinkle over apple-currant mixture. Bake at 375°F until topping is brown and apples are tender. Portion into squares.
Pecans, chopped	1 cup	$1\frac{1}{2}$ qt.	
Flour, all purpose	$\frac{3}{4}$ cup	1 lb. + $\frac{1}{2}$ cup	
Granulated sugar	$\frac{1}{3}$ cup	2 cups	
Brown sugar, light	$\frac{1}{3}$ cup	2 cups	
Butter, cold, chopped	$\frac{1}{2}$ cup	3 cups	
Orange rind, grated	of 1	of 6	
Lemon rind, grated	of 1	of 6	
Cinnamon, ground	$\frac{1}{2}$ tsp.	2 tbsp.	
Ginger, ground	$\frac{1}{4}$ tsp.	$1\frac{1}{2}$ tsp.	

SPECIAL HANDLING FOR BUFFETS: *Serve warm from shallow insert pan(s) set over single heating unit. Keep covered. Offer with side dishes of unsweetened whipped cream.*

Swedish Sandbakker Tarts

INGREDIENTS	TEST QUANTITY: 8	SERVICE QUANTITY: 50	METHOD
Butter	$\frac{1}{2}$ cup	3 cups	Work together until mixture forms coarse crumbs.
Flour, all purpose, unsifted	1 cup	$1\frac{1}{2}$ lb.	
Orange peel, grated	1 tsp.	2 tbsp.	
Sugar	$\frac{1}{4}$ cup	$1\frac{1}{2}$ cups	
Egg yolks	1	6	Add; stir with fork to blend. Spoon 1 tbsp. of mixture into waxed-paper–lined tart pans. Smooth into shape and bake at 400°F until golden, about 10 to 12 minutes. Remove when cool. Reserve.
Pecans, ground	1 tbsp.	$\frac{1}{3}$ cup	
Almonds, ground, blanched	1 tbsp.	$\frac{1}{3}$ cup	
Almond extract	$\frac{1}{2}$ tsp.	1 tbsp.	
Cinnamon, ground	$\frac{1}{4}$ tsp.	$1\frac{1}{2}$ tsp.	
Ginger, ground	$\frac{1}{8}$ tsp.	$\frac{3}{4}$ tsp.	
Vanilla extract	$\frac{1}{2}$ tsp.	1 tbsp.	Combine over hot water.
Eggs	3	$1\frac{1}{2}$ dozen	
Egg yolks	1	6	
Sugar	1 cup	3 lb.	
Lemon rind	of 2	of 12	Add. Cook, stirring, over boiling water until very thick. Do not boil. Chill very well and fill tart shells prior to service.
Lemon juice	of 2	of 12	
Orange brandy	1 tbsp.	$\frac{1}{3}$ cup	
Butter	$\frac{1}{2}$ cup	3 cups	

SPECIAL HANDLING FOR BUFFETS: *Serve chilled. Top with meringue and bake until golden before chilling.*

Swiss Chocolate Torte

INGREDIENTS	TEST QUANTITY: 8	SERVICE QUANTITY: 50	METHOD
Chocolate, sweet, dark, grated	$\frac{1}{2}$ lb.	3 lb.	Combine in bain marie. Stir. Melt completely.
Coffee liqueur	1 tbsp.	$\frac{1}{3}$ cup	
Butter, soft	$\frac{1}{2}$ cup	3 cups	
Sour cherries, chopped, drained	$\frac{1}{2}$ cup	3 cups	
Sugar	1 cup	3 lb.	
Cinnamon	$\frac{1}{4}$ tsp.	$1\frac{1}{2}$ tsp.	
Egg yolks	5	$2\frac{1}{2}$ dozen	Add individually. Stir well after each addition.
Vanilla extract	$\frac{1}{2}$ tsp.	1 tbsp.	Add. Stir well.
Cherry liqueur	1 tbsp.	$\frac{1}{3}$ cup	
Orange extract	$\frac{1}{2}$ tsp.	1 tbsp.	
Flour, all purpose, sifted	1 cup	$1\frac{1}{2}$ lb.	Combine. Add gently.
Baking powder	1 tsp.	2 tbsp.	
Pecans, chopped finely	1 tbsp.	$\frac{1}{3}$ cup	
Egg whites	5	$2\frac{1}{2}$ dozen	Whip until stiff. Fold in. Pour into buttered and paper-lined 9-in. springform pan(s). Bake at 350°F until cake(s) test done, about 40 minutes. Remove and place on service piece(s).
Cream of tartar	$\frac{1}{8}$ tsp.	$\frac{3}{4}$ tsp.	
Powdered sugar	as desired	as desired	Sift over top.

SPECIAL HANDLING FOR BUFFETS: *Serve at room temperature. Serve with fresh or stewed berries.*

Whiskey Sauce for Bread Pudding

INGREDIENTS	TEST QUANTITY: 8	SERVICE QUANTITY: 50	METHOD
Sugar	1 cup	3 lb.	Mix until thick in bain marie over very hot water.
Honey	1 tbsp.	$\frac{1}{3}$ cup	
Eggs, beaten	1	6	
Vanilla extract	$\frac{1}{2}$ tsp.	1 tbsp.	
Butter, melted	$\frac{1}{4}$ lb.	$1\frac{1}{2}$ lb.	Add to mixture. Stir over hot water until sugar dissolves and mixture thickens. Do not boil. Remove from heat. Let cool.
Lemon peel, grated	$\frac{1}{2}$ tsp.	1 tbsp.	
Pecans, chopped	$\frac{1}{4}$ cup	$1\frac{1}{2}$ cups	
Cognac	2 tbsp.	$\frac{3}{4}$ cup	Stir into cool mixture.
Whiskey	$\frac{1}{2}$ cup	3 cups	

SPECIAL HANDLING FOR BUFFETS: *See recipe for Bread Pudding. Substitute rum for the whiskey.*

Review Questions

1. Name two traditional desserts made with pâte à chou.

2. Describe a Bavarian cream.

3. How do French, Italian, and Swiss meringues differ?

4. What do gateau and kuchen have in common?

5. What is needed for French millefeuille?

6. Describe zabaglione.

Eleven
Brunch: What's in a Name

Brunch is an occasion seemingly designed for culinary dramatics. Buffet tables spring to life with ornate displays, brimming trays, and steaming chafers of every description. From steamship rounds to pastry squares, from cold seafood to hot pastrami, brunch is a time for buffet creativity. Brunch is also a time for classic presentations of eggs. According to French tradition, the pleats of a chef's tall white hat represent the hundred ways one must know to prepare eggs. We turn now to classic French cooking for brunch buffet menu specialties that feature eggs in many forms.

SCRAMBLED

Scrambled eggs receive a touch of high fashion when the following garnishes are mixed in or offered on the side. Classic French names add buffet sophistication.

Antoine. A touch of diced fried bacon, herbs, and capers.

Arlesian. Sautéed diced eggplant, chopped tomatoes, and minced green pepper.

Brazilian. Julienne of red pepper with chopped tomatoes and ham, served in pastry.

Brioche. Sautéed mushrooms and parsley, served in hollowed brioche shells.

Cambridge. Diced lobster, mushrooms, and peppers in cream sauce.

Chantilly. Partially whipped, unseasoned heavy cream with snipped chives.

Chatillion. Sautéed sliced mushrooms, chopped chives, and parsley.

Countess. Chopped cooked shrimp and tips of asparagus in cream sauce.

Figaro. Sliced or chopped sausage, with a tomato béarnaise sauce on the side.

Fines Herbes. With finely chopped chives, parsley, tarragon, and chervil.

Green Meadow. Served in small tart shells on purée of spinach with chopped herbs.

Hamburg. Strips of smoked herring, chopped capers, and minced scallion.

Joinville. Diced shrimp, mushrooms, and truffles served in pastry shell.

Leuchtenberg. Chopped chives and caviar, with minced scallion and sour cream.

Madrid. Sautéed chopped tomatoes bound with a light cream sauce.

Marie. Grated Parmesan cheese, served in pastry shells and sprinkled with mushrooms.

Mercedes. Chopped chives and sautéed tomato, with tomato sauce on the side.

Mexican. Sautéed tomato, onion, and green peppers, with tomato sauce on the side.

Montbarry. Diced mushrooms and asparagus tips with grated Parmesan cheese.

Moorish. Chopped sautéed sausages with diced ham and pimiento.

Oriental. Sautéed julienne of peppers and onions, with diced tomatoes and brown sauce.

Parmetier. Sautéed diced potatoes and chopped parsley.

Provençale. Sautéed onion, garlic, chopped tomato, and parsley.

St. Denis. Served in large sautéed mushroom caps, red wine sauce on the side.

Saragossa. Sautéed diced ham, with fried bananas and corn fritters with tomato sauce.

Spanish. Served on sautéed slices of tomato, with fried onion rings.

Swiss. Served in tart shells and topped with grated and browned Swiss cheese.

Turkish. Saffron, chopped eggplant, onion, and tomato, served on sautéed eggplant slice.

Yvette. Asparagus tips and poached crayfish tails with tomato sauce on the side.

"EN COCOTTE"

Eggs *en cocotte* are actually baked in crêpe-lined muffin tins. Put the filling in the crêpe, follow with the whole eggs, and bake until done. Offer sauces on top or in small ramekins. These brunch "packages" are easy to serve and provide another outlet for buffet creativity.

Carnegie. Lined with mushroom purée and diced peppers, tomato sauce.

Commander. Buttered crêpes and eggs, served with béarnaise sauce.

Cuban. Lined with creamed crab meat, baked, sprinkled with chopped parsley.

Florentine. Lined with creamed spinach, sprinkled with grated cheese, baked.

Forester. Lined with minced morels and sautéed bacon, sprinkled with herbs.

Josephine. Lined with mushroom purée, topped with chopped tomatoes, cheese sauce.

Marigny. Lined with poached oysters, cream sauce, and grated Parmesan cheese.

Parisian. Lined with minced chicken, ham, tongue, mushrooms; topped with a rich brown sauce.

Puerto Rico. Lined with diced tomatoes, ham, and asparagus; served with cream sauce.

Portuguese. Lined with chopped tomato, tomato sauce.

Princess. Lined with creamed asparagus tips, cream sauce, and grated cheese.

Queen's Style (à la reine). Lined with minced poached chicken, cream sauce.

St. George. Lined with onion purée, topped with cream sauce and grated cheese.

Tosca. Lined with sour cream, sprinkled with grated cheese, baked.

Valentine. Lined with tomato purée and chopped mushrooms, topped with cream sauce.

Voltaire. Lined with chicken hash, topped with cream sauce with grated cheese, and baked.

POACHED

Poached eggs served atop toasted English muffins have spawned a number of brunch classics, including legendary eggs Benedict. Tart shells and toast join muffins and vegetables for creative poached egg menus.

African. Toasted muffin topped with bacon and sautéed tomatoes; tomato sauce.

Americaine. Sautéed tomato slices, topped with cooked lobster, lobster sauce.

Andalusian. Sautéed eggplant slices, tomato sauce with strips of grilled pepper.

Bakers. Toasted muffin lined with sautéed mushrooms, cheese sauce and grated Parmesan.

Baltic. Toasted crouton sprinkled with caviar, cheese sauce and grated Parmesan.

Barcelona. Halved baked tomatoes topped with sautéed green pepper, rich brown sauce.

Bar-le-Duc. Poached artichoke bottoms, cream sauce with chopped tarragon.

Bernadotte. Tart shell with chopped anchovy, cream sauce with chopped olives.

Buckingham Palace. Toasted muffin, cover with ham slice, cream sauce, and grated cheese.

Cardinal. Tart shell with creamed lobster and lobster sauce.

Chambery. Crouton spread with chestnut purée and Madeira sauce.

Cinderella. Slice of baked potato topped with truffles, cream sauce, grated cheese.

Creole. Flat rice croquettes, chopped mushrooms, and creole sauce.

Danish. Tart shell lined with chopped smoked salmon, hollandaise sauce.

Dufferin. Large grilled mushroom caps, horseradish sauce.

English. Croutons covered with Cheddar cheese sauce, paprika, and grilled bacon.

Flemish. Tart shell lined with puréed brussels sprouts and cream sauce.

Fontainbleu. Crouton lined with chopped tomato, topped with cream sauce with diced red pepper.

Gascon. Tomato halves lined with lamb hash, garlic, and herbs, topped with tomato sauce.

Henri IV. Artichoke bottom and béarnaise sauce.

Hungarian. Tart shell lined with stewed onion and tomato, cream sauce and paprika.

Lafayette. Toasted muffin lined with chopped tomatoes and béarnaise sauce.

Louisville. Corn fritters, fried bacon, and banana, topped with tomato sauce.

Maltese. Tart shell lined with asparagus tips, maltaise sauce.

New York. Rounds of fried corn mush, cream sauce with diced red pepper.

Orleans. Tart shell lined with chopped chicken, topped with tomato sauce and chopped pistachios.

Richelieu. Duchess potato nests lined with grilled mushrooms, topped with rich brown sauce.

Ritz. Tart shells lined with chopped shrimp and green pepper, shrimp cream sauce.

Sardinian. Grilled tomato half, cheese sauce and grated cheese, browned.

Sully. Tart shell with chicken hash, béarnaise sauce.

Swiss. Toasted muffin lined with Swiss cheese, cream sauce with grated cheese.

Trouville. Mushroom caps with poached oysters and mussels, shrimp sauce.

Viroflay. Miniature brioche shells lined with creamed spinach, cream sauce.

Washington. Ramekin with creamed corn, cheese sauce with grated cheese, browned.

OMELETS

Omelets, universal favorites, are especially popular at brunch, where they can be offered with a variety of fillings. Perhaps the following list of French classics will bolster your menu as it rounds out our discussion of brunchtime egg specialties.

Beranger. Chopped tomatoes, fried bacon, herbs, tomato sauce.

Breton. Sautéed chopped onions, leeks, and mushrooms.

Bonne Femme. Fried bacon in egg mixture, with fried onions and mushrooms as filling.

Butcher Style. Chopped ham and bacon, served with mustard sauce.

Cherbourg. Chopped shrimps in cream sauce, garnish of chopped shrimp.

Continental. Chopped parsley in egg mixture, diced fried potatoes and mushrooms.

Gypsy. Chopped tomatoes, ham, mushrooms, and truffles; served with rich brown sauce.

Grenoble. Sautéed spinach with garlic and crumbled fried onions.

Guilford. Sautéed morels or other mushrooms with diced red pepper.

Havana. Fried chicken livers, diced green peppers, and tomatoes, in tomato sauce.

Jessica. Sliced morels and asparagus tips; rich brown sauce.

Lyonnaise. Sautéed sliced onions and chopped parsley.

Mazarin. Sliced Italian chipolata sausage and sautéed mushrooms in Madeira sauce.

Mireille. Chopped tomato and garlic in saffron cream sauce.

Olympia. Diced crab meat and green pepper in light cream sauce.

Raspail. Chopped beef, ham, and mixed herbs in rich brown sauce.

Richemonde. Sautéed mushrooms with port, in light cheese sauce.

Russian. Paprika in egg mixture, with caviar, sour cream, and minced onions.

Saratoga. Crab meat and sautéed peppers in creole sauce.

Seville. Tomatoes and chopped green olives and garlic, in tomato cream sauce.

Villager. Sautéed chopped mushrooms with mixed herbs.

Alsatian Apple Crêpes

INGREDIENTS	TEST QUANTITY: 8	SERVICE QUANTITY: 50	METHOD
Peanut oil, hot	$\frac{1}{4}$ cup	$1\frac{1}{2}$ cups	Sauté until soft, turning often. Reduce heat.
Butter, hot	3 tbsp.	1 cup + 2 tbsp.	
Ginger, grated	$\frac{1}{4}$ tsp.	$1\frac{1}{2}$ tsp.	
Green apples (medium), firm, peeled, cored, sliced	2 lb.	12 lb.	
Raisins, golden	$\frac{1}{2}$ cup	3 cups	
Brown sugar, light	$\frac{1}{3}$ cup	2 cups	Add until dissolved.
Cinnamon	1 tsp.	2 tbsp.	
Nutmeg	$\frac{1}{4}$ tsp.	$1\frac{1}{2}$ tsp.	
Cloves	$\frac{1}{8}$ tsp.	$\frac{3}{4}$ tsp.	
Sugar	3 tbsp.	1 cup + 2 tbsp.	Add; stir gently until dissolved. Remove from heat.
Almonds, slivered	1 tbsp.	$\frac{1}{3}$ cup	Add; stir gently. Remove from pan. Cool.
Vanilla extract	1 tsp.	2 tbsp.	
Cognac	1 tbsp.	$\frac{1}{3}$ cup	
Orange juice	of 1	of 6	
Orange rind, grated	of 1	of 6	
Crêpes	16	100	Divide mixture along centers of the crêpes. Fold edges over and place seam side down in buttered sheet pans. Reserve extra mixture for service.
Butter, melted	3 tbsp.	1 cup	Sprinkle over crêpes. Bake at 350°F until lightly brown, about 3 to 5 minutes.
Honey	1 tbsp.	$\frac{1}{3}$ cup	

SPECIAL HANDLING FOR BUFFETS: *Serve very warm from shallow insert pan(s) set over dual heating units. Keep covered. Add some chopped nuts to the filling. Offer with whipped cream or crème frâiche. Serve with extra apple mixture.*

Apple Dumplings

INGREDIENTS	TEST QUANTITY: 8	SERVICE QUANTITY: 50	METHOD
Butter, unsalted	6 oz.	2¼ lb.	Combine and work until crumbly. Keep mixture chilled.
Lard	4 oz.	1½ lb.	
Almonds, ground	¼ cup	1½ cups	
Flour, all purpose	3 cups	4½ lb.	
Lemon rind, grated	1 tsp.	2 tbsp.	
Salt	¼ tsp.	1½ tsp.	
Sugar	2 tbsp.	¾ cup	
Cinnamon	½ tsp.	1 tbsp.	
White wine, ice cold	⅓ to ½ cup	2 to 3 cups	Add gradually and work into a ball; add more wine if needed. Dust with flour; wrap and chill for at least 1 hour. Roll out the dough ¼ in. thick and cut into 8-in. circles. Chill.
Butter	⅓ cup	2 cups	Cream well.
Brown sugar, light	⅔ cup	2 lb.	
Apple brandy	1 tbsp.	⅓ cup	Combine well with sugar. Reserve.
Lemon juice	⅓ cup	2 cups	
Pecans, chopped	¼ cup	1½ cups	
Lemon peel	1 tbsp.	⅓ cup	
Raisins	⅓ cup	2 cups	
Nutmeg	¼ tsp.	1½ tsp.	
Cinnamon	½ tsp.	1 tbsp.	
Apples, tart, peeled, cored	8	50	Rub with lemon juice. Pack core cavity with sugar/fruit mixture. Place each in center of dough round. Wrap with dough; twist to seal. Arrange on buttered sheet pan(s) and bake in 375°F oven until barely tender.
Lemon juice	1 tbsp.	⅓ cup	
Brandy	as needed	as needed	Brush tops with brandy and sprinkle with sugar. Continue baking until golden brown, about 10 minutes.
Sugar	¼ cup	1½ cups	

SPECIAL HANDLING FOR BUFFETS: *Serve very warm from shallow insert pan(s) set over dual heating units. Keep covered. Substitute firm pears for apples. Serve with whipped cream or vanilla sauce.*

Bacon Muffins

INGREDIENTS	TEST QUANTITY: 8	SERVICE QUANTITY: 50	METHOD
Flour, all purpose	2 cups	3 lb.	Sift together.
Baking powder	4 tsp.	$\frac{1}{2}$ cup	
Lemon peel, grated	$\frac{1}{2}$ tsp.	1 tbsp.	
Salt	$\frac{1}{2}$ tsp.	1 tbsp.	
White pepper	$\frac{1}{4}$ tsp.	$1\frac{1}{2}$ tsp.	
Sugar	2 tbsp.	$\frac{3}{4}$ cup	
Eggs, beaten	2	12	Combine and add to dry ingredients. Barely mix; do not overblend.
Milk	1 cup	$1\frac{1}{2}$ qt.	
Bacon drippings, strained	$\frac{1}{4}$ cup	$1\frac{1}{2}$ cups	Combine and add. Portion into preheated greased muffin tins. Bake at 425°F until golden, about 25 minutes.
Bacon, fried, crumbled	$\frac{1}{2}$ cup	3 cups	
Onions, chopped, sautéed	$\frac{1}{4}$ cup	$1\frac{1}{2}$ cups	
Cheddar cheese, grated	$\frac{1}{4}$ cup	$1\frac{1}{2}$ cups	

SPECIAL HANDLING FOR BUFFETS: *Serve very warm from shallow insert pan(s) set over dual heating units. Do not cover.*

Baked Apples in Brandy Sauce 2

INGREDIENTS	TEST QUANTITY: 8	SERVICE QUANTITY: 50	METHOD
Sugar	2 cups	6 lb.	Combine and boil for 5 minutes.
Vanilla extract	1 tsp.	2 tbsp.	
Water	2 cups	3 qt.	
Cognac	$\frac{1}{4}$ cup	$1\frac{1}{2}$ cups	
Currant jelly	$\frac{1}{2}$ cup	3 cups	
Pecans, chopped	$\frac{1}{4}$ cup	$1\frac{1}{2}$ cups	
Apple jelly	$\frac{1}{2}$ cup	3 cups	
Orange rind, grated	1 tsp.	2 tbsp.	
Tart apples (small), cored, peeled	8	50	Drop into syrup. Simmer for 10 minutes. Place apples in roasting pan(s) and pour syrup over. Cover tightly and bake at 350°F until the apples are tender. Cool in pan(s). Transfer apples with slotted spoon to shallow insert pan(s). Ladle syrup over apples as desired.
Brandy	1 oz.	6 oz.	Pour over apples.
Heavy cream	$\frac{1}{2}$ cup	3 cups	Combine and beat until stiff.
Sugar	to taste	to taste	
Cinnamon	to taste	to taste	
Apple brandy	1 oz.	$\frac{3}{4}$ cup	Add to cream. Spoon on top of each apple or offer on the side.
Orange brandy	1 tbsp.	$\frac{1}{3}$ cup	
Almonds, chopped	$\frac{1}{2}$ cup	3 cups	Sprinkle over apples.

SPECIAL HANDLING FOR BUFFETS: *Serve warm from shallow insert pan(s) set over single heating unit. Keep covered. Offer with small vanilla wafers and additional whipped cream if desired. Note: A similar procedure can be found in the Desserts chapter, page 294.*

Belgian Beer Waffles

INGREDIENTS	TEST QUANTITY: 8	SERVICE QUANTITY: 50	METHOD
Flour, all purpose, sifted	$1\frac{3}{4}$ cups	$2\frac{2}{3}$ lb.	Combine. Let rest for 2 hours. Spread thinly
Almonds, powdered	$\frac{1}{3}$ cup	2 cups	on hot waffle iron. Cook until steam stops.
Salt	$\frac{1}{4}$ tsp.	$1\frac{1}{2}$ tsp.	Keep warm on paper-lined sheet pans at 250°F.
Butter, melted	$\frac{1}{4}$ cup	$1\frac{1}{2}$ cups	
Beer	$1\frac{1}{2}$ cups	$2\frac{1}{4}$ qt.	
Eggs	1	6	
Lemon rind, grated	of 1	of 6	
Orange rind, grated	1 tsp.	2 tbsp.	
Lemon juice	1 tbsp.	$\frac{1}{3}$ cup	
Vanilla extract	$\frac{1}{4}$ tsp.	$1\frac{1}{2}$ tsp.	
Sugar	1 tsp.	2 tbsp.	
Cinnamon	$\frac{1}{4}$ tsp.	$1\frac{1}{2}$ tsp.	
Strawberries, sliced	$\frac{1}{2}$ cup	3 cups	Combine. Offer with waffles.
Sour cream	1 cup	$1\frac{1}{2}$ qt.	
Pecans, chopped	$\frac{1}{4}$ cup	$1\frac{1}{2}$ cups	
Brown sugar, light	$\frac{1}{3}$ cup	1 lb.	
Honey	1 tbsp.	$\frac{1}{3}$ cup	

SPECIAL HANDLING FOR BUFFETS: *Serve very warm from shallow insert pan(s) set over dual heating units. Do not cover or waffles will lose their crispness. Serve with assorted puréed berries.*

Black Forest Cherry Crêpes

INGREDIENTS	TEST QUANTITY: 8	SERVICE QUANTITY: 50	METHOD
Flour, all purpose	$\frac{2}{3}$ cup	1 lb.	Combine. Let rest 1 hour. Spoon $\frac{1}{4}$ cup of
Milk	$\frac{2}{3}$ cup	1 qt.	batter into heated pan. Pour excess back in
Kirschwasser brandy	1 tbsp.	$\frac{1}{3}$ cup	bowl. Cook at moderate heat until done,
Eggs, beaten	3	$1\frac{1}{2}$ dozen	about 45 seconds on each side. Reserve.
Orange rind, grated	$\frac{1}{2}$ tsp.	1 tbsp.	
Salt	pinch	to taste	
Ginger, ground	$\frac{1}{4}$ tsp.	$1\frac{1}{2}$ tsp.	
Butter, unsalted, soft	$\frac{3}{4}$ cup	$2\frac{1}{4}$ lb.	Combine. Whip until smooth.
Powdered sugar	$\frac{1}{2}$ cup	3 cups	
Honey	1 tbsp.	$\frac{1}{3}$ cup	
Cinnamon	$\frac{1}{4}$ tsp.	$1\frac{1}{2}$ tsp.	
Pecans, chopped	$\frac{1}{4}$ cup	$1\frac{1}{2}$ cups	Combine. Stir in. Spread over crêpes. Fold
Cherries, sour, chopped	$\frac{1}{3}$ cup	2 cups	crêpes into fourths.
Orange brandy	1 tbsp.	$\frac{1}{3}$ cup	
Kirschwasser brandy	2 oz.	$1\frac{1}{2}$ cups	
Chocolate, semisweet, shaved	$\frac{1}{4}$ cup	$1\frac{1}{2}$ cups	
Powdered sugar	as needed	as needed	Sprinkle over before service.

SPECIAL HANDLING FOR BUFFETS: *Serve very warm from shallow insert pan(s) set over dual heating units. Keep covered. Offer with sour cream.*

Blintzes with Cheese

INGREDIENTS	TEST QUANTITY: 8	SERVICE QUANTITY: 50	METHOD
Flour, all purpose, sifted	$\frac{3}{4}$ cup	$1\frac{1}{4}$ lb.	Combine in blender and mix well for 20 seconds. Cover and refrigerate for 1 hour or more.
Milk	$1\frac{1}{2}$ cups	$2\frac{1}{4}$ qt.	
Eggs, beaten	1	6	
Salt	1 tsp.	2 tbsp.	
Butter, clarified, melted	as needed	as needed	Wipe over surface of moderately hot 6-in. pan. Pour in $\frac{1}{4}$ cup of crêpe mixture, rotate pan, and pour out excess. Cook on one side until golden. Flip with fork or fingers and repeat. Continue to wipe pan with butter as needed. Reserve crêpes.
Cottage cheese	1 pt.	6 lb.	Combine and adjust seasoning. Put 1 ounce (2 tbsp.) of this mixture one-third of way toward center of each blintz. Fold sides over and roll up; reserve.
Eggs, lightly beaten	1	6	
Sugar	3 tbsp.	1 cup	
Vanilla	2 tsp.	$\frac{1}{4}$ cup	
Salt	to taste	to taste	
Butter, clarified	$\frac{1}{4}$ cup	as needed	Heat in skillet. Add blintzes, seam side down. Turn and add butter as needed, until blintzes are golden. Transfer to service pan.

SPECIAL HANDLING FOR BUFFETS: *Serve very warm from shallow insert pan(s) set over dual heating units. Keep covered. Sprinkle with powdered sugar. Offer with fruit sauces.*

Blueberry Tea Scones

INGREDIENTS	TEST QUANTITY: 8	SERVICE QUANTITY: 50	METHOD
Flour, all purpose, sifted	2 cups	3 lb.	Sift together.
Lemon peel, grated	1 tsp.	2 tbsp.	
Sugar	3 tbsp.	1 cup + 2 tbsp.	
Baking powder	1 tbsp.	6 tbsp.	
Salt	$\frac{1}{2}$ tsp.	1 tbsp.	
Orange peel, grated	1 tbsp.	6 tbsp.	Cut into flour mixture.
Pecans, chopped	$\frac{1}{4}$ cup	$1\frac{1}{2}$ cups	
Butter	6 tbsp.	1 lb. + $\frac{1}{4}$ cup	
Cinnamon	$\frac{1}{4}$ tsp.	$1\frac{1}{2}$ tsp.	
Blueberries, fresh or frozen	$1\frac{1}{2}$ cups	9 cups	Toss together and add.
Flour, all purpose	$\frac{1}{2}$ cup	3 cups	
Vanilla	$\frac{1}{2}$ tsp.	1 tbsp.	Combine with mixture to form a ball. Roll out
Buttermilk	$\frac{1}{3}$ cup	2 cups	to $\frac{1}{2}$-in. thick circle. Cut into wedges. Place on
Eggs, beaten	1	6	buttered sheet pan(s).
Sugar	2 tbsp.	$\frac{3}{4}$ cup	Combine. Sprinkle over. Bake at 350°F until
Cinnamon	1 tsp.	2 tbsp.	nicely browned, about 15 minutes.
Nutmeg	$\frac{1}{4}$ tsp.	$1\frac{1}{2}$ tsp.	

SPECIAL HANDLING FOR BUFFETS: *Serve very warm from shallow insert pan(s) set over dual heating units. Do not cover. Offer with sweet butter and marmalade.*

Brandied Orange Crêpes

INGREDIENTS	TEST QUANTITY: 8	SERVICE QUANTITY: 50	METHOD
Milk	$1\frac{1}{2}$ cups	$2\frac{1}{4}$ qt.	Heat just to scalding.
Orange peel, grated	1 tsp.	2 tbsp.	Whip together until thick and lemony. Add milk. Return to heat. Stir over moderate heat until mixture thickens. Do not boil. Chill.
Lemon peel, grated	1 tbsp.	$\frac{1}{3}$ cup	
Orange brandy	1 tbsp.	$\frac{1}{3}$ cup	
Egg yolks	3	$1\frac{1}{2}$ dozen	
Mandarin orange segments, drained	$\frac{1}{2}$ cup	3 cups	
Sugar	3 tbsp.	1 cup + 2 tbsp.	
Flour, all purpose	3 tbsp.	1 cup + 2 tbsp.	
Salt	$\frac{1}{4}$ tsp.	$1\frac{1}{2}$ tsp.	
Ginger, ground	$\frac{1}{4}$ tsp.	$1\frac{1}{2}$ tsp.	
Dessert crêpes	16	100	Spoon 1 tbsp. of mixture onto each crêpe. Fold into quarters. Place on sheet pan(s).
Powdered sugar, sifted	$\frac{1}{4}$ cup	$1\frac{1}{2}$ cups	Sprinkle over. Place under broiler until bubbly, about 2 minutes. Place in service piece(s).
Honey	$\frac{1}{4}$ cup	$1\frac{1}{2}$ cups	Whip together. Simmer. Flame. Pour over crêpes.
Cognac	2 oz.	$1\frac{1}{2}$ cups	
Orange brandy	2 oz.	$1\frac{1}{2}$ cups	
Butter, melted	$\frac{1}{4}$ cup	$1\frac{1}{2}$ cups	
Pecans, chopped	1 tbsp.	$\frac{1}{3}$ cup	

SPECIAL HANDLING FOR BUFFETS: *Serve very warm from shallow insert pan(s) set over dual heating units. Keep covered. Offer with sour cream or crème frâiche.*

Cajun Rice Calas (deep-fried rice bread)

INGREDIENTS	TEST QUANTITY: 8	SERVICE QUANTITY: 50	METHOD
Dry yeast	1 tbsp.	6 tbsp.	Combine. Let dissolve until foamy.
Water, warm	$\frac{1}{4}$ cup	$1\frac{1}{2}$ cups	
Honey	1 tsp.	2 tbsp.	
Rice, cooked, cool, drained	2 cups	3 qt.	Add. Combine well. Cover. Let stand in
Raisins, plumped, drained	$\frac{1}{2}$ cup	3 cups	warm spot overnight.
Pecans, chopped	$\frac{1}{4}$ cup	$1\frac{1}{2}$ cups	
Eggs, beaten	3	$1\frac{1}{2}$ dozen	Add gradually, mixing thoroughly.
Brown sugar, light	$\frac{1}{3}$ cup	2 cups	Combine and beat in.
Vanilla extract	$\frac{1}{2}$ tsp.	1 tbsp.	
Orange rind, grated	1 tsp.	2 tbsp.	
Lemon rind	1 tsp.	2 tbsp.	
Salt	to taste	to taste	
Cinnamon, ground	$\frac{1}{4}$ tsp.	$1\frac{1}{2}$ tsp.	
Mace, ground	$\frac{1}{4}$ tsp.	$1\frac{1}{2}$ tsp.	
Nutmeg, grated	$\frac{1}{4}$ tsp.	$1\frac{1}{2}$ tsp.	
Flour, all purpose	$1\frac{1}{2}$ cups	$2\frac{1}{4}$ lb.	Add to mixture. Cover and let rise until
Vegetable oil	as needed	as needed	mixture bubbles actively. Spoon into 375°F oil and fry until calas are golden brown.

SPECIAL HANDLING FOR BUFFETS: *Serve very warm from shallow insert pan(s) set over dual heating units. Offer with powdered sugar.*

Chipped Beef with Cheddar Cream

INGREDIENTS	TEST QUANTITY: 8	SERVICE QUANTITY: 50	METHOD
Chipped beef	1 lb.	6 lb.	Soak to soften, about 5 minutes. Drain. Chop coarsely. Reserve.
Beer, dark	$\frac{1}{2}$ cup	3 cups	
Water, boiling	to cover	to cover	
Sherry, dry	1 oz.	$\frac{3}{4}$ cup	
Cream sauce	$1\frac{1}{2}$ cups	$2\frac{1}{4}$ qt.	Combine in bain marie. Stir until cheese melts. Add reserved beef.
Garlic, minced	$\frac{1}{2}$ tsp.	1 tbsp.	
Cheddar cheese, grated	$\frac{1}{2}$ lb.	3 lb.	
Scallions (greens and whites), chopped	$\frac{1}{4}$ cup	$1\frac{1}{2}$ cups	
Sherry, dry	$\frac{1}{2}$ oz.	3 oz.	
Parsley, chopped	$\frac{1}{4}$ cup	$1\frac{1}{2}$ cups	
Brandy	$\frac{1}{2}$ oz.	3 oz.	
Mustard, dry	$\frac{1}{2}$ tsp.	1 tbsp.	
Mustard, Dijon type	1 tsp.	2 tbsp.	
Worcestershire sauce	$\frac{1}{2}$ tbsp.	3 tbsp.	
Nutmeg, ground	$\frac{1}{4}$ tsp.	$1\frac{1}{2}$ tsp.	
Hot pepper sauce	to taste	to taste	Adjust seasoning.
Salt	to taste	to taste	
Black pepper	to taste	to taste	

SPECIAL HANDLING FOR BUFFETS: *Serve very warm from shallow insert pan(s) set over dual heating units. Keep covered. Offer with English muffins or Southern Biscuits (see Recipe Index).*

Cornmeal Johnny Cakes

INGREDIENTS	TEST QUANTITY: 8	SERVICE QUANTITY: 50	METHOD
Milk	$1\frac{1}{4}$ cups	$7\frac{1}{2}$ cups	Heat just to a simmer.
Water	1 cup	$1\frac{1}{2}$ qt.	
Cornmeal, yellow	$\frac{1}{2}$ cup	3 cups	Add gradually. Cool and reserve.
Corn, whole kernel, drained or frozen	$\frac{1}{2}$ cup	3 cups	
Eggs, beaten	2	12	Combine and add to reserved corn mixture.
Butter, melted	$\frac{1}{2}$ cup	3 cups	Portion onto hot, lightly greased griddle.
Flour, all purpose	$1\frac{1}{4}$ cups	$7\frac{1}{2}$ cups	Turn when golden and repeat on second side.
Baking powder	1 tsp.	2 tbsp.	
Salt	$\frac{1}{2}$ tsp.	1 tbsp.	
Baking soda	$\frac{1}{2}$ tsp.	1 tbsp.	
Maple syrup	1 tbsp.	$\frac{1}{3}$ cup	
Cinnamon	$\frac{1}{4}$ tsp.	$1\frac{1}{2}$ tsp.	

SPECIAL HANDLING FOR BUFFETS: *Serve very warm from shallow insert pan(s) set over dual heating units. Keep covered. Offer with creamed shellfish.*

Country Apples

INGREDIENTS	TEST QUANTITY: 8	SERVICE QUANTITY: 50	METHOD
Green apples, peeled, cored, cut into eighths	2 lb.	12 lb.	Combine in bowl. Toss well and place in baking pan(s). Bake at 375°F until apples are soft.
Raisins, golden	$\frac{1}{2}$ cup	3 cups	
Sugar	1 cup	3 lb.	
Ginger, ground	$\frac{1}{4}$ tsp.	$1\frac{1}{2}$ tsp.	
Cinnamon, ground	2 tsp.	$\frac{1}{4}$ cup	
Nutmeg, ground	$\frac{1}{2}$ tsp.	1 tbsp.	
Cognac	1 oz.	$\frac{3}{4}$ cup	
Orange peel, grated	1 tsp.	2 tbsp.	
Lemon juice	of 1	of 6	
Apricots, dried, diced	$\frac{1}{2}$ cup	3 cups	
Butter, melted	$\frac{1}{4}$ cup	$1\frac{1}{2}$ cups	
Apple brandy	1 tbsp.	$\frac{1}{3}$ cup	Combine and offer with apples.
Sour cream	$\frac{1}{2}$ cup	3 cups	
Lemon peel, grated	1 tsp.	2 tbsp.	
Honey	1 tbsp.	$\frac{1}{3}$ cup	

SPECIAL HANDLING FOR BUFFETS: *Serve very warm from shallow insert pan(s) set over dual heating units. Keep covered. Add chopped pecans to mixture; proceed.*

Country Sausage

INGREDIENTS	TEST QUANTITY: 8	SERVICE QUANTITY: 50	METHOD
Pork, boneless, cubed	2 lb.	12 lb.	Grind together through fine disc. Keep mixture very cold.
Pork fat, diced	$\frac{1}{3}$ lb.	2 lb.	
Bacon, chopped	1 cup	$1\frac{1}{2}$ qt.	
Salt	1 tbsp.	$\frac{1}{3}$ cup	Combine. Add quickly to meat. Combine well. Chill overnight. Shape into patties.
Thyme, dried	$\frac{1}{2}$ tsp.	1 tbsp.	
Sage, dried	$1\frac{1}{2}$ tsp.	3 tbsp.	
Marjoram, dried	$\frac{1}{2}$ tsp.	1 tbsp.	
Black pepper	$1\frac{1}{2}$ tsp.	3 tbsp.	
Red pepper, crushed	$\frac{1}{2}$ tsp.	1 tbsp.	
Olive oil	2 tbsp.	$\frac{3}{4}$ cup	Sauté patties until browned on both sides.

SPECIAL HANDLING FOR BUFFETS: *Serve very warm from shallow insert pan(s) set over dual heating units. Keep covered. Form mixture into balls and cook; offer with baked acorn squash and apple sauce.*

Crêpes Brulatour

INGREDIENTS	TEST QUANTITY: 8	SERVICE QUANTITY: 50	METHOD
Milk	1 cup	$1\frac{1}{2}$ qt.	Combine in blender; process until smooth. Let rest 1 hour. Make crêpes in buttered pan. Reserve.
Eggs, beaten	3	$1\frac{1}{2}$ dozen	
Vanilla extract	1 tsp.	2 tbsp.	
Lemon peel, grated	$\frac{1}{2}$ tsp.	1 tbsp.	
Flour, all purpose	$\frac{3}{4}$ cup	$4\frac{1}{2}$ cups	
Peanut oil	$\frac{1}{4}$ cup	$1\frac{1}{2}$ cups	
Cream cheese, room temperature	5 oz.	2 lb.	Cream together.
Orange peel, grated	$\frac{1}{2}$ tsp.	1 tbsp.	
Brown sugar, light	$\frac{1}{3}$ cup	2 cups	
Cinnamon	$\frac{1}{4}$ tsp.	$1\frac{1}{2}$ tsp.	
Cognac	1 tbsp.	$\frac{1}{3}$ cup	Add; blend; refrigerate 30 minutes. Then portion 2 tbsp. of filling onto each crêpe. Roll up. Reserve.
Vanilla	2 tsp.	$\frac{1}{4}$ cup	
Walnuts, chopped	3 tbsp.	1 cup + 2 tbsp.	
Pecans, chopped	3 tbsp.	1 cup + 2 tbsp.	
Light cream	2 tsp.	$\frac{1}{4}$ cup	
Heavy cream	1 cup	$1\frac{1}{2}$ qt.	Whip together until stiff. Chill.
Vanilla	$1\frac{1}{2}$ tsp.	3 tbsp.	
Powdered sugar	$\frac{1}{4}$ cup	$1\frac{1}{2}$ cups	
Butter	4 oz.	$1\frac{1}{2}$ lb.	To prepare for service: melt in sauté pan or chafer.
Strawberries, halved	1 qt.	6 qt.	Add; simmer until sugar is melted.
Brown sugar, light	$\frac{1}{4}$ cup	$1\frac{1}{2}$ cups	
Orange brandy	$\frac{1}{2}$ cup	3 cups	Add; flame; let reduce. Add filled crêpes and simmer until warmed. Serve crêpes with sauce, whipped cream, and commercial Melba sauce.
Rum	$\frac{1}{4}$ cup	$1\frac{1}{2}$ cups	

SPECIAL HANDLING FOR BUFFETS: *Serve very warm from shallow insert pan(s) set over dual heating units. Keep covered. Substitute raspberries or cherries. Offer with sour cream.*

Crêpes Maison, Galatoire's of New Orleans

INGREDIENTS	TEST QUANTITY: 8	SERVICE QUANTITY: 50	METHOD
Eggs, beaten	3	$1\frac{1}{2}$ dozen	Combine.
Milk	$\frac{3}{4}$ cup	1 qt. + $\frac{1}{2}$ cup	
Flour, all purpose	$\frac{3}{4}$ cup	$1\frac{1}{4}$ lb.	Sift together and add. Blend until smooth. Let
Sugar	2 tsp.	$\frac{1}{4}$ cup	rest 1 hour. Make crêpes and reserve.
Salt	$\frac{1}{2}$ tsp.	1 tbsp.	
Red currant jelly	1 cup	$1\frac{1}{2}$ qt.	Spread 2 tbsp. on each crêpe. Fold into thirds. Place on sheet pan.
Powdered sugar, sifted	$\frac{1}{4}$ cup	$1\frac{1}{2}$ cups	Combine and sprinkle on top. Prior to service,
Almonds, sliced	$\frac{2}{3}$ cup	2 lb.	broil until almonds are toasted.
Triple sec	$\frac{1}{3}$ cup	2 cups	Sprinkle over before service.

SPECIAL HANDLING FOR BUFFETS: *Serve very warm from shallow insert pan(s) set over dual heating units. Keep covered. Substitute peach preserves and pecans. Galatoire's is one of New Orleans' most eminent restaurants.*

Ham Hash

INGREDIENTS	TEST QUANTITY: 8	SERVICE QUANTITY: 50	METHOD
Baked ham, minced	1 lb.	6 lb.	Combine; adjust seasoning. Form into patties.
Potatoes, peeled, cooked, diced	2 cups	6 lb.	
Onion, minced	$\frac{1}{2}$ cup	3 cups	
Horseradish, grated	1 tsp.	2 tbsp.	
Green pepper, minced	$\frac{2}{3}$ cup	1 qt.	
Red bell pepper, minced	$\frac{2}{3}$ cup	1 qt.	
Parsley, chopped	$\frac{1}{4}$ cup	$1\frac{1}{2}$ cups	
Mustard, dry	$\frac{1}{2}$ tsp.	1 tbsp.	
Salt	to taste	to taste	
Black pepper	to taste	to taste	
Cayenne	to taste	to taste	
Clarified butter	$\frac{1}{4}$ cup	$1\frac{1}{2}$ cups	Heat in skillet. Add hash. Cook until first side is browned.
Worcestershire sauce	1 tsp.	2 tbsp.	
Scallions (greens and whites), chopped	$\frac{1}{4}$ cup	$1\frac{1}{2}$ cups	
Clarified butter	$\frac{1}{4}$ cup	$1\frac{1}{2}$ cups	Heat in additional skillet(s); turn patty(s) from first pan. Continue cooking until done. Remove from skillet(s) and place in service pans. (Note: if care is taken, all cooking can be done in same pan(s)).
Parsley, chopped	as desired	as desired	Garnish.

SPECIAL HANDLING FOR BUFFETS: *Serve very warm from shallow insert pan(s) set over dual heating units. Keep covered. Serve with poached eggs.*

Lingonberry Crêpes

INGREDIENTS	TEST QUANTITY: 8	SERVICE QUANTITY: 50	METHOD
Water, warm	$1\frac{1}{4}$ cups	$7\frac{1}{2}$ cups	Combine gradually to form batter. Let rest 30 minutes.
Cranberry liqueur	1 tbsp.	$\frac{1}{3}$ cup	
Egg yolks, beaten	2	12	
Lemon peel, grated	$\frac{1}{2}$ tsp.	1 tbsp.	
Sugar	$1\frac{1}{2}$ tbsp.	$\frac{1}{2}$ cup + 1 tbsp.	
Flour, all purpose, sifted	1 cup	$1\frac{1}{2}$ lb.	
Pecans, chopped finely	1 tbsp.	$\frac{1}{3}$ cup	
Egg whites, beaten stiff	2	12	Fold in.
Heavy cream	$\frac{1}{2}$ cup	3 cups	Whip and fold in.
Orange brandy	1 oz.	$\frac{3}{4}$ cup	
Orange rind, grated	1 tbsp.	$\frac{1}{3}$ cup	
Butter, melted	1 tbsp.	$\frac{1}{3}$ cup	Stir in gently. Ladle $\frac{1}{4}$-cup mixture onto hot crêpe pan; pour off excess. Cook until both sides are lightly golden.
Lingonberry preserves	1 cup	3 lb.	Spread on crêpes. Roll up into tubes. Place on service piece.
Orange brandy	1 tbsp.	$\frac{1}{3}$ cup	
Honey	1 tbsp.	$\frac{1}{3}$ cup	
Powdered sugar	as needed	as needed	Dust over crêpes before service.

SPECIAL HANDLING FOR BUFFETS: *Serve very warm from shallow insert pan(s) set over dual heating units. Keep covered. Omit powdered sugar and mint leaves and offer as a unique garnish for roasted game.*

Open-Faced Shrimp and Cheese Muffins

INGREDIENTS	TEST QUANTITY: 8	SERVICE QUANTITY: 50	METHOD
Boiled shrimp, finely chopped	1 lb.	6 lb.	Combine and reserve.
Scallions (greens and whites), chopped	1 tbsp.	$\frac{1}{3}$ cup	
Colby cheese, grated	$\frac{1}{4}$ cup	$1\frac{1}{2}$ cups	
Red pepper, crushed	$\frac{1}{4}$ tsp.	$1\frac{1}{2}$ tsp.	
Butter, melted	1 tbsp.	$\frac{1}{3}$ cup	Combine off the heat. Return to moderate heat.
Flour, all purpose	1 tbsp.	$\frac{1}{3}$ cup	
Milk	$\frac{1}{4}$ cup	$1\frac{1}{2}$ cups	Add; stir until thick. Pour into mixing bowl.
Worcestershire sauce	$\frac{1}{2}$ tsp.	1 tbsp.	
Parsley, chopped	$\frac{1}{4}$ cup	$1\frac{1}{2}$ cups	Add with reserved shrimp and cheese. Form into small patties and dust with any remaining bread crumbs.
Onion, chopped	1 tbsp.	$\frac{1}{3}$ cup	
Garlic, minced	$\frac{1}{2}$ tsp.	1 tbsp.	
Salt	$\frac{1}{2}$ tsp.	1 tbsp.	
Black pepper	to taste	to taste	
Curry powder	$\frac{1}{4}$ tsp.	$1\frac{1}{2}$ tsp.	
Cayenne	$\frac{1}{4}$ tsp.	$1\frac{1}{2}$ tsp.	
Bread crumbs, finely crumbled	$\frac{1}{2}$ cup	3 cups	
Butter, melted	2 tbsp.	$\frac{3}{4}$ cup	Sauté patties until golden.
English muffin halves, toasted	8	50	Cover with patties. Broil quickly to warm patties.

SPECIAL HANDLING FOR BUFFETS: *Serve very warm from shallow insert pan(s) set over dual heating units. Keep covered. Omit English muffins and offer as a base for poached eggs.*

Orange Honey Butter

INGREDIENTS	TEST QUANTITY: 8	SERVICE QUANTITY: 50	METHOD
Butter, soft	1 cup	3 lb.	Whip together until fluffy.
Honey	$1\frac{3}{4}$ cups	8 lb.	
Brown sugar, light	$\frac{2}{3}$ cup	2 lb.	
Cinnamon	$\frac{1}{4}$ tsp.	$1\frac{1}{2}$ tsp.	
Orange brandy	1 oz.	$\frac{3}{4}$ cup	Combine. Whip into mixture.
Lemon peel, grated	1 tsp.	2 tbsp.	
Orange peel, grated	1 tbsp.	$\frac{1}{3}$ cup	
Pecans, chopped	1 tbsp.	$\frac{1}{3}$ cup	

SPECIAL HANDLING FOR BUFFETS: *Serve in small $\frac{1}{2}$-cup crocks with brunchtime breads and muffins.*

Pennsylvania Dutch Pork 'n Chicken Scrapple

INGREDIENTS	TEST QUANTITY: 8	SERVICE QUANTITY: 50	METHOD
Butter	2 tbsp.	$\frac{3}{4}$ cup	Sauté until soft.
Onion, minced	$\frac{1}{4}$ cup	$1\frac{1}{2}$ cups	
Garlic, minced	1 tsp.	2 tbsp.	
Celery, minced	$\frac{1}{4}$ cup	$1\frac{1}{2}$ cups	
Carrots, julienned	$\frac{1}{4}$ cup	$1\frac{1}{2}$ cups	
Cornmeal, yellow	$1\frac{1}{2}$ cups	3 lb.	Add. Stir to combine.
Salt	$\frac{1}{2}$ tsp.	1 tbsp.	
Oregano, dried	$\frac{1}{4}$ tsp.	$1\frac{1}{2}$ tsp.	
Sage, chopped	$\frac{1}{4}$ tsp.	$1\frac{1}{2}$ tsp.	
Marjoram, dried	$\frac{1}{4}$ tsp.	$1\frac{1}{2}$ tsp.	
Thyme, dried	$\frac{1}{4}$ tsp.	$1\frac{1}{2}$ tsp.	
Black pepper	$\frac{1}{4}$ tsp.	$1\frac{1}{2}$ tsp.	
Red pepper, crushed	$\frac{1}{4}$ tsp.	$1\frac{1}{2}$ tsp.	
Chicken stock, strong	2 cups	3 qt.	Stir in. Bring just to a boil. Simmer 15 minutes.
White wine	1 cup	$1\frac{1}{2}$ qt.	
Chicken, poached, chopped	$1\frac{1}{2}$ cups	$2\frac{1}{4}$ qt.	Add. Stir to combine. Adjust seasoning. Pour into buttered loaf pan(s). Chill overnight. Slice into $\frac{1}{2}$-in. thick slices.
Pork, cooked, shredded	$1\frac{1}{2}$ cups	$2\frac{1}{4}$ qt.	
Flour, all purpose	as needed	as needed	Dredge. Shake off excess.
Black pepper	as needed	as needed	
Butter, melted	as needed	as needed	Sauté slices until golden brown. Change butter as needed.

SPECIAL HANDLING FOR BUFFETS: *Serve very warm from shallow insert pan(s) set over dual heating units. Keep covered. Offer with maple syrup or honey or as a base for fried eggs.*

Poached Eggs Sardou

INGREDIENTS	TEST QUANTITY: 8	SERVICE QUANTITY: 50	METHOD
Butter, melted	$\frac{1}{4}$ cup	$1\frac{1}{2}$ cups	Sauté until soft.
Scallions (greens and whites), chopped	$\frac{1}{4}$ cup	$1\frac{1}{2}$ cups	
Garlic, minced	1 tsp.	2 tbsp.	
Spinach, cooked, squeezed, chopped	$1\frac{1}{2}$ cups	$\frac{1}{2}$ gal.	Add. Stir to combine.
Nutmeg, ground	$\frac{1}{4}$ tsp.	$1\frac{1}{2}$ tsp.	
Yogurt	$\frac{3}{4}$ cup	$2\frac{1}{4}$ lb.	Combine and add. Mix well.
Parmesan cheese, grated	3 tbsp.	1 cup + 2 tbsp.	
Cognac	1 tbsp.	$\frac{1}{3}$ cup	
Lemon juice, strained	1 tbsp.	$\frac{1}{3}$ cup	
Worcestershire sauce	$\frac{1}{2}$ tsp.	1 tbsp.	
Mustard, Dijon type	1 tsp.	2 tbsp.	
Red pepper, crushed	$\frac{1}{8}$ tsp.	$\frac{3}{4}$ tsp.	
Salt	to taste	to taste	
Black pepper	to taste	to taste	
Artichoke bottoms, poached, trimmed	8	50	Place on buttered sheet pan(s). Spoon mixture into artichokes, pressing with teaspoon to create a round well.
Eggs, poached soft, trimmed	8	50	Place one egg in each well.
Hollandaise sauce	$\frac{1}{2}$ cup	3 cups	Spoon 1 tbsp. over each egg.
Paprika, sweet	as needed	as needed	Sprinkle over top. Broil to glaze sauce.

SPECIAL HANDLING FOR BUFFETS: *Serve very warm from shallow insert pan(s) set over dual heating units. Keep covered. Season spinach with nutmeg or a trace of balsamic vinegar.*

Pumpkin Nut Bread

INGREDIENTS	TEST QUANTITY: 8	SERVICE QUANTITY: 50	METHOD
Shortening, soft	$\frac{1}{3}$ cup	2 cups	Whip together until creamed.
Sugar	$1\frac{1}{3}$ cups	4 lb.	
Eggs	2	12	Add individually. Beat well after each addition.
Pumpkin purée, cooked	1 cup	3 lb.	Combine. Add to sugar mixture. Blend well.
Vanilla extract	$\frac{1}{2}$ tsp.	1 tbsp.	Reserve.
Orange brandy	1 tbsp.	$\frac{1}{3}$ cup	
Orange peel, grated	1 tsp.	2 tbsp.	
Ginger, ground	$\frac{1}{4}$ tsp.	$1\frac{1}{2}$ tsp.	
Flour, all purpose	$1\frac{2}{3}$ cups	$2\frac{1}{2}$ lb.	Sift together.
Salt	1 tsp.	2 tbsp.	
Baking powder	$\frac{1}{4}$ tsp.	$1\frac{1}{2}$ tsp.	
Baking soda	1 tsp.	2 tbsp.	
Cinnamon	$\frac{1}{2}$ tsp.	1 tbsp.	
Nutmeg	$\frac{1}{2}$ tsp.	1 tbsp.	
Cloves, ground	$\frac{1}{4}$ tsp.	$1\frac{1}{2}$ tsp.	
Cola soda	$\frac{1}{3}$ cup	2 cups	Add to reserved pumpkin mixture alternately with dry ingredients.
Pecans, chopped	$\frac{1}{3}$ cup	2 cups	Fold in. Pour mixture into buttered and floured loaf pan(s). Bake at 350°F until skewer comes out clean.
Walnuts, chopped	$\frac{1}{3}$ cup	2 cups	
Raisins	$\frac{1}{3}$ cup	2 cups	

SPECIAL HANDLING FOR BUFFETS: *Serve very warm from shallow insert pan(s) set over dual heating units. Keep covered. Offer with Orange Honey Butter (see Recipe Index).*

Scottish Currant Scones

INGREDIENTS	TEST QUANTITY: 8	SERVICE QUANTITY: 50	METHOD
Dried currants	$\frac{1}{2}$ cup	3 cups	Macerate overnight. Drain well. Reserve.
Orange peel, grated	1 tsp.	2 tbsp.	
Dark rum	1 tbsp.	3 oz.	
Flour, all purpose	2 cups	3 lb.	Sift together.
Brown sugar, light	$\frac{1}{2}$ cup	3 cups	
Cream of tartar	2 tsp.	$\frac{1}{4}$ cup	
Baking soda	1 tsp.	2 tbsp.	
Salt	$\frac{3}{4}$ tsp.	$1\frac{1}{2}$ tbsp.	
Cinnamon	$\frac{1}{4}$ tsp.	$1\frac{1}{2}$ tsp.	
Butter	$\frac{1}{2}$ cup	3 cups	Combine and add to flour mixture. Work until mixture is crumbly. Add reserved currants and combine well.
Lemon peel, grated	$\frac{1}{2}$ tsp.	1 tbsp.	
Eggs, beaten	2	12	Combine and add. Work into mixture with a fork. Divide into two parts and flatten each into a $\frac{1}{2}$-in. thick circle. Place each circle into a greased and floured 8-in. cake pan. Score the top of each circle into eight wedges. Bake at 425°F until golden brown. Reheat at 300°F.
Milk	$\frac{1}{4}$ cup	$1\frac{1}{2}$ cups	
Cognac	1 tbsp.	$\frac{1}{3}$ cup	
Almonds, chopped	$\frac{1}{4}$ cup	$1\frac{1}{2}$ cups	

SPECIAL HANDLING FOR BUFFETS: *Serve very warm from shallow insert pan(s) set over dual heating units. Keep covered. Offer with marmalade and sweet butter.*

Shirred Eggs on English Muffins

INGREDIENTS	TEST QUANTITY: 8	SERVICE QUANTITY: 50	METHOD
Egg whites	8	50	Whip until just stiff.
Cream of tartar	pinch	½ tsp.	
English muffin halves, toasted	8	50	Mix butter and other ingredients and spread
Butter	as needed	as needed	on each muffin half. Place on sheet pans.
Mustard, Dijon type	3 tbsp.	1 cup + 2 tbsp.	Portion egg whites on each half. Form a nest
Mayonnaise	2 tbsp.	¾ cup	with back of spoon.
Ginger, ground	½ tsp.	1 tbsp.	
Chili sauce	3 tbsp.	1 cup + 2 tbsp.	Divide among "nests."
Worcestershire sauce	1 tsp.	2 tbsp.	
Egg yolks, whole	8	50	Place a yolk on each muffin.
Cheddar cheese, grated	¼ cup	1½ cups	Sprinkle over. Bake at 350°F until yolks are
Salt	to taste	to taste	set and whites are light brown.
White pepper	to taste	to taste	
Red pepper, crushed	to taste	to taste	
Chives, chopped	¼ cup	1½ cups	Sprinkle over.

SPECIAL HANDLING FOR BUFFETS: *Serve very warm from shallow insert pan(s) set over dual heating units. Keep covered. Add grated Cheddar cheese to mixture after chili sauce; proceed.*

South American Doughnuts

INGREDIENTS	TEST QUANTITY: 8	SERVICE QUANTITY: 50	METHOD
Dry yeast	1 tbsp.	6 tbsp.	Combine. Let sit for 5 minutes.
Water, barely warm	$\frac{1}{2}$ cup	3 cups	
Honey	1 tsp.	2 tbsp.	
Flour, all purpose	$1\frac{3}{4}$ cups	$2\frac{1}{2}$ lb.	Combine well. Add yeast mixture.
Sweet potato, cooked, puréed	$\frac{1}{2}$ cup	3 cups	
Orange peel, grated	1 tsp.	2 tbsp.	
Salt	$\frac{1}{4}$ tsp.	$1\frac{1}{2}$ tsp.	
Cinnamon, ground	$\frac{1}{4}$ tsp.	$1\frac{1}{2}$ tsp.	
Mace, ground	$\frac{1}{4}$ tsp.	$1\frac{1}{2}$ tsp.	
Nutmeg, ground	$\frac{1}{8}$ tsp.	$\frac{3}{4}$ tsp.	
Eggs, beaten	2	12	Add; stir until smooth. Cover and let rise in warm spot for 2 hours. Drop by spoons into 375°F oil. Fry until nicely golden. Drain.
Cognac	$\frac{1}{4}$ cup	$1\frac{1}{2}$ cups	

SPECIAL HANDLING FOR BUFFETS: *Serve very warm from shallow insert pan(s) set over dual heating units. Do not cover or doughnuts will become soft. Offer with assorted preserves.*

Southern Biscuits

INGREDIENTS	TEST QUANTITY: 8	SERVICE QUANTITY: 50	METHOD
Flour, all purpose	2 cups	3 lb.	Sift together into bowl.
Salt	$\frac{1}{2}$ tsp.	1 tbsp.	
White pepper	$\frac{1}{4}$ tsp.	$1\frac{1}{2}$ tsp.	
Baking powder	1 tbsp.	$\frac{1}{3}$ cup	
Shortening (lard)	2 tbsp.	$\frac{3}{4}$ cup	Cut in until crumbly.
Bacon grease	2 tbsp.	$\frac{3}{4}$ cup	
Milk	$\frac{3}{4}$ cup	1 qt. + $\frac{1}{2}$ cup	Work in with fork until dough forms a ball. Knead gently. Roll out $\frac{1}{2}$ in. thick. Cut with 2-in. cutter. Bake on ungreased sheet pan(s) at 450°F, 15 minutes.
Chives, minced	1 tsp.	2 tbsp.	
Chili sauce	1 tbsp.	$\frac{1}{3}$ cup	

SPECIAL HANDLING FOR BUFFETS: *Serve very warm from shallow insert pan(s) set over dual heating units. Keep covered. Offer with assorted butters and preserves. Use as a base for creamed shellfish.*

Swiss Apple Fritters

INGREDIENTS	TEST QUANTITY: 8	SERVICE QUANTITY: 50	METHOD
Cake flour	1 cup	$1\frac{1}{2}$ lb.	Sift together.
Sugar	1 tbsp.	$\frac{1}{3}$ cup	
Lemon rind, grated	1 tsp.	2 tbsp.	
Baking powder	1 tsp.	2 tbsp.	
Salt	$\frac{1}{4}$ tsp.	$1\frac{1}{2}$ tsp.	
Eggs, beaten	2	12	Combine; add to flour. Mix only until smooth.
Pecans, chopped	$\frac{1}{4}$ cup	$1\frac{1}{2}$ cups	
Milk	$\frac{1}{3}$ cup	2 cups	
White wine	$\frac{1}{3}$ cup	2 cups	
Shortening, melted	2 tsp.	$\frac{1}{4}$ cup	
Apples (medium), peeled, cored, sliced	4	25	Dip slices into mixture and drain on rack. Fry in 375°F oil until crisp and golden.
Powdered sugar	$\frac{1}{4}$ cup	$1\frac{1}{2}$ cups	Sift together and sprinkle on.
Ginger	$\frac{1}{4}$ tsp.	$1\frac{1}{2}$ tsp.	
Cinnamon	$\frac{3}{4}$ tsp.	$1\frac{1}{2}$ tbsp.	
Nutmeg	$\frac{1}{4}$ tsp.	$1\frac{1}{2}$ tsp.	

SPECIAL HANDLING FOR BUFFETS: *Serve very warm from shallow insert pan(s) set over dual heating units. Keep covered. Offer with sour cream or crème frâiche.*

Tropical Banana Fritters

INGREDIENTS	TEST QUANTITY: 8	SERVICE QUANTITY: 50	METHOD
Light rum	$\frac{1}{2}$ cup	3 cups	Combine to dissolve.
Orange brandy	1 tbsp.	$\frac{1}{3}$ cup	
Lime juice, fresh, strained	2 tbsp.	$\frac{3}{4}$ cup	
Lime peel, grated	$\frac{1}{2}$ tsp.	1 tbsp.	
Sugar	$\frac{1}{4}$ cup	$1\frac{1}{2}$ cups	
Molasses	$\frac{1}{4}$ cup	$1\frac{1}{2}$ cups	
Bananas, ripe, peeled	4	25	Slice into 1-in. pieces. Marinate for 1 hour. Drain and dry well.
Flour, all purpose	3 cups	$1\frac{1}{2}$ lb.	Process until completely smooth. Let rest for 1 hour. Dip bananas into batter. Shake off excess. Fry in 375°F oil until golden on both sides.
Lime peel, grated	1 tsp.	2 tbsp.	
Sugar	3 tbsp.	1 cup + 2 tbsp.	
Ginger, ground	$\frac{1}{4}$ tsp.	$1\frac{1}{2}$ tsp.	
Baking powder	$1\frac{1}{2}$ tsp.	3 tbsp.	
Salt	$\frac{1}{2}$ tsp.	1 tbsp.	
Milk	1 cup	$1\frac{1}{2}$ qt.	
Eggs	2	12	
Butter, melted	$1\frac{1}{2}$ tbsp.	$\frac{1}{2}$ cup	
Vegetable oil	as needed	as needed	

SPECIAL HANDLING FOR BUFFETS: *Serve very warm from shallow insert pan(s) set over dual heating units. Do not cover or fritters will become soft. Offer with molasses or maple syrup.*

Welsh Rabbit

INGREDIENTS	TEST QUANTITY: 8	SERVICE QUANTITY: 50	METHOD
Cheddar cheese, sharp, grated	1 lb.	6 lb.	Stir in pan over low heat until melted.
Bacon, sautéed, crumbled, drained	$\frac{1}{2}$ cup	3 cups	
Scallions (greens and whites), chopped	$\frac{1}{4}$ cup	$1\frac{1}{2}$ cups	
Lager beer or stout	1 pt.	3 qt.	Combine and add to cheese. Stir while the mixture thickens, approximately 10 minutes. Pour into service piece(s).
Tomatoes, peeled, seeded, chopped	1 cup	$1\frac{1}{2}$ qt.	
Eggs, lightly beaten	2	12	
Mustard, dry	$\frac{1}{3}$ cup	2 cups	
Cayenne pepper or hot paprika	$\frac{1}{2}$ tsp.	1 tbsp.	
Worcestershire sauce	to taste	to taste	
Salt	to taste	to taste	
Black pepper	to taste	to taste	

SPECIAL HANDLING FOR BUFFETS: *Serve very warm from shallow insert pan(s) set over dual heating units. Keep covered. Offer with diagonally sliced toast points or English muffins. Line desired bread with tomato slices and garnish with grilled bacon.*

Williamsburg Sweet Potato Muffins

INGREDIENTS	TEST QUANTITY: 8	SERVICE QUANTITY: 50	METHOD
Butter	$\frac{1}{4}$ cup	$1\frac{1}{2}$ cups	Cream well.
Brown sugar, light	$\frac{2}{3}$ cup	2 lb.	
Orange peel, grated	1 tsp.	2 tbsp.	
Eggs, beaten	1	6	Add. Mix thoroughly.
Sweet potatoes, cooked, peeled, mashed	$\frac{3}{4}$ cup	3 lb.	Add. Blend well.
Bacon, sautéed, crumbled, drained	$\frac{1}{4}$ cup	$1\frac{1}{2}$ cups	
Flour, all purpose	$\frac{3}{4}$ cup	$1\frac{1}{2}$ lb.	Sift together.
Baking powder	1 tsp.	2 tbsp.	
Salt	$\frac{1}{8}$ tsp.	$\frac{3}{4}$ tsp.	
White pepper	$\frac{1}{8}$ tsp.	$\frac{3}{4}$ tsp.	
Cinnamon	$\frac{1}{2}$ tsp.	1 tbsp.	
Nutmeg	$\frac{1}{8}$ tsp.	$\frac{3}{4}$ tsp.	
Ginger	$\frac{1}{8}$ tsp.	$\frac{3}{4}$ tsp.	
Milk	$\frac{1}{2}$ cup	3 cups	Add to sweet potato mixture, alternating with dry ingredients.
Flour	as needed	as needed	Dredge in flour and fold in. Spoon mixture into greased muffin tins. Bake at 400°F until muffins test done, about 25 minutes.
Pecans, chopped	2 tbsp.	$\frac{3}{4}$ cup	
Walnuts, chopped	$\frac{1}{4}$ cup	$1\frac{1}{2}$ cups	

SPECIAL HANDLING FOR BUFFETS: *Serve very warm from shallow insert pan(s) set over dual heating units. Keep covered. Offer with Orange Honey Butter (see Recipe Index) or marmalade.*

Yankee Red Flannel Hash

INGREDIENTS	TEST QUANTITY: 8	SERVICE QUANTITY: 50	METHOD
Beets, cooked, drained, chopped	1½ cups	3 lb.	Combine in large bowl. Mix well. Portion into patties.
Corned beef, cooked, chopped	1½ cups	3 lb.	
Ham, cooked, chopped	¾ cup	1½ lb.	
Potatoes, cooked, diced	1 cup	2 lb.	
Onion, chopped	½ cup	3 cups	
Celery, chopped	¼ cup	1½ cups	
Scallion (green only), chopped	½ cup	3 cups	
Garlic, minced	1 tsp.	2 tbsp.	
Parsley, chopped	½ cup	3 cups	
Bacon, fried, crumbled, drained	½ cup	3 cups	
Red pepper, crushed	½ tsp.	1 tbsp.	
Salt	to taste	to taste	
Black pepper	to taste	to taste	
Eggs, beaten	2	12	
Beer, dark	⅓ cup	2 cups	
Worcestershire sauce	1 tsp.	2 tbsp.	
Flour, all purpose	2 tbsp.	¾ cup	
Butter, melted	2 tbsp.	¾ cup	Heat on griddle or in large pan(s). Sauté patties until crisp on each side.
Bacon drippings, strained, melted	2 tbsp.	¾ cup	
Parsley, chopped	¼ cup	1½ cups	Sprinkle over.

SPECIAL HANDLING FOR BUFFETS: *Serve very warm from shallow insert pan(s) set over dual heating units. Keep covered. Offer with poached eggs and side dishes of sour cream or chili sauce.*

Review Questions

1. What is the term for eggs cooked in a crêpe shell?

2. How are Spanish scrambled eggs served?

3. What is the name for poached eggs served on baked tomatoes?

4. What is a Cherbourg omelet?

5. What do eggs have to do with a chef's hat?

6. How are Princess eggs served?

Twelve

Equipment: The Right Stuff

"Hot food hot, cold food cold"—that is a continuing challenge for the food-service industry. This hot and cold issue is especially critical to buffet service. The maintenance of correct service temperatures ensures not only that your patrons will savor your fare at its very best but also that they will enjoy a certainty of safety in regard to food science and sanitation. Luckily, the industry has access to a wealth of equipment that permits the tether from kitchen to service area to be as long as your needs demand.

"SOME LIKE IT HOT"

THE CHAFING DISH

Probably the universal favorite for service of hot food, the chafing dish is used (1) to keep food warm without scorching and (2) to present that food to what can be a multitude of people. What makes it a truly versatile buffet tool is its ability to take many forms and sizes, to thus serve several varieties of related foods in an attractive manner. Further, chafing dishes are portable and can be set up in a flash — ready to be tended by an economically feasible number of staff or made available to patrons who serve themselves. Chafers are available in myriad shapes and in several materials, finishes, and heat sources.

THE SHAPE OF THINGS TO COME

Chafers can be purchased in round, square, oval, and rectangular shapes, the rectangle being the clear favorite in terms of flexibility. Built as portable steam tables, these units accommodate standard two-inch or four-inch deep insert pans as well as a variety of partial sizes (see the table of insert pans in the Appendix). The volume range of this style reaches as high as four gallons, an amount that can easily serve 120 half-cup portions of barbecued beans. Or you can offer spareribs and their Chinese dipping sauce from separate inserts within the same chafer.

When covered with their fitted domes (or "heads"), square insert pans are often used for breads, buns, and stuffings. They can also be used for serving smaller groups of people virtually any item you wish.

While they are pretty to look at, oval chafers are not prevalent in food service, in large part because they are not fitted with variable inserts. In other words, oval chafers lack versatility, and very few manufacturers bother to produce them.

Round units (normally with capacities that range from a quart to a gallon) are used to service smaller groups; the lower volumes preclude the use of or need for fractional inserts. Some catalogs list five- or six-gallon round chafers, often with revolving dome covers; their presence on buffet lines, while impressive, is reserved for high-volume operations or functions.

A MATTER OF MATERIAL

The perennial leader of the chafing dish pack is stainless steel. Easy to clean and maintain, stainless steel can withstand the rigors of daily use. Available in brushed (satin) finish for high-traffic use, stainless steel can be upgraded to a mirror-image polished finish; very nice to look at, but remember all those fingerprints! You must decide on light-, medium-, or heavy-gauge stainless steel in these units; original cost must be balanced by hours of use and expected life of service.

Next up the cost ladder are stainless steel units with brass fittings. These are "dressmaker's" features, but you shouldn't deny the aesthetics of these pleasing (if difficult to keep shiny) nuances.

Copper and brass chafers are often as expensive as they are appealing, but when a sophisticated warm glow is an important part of your buffet, their selection might be mandated. Both these metals are too soft in their own right to constitute the entire chafing unit, and they are also potentially toxic when exposed to certain foods and heat; they are thus lined with tin, nickel, silver, or stainless steel in the form of an exterior lamination. A note on copper: Although an excellent heat conductor when used in thicknesses above an eighth of an inch, the usual coating of copper on chafer units should be considered only in an aesthetic sense.

There has been a recent trend toward "sandwiching" diverse metals to use the best qualities of each. An inner lining of stainless steel (for sanitation and maintenance), a "filling" of aluminum (excellent heat conductor), and an outer shell of copper (for beauty) all combine for effective, appealing service ware.

Silver chafers are expensive investments and should be considered from several vantages. Ultimate satisfaction and term of use each depend on (1) thickness of silver plate, (2) type of base metal used, (3) type of metal used for decorative "gadroon" work, (4) type of soldering used throughout, and (5) the type of finish applied, either polished or butler style. Because there are so many factors to consider when buying silver chafers, one should work with reputable dealers and manufacturers who can answer all questins and provide certainty of quality. Remember, too, some basic food chemistry: dishes that contain eggs or some mild acid (lemon juice, wine, vinegar, mayonnaise) will tarnish the silver and become discolored in the bargain. The solution is to use chafers with polished stainless steel or chrome liners. Minor color variations (chrome often appears bluish, whereas silver plate tends to be pinkish in hue) fade away when food fills the dishes.

LET THERE BE HEAT!
There are three major sources of heat for chafing dishes: electricity, liquid alcohol, and solid alcohol.

Electric units might have a place in the home, but they are less than ideal for use by food-service operators. Rheostats take a beating, are misplaced, or are often doused with damaging liquids; cords disappear or become damaged. Additionally, the need to run extension cords hither, thither, and yon can create problems, not the least of which is the constant danger of tripping or pulling the chafer off the service tables.

The leader in heat sources continues to be liquid alcohol, dating back to the nineteenth century. The prevalence of this style of chafer is definitely on the wane, however, largely because of the obvious dangers of spilling and excessive volatility. "Spirit lamps," as they have been called, are not practical in a food-service sense.

This brings us to solid alcohol fuel. Available in a variety of conveniently sized cans, these fuels are not spillable, they burn with a charming blue flame, and they consume less oxygen than their liquid counterpart. The cans that fit into universal chafer units typically burn efficiently for an hour or more—often for your main period of buffet service. If service extends past an hour, cans can be quickly and safely replaced.

But the real use of fuel cans begins well before service. Chafing dish water pans should be filled to a depth of up to an inch with hot water, depending on the size of inserts and the foods served. This water should reach about a half-inch up the sides of the insert pan. Light the fuel and cover the chafing units about 30 minutes prior to service; this will provide plenty of time for water temperature to reach optimum holding temperature. Keep foods

covered at all times because there is a tremendous loss of heat from exposed food (there are exceptions in some instances—consult specific recipes). If handled and maintained correctly, your food-service chafer will last for years.

BUT WHAT ABOUT SOURCES?
Your local supplier will doubtless offer you many options for chafers, but we list some of the major manufacturers for your information: Bell Mark Sheffield Silver, Bloomfield Industries, Legion Utensils, Regency Service Carts, Spring of Switzerland, Sterno, and Volrath.

"THE BIG CHILL"

The "salad bar age" is upon us. Many considerations are often overlooked in the selection and use of this important piece of buffet equipment. Cold food deserves to be served cold, so many of the following thoughts should be considered, even if you opt to create your own salad and cold food display.

Will your salad area be permanent or temporary?

Will it (or should it) be a drop-in unit or freestanding?

Will it be chilled by ice or by compressor?

If ice, how deep must its holding pan be?

Will the unit offer storage for chilled plates or bowls?

Should a rail be provided for trays?

What about a sneeze guard? Hanging or attached?

Do you need lights? A drain container? An evaporator?

Do you plan to offer a "Soup 'n Salad" feature? Where will you put the soup?

Will there be a bread board? Plate levelers? Carving boards?

How many bowls will it fit? What sizes?

Will you feature ice carvings? How will they be supported? How will they drain?

The "big chill" is indeed a big question. Consider your cold food buffet long and hard. The food must be held at correct low temperatures (less than 40°F) for extended times, and a correctly designed salad bar or other buffet arrangement will help to assure that this condition is addressed—and met.

"TAKING IT ON THE ROAD"

Food-service operators are entering the off-premise catering market in ever-increasing numbers. Buffets find themselves being served in countless locations, often far from the control of "friendly" kitchens and service space. The following checklist highlights just some of the considerations you should make before you "take your act on the road."

How will you transport food? Equipment?

Are your sheet pan racks mobile?

Do you have a mobile bar?

If not, where will you set it up on location?

How about ice storage on site?

Checklist of chafing dishes?

Extra solid alcohol fuel?

Linens?

Service trays?

Bus trays?

China?

Glassware (service and bar)?

Coffee pots?

Beverage pitchers?

Table skirts?

Ice sculpture molds?

All food and garnish?

ID tags for foods on the buffet line?

Service forks and spoons?

Side towels?

The list can go on, and it does. You will learn from every experience. Keep a journal from one function to the next: What did you do right? And wrong? Where were the bottlenecks? How about your staff? And so on, and so on.

One final note: There is an old expression that states, "It is a poor workman who blames his tools." Don't be a victim of poor equipment or poor planning.

Review Questions

1. Offer two benefits of chafing dishes.

2. Describe the benefits and limitations of stainless steel, copper, and silver chafers.

3. Are electric chafers predominant in food service? Why?

4. List 10 concerns of cold food service.

5. List 10 concerns of a mobile buffet.

6. What is the oldest form of chafing dish heat?

Thirteen
Buffet Layout: The Master Plan

From the simple to the "haute sublime," buffets can enhance your food-service operation in countless ways. There must be a plan for your buffets, however — a master plan for you to follow before you embark on any scheduled function. This plan — a map, really — should address every why, when, where, how, and with whom that comes up in communication with client and staff. Every step along the way that you can plan opens the door to profits just a little wider.

BUT WHY BUFFETS?

First, we should consider some of the benefits provided by this style of food service. Just why does a buffet answer so many questions? Let's start with 10 quick responses.

1. "More with less." With buffets, you can produce quantities of food and serve it with a minimum of service staff. Guests serve themselves, remember, so front-line staff can be limited to a carver or two and people to replenish food and china. Cleanup crews are necessary, but they always are.

2. Cooking in quantity. If a kitchen is able to cook in multiple units, the per guest labor cost is lowered. Dish for dish, it is less expensive to cook for 500 than it is for 50. Buffets let the kitchen "strut its stuff" for less.

3. Productive cooking. Not only is buffet cooking less expensive, it is also more productive. Think about the time it takes to set up a mise en place. From that point on, cooks can generate more units of food in fewer units of time. Productivity results, and that's money.

4. Food cost savings. Not designed solely as a catchall for leftovers, buffets do serve as a creative outlet for the profitable use of these food-service constants. The result is a beneficial reduction in food cost.

5. Help in menu planning. Buffets allow an operator to cover all the bases in menu planning. There is no need to second-guess an entire menu: Who will order veal, how many soups should be prepared, how many chef's salads — a buffet is a one-shot menu planner. Leftovers can be used, not created, and you can adjust the menu for each occasion.

6. No printed menus. You save on menu printing costs. You might post one or two menus or opt for individual cards for each dish, and that sure beats printing 500 menus.

7. Show off a little. Buffets can be extravagant springboards for your food-service creativity. They give your staff an outlet for expression, and they give the operator a true sense of pride.

8. Show off a lot! Each buffet you offer increases the overall reputation of your operation. "Knock 'em flat," so to speak, at one affair, and you are bound to get opportunities for more.

9. Increase business. When you prove that you are capable of pulling off a super show, business will come back, joined by new opportunities.

10. It's easier! Face it, buffets serve more people in less time with fewer people than do other styles of food service. You can change the occasion, but not the facts: Buffets make sense and cents in contemporary food service.

THE MASTER PLAN

So you've decided that buffets can work for you. Now what? The first thing to do — the very first thing — is to draw up your plans. Include every aspect of food, service, theme, and client — and then stick to it.

First, discuss with your client or manager such factors as number of patrons, price per person, built-in gratuities, menu, date, and expected time of service. Once the details have been determined, literally draw up a layout of the best plan to serve each guest with the most ease. Post this plan and discuss it with your management and staff. This "map" should include every dish, every platter, everything that is to be served on the buffet; show where everything is to be positioned. More details on this later.

Next, prepare a time schedule to accomplish everything—easily—by service time.

1. *In advance.* Prepare nonedible garnishes and centerpieces. These can include ice carvings, mock hams or chickens, blown sugar, and the like. Arrange for storage too. Any required carpentry work (risers, for example), should be done well in advance. Mirrors should be built, ordered or polished, as should silver candelabra and platters. Linens should be ordered in plenty of time; don't forget skirting for tables.

2. *Prepare foods to refrigerate.* Some foods can be prepared two to three days in advance. Pâtés and galantines; gelatin molds; poached salmon, lobsters, shrimp, and the like—can be cooked and held for service.

3. *Prepare platters.* The day before the affair, platters, aspics, chaud-froid pieces, and large, cold items can be prepared and refrigerated.

4. *Today is the day.* Prepare all foods for service. Set up all chafers and arrange platters. Plan the day so that nothing comes down to last (often frantic) moments before service.

THE BUFFET LAYOUT

This will be greatly influenced by the number of people, the theme, and the space allotted. If there are to be more than 80 people (a rough rule of thumb), it is a good idea to serve in zones.

Plan the zones so that guests can enter and exit a line without interfering with another line; they should be able to walk with their plates to their table in the fewest possible steps. Each zone must have its own set of chafers, platters, bowls, carvers, and china. All foods should be the same for each zone, but may be garnished or decorated individually. Each zone should have a staff member to refill chafers, bowls, and platters and to be available to help patrons in any way. Each zone should have adequate china for service; silver and glassware will be placed on individual tables. The zones must be designed with such factors in mind as emergency exits (these must not be blocked) and columns or pillars (these simply can neither be moved nor overlooked). Access to the kitchen is a must for any setup.

There are several shapes available for zone service, and each can be suitable to certain room conditions.

1. *Center or hollow squares.* Normally set up in the middle of a room, this design is often dominated by a large floral display, ice carving, or *grosse pièce* in the center. Many tables and zones can be accommodated.

2. *Circular.* This shape should also permit full-sided access to all zones, similar to hollow squares.

3. *T-shape.* Set up in the middle of the room, this design permits dual access (and egress) for many, many patrons. A constant flow, with a simple turn to left or right to tables, helps patrons to ease through the process.

4. *U-shape.* These also permit dual access, but two complete buffets must be arranged, one for each arm. This design permits simplified restocking of foods, right down the center. Once again, a turn right or left directs patrons to their tables.

5. *L-shape.* This design is functional when placed in the corner of a room.

6. *Straight.* This design helps utilize wall space. Remember to save room from behind to replace foods.

7. *Satellite tables.* Many operators prefer to put all appetizers on one table, soups on another, salads on another, and so on. Patrons help themselves, return to the table, and then repeat the process throughout courses.

No matter what design you choose for buffet service, access to the kitchen is important. Also try to reduce to a minimum the number of steps a patron must walk. If soup is served, many operators have the service staff carry it to the table for the guest or serve it separately at the table.

BRING ON THE FOOD

Of course, no buffet plan means a thing without your culinary specialties. Once your theme and menu have been chosen, there are several guidelines to help you get the most out of your selections—and your patrons' appreciation.

1. *Arrange food by types.* Keep salads together with cold foods; side dishes with the like; desserts by themselves. Start with less expensive foods (plates fill quickly) and work up to that expensive entree or *pièce de résistance.*

2. *Vary the level.* For a buffet to have true appeal, vary the height and breadth of displays. Usually the more expensive items are raised and offered from behind a row of less expensive items.

3. *Arrange with care.* Don't put too much light with light, dark with dark.

Don't overcrowd any platter or bowl. Never garnish with something inappropriate or inedible! Even if a garnish is edible (e.g., a tomato rose), don't automatically put it with food; it might be more effective in a bed of greens. Never overdecorate: remember, the key is garnish, not garish. Never use brightly colored aspic or chaud-froid—that's garish. Make sure that show pieces are clearly positioned as just that; don't intersperse them among the foods. Don't spend a lot of valuable time creating inedible garnishes.

4. *Choose and use service pieces with care.* It doesn't all have to be silver: mirrors, ceramics, glass, and stainless steel all have their places on a buffet line. Be sure to select the right piece for the food shown. Food should never extend past (or even onto) the rim of platter, plate, or bowl. Use oblong or round trays with handles for small items; use square or rectangular trays or platters for large, heavy items. Each platter or bowl should be garnished nicely and appropriately (e.g., no shrimp on the veal platter). Salads must be placed in bowls that will not be affected (discolored or altered taste) by dressings; sparkling clean glass, stainless steel, or wood are recommended. Do not place food far out of the reach of patrons, and never, never, have a bowl, tray, or chafer extend off the edge of the table. That is just inviting trouble. If soup is served, offer it at the end of the buffet or provide table service. If a carver is used, position the station at the beginning of the entree section. Always replenish bowls, trays, platters, and chafers before they are empty: every guest should be treated to first-class foods and service.

GARNISH, NOT GARISH

The expression "less is more" applies to garnishing. Never overdo, but do it with style: the idea is to decorate, not to dominate. Several foods are ideal for a variety of buffet uses.

1. *Anchovies.* Blanch and shape into curls or spindles. Use for seafood buffet items.

2. *Apples.* Sliced or carved, plain or pickled, large or small. Good with salads, pork, game.

3. *Asparagus.* A little expensive, but nothing beats the bright green tips or spears when they appear in salads and Chinese dishes and with roast beef. Just blanch and garnish.

4. *Beets.* Be careful; they bleed and stain almost anything. Uncooked beets can be used in vegetable assortments.

5. *Broccoli.* Use tiny flowerets in salads. Blanch or stir-fry to get and set the brilliant green.

6. *Caviar.* It can get costly, but it is available in almost rainbows of types. Use on canapés, shellfish, and seafood in general.

7. *Celery leaves.* These often rejected lovelies can treat the side of a bowl of cottage cheese or the flanks of a poached salmon. Can be used as a chaud-froid garnish too. Sometimes a gentle blanching will increase color.

8. *Cucumbers.* Skinned, sliced, or diced, cucumbers are a real buffet favorite. Use on salads and seafood, appetizer to entree.

9. *Dill.* Elegant, delicate, beautiful with eggs and seafood, get dill before it blooms.

10. *Leeks.* One of the naturals, either trimmed or whole, leeks can be used throughout buffet work. Blanch the leaves and cut into desired shapes for aspic or chaud-froid pieces. Use blanched sliced rings for salads, potatoes, and seafood casseroles.

11. *Mushrooms.* Caps or slices, cooked or raw, mushrooms can even be stuffed and served by themselves. Dip in lemon juice to help maintain color.

12. *Olives.* Ripe olives can be sliced in a variety of ways and have even been used as a substitute for truffles. Use them for canapés, salads, pâtés and more.

13. *Peppers.* Sweet or hot (be careful with these), red or green, peppers can be used in many buffet settings. Whether carved as the top of a carrot palm tree or laced around greens in a Mexican fiesta, peppers can be creatively employed.

14. *Pimientos.* A canned variation of the pepper theme, pimientos can be sliced or cut into many decorative forms. Use dots to rim a shrimp canapé, wedges to punctuate potato salad, or rings to set off a poached salmon. Limitless uses.

15. *Radishes.* A tiny rose or tinier petals for an olive sunflower; dices and slices and little wedges in salad. Use cutouts from bright red skin under a coating of aspic. When you can get them, radishes with bright-green tops spruce up any display of greens.

16. *Tomatoes.* Of course, there's that wonderful rose made from the peel. But small segments can be used for smaller flowers; use in conjunction with cucum-

ber stems and leaves. Hollow out cherry tomatoes and stuff with all types of purées.

17. *Truffles*. Now it's the big time, be-cause truffles are expensive. Slice paper thin and then use little cutters of different shapes. To make a little go a long way, purée the truffles and mix with gelatin. Pour out onto a flat surface, spread the mixture thin, and chill. Then cut the sheet into desired shapes. Keep chilled. Store leftover truffles in sherry or Madeira; use the liquid as a flavoring.

Review Questions

1. Name six benefits of buffets.

2. Describe the uses of six styles of buffet table layouts.

3. Discuss the use of garnishes.

4. Are beets suggested as garnish? Why?

5. What are some foods that can be prepared in advance?

6. What is the "magic number" for zone service?

Glossary

Abass bi hamod: Lebanese lentil soup.

Abbachio al forno: Italian barbecued lamb.

Akadashi: Japanese soup with tofu in light fish stock.

Ajiaco Bogotano: Colombian chicken soup.

Arrostino annegato: Italian shish kebabs.

Arroz con pato: Peruvian marinated and beer-braised duck with rice.

Assida: Tunisian sweet pastry with cream.

Asopao: Puerto Rican chicken and rice stew.

Bagna cauda: Italian dipping sauce for raw vegetables.

Balletjes: East Indian beef meatballs.

Bayerisher linsentopf: German smoked pork with lentils.

Bento: Japanese "picnic box" foods served (often as an appetizer) warm or at room temperature.

Berner platte: Swiss assortment of sausages, beans, and sauerkraut.

Blinis: Small buckwheat crêpes.

Boereks: Turkish appetizers made of phyllo dough with savory stuffings.

Borju porkholt: Hungarian pork stew.

Borscht: Russian cold beet soup.

Bouillabaise: French Mediterranean fish stew.

Braciolli: Italian rolled stuffed beef.

Brunkalsuppa: Danish cabbage soup.

Bully beef: British version of creamed chipped beef.

Callaloo: Caribbean crab soup.

Caldillo de congria: Ceylonese (Sri Lankan) fish stew.

Cantonese duck: Chinese marinated and roasted duck.

Casik: Turkish cucumber and mint soup.

Cassoulet: Classic French bean and sausage casserole with preserved goose or duck.

Ceviche: Marinated salad in which seafood is served that has "cooked" in citrus juices.

Cha shu bok tsoi: Cantonese stir-fried pork with vegetables.

Chupe de camarones: Peruvian shrimp soup with corn.

Chupin de pescado: Uruguayan fish stew with sherry.

Clodnick: Polish cold vegetable soup.

Chorizo: Spanish or Mexican sausage.

Chupattas: Indian breads.

Cochiniat pibl: Mexican pit-roasted pork.

Cock-a-leekie soup: British chicken soup with barley.

Confit d'oie: French preserved goose used in cassoulet.

Couscous: North African dish of steamed grain with vegetables and meat or chicken.

Csirka paprikas: Hungarian chicken dish.

Cuscuz de galinha: Brazilian chicken and cornmeal mosaic.

Czarnina: Polish duck soup with cinnamon and mace.

Dhansak: Indian lamb stew.

Dim sum: Chinese appetizer dumplings.

Dindonneau truffe: French roast turkey with truffles.

Dolmades: Greek stuffed grape leaves.

Fafa: Tahitian steamed chicken with coconut.

Finnan haddie: Scottish smoked haddock, often served in cream sauce.

Frittata: Italian open-faced omelet.

Ga li gai goh: Chinese appetizer with curried chicken on pie dough strips.

Gazpacho: Spanish tomato-based cold vegetable soup.

Geoducks: Pacific coast clams.

Gnocchi: Italian dumplings made from various flours or cornmeal; served as appetizer or accompaniment.

Gohan: Japanese steamed rice.

Gronsaksuppe: Swedish vegetable soup.

Guiso de puerco: Mexican pork stew.

Gulyas: Hungarian goulash.

Hama guri no ushio jiru: Japanese clam consommé.

Hanim parmagi: Turkish appetizer, strips of fried spiced beef.

Hernekeitto: Finnish split pea soup.

Hwang gwa ro pien: Shanghai pork with peanuts.

Hwei gwo ro: Szechuan twice-cooked pork.

Ikebana: Japanese flower arranging.

Jaegerschnitzle: German fried pork with mushrooms.

Jao tse: Chinese "pot sticker" dumplings; filled with seasoned pork and steamed or fried.

Julebord: Norwegian Christmas buffet.

Kadin budu: Turkish beef patties.

Kartoffelsuppe: German potato soup.

Kasseri tighanito: Greek fried cheese.

Kengphed: Laotian fish and potato soup.

Kippesoep met balletzes: Dutch chicken soup with pork meatballs.

Kota kapama: Greek macaroni and chicken casserole.

Kubba shalgum: Iraquian meatball soup.

Kufta: Jordanian chicken broth.

Lablabi: Tunisian chick pea soup.

Lancashire hot pot: British lamb stew.

Lengenysolt: Hungarian rolled stuffed beef.

Loukania: Greek sausage.

Ma ho: Thai pork meatballs.

Makemon: Japanese "hot pot" one-dish cooking method.

Mang tang naw cua: Vietnamese crab and asparagus soup.

Manzo: Italian beef.

Meggykeszue: Hungarian cold cherry soup.

Melagrana: Italian pomegranate sauce for turkey.

Metais: Indian dessert pastries.

Mezes: Greek appetizers.

Minestrone: Italian vegetable soup.

Mole poblano de guajolote: Classic Mexican turkey preparation with chocolate-laced sauce.

Mortadella: Italian bologna-style sausage.

Moussaka: Greek casserole of eggplant and ground lamb.

Mulligatawny: Indian spiced soup.

Mu shu pork: Peking shredded pork wrap in crêpelike pancakes.

Nargisi koftas: East Indian beef meatballs.

Nimono: Japanese poached beef.

Onigariyaki: Japanese seafood kebab with shrimp or mussels.

Ouzo: Greek anise-flavored spirit.

Paella: Spanish specialty saffron rice dish with shellfish, chicken, and sausage.

Pappadams: Indian spiced bread wafers.

Pecena husa se zelim: Czechoslovakian sauerkraut-stuffed goose.

Peking duck: Chinese dried and roasted duck served with scallions and thin pancakes.

Pepper pot: Spicy Jamaican beef soup.

Piazziola di manzo: Italian fried steak with tomatoes.

Pollo boracho: Spanish "drunken chicken" stew.

Popetone: Italian meatloaf.

Potage jardiniere: Luxembourg vegetable soup.

Potlach: Pacific Northwest Indian traditional gala.

Pot stickers: Chinese appetizer dumplings; filled with seasoned pork and steamed or fried.

Raclette: Swiss presentation of slightly melted cheese with breads.

Raki: Turkish anise-flavored spirit.

Raki table: Turkish appetizer assortment.

Rellenong manok: Philippine pork-stuffed chicken.

Retsina: Greek white wine; resiny flavor.

Rijsttafel: Indonesian buffet extravaganza.

Roditys: Greek rośe wine.

Rostelyos: Hungarian casseroles of thinly sliced beef and vegetables.

Rouille: Garlic mayonnaise served with fish stew.

Rouladen: German rolled, stuffed beef.

Sambals (Indian): Appetizers.

Sambal (Indonesian): Condiments.

Samoosas: Indian fried puffs with various fillings.

Sangria: Spanish fruited wine beverage.

Sashimi: Japanese presentation of skillfully sliced raw fish.

Satés: Indonesian kebabs of pork or chicken strips.

Sauerbraten: German marinated braised beef.

Schlact platte: German sausage platter.

Sertes porkholt: Hungarian pork stew.

Shanghai duck: Chinese poached duck with soy sauce and hoisin.

Shorba: Sudanese peanut soup.

Smorgasbord: Classic Swedish buffet.

Smorrebrod: Danish open-faced sandwich buffet.

Sopa de frijoles: Bean soup.

Sopa de lima: Mexican chicken soup with lime.

Sopa Portuguesa: Portuguese fish and shrimp soup.

Soupa sus topcheta: Bulgarian meatball soup.

Soupe à la Malgache: Madagascar vegetable soup.

Soupe au giraumon: Haitian chicken and vegetable soup.

Souvlakia: Greek appetizer kebabs.

Spinatsuppe med ostebrod: Norwegian spinach soup with cheese toast.

Stefado: Greek stew with rabbit, lamb, or beef.

Stekt gas: Swedish roast goose.

Siu mai: Chinese steamed appetizer dumpling; filled with seasoned shrimp or pork.

Sumashijura: Japanese clear chicken soup.

Sumashi wan: Japanese tofu and shrimp soup.

Sushi: Various Japanese presentations of raw fish with gelatinous rice.

Swan la tong: Chinese hot and sour soup.

Szechuan duck: Chinese steamed and fried duck served with soy sauce and coriander.

Tandoori: Indian method for kiln-roasting chicken.

Tandoori murgh: Indian kiln-roasted chicken.

Tapas: Spanish appetizer assortment.

Tarator: Turkish dipping sauce with pimiento and garlic.

Tempura: Japanese frittered items served with dipping sauces.

Teriyaki: Japanese marinated/grilling cooking style.

Tinola: Chicken soup with ginger and onions.

Tom yum gai: Thai hot and sour soup.

Vatapa: Brazilian seafood soup.

Vicknings table: Swedish buffet for "the morning after the night before."

Vienna breads: Danish term for what is elsewhere called "Danish pastries."

Vitello: Italian veal.

Wasabe: Japanese piquant green horseradish.

Waterzooi: Belgian chicken stew with lemon.

Weiss kartoffelsupa: Swiss potato soup.

Wontons: Chinese pastry squares, filled or plain, fried or steamed.

Yakitori: Japanese skewers of grilled chicken strips.

Yalanci dolma: Turkish stuffed grape leaves.

Zakuski: Russian appetizer assortment.

Zensai: Japanese appetizers.

Bibliography

There is wealth to be learned from books, and many of those whose titles follow offered great inspiration during the writing of *Buffets*.

American Spice Trade Association. *Food Service Seasoning Guide*. New York: American Spice Trade Association, 1969.

Anderson, Frederick O. *How to Grow Herbs for Gourmet Cooking*. New York: Meredith, 1967.

Bailey, Adrian. *The Cooking of the British Isles*. New York: Time-Life Books, 1971.

Beard, James. *Barbecue with Beard*. New York: Golden Press, 1975.

Beard, James. *Delights and Prejudices*. New York: Atheneum, 1981.

Beck, Simone. *Simca's Cuisine*. New York: Alfred A. Knopf, 1972.

Better Homes and Gardens. *Heritage Cook Book*. Meredith, 1975.

Bickel, Walter. *Herring's Dictionary of Classical and Modern Cookery*. Germany: Pfanneberg, 1974.

Billik, Crownie, and Kathy Kaufman. *The Brunch Cookbook*. New York: Hawthorn, 1972.

Birchfield, John. *Contemporary Quantity Recipe File*. Boston: Cahners, 1975.

Bocuse, Paul. *Paul Bocuse's French Cooking*. New York: Pantheon, 1977.

Brooks, Karen Gail, and Gideon Bosker. *The Global Kitchen*. New York: Andrews and McMeel, 1981.

Brown, Dale. *American Cooking*. New York: Time-Life Books, 1971.

Brown, Dale. *American Cooking: The Northwest*. New York: Time-Life Books, 1973.

Brown, Helen. *West Coast Cookbook*. New York: Bonanza, 1952.

Brunet, E. *Le Repertoire de la Cuisine*. Woodbury, N.Y.: Barron's, 1967.

Campbell Soup Company. *The International Cook*. Camden, N.J.: Campbell Soup Company, 1980.

Chang, Wonona W., B. Irving, Helene W. Kutshcer, and H. Austin. *An Encyclopedia of Chinese Food and Cookery*. New York: Crown, 1970.

Chiffriller, T. F., Jr. *Successful Restaurant Operation*. Boston: CBI, 1982.

Child, Julia. *The French Chef Cookbook*. New York: Alfred A. Knopf, 1968.

Child, Julia, Louisette Berthole, and Simone Beck. *Mastering the Art of French Cooking*, Vols. I and II. New York: Alfred A. Knopf, 1961 and 1970.

Claiborne, Craig. *Cooking with Herbs and Spices*. New York: Harper & Row, 1970.

Claiborne, Craig, and Pierre Franey. *Classical French Cooking*. New York: Time-Life Books, 1972.

Courtine, Robert J. *The Master Chefs of France Recipe Book*. New York: Everest House, 1981.

Culinary Institute of America. *The American Bounty Sampler*. Hyde Park, N.Y.: Culinary Institute of America, 1982.

Dannenbaum, Julie. *Menus for All Occasions*. New York: E. P. Dutton, 1974.

Davis, Frank. *The Frank Davis Seafood Notebook*. Gretna, La.: Pelican, 1983.

Demos, Stanley. *The Stanley Demos Cookbook*, 7th ed. Cincinnati: C. J. Krehbiel, 1979.

Dutton, Joan Parry. *The Williamsburg Cookbook*. Williamsburg, Va.: The Colonial Williamsburg Foundation, 1975.

Dyer, Ceil. *The Perfect Dinner Party Cookbook*. New York: David McKay, 1974.

Eren, Neset. *The Art of Turkish Cooking*. New York: Doubleday, 1969.

Escoffier, Auguste. *The Escoffier Cookbook*. New York: Crown, 1969.

Ets-Hokin, Judith. *The San Francisco Dinner Party Cookbook*. Millbrae, Calif.: Celestial Arts, 1982.

Fisher, M. F. K. *The Cooking of Provincial France*. New York: Time-Life Books, 1968.

Fowler, Sina Faye, Bessie Brooks West, and Grace Severance Shugart. *Food for 50*, 5th ed. New York: John Wiley, 1971.

Freson, Robert. *The Taste of France*. New York: Stewart, Tabori & Chang, 1983.

Gaede, Sarah. *The Pirate's House Cook Book*. Memphis, Tenn.: Wimmer Brothers, 1982.

Gibbons, Barbara. *The Year-Round Turkey Cookbook*. New York: McGraw-Hill, 1980.

Gibbons, Euell. *Stalking the Blue-eyed Scallop*. New York: David McKay, 1964.

Gisslen, Wayne. *Professional Cooking*. New York: John Wiley, 1983.

Goock, Roland. *The World's 100 Best Recipes*. Melrose Park, Ill.: Culinary Arts Institute, 1973.

Guste, Roy, Jr. *Antoine's Restaurant Cookbook*. New York: W. W. Norton, 1980.

Guste, Roy, Jr. *The Restaurants of New Orleans*. New York: W. W. Norton, 1982.

Hammersley, Evadna. *Lamb Around the World*. New York: Random House, 1970.

Harris, Gertrude. *Pasta International*. San Francisco: 101 Productions, 1978.

Hazelton, Nika Standen. *The Swiss Cookbook*. New York: Atheneum, 1967.

Heatter, Maida. *Book of Great Cookies*. New York: Alfred A. Knopf, 1977.

Idone, Christopher. *Glorious Food*. New York: Stewart, Tabori & Chang, 1982.

Jones, Evan. *American Food: The Gastronomic Story*, 2nd ed. New York: Vintage Books, 1981.

Junior Charity League of Monroe. *The Cotton

Country Collection. Monroe, La.: Junior Charity League, 1982.

Junior League of Charleston. *Charleston Receipts,* 13th ed. Charleston, S.C.: Junior League, 1981.

Junior League of Lafayette. *Talk About Good II.* Lafayette, La.: Junior League, 1979.

Junior League of New Orleans. *The Plantation Cookbook.* Garden City, N.Y.: Doubleday, 1972.

Kennedy, Diana. *The Cuisines of Mexico.* New York: Harper & Row, 1972.

Kotschevar, Lendal H. *Quantity Food Production,* 3rd ed. Boston: Cahners, 1974.

Kotschevar, Lendal H., and Margaret McWilliams. *Understanding Food.* New York: John Wiley, 1969.

Kraus, Barbara. *The Cookbook of the United Nations.* New York: Simon & Schuster, 1970.

Krohn, Norma Odya. *Menu Mystique.* Middle Village, N.Y.: Jonathan David, 1983.

Kuo, Irene. *The Key to Chinese Cooking.* New York: Alfred A. Knopf, 1980.

Lang, George. *The Cuisine of Hungary.* New York: Bonanza, 1971.

Lem, Arthur, and Dan Morris. *The Hong Kong Cookbook.* New York: Funk and Wagnalls, 1970.

Lenotre, Gaston. *Lenotre's Desserts and Pastries.* Woodbury, N.Y.: Barron's, 1977.

Lenotre, Gaston. *Lenotre's Ice Cream and Candies.* Woodbury, N.Y.: Barron's, 1979.

Leonard, Jonathan Norton. *Latin American Cooking.* New York: Time-Life Books, 1971.

Leonard, Jonathan Norton. *American Cooking: The Great West.* New York: Time-Life Books, 1974.

Leonard, Jonathan Norton. *American Cooking: New England.* New York: Time-Life Books, 1976.

Lesberg, Sandy. *Sandy Lesberg's 100 Great Restaurants of America.* New York: Crown, 1981.

Lucas, Dione. *The Cordon Bleu Cook Book.* Boston: Little, Brown, 1947.

Lundberg, Donald E., and Lendal H. Kotschevar. *Understanding Cooking.* Holyoke, Mass.: Marcus Printing, 1965.

MacDonald, Barbara, Carolyn Boisvert, and Peggy Miller. *The Fifty States' Cookbook.* Chicago: Culinary Arts Institute, 1977.

Mario, Thomas. *Playboy's Wine & Spirits Cookbook.* Chicago: Playboy Press, 1974.

Martini, Anna. *The Mondadori Regional Italian Cookbook.* New York: Harmony, 1982.

Matthews, Ruth H., and Young J. Garrison. *Food Yields Summarized by Different Stages of Production.* Washington, D.C.: U.S. Department of Agriculture, 1975.

Mazanec, Bernice, and Ruth Cech. *Come to Lunch.* Lake Toxaway, N.C.: The Red Barn, 1981.

McClane, A. J. *The Encyclopedia of Fish Cookery.* New York: Holt, Rinehart and Winston, 1977.

McClane, A. J. *North American Fish Cookery.* New York: Holt, Rinehart and Winston, 1981.

Montagne, Prosper. *Larousse Gastronomie.* New York: Crown, 1961.

Nicolas, Jean F. *The Complete Cookbook of American Fish and Shellfish.* Boston: CBI, 1981.

Nicolas, Jean F., and Frederic Sonnenschmidt. *The Professional Chef's Art of Garde Manger.* Boston: Cahners, 1973.

Oliver, Raymond. *La Cuisine.* New York: Leon Amiel, 1969.

Pauli, Eugene. *Classical Cooking the Modern Way.* Boston: CBI, 1979.

Pederson, Raymond. *Prize Winners.* Boston: CBI, 1983.

Pers, Meijer. *Cooking Without Frontiers.* New York: Newsweek, 1972.

Point, Fernand. *Ma Gastronomie.* Wilton, Conn.: Lyceum Books, 1974.

Pucillo, Constanzo. *Recipes of the Famous Petite Marmite.* Miami: Argos, 1970.

Queen's Daughters, Inc. *Entertaining the Louisville Way.* Louisville, Ky.: The Queen's Daughters, 1969.

Rau, Santha Rama. *The Cooking of India.* New York: Time-Life Books, 1972.

Romagnoli, Margaret, and G. Franco. *The Romagnoli's Table.* Boston: Little, Brown, 1975.

Root, Waverly. *The Cooking of Italy.* New York: Time-Life Books, 1968.

Rozin, Elisabeth. *The Flavor-Principle Cookbook.* New York: Hawthorne, 1973.

Rudkin, Margaret. *The Margaret Rudkin Pepperidge Farm Cookbook.* New York: Grosset & Dunlop, 1963.

Savage, Mary. *Savory Stews.* Garden City, N.Y.: Doubleday, 1969.

Schuler, Elizabeth. *German Cookery.* New York: Crown, 1955.

Scott, Natalie V. *Mandy's Favorite Louisiana Recipes.* Gretna, La.: Pelican, 1980.

Scriven, Carl, and James Stevens. *Food Equipment Facts.* Troy, N.Y.: Conceptual Design, 1980.

Seelig, R. A. *When You Advertise . . .* Washington, D.C.: United Fresh Fruits and Vegetables Association, 1970.

Simmons, Adelma Grenier. *Herbs to Grow Indoors.* New York: Hawthorne, 1973.

Steinberg, Rafael. *The Cooking of Japan.* New York: Time-Life Books, 1971.

Steinberg, Rafael. *Pacific and Southeast Asian Cooking.* New York: Time-Life Books, 1972.

Stockli, Albert. *Splendid Fare: The Albert Stockli Cookbook.* New York: Alfred A. Knopf, 1970.

Stouffer Corporation. *The Stouffer Cookbook of Great American Food & Drink.* New York: Random House, 1973.

Stratton, Eula Mae. *Ozark Cookery.* Branson, Mo.: The Ozark Mountaineer, 1976.

Stroman, James. *Prize Recipes from Great Restaurants: The Western States.* Gretna, La.: Pelican, 1979.

Stroman, James. *Prize Recipes from Great Restaurants: The Southern States and Tropics.* Gretna, La.: Pelican, 1983.

Time-Life Books. *Pasta.* Alexandria, Va.: Time-Life, 1980.

The Times-Picayune. *The Original Picayune Creole Cook Book,* 9th ed. New Orleans: The Times-Picayune, 1942.

Toklas, Alice B. *The Alice B. Toklas Cook Book.* New York: Harper & Brothers, 1954.

Truax, Carol. *The Art of Salad Making.* Garden City, N.Y.: Doubleday, 1968.

Trustees Garden Club. *Recipes,* 2nd ed. Savannah, Ga.: Trustees Garden Club, 1983.

Turgeon, Charlotte. *Holiday Magazine Award Cookbook.* Indianapolis: Curtis, 1976.

Verdon, René. *The White House Chef Cookbook.* Garden City, N.Y.: Doubleday, 1967.

Wallace, Lily Haxworth. *Sea Food Cookery.* New York: Blue Ribbon, 1949.

Ward, James. *Restaurants Chicago-Style.* Boston: CBI, 1979.

Waters, Alice. *Chez Panisse Menu Cookbook.* New York: Random House, 1982.

Wells, Dean Faulkner. *The Great American Writers' Cookbook.* Oxford, Miss.: Yoknapatawpha Press, 1981.

Wilkinson, Jule. *Selected Recipes from IVY Award Winners.* Boston: Cahners, 1976.

Wolfe, Linda. *The Cooking of the Caribbean Islands.* New York: Time-Life Books, 1972.

Women of St. Paul's Greek Orthodox Church. *The Art of Greek Cookery.* Garden City, N.Y.: Doubleday, 1963.

Recipe Index

Index

RECIPE EXPANSION TABLE

To expand or reduce recipes, simply read across for the desired amount. For example, if your recipe is for 50 portions, and you need to reduce it to 8, read from right to left; if your recipe is for 8 and you want 75, read from left to right.

8	20	25	50	75	100
$\frac{1}{4}$ tsp.	$\frac{1}{2}$ tsp.	$\frac{3}{4}$ tsp.	$1\frac{1}{2}$ tsp.	$2\frac{1}{4}$ tsp.	1 tbsp.
$\frac{1}{2}$ tsp.	1 tsp.	$1\frac{1}{2}$ tsp.	1 tbsp.	$1\frac{2}{3}$ tbsp.	2 tbsp.
$\frac{3}{4}$ tsp.	$1\frac{1}{2}$ tsp.	$2\frac{1}{4}$ tsp.	$1\frac{1}{2}$ tbsp.	$2\frac{2}{3}$ tbsp.	3 tbsp.
1 tsp.	2 tsp.	1 tbsp.	2 tbsp.	3 tbsp.	$\frac{1}{4}$ cup
$1\frac{1}{2}$ tsp.	1 tbsp.	$1\frac{1}{2}$ tbsp.	3 tbsp.	5 tbsp.	$\frac{1}{3}$ cup
2 tsp.	$1\frac{2}{3}$ tbsp.	2 tbsp.	$\frac{1}{4}$ cup	$\frac{1}{3}$ cup	$\frac{1}{2}$ cup
$2\frac{1}{2}$ tsp.	2 tbsp.	$2\frac{1}{2}$ tbsp.	5 tbsp.	$\frac{1}{2}$ cup	5 oz.
1 tbsp.	$2\frac{1}{2}$ tbsp.	3 tbsp.	3 oz.	9 tbsp.	$\frac{3}{4}$ cup
2 tbsp.	5 tbsp.	3 oz.	$\frac{3}{4}$ cup	9 oz.	$1\frac{1}{2}$ cup
$\frac{1}{4}$ cup	5 oz.	$\frac{3}{4}$ cup	$1\frac{1}{2}$ cup	2 cup	3 cup
$\frac{1}{2}$ cup	$1\frac{1}{4}$ cup	$1\frac{1}{2}$ cup	3 cup	1 pt.	3 pt.
$\frac{3}{4}$ cup	15 oz.	$2\frac{1}{4}$ cup	$4\frac{1}{2}$ cup	$1\frac{1}{2}$ pt.	$4\frac{1}{2}$ pt.
1 cup	$2\frac{1}{2}$ cup	3 cup	$1\frac{1}{2}$ qt.	1 qt.	3 qt.